"Father Porter has written a ⸻⸻⸻⸻⸻⸻ of the Church. Its biblical basis makes it an especially appropriate text for college or seminary classroom."

Joseph Augustine DiNoia, OP
Undersecretary of the Vatican's Congregation for the Doctrine of the Faith and author of *The Diversity of Religions: A Christian Perspective*

"It is not easy to teach ecclesiology today. Where to begin? How to be faithful to the Catholic tradition and at the same time ecumenically open-minded and attentive to questions of credibility? How to negotiate the many controverted questions in a fair yet decisive manner? Ecclesiology is a theological 'minefield'!

"In *A Guide to the Church*, Fr. Lawrence Porter has succeeded in finding a way into the topic that is at the same time fresh and familiar. He confidently proposes a biblically-grounded exposition of the nature and purpose of the Church, its mission and its ministries — without ignoring the many competing claims found among Catholic theologians and within the ecumenical movement. By staying close to the biblical and patristic sources, he paints a portrait of the Church which many Christians will find illuminating and faithful. Porter stays in dialogue with other opinions, but skillfully sets out his own views in a non-polemical and engaging style. He hopes to persuade, so he does not propose and defend the tenets of Catholic dogmatic theology in a systematic way, but confines himself to laying out its biblical foundations in dialogue with contemporary Christian scholarship. He is very attentive to questions of credibility, and takes the time to explain and defend each point in a personal, even conversational tone. While Porter clearly writes with the theological novice in mind, his book will benefit anyone who wants an up-to-date, insightful, and stimulating treatise on ecclesiology."

Sister Sara Butler, MSBT, STL, PhD
Professor of Dogmatic Theology, St. Joseph's Seminary, Yonkers, NY

"Father Porter is a well-respected professor and lecturer. In his new book, he surveys the Church with the keen eye of a theologian. He presents his understanding of the Church in such a way as to help others come to a deeper appreciation of this great mystery."

Most Rev. Arthur Serratelli, STD, SSL, Bishop of Paterson and Former Chair of the Committee on Doctrine of the United States Conference of Catholic Bishops

A GUIDE TO THE CHURCH

A Guide to the Church

Its Origin and Nature,
Its Mission and Ministries

LAWRENCE B. PORTER, Ph.D.

ST PAULS

Library of Congress Cataloging-in-Publication Data

Porter, Lawrence B.
    A guide to the church : its origin and nature, its mission and
ministries / Lawrence B. Porter.
        p. cm.
    Contents: The church as a form of community — The church as sacred assembly—
The origin of the church — The church and the kingdom of God — Models of the
church — A biblical image of the church : Jesus, little flock — More biblical images :
people of God and body of Christ — Am image from three North African theologians
— Introduction to the essential attributes or marks of the church — The unity of the
church — The holiness of the church — The church's Catholic character — A church
that is Apostolic — The church is a communion — Its mission and ministries — The
church's mission : its origin and goals — The home mission : biblical portraits — The
foreign mission : Paul's inculturation of the Gospel — The church's mission and other
religions — Relations between church and state — Introduction to the concept of
ministry — The ordering of Christian ministries — Promotion to ministry — Priestly
ministry — Diaconal ministry — The petrine ministry — The teaching ministry —
Women and ministry — The ministry of a consecrated life.
    ISBN-13: 978-0-8189-1255-9
    ISBN-10: 0-8189-1255-3
    1. Church.   I. Title.

BV600.3.P67 2007
262—dc22

                                          2007017711

Nihil Obstat:
Rev. Msgr. Gerard H. McCarren, STD
Censor Librorum
September 19, 2007

Imprimatur:
✠ Most Rev. John J. Myers, DD, JCD
Archbishop of Newark
September 24, 2007

The Nihil Obstat and Imprimatur are official declarations that a book or
pamphlet is free of doctrinal or moral error. No implication is contained
therein that thosewho have granted the Nihil Obstat and Imprimatur
agree with the contents, opinions or statements expressed.

Produced and designed in the United States of America by the
Fathers and Brothers of the Society of St. Paul,
2187 Victory Boulevard, Staten Island, New York 10314
as part of their communications apostolate.

ISBN: 978-0-8189-1255-9

Printing Information:

Current Printing - first digit									
2	3	4	5	6	7	8	9	10	

Year of Current Printing - first year shown

2017	2018	2019	2020	2021	2022	2023	2024	2025

In Loving Memory of My Parents

Roy Amber Porter
Anna Domenica Volpe

Contents

PART III
APPENDICES

Introduction

In the year 1190, a Jewish scholar, Moses Maimonides, produced a literary work which he called *A Guide for the Perplexed*. Maimonides had written this work for the consolation of pious and thoughtful Jews of his day who were very perplexed as to how claims for their God of the Bible could be reconciled with the claims of modern science.

My aim is similar to that of Maimonides. I too want to give guidance to the perplexed. But my focus and audience are considerably different. Though some people today are still concerned as to how one might reconcile the biblical doctrine of God with the claims of modern science, I believe there are many more people today who are perplexed not by the relation between God and science but by the why and wherefore of this thing we call the Church. Indeed, I can readily identify several groups in contemporary society who are often and considerably perplexed as regards the Church.

Contemporary society, whether in Europe or America, is rapidly becoming highly pluralistic and diverse. For example, while a large portion of American citizens, the majority even, still claim to be Christian, nevertheless, there are also present here significant numbers of people of other faiths, for example, Jews, Muslims, Hindus, etc.. But, in addition to people of other faiths, there are also significant numbers of Americans who have no discernible religious commitment at all. Both of these groups find the Church perplexing. That is, both believers and skeptics alike — Jews, Muslims, Hindus, free-thinkers, humanists and atheists in American society — are at times considerably perplexed not so much by individual Christian faith but by those organized Christians who not only claim to have a special relationship with God but also an urgent, indeed, compelling need to reshape the world. These non-Christians or non-believers are made anxious by the ability of the Church as a social institution to not only command the loyalty of its own members but to go on to challenge the laws and values of society at large.

But contemporary perplexity regarding the Church does not end with an account of non-Christians and non-believers. There are yet others among us who find the Church perplexing. And these others come from the ranks of pious Christians themselves. For example, even among Christians there are widely varying notions as to what the Church is or ought to be. More precisely, there are many Evangelical Christians and many Liberal Protestants who find the structure of authority and exclusive claims of those Christian assemblies which form the Catholic Church more than just perplexing, that is, not just unnecessary but ominous. Indeed, they find not only the Catholic Church's demands upon the consciences of its own members perplexing but these Evangelical Christians and Liberal Protestants are often offended, even outraged, by the Catholic Church's unwillingness to recognize Evangelical and Liberal Protestant communities of faith as worthy of the designation "Church."

But, as we all know, even before the Protestant Reformation there had arisen serious divisions among Christians over the idea of the Church. To this day there are Orthodox Christians among us who find the claims of the Catholic Church especially annoying and perplexing. For Orthodox Christians know that, despite the fact they hold many doctrinal teachings in common with the Catholic Church, it is precisely with regard to the doctrine of authority in the Church that they most strongly disagree with Catholics.

But even these groups do not exhaust the number of those vexed by the idea of the Church and its historic manifestation among us today. For it is readily demonstrable: there are several more groups of pious Christians who find the Church a perplexing social phenomenon as well as a mysterious, often controversial, doctrine. And these groups are to be found among Catholics themselves. Today there are many Catholics who readily admit to being plagued by troublesome, unanswered questions regarding the Church. For example, there are those who describe themselves as conservative or traditionalist Catholics. For these people the reforms initiated by the Second Vatican Council (1962-1965) have been very perplexing. Indeed, some of these conservative Catholics even feel betrayed by that Council. They feel that those conciliar reforms have rendered the Church they knew and loved quite unrecognizable or only a vestige of what it once was. On the other hand, there is also clearly discernible today among Catholics yet another group, for there are many Catholics who are equally quick to describe themselves as theological and social liberals. They find their Church just as perplexing though for quite different reasons. Catholic liberals or progressives are very perplexed by what they feel is the failure of the post-Vatican II Church to not just implement but to continue and even go beyond the reforms inaugurated by the Second Vatican Council. Members of this group often feel oppressed by the historic Church of the past which they consider still too much with us. They want to see the Church even more radically transformed. Finally, there are among pious Catholics today those who, while they would not readily identify themselves with either Liberal or Conservative Catholics, nonetheless, they too find the Church and its ways very perplexing. And this group is perhaps quite numerous, for, while I described above the consternation of many at the ease with which the Church commands the loyalty of most of its members, there is reason to suspect that in our time loyalty to the Church even among "practicing" members is often tenuous and, indeed, at times discreetly compromised when particular teachings of the Church are disregarded in the privacy of conscience. And thus I do not feel I am exaggerating when I say: for a great many to-day — pious Catholics, as much as Protestants, Orthodox, devout adherents of other religions, humanists, and atheists — it is not at all clear where the Church is coming from, or from whence comes its authority, the justification for its claims upon its members and upon others. For all too many today it is not clear what the Church should be doing or how it should go about doing this, where it should be going, what direction it should take or why it should even exist.

As something of a remedy for this lamentable situation what I try to do in this book is to set forth in clear and understandable terms a contemporary exposition of the historic or classical theology of the Church, its origins, its claims, its structures, its aims and endeavors, its mode of operation. For this formidable task, I have divided this book into three parts, each with several chapters. Part I is entitled, "The Church: Its Origin and Nature." There I treat such basic questions as where did the idea of the Church even come from, what are some of the historic claims made about the Church, what is the origin and history of those claims. This includes an examination of classic biblical images of the Church, the contemporary concept of models of the Church as well as ancient creedal affirmations that set forth such particularly perplexing claims as that the Church is, or at least should be, one, holy, catholic and apostolic, a communion. Part II is entitled, "The Church: Its Mission and Ministry." There I examine such questions as what is the Church expected to do in the world and how does it go about doing that. This includes not only a treatment of the historic mission of the Christian Church but also how that mission is conceived of today. I also treat of the origin and development of Christian ministries, surveying each of the most prominent ministries operative today, the rationale for them. Finally, I have appended two essays which treat of topics that either do not fit into the principal divisions of this book or are further elaborations on the material treated in the two principal divisions. One is an essay treating the considerable significance given to Mary, the Mother of Jesus, in the oldest Christian Churches. The second is a consideration of the Second Vatican Council as an example of the Church as not just a worshiping but also a deliberative assembly.

At first thought, this program may seem overly ambitious. Indeed, even just a glance at the table of contents of this book may well strike some with the thought the reading of this book might prove an all too daunting task. But be advised: this book need not be read methodically from cover to cover. While, indeed, there is an overall program dictating the disposition of these chapters into an ongoing, logical argument — and some may want to read it that way — on the other hand, I have intentionally treated each of the themes in a relatively concise and summary fashion. That is, all three sections of this book, Parts I and II and the Appendices, consist of numerous but short and intentionally concise or summary treatments of the issues at hand. And thus we have here chapters that can be read independently and in a brief period of time in a manner that will familiarize the reader with the major issues pertinent to each topic heading. Which is to say: this book has been intentionally cast more as a "handbook," a manual guide, rather than as a treatise, that is, one sustained argument to be considered as a whole.

It is also important that the reader know something about the author of this book, the point of view from which I write, and the approach I take to the subject matter at hand, and know this at the beginning. It may already be apparent to many readers that the principal focal point for my remarks herein is the historic Catholic Church, the Church sometimes referred to as the Roman Catholic Church. This, my identification with one particular historic expression of the phenomenon called Church might appear to some readers to prejudice my arguments and render them as merely apologetic for that one Christian tradition. Some therefore will be tempted to put this book aside and read no further. But I ask such readers to first consider: It is true that I am a member of the Catholic Church, and, in fact, I am an ordained minister of that Church. Moreover, I readily admit as a Catholic theologian I am self-consciously an exponent of the Catholic Church's traditional doctrine. That is, I am not a self-conscious dissenter from official Church teaching. Nor do I try to reinvent the Church. Nothing I say here is intended as a significant innovation beyond what the Church has traditionally taught about itself. Even so, the reader need not be put off by this my point of view, my precise and unqualified institutional affiliation. Any author writing about the Church will represent some personal, existential decision regarding the historic phenomenon called Church. The author will either be a member of some one particular Church or represent a decision against any membership, by labeling him or herself a generic Christian, an atheist or a member of some other faith, perhaps a Jew, a Muslim, a Hindu. Moreover, that I should presume to address others from a standpoint emphatically within the Catholic tradition need not be seen as entirely and simply apologetic. Indeed, I insist the Catholic Church is my focus not just because I am a member of it, but because, arguably, we find in it the most historic and ambitious form of Church. As for the historic character of the Catholic Church: here it is important to recall it was the thesis not of a Catholic theologian but of a German Lutheran that the Catholic Church, Roman Catholicism, has its roots within the New Testament itself. Ernst Käsemann (1906-1998) long ago argued for a thing he called *Frühkatholizismus.* That is a German word meaning "early Catholicism." Käsemann claimed, and he was not alone in this claim, it is patently observable that certain characteristics of the historic Catholic Church — for example: hierarchy, ordination, sacramentalism, dogma — are already present in the earliest documents of the Christian movement, that is, in those literary works that comprise the New Testament. As for the ambitious character of the Catholic Church: to be sure, Käsemann and his fellow thinkers were insistent that this early appearance is a corruption and deviation, that is, this "early Catholicism" is a distortion of the original gospel message. I, of course, do not concur in that judgment. In fact, I hope to show how this phenomenon of early Catholicism is not only evident earlier than Käsemann allows but is often rooted in the very words and deeds of the historical Jesus. As for those readers who do not share my convictions, they will still profit from reading this book because they will feel confident that herein they can examine temptations or distortions regarding the Church which have been present not only from the beginning but are still advocated by some to this very day. And thus I feel confident there is a lesson here for everyone, even those least sympathetic to the Catholic Church and its rationale.

But the reader should also realize that this book is not merely an exercise in defensive apologetics. It is also intended to be a work of constructive theology. More precisely, what I present here is intended to be not just the defense of a tradition but a genuine dialogue with current as well as historical voices. For example, even if most often herein I am describing the outlines of a Catholic ecclesiology, I do not ignore the significant differences between it and the self-conception of other Christian assemblies who call themselves Church. Nor am I impervious to the particular values, moral as well as intellectual, embodied in other ecclesial traditions. Indeed, I have a dual religious heritage, both personally and intellectually. And this dual heritage has figured significantly in the formation of my mind and character and the composition of this book. More precisely, while my mother's religious heritage was Italian Catholic, my father's was that of English Anabaptists. Moreover, though I was raised in the Catholic Church, my father's religious witness, his strict sabbatarianism and biblicism, also had a formative influence upon me. And, while I hold standard pontifical degrees (baccalaureate, licentiate, lectorate) acquired in a Catholic seminary — the Dominican Studium in Washington, D.C. — I also earned a master's degree and a doctorate from an historic Protestant institution — the Oberlin School of Divinity at Vanderbilt University in Nashville, Tennessee. This, my dual-religious heritage, has left me with strong convictions about method in our study of the Church especially with regard to the importance of inclusion and balance.

I am convinced theology is different from empirical science. With empirical science the difference between right and wrong is often not just demonstrable but precisely measurable. For example, in mathematics with base ten, two and two are always four. This is indisputable and any other claim is not just chicanery but demonstrably incorrect. Such mathematical precision has tremendous practical implications. For example, shortly after the orbiting telescope called the Hubble Spacecraft was first launched into space, it was discovered that there was an error in the curvature of its lens. The error was only the smallest fraction of an inch. But that was enough to render that space telescope useless until it was corrected. Theology is not like that. Theological error is rarely totally wrong. Indeed, the very durability of theological error, the persistence of heresies, is due to the fact that more

often than not a heresy is built upon a truth of the faith. It may
be an isolated truth, an exaggerated truth, perhaps only a half-
truth, but rarely is a heresy without any truth. And that small or
partial or exaggerated truth cannot be discarded or dismissed in
the way a defective lens can be replaced. (In fact, Hubble's defective lens was not replaced but compensated for by the addition
of something like a contact lens.) This means that herein I have
tried to do two things. First, I have self-consciously attempted
to avoid both the exaggerations implicit in extreme or polarized
positions and the exclusivity of either/or positions. Second,
whenever and wherever possible, I try to include and balance
the demands of two apparently opposing insights. And thus at
times I will attempt to demonstrate the reconcilability into one
unitary vision of the historic concerns of Orthodox, Protestant,
liberal and conservative Catholic, and even secularist mentalities
in the belief that each represents a partial vision of a larger truth.
The only time I avoid inclusion is in my option to quote from the
Revised Standard Version of the Bible rather than use the New
Revised Standard Version. The reason for this option is: my arguments require precise historical references but the NRSV's use of
inclusive language renders that translation at times imprecise or
less than accurate.

This latter point serves to introduce another thing the potential reader should be made aware of and that is the fact that
the Bible figures significantly in all the thoughts, arguments,
explanations or elaborations I set forth herein. There are several
reasons for this. For one thing, the Bible is the common language
of the Christian tradition. Catholic, Orthodox and Protestant all
quote from it. And thus it supplies a logical common ground for
dialogue among these groups. But the Bible, especially that part
of the Christian Bible that we call the New Testament, is also of
fundamental importance because it contains the earliest witness
to the origin and development of the Church, its earliest rationale.
No one can afford to ignore this earliest witness. Indeed, many
will feel this earliest witness, because it records or represents the
experience of the first generation of Christians, some of whom
knew the historical Jesus, is a privileged vision of the Church,

one which must stand as the criterion against which we judge everything that comes after it. Moreover, as a Catholic theologian, I am in good company when I give the Bible such a place not just of prominence but even pre-eminence. Thomas Aquinas is considered by many as the foremost example of a Catholic systematic theologian, that is, a theologian who has thought through all the implications, every related angle of his faith employing an acute rational tool, the result of his careful study of and commentary upon philosophical — Platonic, Neo-Platonic and Aristotelian — sources. However, what is not always sufficiently acknowledged is that Aquinas was also an accomplished biblical exegete. When he taught at the University of Paris, he held the title of *Magister in Sacra Pagina*, "Master of the Sacred Page." And the book to which that phrase referred was not Aristotle's *Metaphysics* but the Bible. Indeed, much of Aquinas's theology and spirituality is contained in his exegetical commentaries on Isaiah, Jeremiah, the Psalms and Job, along with the Gospels and Epistles of the New Testament. Moreover, even a casual look at his great encyclopedic and systematic summary of theology, the *Summa theologiae*, is enough to make it obvious to the reader that for all of Aquinas's philosophical acumen and erudition, he knew the Bible thoroughly and quoted from it profusely. Indeed, in his *Summa theologiae*, all of Aquinas' questions and answers begin or end with biblical quotations.

Though I too quote constantly from the Bible herein, in doing this I hope to avoid the common error of biblical "prooftexting." Instead, I aim to employ a method of exposition that is historical and critical. That is, I will not just quote a biblical passage as proof of the ideas, thoughts, arguments, explanations or elaborations I am setting forth. While I shall be keen to point out to the reader those biblical passages that long ago became fundamental departure points, foundational reference points, for a theology of the Church, I shall also try to explain how our understanding of those classic biblical passages has changed over the centuries. Also I shall be conscientious to point out the particularly challenging, alternative readings or interpretations of those classic passages given by modern biblical scholars. As my models for biblical interpretation I claim such eminent twentieth century exegetes as John L. McKenzie (1910-1991) and Raymond E. Brown (1928-1998) and Rudolf Schnackenburg (1914-2002). Hopefully, I have learned my lessons well from them and, if they could, they would not disown me.

Finally, it is important that the reader be advised how derivative is my thought herein. What is true and valuable in this book I owe to others. The errors alone are mine. In this regard, what John of Salisbury (ca. 1115-80) once attributed (in his *Metalogicon*, Bk 3, Ch. 4) to a contemporary scholar of his time is equally applicable to me today: "Bernard of Chartres used to compare us to dwarfs perched on the shoulders of giants. He pointed out that we see more and farther than our predecessors, not because we have keener vision or greater height, but because we are lifted up and borne aloft on their gigantic stature." I do not claim to see more and farther, but that I can see at all is due in great measure to what I have learned from others. But, I have also decided that, since my concern here is to outline and explain basic ideas, to specify the precise literary origin of each turn in the development of these ideas would only encumber the text (and the reader) with technicalities. Moreover, that I do not always acknowledge my sources is a lacuna which the theologically informed reader will not only readily recognize but easily supply for. Even so, I have decided I should at least take the opportunity here in this preface to acknowledge my general indebtedness to others. In addition to the three exegetes whose work I have already acknowledged as having greatly influenced my method — McKenzie, Brown, and Schnackenburg — I also willingly recognize I have learned much in terms of the content of ecclesiology from theologians such as Angel Antón, Johann Auer, Louis Bouyer, Yves Congar, Avery Dulles, Miguel Garijo-Guembe, Monika Hellwig, Charles Journet, Hans Küng, René Latourelle, Gerhard Lohfink, Henri de Lubac, Jürgen Moltmann, Christopher O'Donnell, Wolfhart Pannenberg, Edward Schillebeeckx, Elizabeth Schüssler-Fiorenza, Juan Luis Segundo, Francis Sullivan, Paul Tillich, Miroslav Volf, and John Zizioulas. Even when I disagree with them, and in some cases the disagreements are considerable, I owe much to these eminent theologians. In addition to my debt to these eminent scholars, I want also to acknowledge my dependence upon those scholars who contributed entries on ecclesiological themes in numerous biblical reference works such as dictionaries and encyclopedias.

Finally, I want to thank my friend and colleague, Monsignor Gerard McCarren, S.T.D. He read this book in manuscript. His wise comments and discerning observations helped me to improve it in many ways.

Lawrence B. Porter, PhD
Seton Hall University
30 June 2007

Biblical Abbreviations

OLD TESTAMENT

Genesis	Gn	Nehemiah	Ne	Baruch	Ba
Exodus	Ex	Tobit	Tb	Ezekiel	Ezk
Leviticus	Lv	Judith	Jdt	Daniel	Dn
Numbers	Nb	Esther	Est	Hosea	Ho
Deuteronomy	Dt	1 Maccabees	1 M	Joel	Jl
Joshua	Jos	2 Maccabees	2 M	Amos	Am
Judges	Jg	Job	Jb	Obadiah	Ob
Ruth	Rt	Psalms	Ps	Jonah	Jon
1 Samuel	1 S	Proverbs	Pr	Micah	Mi
2 Samuel	2 S	Ecclesiastes	Ec	Nahum	Na
1 Kings	1 K	Song of Songs	Sg	Habakkuk	Hab
2 Kings	2 K	Wisdom	Ws	Zephaniah	Zp
1 Chronicles	1 Ch	Sirach	Si	Haggai	Hg
2 Chronicles	2 Ch	Isaiah	Is	Malachi	Ml
Ezra	Ezr	Jeremiah	Jr	Zechariah	Zc
		Lamentations	Lm		

NEW TESTAMENT

Matthew	Mt	Ephesians	Eph	Hebrews	Heb
Mark	Mk	Philippians	Ph	James	Jm
Luke	Lk	Colossians	Col	1 Peter	1 P
John	Jn	1 Thessalonians	1 Th	2 Peter	2 P
Acts	Ac	2 Thessalonians	2 Th	1 John	1 Jn
Romans	Rm	1 Timothy	1 Tm	2 John	2 Jn
1 Corinthians	1 Cor	2 Timothy	2 Tm	3 John	3 Jn
2 Corinthians	2 Cor	Titus	Tt	Jude	Jude
Galatians	Gal	Philemon	Phm	Revelation	Rv

Part I

THE CHURCH: ITS ORIGIN AND NATURE

CHAPTER 1

The Church as a Form of Community

"We live in St. Mark's parish. But on Sunday mornings we go to St. Cunegunde's. There is much more of a sense of *community* at St. Cunegunde's." This is a sentiment I have heard expressed fairly frequently. And as I drive around I increasingly come across a sign announcing "St. Mary's Catholic *Community*" rather than the more conventional "St. Mary's Catholic Church." "Community" seems to be something of a "buzz" word, a fashionable expression these days. Its popularity is perhaps symptomatic of a general social problem. That is, modern society tends to be anonymous, people see themselves as but a small cog in a large social process, and so people look for social situations that suggest more intimacy. These people who want to see the Church as a form of community are "on to something." That is, one could well argue community has always been an important part of biblical faith.

Doubtless Moses, when he encountered God on Horeb (Ex 3) and Sinai (Ex 19), was something of a lone mystic. But Moses eventually came down the mountain and shared with others the visions he had experienced in solitude. Moreover, the message he brought down with him had a strong component of community responsibility. True, the first four commandments concern duties toward God. But the final six address our relations with family and neighbor (cf. Ex 20 and Dt 5). Without doubt, Jesus too is at times presented in the Gospels as something of a lone religious mystic. That is, at times he goes off by himself to pray to his Father in solitude (Mk 1:35, 6:46; Mt 14:23; Lk 6:12).

However, there can be little doubt that Jesus is also presented in the Gospels as supremely a man of the people. One of the very first things he does at the beginning of his public ministry is to gather a community of disciples, and from then on wherever Jesus goes he gathers a crowd, a crowd whom he not only prophetically alerts to relationships in their own lives but invites into a deeper communion with God, himself and each other. Moreover, the communal character of Jesus' preaching is especially strong. Indeed, some have argued that in this matter of communal awareness Jesus' preaching went beyond traditional Jewish piety. For example, while it may be alleged Jesus often simply repeats Jewish piety, it can also be argued when he repeats it he stresses its communal dimension, as when Jesus yokes together the injunction of Deuteronomy 6:4, to "love the Lord your God with all your heart and with all your soul and with all your might" with that of Leviticus 19:18 to "love your neighbor as yourself" (Mk 12:31; Mt 22:39; Lk 10:27). Also, apparently, Jesus made love of neighbor the test for the genuineness of one's love of God, as when in Matthew 5:23 he is quoted as saying, "If on the way to the temple, you remember that your neighbor has something against you, put your gift aside. Go first and be reconciled with your neighbor." Moreover, Jesus makes a special point of promising his presence to the community of his disciples, "Where two or three are gathered in my name there I am in your midst" (Mt 18:20). Jesus sends forth his disciples "two by two" (Mk 6:7, 11:1; Lk 10:1, 19:29). And from early in Christian history commentators on the Gospels insisted upon the significance of Jesus' having taught us to pray "*Our* Father" not "*My* Father" (Mt 6:9). All this can be used to argue that Christianity is a peculiarly communal faith wherein the drama of the search for self-identity is strongly yoked to the drama of communal existence. For this reason I begin our study of the Church by exploring the phenomenon of community. Insofar as the Church is made up of human beings it is a form of community. And so we need to understand something about what human community is if we are to understand what form of community the Church is. And so what I would like to do here is first to start with a consideration of the general phenomenon of human community. Human community comes in various forms but these various forms exhibit some common dynamics. It would be helpful if we could identify these common dynamics and then see how they apply to the form of community that is the Church.

It is arguable that one of the major characteristics of the human species as a phenomenon, an observable event or thing, is that whenever and wherever we find human beings, human beings exhibit a social aspect, that is, they tend to form associations among themselves. And, when these associations exhibit a certain measure of stability, when they become meaningful bonds, reliable networks of social transference, and not just fleeting purely adventitious encounters, we call them communities. The science of anthropology, the study of historical evidence for primitive human beings, seems to indicate that from as far back in time as we have evidence, human beings have tended to band together in various forms of community.

In ancient times, one of the most basic forms of association or community was the family. It also tended to be (and still can be) one of the strongest of human associations. And this is because of its affective component. That is, one not only becomes emotionally attached to a caring parent or a helpless child but strongly attached to them. Moreover, since in primitive times it was very difficult to survive on one's own, the social bonds represented by family or the confederation of families we call a tribe were absolutely vital, a matter of life and death. But even in ancient times, besides these two basic forms of community, family and tribe, there appeared other forms of human association with small but well defined aims, communities or associations formed to facilitate common tasks or common interests, for example, hunting parties in search of food or fuel or defensive units for protection from aggressors, human or animal. This pattern of behavior is evident even today, that is, if we look around us, we see that most human beings are born into a family and then they tend, sometimes self-consciously, other times unselfconsciously, to organize themselves into other forms of community. For example, children move away to attach themselves to an academic community, a college or university, or later marry and form a family of their own or join a subculture. And as in the ancient world so today many forms of community are based upon common tasks. While primitive human beings may have gathered together in hunting parties, today we have labor unions and professional associations. In every modern society we can discern a legal community, a medical community, an academic community and the religious communities that assemble at mosques, churches, temples, synagogues and shrines. All these forms of community are examples of people coming together to pursue a common goal or task, to foster a tradition or perfect a vision.

Another thing that the reader must understand is that there are certain dynamics present in every form of community. For example, one of the basic dynamics of human community is that every form of human association implies some measure of give and take, some form of commitment and responsibility to as well as benefit from the association. Indeed, one could easily compile a list of various forms of human community ranking them in growing order according to increasing intensity of relationship, increasing demands on giving and receiving. I adapt here a list used by Johann Auer in his book on *The Church*: acquaintanceship, comradeship, friendship, marriage, family, clan or people, nation. Each form of community in this list, from the simplest to the most complex, represents increasing levels of involvement and commitment. Acquaintanceship is the simplest level of community. Our neighbors are not total strangers. We know where they live and some of their habits. And simply because we live closely together in a geographic area we share some vital concerns with our neighbors. For example, as neighbors, we are concerned that our streets are plowed when it snows, that the garbage is picked up regularly. Comradeship is a little more intense form of human community. The faculty in a university community is, in a sense, comrades sharing a common task. That is, they too may not be emotionally attached to each other as the members of a family are, yet their common task brings them even closer together than mere territorial neighbors. An academic faculty is formed to see that students are educated, exposed to a body of literature containing ancient wisdom, not just to repeat it but to be able to work with it and apply it to new tasks and situations. However, there is also discernible in every academic community a smaller and even more intense form of community called friendship. There are students who share more than lecture notes. There are professors who are friends and not just colleagues, who share personal and not just professional interests. And some of those friendships develop into marriages.

Marriage is an even more intense and demanding form of community in that here two people promise to be with and for each other more exclusively and permanently than a mere friendship, however intense, could avail. Indeed, even the best of friends might have to part, at graduation time, for example, or to take a new faculty position at another school. If children issue from a marriage bond, then further intensive relationships are formed. Indeed, family, especially in older times was often the community for whom one was expected to attempt and sacrifice the most. For some people, race or ethnic identity is an important bond, that is, form of community. For example, in the U.S.A. some ethnic groups maintain an intense bond to their ancestral home, to preserving ethnic traditions such as food and drink, dance and music. Finally, there is the State. The State is a geographically situated form of community like one's neighborhood, that is, one is born in a particular geographical location. But the State is also a comprehensive form of community regulating many aspects of human life: health services, highway construction, educational institutions.

Moreover, the State can make supreme demands upon its members. For example, in times of war when the welfare or very existence of one's political community is at issue, the State can demand that the individual be recruited for dangerous assignment to protect the State, a dangerous assignment that could lead to one's death.

Yet another observable aspect of human community is

that of traditions or customs. Traditions or customs are not just tried and tested ways of doing things, they also represent the inherited experience of the community. In primitive societies, in the company of a hunting party one learned the technique of hunting and heard of the experiences of great hunters. When these experiences and methods are written down they become rules or even laws. At the level of the family, the process of "inculturation" — learning traditions and customs — begins when one is very young. From early on a parent starts to teach a child what are acceptable and what are not acceptable forms of behavior within the community called family. Moreover, every family has its own distinctive history and to the degree that it is known and recalled, or celebrated, that experience weighs upon all members of that family as a precedent or an ideal, even if it is a simple tradition or custom such as "We always get together as a family for a Fourth of July picnic or to celebrate Christmas or grandma's birthday." Professional communities such as the medical or legal community often place great emphasis upon the observance of traditional procedures and in their meeting places they often have framed portraits of principal figures in the history of their professions. The State mandates that on certain days labor must cease so that some event in that political community's history can be observed with appropriate festivity or solemnity. Even local communities have laws as to where one might park or where one might empty the garbage.

Until now, I have been emphasizing community as a common identity or cooperation in a common task or effort. But we must also recognize the dynamics of freedom in any form of community. The phenomenon of freedom is an aspect of all human communities. True, some have distinguished the various forms of human association or community into two types: either natural associations or free associations. *"Natural" Associations*: it is observable that there are some forms of community that have a "given-ness" to them, that is, they appear to be simple casual or natural associations, not based upon any self-conscious, free decision of or by the individual. Examples of this would be those associations that we call neighborhoods or families. Initially, at

natural associations - we don't have a choice

least, we do not usually choose our neighbors but simply find ourselves living next to someone. The same thing with a family; most people were born into a family. We are born in such and such a place or are born into such and such a family or institution. Then there are *"Free" Associations* such as friendships, work and Church. However, it is also arguable all human associations involve some free decision. Even if we are born into a family and into a neighborhood, there will come some point in life when we will have to make a decision to enhance or to dissolve these "given" or "natural" relationships. With most human beings there comes a point in life when they begin to weigh the decision whether they want to continue their relationships with the communities they have found themselves part of from birth or whether they want to lessen, even end, those ties. And thus we at times find ourselves in the process of making decisions to confirm and even intensify this relationship in which we find ourselves by joining with our family and neighbors or to lessen these relationships or maybe even end these relationships by moving away from the neighborhood and cutting off all contact even with family. Indeed, occasionally it happens that some people decide to abandon all such free associations and move into the woods or by the sea or on a rock to live as a solitary. The element of freedom in community, the decision to stay with or remove oneself from a community can often be a very intense and dramatic struggle. It is probably for that reason that Auer describes this dynamic as the tension between "self-preservation and self-abandonment."

Yet another part of the dynamics of freedom is also wrestling with the demands of tradition, sacred memories or history. If, indeed, customs and traditions are the community's means of appropriating the wisdom of ancient experiences, ways that are not only tried and true but effectively embody and communicate the history, the historic experiences of that community, observance of these traditions and customs weighs heavily on everyone in the community. Innovative minds will often find community a great challenge in this regard. It is always difficult for any community to discern who among them is a genuinely insightful and thus beneficial innovator and who is a wild-eyed willful maverick. This leads to the next dynamic of human community which we must consider.

Finally, there is the drama of freedom which has its focus not in the individual but the community itself. This we might call the dynamic of disassociation, exile or banishment. If every member of a community experiences the tension between self-preservation and self-abandonment to the demands of community, the community itself must at certain times judge and exercise its freedom as to whether an individual member meets the least demands for membership or perhaps constitutes a lethal challenge to the community. For example, all forms of community imply a reciprocal relationship but if one is not "carrying one's load," if one is indulging in more taking than giving, in a friendship, in a marriage, or at work, that will put a strain on the relationship. And, if it is enough of a strain, it will lead to a separation. Sometimes in professional associations such as legal communities or medical communities this form of separation takes dramatic expression as disbarment or loss of license to practice.

It is arguable that the Church is a form of community. It is a community of faith. This means it too, insofar as it is made up of human beings, will exhibit many of the characteristics of other forms of human community, the various forms we have been observing. The Church too is made up of people with a common interest. It too has both the benefits and the requirements of membership. The Church too has certain criteria for membership which if not lived up to can lead to formal separation. It too involves the individual member's wrestling with the drama of self-preservation and self-abandonment, the personal appropriation or rejection of communal values and traditions. But it is arguable that in the Church all these dynamics and tensions are heightened such that the Church represents, if not *the* most, certainly one of the most comprehensive, challenging and ambitious forms of community.

That the Church is one of the most comprehensive forms of community is arguable from the fact that it comprises many people from many lands. It is not identified with any one ethnic or geographical group. The Church, while indeed it began with significant Semitic roots quickly abandoned that Semitic identity and has historically exhibited itself as capable of rooting itself in many cultures. Indeed, it could be argued that the Church is more comprehensive and inclusive than the United Nations. For, while world peace is universally desired, the Church comprises a more intensive relationship than merely the quest for political harmony. It is the most challenging form of community in that it makes the greatest demands upon give and take, that is, it makes demands upon the most personal human resources of faith, hope and love, asking for a great deal of each of these virtues. It asks its members to believe that despite much chaos and confusion this life has a meaning. It asks us to hope this life is not all there is. There is a further life to come. It asks its members to love unto death (especially in marriage). It places supreme importance upon the transmission and appropriation of its historic, formative experiences (the life and death of Jesus of Nazareth). It is the most ambitious form of community in that it is not only convinced it can bring a depth of meaning to each individual life but also peace to the world. No doubt some people will find these claims of the Church too daunting or even gratuitous, groundless. But no one should doubt their importance. The things one believes in make a great difference in the way one lives. If one believes that there is nothing beyond this life, one can easily become very greedy, grabbing all one can get here and now. If one believes that there is no judgment but the judgment of men, one will be greatly tempted by the prospect of eluding or confounding human judgment.

However, after having said all these things about the universally observable phenomenon of community, we must also address the fact that many people have suggested modernity has put severe strains upon the viability of any significant form of community beyond the most casual, merely adventitious, associations. That is, it is arguable there are factors in modern society that raise serious obstacles against the formation of any truly serious sense of community as a formative social tool that gives identity and value to peoples' lives. In ancient times, community was often so formative an influence on people's lives that separation from community was tantamount to the most extreme act of violence. And thus Socrates preferred self-inflicted death to banishment from Athens. The Christian, Dante, had no such option. And thus for the rest of his life he mourned grievously his separation from Florence. The societies of Athens and Florence had so impressed their values on these men that even though they might raise what their fellows regarded as lethal challenges to those societies, they themselves felt a tragic, frightening loss at the prospect of their being banished from those historic communities. It is doubtful that many feel that way today about any community of which they have been a member unless that be a professional association to which they have dedicated their whole life or from which they gain their livelihood.

Modern-day capitalist and consumer-oriented societies provide the individual with the means to be self-sufficient, to live quite independently of family, tribe and sometimes even friends. Today the material things needed to enable one, not just to survive, but to enjoy a high level of existence, can be readily bought and stored on one's own. And then there are the obstacles to community created by the culture of technology. There are ambiguities inherent in so-called technological "advances." For example, while technological devices such as the television and the telephone can facilitate communication, it is always communication from a distance. While televisions and cell phones enable us to readily communicate verbally or visually, they cannot entirely overcome our moral distance from people and events. And a considerable argument could be made that there is no substitute for "real presence." Being virtually present is not the same thing as being truly there. Indeed, one of the basic requirements for any form of community is that one be present to the other, surely not at all times, but at least for significant moments. Even such loose affiliations as professional societies do not exist merely by correspondence. They meet at least once a year for their annual convention. Moreover, while modern technological society with its ready mobility (planes, trains and automobiles) makes it more than ever possible to be at least physically present, it also makes it easy to rapidly distance oneself from a situation, to withdraw from the closest community of family, friends and neighbors as when job opportunities make it economically desirable to move far away. No doubt television and the internet supply a sense of community, the global village, but there is also evidence much of this is an illusion in that they make community only more elusive, enabling the emotionally remote to enter voyeuristically upon an experience that should require personal intimacy. Indeed, one of the tell-tale indications that the sense of community is rare in modern society is the phenomenon by which many Christians choose the local church they attend on the criterion of whether or not it provides a sense of social community as well as the opportunity to celebrate a common faith. And thus parishes sometimes are under considerable pressure to provide not just an intense worship experience, an encounter with the transcendent, but also a significant amount of social interaction.

Yet another formidable challenge to the achievement of community is the fact that, as children of the Enlightenment, we moderns tend to champion personal freedom over and against the legitimate demands of community, and foster independent thinking over against the common norms of tradition. Indeed, nineteenth century romanticism has created the image of the genius as necessarily rebellious. A simple practical effect of this is that no one is surprised to see a freshman arrive on campus wearing a t-shirt that says "Question Authority." No doubt, there will be times when authority should be not just questioned but even challenged. But, out of a sense of fairness, this should be done only after authority has been given a fair hearing. But to truly hear requires study, careful listening, indeed, entering into the other's experience. Even Beethoven, often portrayed as the archetype of artistic rebellion, broke the traditional laws of harmony only after years of careful learning and study of them.

What we have said here can easily lead us to think, the antique form of community that is Church, the formative bond and corporate witness it is meant to be, cannot help but experience new challenges in the modern era. When one has been taught to question all authority even before hearing it, to question on principle, what is the chance that one will take the time and effort to give Christianity, the experience of Christ, a fair hearing? But in the end, one might take comfort from the idea that community is a deeply inscribed human need. The phenomenon of human community may not be purely adventitious, simply a survival tactic; it may instead be the expression of an individuality looking to another or others for fulfillment, and not just any others, but truly significant others. Our next chapter will introduce us to the One "Other" whose significance is of paramount importance in the community called Church, an Other who has spoken loudly and deeply though often mysteriously through events and experiences whose narration is listened to and pondered repeatedly and often, such that Christians to this day gather regularly to hear those words and ponder those events and experiences.

Further Reading

In Johann Auer's *The Church: The Universal Sacrament of Salvation* (Catholic University of America Press, 1993), Chapter I is an example of a classical treatment of this theme.

In T. Howland Sanks' *Salt, Leaven and Light: The Community Called Church* (Crossroad, 1997), Chapter 1 is a perceptive analysis of the challenging setting for the community called Church in contemporary American society.

CHAPTER 2

The Church as Sacred Assembly

Words are powerful things. For example, there are some people right now pacing the lobby of a courtroom or a hospital corridor waiting for a few words or even just one word. And that word once uttered will either plunge them into despair or open up vistas of hope. Words are powerful things, but sometimes we use words quite idly, that is, with little regard for the fullness of their meaning. This is particularly true of the word "Church." It conjures up various thoughts for various people. Not all these connotations are equally valid. In fact, its most common meaning in the English language can be very misleading. So in this chapter we shall have to try to get at a more theologically correct definition of this important word, "Church."

German theologian Paul Tillich (1886-1965) took refuge from the Nazis by coming to the United States where he soon mastered the English language and spent the rest of his life teaching and writing in English. Even so, Tillich was never entirely comfortable with the English language as a tool for theological thought. For example, he never stopped lamenting the fact that the word "spirit" in the English language has none of the philosophical and theological richness it has in European tongues (*Systematic Theology* Part IV "Life and the Spirit," section I.4.b, "The Meaning of Spirit as a Dimension of Life"). That is, in French and German, *esprit* and *geist* have a primarily spiritual meaning referring to movements of the mind and soul. But in the English language while these high-minded connotations are possible, they are also secondary to more common usages of the word "spirit." And these common usages connote many degraded if not dubious notions. More precisely, while the English word "spirit" can refer to a dynamic motivation — we often speak of school spirit — the word is also a common term for a ghost or "things that go bump in the night." And while the word "spirits" in the English language can be used to refer to souls, in popular parlance that word not only connotes ghosts or spectral beings but it is commonly used to refer to alcoholic beverages! There is a similar problem with the word "Church." Here too there is a common even gross use of the word that obscures the important and precise theological meaning.

For example, if in South Orange, New Jersey, the town where I live, a visitor were to ask someone on the street, "Where is Our Lady of Sorrows Church?", no doubt the person to whom this inquiry was addressed would immediately think of the church building on Prospect Street in South Orange and then give the inquirer directions as to how to get to that building. After following those directions, the visitor might arrive at the building only to find it empty but open and then proceed to admire the architectural splendor of that fine church building. But the fact is: the Church is not a building. It is people. The Church of Our Lady in South Orange is the people who meet in that building. The building may indeed reflect their faith. And, moreover, it is indeed the place where those people of faith regularly assemble. And so, in a sense, that building is a sacred space, sacred to those people. But we must never lose sight of the fact that the Church is primarily, essentially, people. That building could burn down. But the people would still be there and they would continue to gather to worship until a new church building was erected.

The reason that the word "church" in the English language refers primarily to a building rather than the people who gather in that building is due to etymology. Etymology is that academic discipline which studies the origin and history of words. Our English word "church" has the same origin and history as the word for church in several other northern European languages

— for example, the German *kirche*, the Slavic *carkov*, the Dutch *kerk*, the Swedish *kyrke* — in that all these words are derived from a Byzantine Greek phrase *kyriakon domos*. *Domos* means building. *Kyriakon* means "of the Lord." And thus the phrase means "house of the Lord." On the other hand, the word for church in Latin, *ecclesia*, and the word for church in the so-called "Romance languages" of southern Europe that derive from Latin (for example, Spanish *iglesia*, French *église*) have their origin in another New Testament Greek phrase, *ekklesia tou theou*. And this New Testament Greek phrase means not "house of the Lord" but "assembly of God." We need to study this phrase carefully. We need to learn first what an assembly was in the ancient world and then what it is that makes an assembly not just any assembly but an assembly *of God*.

The Greek word for assembly, *ekklesia*, has a history that goes back much further than the New Testament. It was a common word in the classical Attic Greek of Thucydides, Plato and Xenophon where its meaning was immediately clear. It is a composite word formed from the verb *kaleo*, "to call," and the prefix *ek* meaning "out." And thus it meant "those who are called out," the *ek-kaloi*. This most often had a very clear political reference in that it designated those members of the community who have been called out and summoned together for a social purpose. In the Greek city-states it referred precisely to those men — and not all men but only those adult males who owned property — who might be called together, assembled, for military purposes to defend the city or for domestic purposes such as deciding some civic matter, a matter of common concern.

Beginning about the year 250 B.C., Greek-speaking Jews in Alexandria, Egypt, produced a comprehensive Greek translation of the Jewish scriptures. In that work they used this classical Greek term, *ekklesia*, which referred primarily to the Hellenistic popular assembly, to translate an important Hebrew word, *qahal*, a word used to refer to the Hebrew sacred assembly. Some scholars have argued that the choice was probably simply dictated by the fact that these two Hebrew and Greek words have a similar etymological background, that is, the Hebrew word is like its

Greek counterpart in that it too meant to call forth. However, it is also possible to argue that the Greek-speaking Jews in Alexandria might also have delighted in using that Greek word because of the implicit contrast between the Hellenistic popular assembly and the Hebrew sacred assembly. That is, while there is a general similarity in that both terms indicate a group of people called forth, there is also considerable difference between the people called forth and the purpose for which they are called forth. More precisely, while the Hellenistic popular assembly consisted of a privileged or select group, namely, adult males, and not all adult males, but adult, land-owning males, the Hebrew sacred assembly made no such elitist distinctions; in the Hebrew sacred assembly all Israel was called forth. For example, while most often the biblical narrative simply refers to the assembly of Israel as "the people," there are a few passages that are more revelatory, that is, a few passages where the comprehensiveness of the Hebrew sacred assembly is given precise description. One example is in Nehemiah 7:2 where we read, "And Ezra the priest brought the law before the assembly, both men and women and all who could hear with understanding." The qualification "hear with understanding" refers not to those without hearing impairment but to children old enough to understand. That is, the Hebrew sacred assembly consisted not just of adult men and women but also children old enough to understand what was said, what was going on. In Deuteronomy 31:12, the composition of the Hebrew sacred assembly is made even more comprehensive and inclusive when we hear Moses give the order, "Assemble the people, men, women, and little ones, and the sojourners within your town." Moreover, while the Hellenistic civic or popular assembly had a democratic character, that is, those assembled had been called together to discern a common threat and each had equal voice, the Hebrew sacred assembly had the character of worship, the recognition of a presence greater than themselves; and it was not their own voices they came to hear but the word of that Other. Several passages in the Torah, the five books of Moses, make it clear the freedom of the Israelite people was not a simple end in itself but rather it was to serve an even higher purpose, Exodus 8:29, "...letting the people go to offer sacrifices to the Lord," Exodus 9:1, "Let my people go, that they may serve me." Exodus 10:3: "Let my people go, so that they may worship me." And in Deuteronomy 4:10, "Assemble the people before me to hear my words."

The importance of these peculiar, distinguishing dynamics of the Hebrew sacred assembly cannot be underestimated for the Hebrew sacred assembly was not just people, it was a people called apart into a relationship with a transcendent reality. The word "transcendent" refers to something above and beyond what is right in front of us. Innate to the religious motive in all human beings is the intuition that beyond the things visible in this world there is a force or intelligence greater than any of the things in this world. However, it was the Hebrew religious imagination that concluded there is but one thing behind this world and it is not only one but friendly, that is pre-eminently personal. This can be seen in an important passage of the Old Testament, the account of the Covenant at Horeb in Deuteronomy 5:1-11. The first passage (5:1-10) is the description of Moses giving the commandments to the people of Israel. The content of those commands is not particularly distinguishing. That is, no civilized society can exist without restrictions against murder, theft, deceit. Certain relationships like marriage and one's parents must be respected. But what makes Israel different is that these precepts are put in the context of the very personal God who lies behind them, not just occasions them but guarantees them, indeed insists on them. We see this in the words that preface the actual Ten Commandments. These words describe the God of Israel in the most personal, anthropomorphic terms as a jealous God:

> I, the Lord, am your God, who brought you out of the land of Egypt, that place of slavery. You shall not have other gods besides me. You shall not carve idols for yourselves in the shape of anything in the sky above, or on the earth below or in the waters beneath the earth; you shall not bow down before them or worship them.

> For I, the Lord, your God, am a jealous God, inflicting
> punishment for their fathers' wickedness on the children
> of those who hate me, down to the third and fourth gen-
> eration; but bestowing mercy down to the thousandth
> generation, on the children of those who love me and
> keep my commandments.

Within the context of this personal relationship with the
Transcendent Other, the rules embodied in the Ten Commandments take on a particular character. First, that personal character
gives them a special urgency. It is as though God were saying
because of what you and I mean to each other, there should be
no lying, stealing, or cheating among you. Also certain other relationships take on a sacral character, marriage becomes a sacred
bond not to be transgressed, human life suddenly has a sacral
aura. Moreover, the recognition of these realities will now separate the Hebrew people from the rest of the world. And thus here
are the great restrictions against mingling with the "nations,"
a term we shall not go into here, but it means all others than the
Hebrews. Here, in a passage from Deuteronomy 7:1-5, we hear
how emphatic that prohibition was:

> When the Lord your God brings you into the land which
> you are entering to take possession of it, and clears away
> many nations before you, the Hittites, the Girgashites,
> the Amorites, the Canaanites, the Perizzites, the Hivites,
> and the Jebusites, seven nations greater and mightier
> than yourselves, and when the Lord your God gives
> them over to you, and you defeat them; then you must
> utterly destroy them; you shall make no covenant with
> them, and show no mercy to them. You shall not make
> marriages with them, giving your daughters to their
> sons or taking their daughters for your sons. For they
> would turn away your sons from following me, to serve
> other gods; then the anger of the Lord would destroy
> you quickly.

It is arguable that in the New Testament we see a similar
prophetic parallelism, that is, a contrast between the Greek civic

assembly and the Christian sacred assembly.

For example, the image of the Greek civic assembly is clearly invoked in the New Testament work called the Acts of the Apostles. In Acts 19:23-41, in a narrative episode detailing an incident that occurred during one of the missionary journeys of Saint Paul, there is a vivid description of an emergency meeting of the *ekklesia* at Ephesus. The incident referred to is commonly called "the riot of the Ephesian silversmiths." According to Acts 19, Saint Paul's preaching of Christianity at Ephesus had caused so many conversions as to threaten the economy at Ephesus. That is, silversmiths at Ephesus made considerable money by fashioning silver shrines of the goddess Artemis whose principal shrine was at Ephesus. Now a group of those silversmiths staged a riot wherein they dragged Paul and his companions into the civic arena and summoned civic officials to deal with this problem. This was a spontaneous, emergency meeting of the civic assembly called *ekklesia* and this is noted in the language of Acts 19, for example, in Acts 19:32, "Now some cried out one thing, some another; for the assembly [*ekklesia*] was in confusion." And in the words of a civic official, the town clerk, who in Acts 19:39, advises the silversmiths to wait for a regularly scheduled meeting of the civic assembly: "But if you seek anything further, it shall be settled in the regular assembly [*ekklesia*]."

But there is another use of the work *ekklesia* in the New Testament and that is to refer to the Christian community. For example, in the earliest literary work of the Christian movement, Paul's First Letter to the Church at Thessalonica, in the very first line we read, "Paul and Silvanus and Timothy to the church of the Thessalonians (*ekklesia Thessalonikeon*). Now, no doubt, a town the size of Thessalonica would have had its own civic assembly, which most certainly would have been called the *ekklesia Thessalonikon*, and so here especially the contrast is paramount. Paul refers here not to the civic assembly of that town rather to the Christian worshipping assembly where this letter would have been read aloud for all to hear. Later in this same letter (1:14), Paul says, "You, brethren, became imitators of the churches of God (*ekklesion tou theou*) in Christ Jesus which are in Judea." In the earliest history of the Christian movement, the Acts of the Apostles (5:11), it is used by Luke to refer to the Christian assembly at Jerusalem, in a reference to the considerable awe provoked by the authority of Peter within that community and among even outsiders, "And great fear came upon the whole church (*ten ekklesion*), and upon all who heard of these things." In Ephesians and Colossians the word is used of the entire worldwide assembly of the followers of Jesus. No doubt there are other terms for the followers of Christ in the NT, for example, they are called (in Ac 9:2) "disciples of the Lord." Paul often refers to them as "the brethren" (1 Th 1:4, 2:1 and 14, Ac 1:15). But it is the word "Church" that is most often used to designate not Christians in their individuality but as a community of faith: 65 times in the New Testament works ascribed to Paul, 23 times in the Acts of the Apostles, 3 times in the Johannine writings, in the Letter of James, and twice it is found on the lips of Jesus (in Mt 16:18 and 18:17), all witnessing to the fact that this word became the common term for the Christian assembly as an alternative society to the Hellenistic public or civic assembly.

From this our word study there emerge several important lessons. First, it must be recognized that the Christian assembly is primarily an encounter with the transcendent. And it is that encounter that binds us to each other in a special way. Secondly, there is a difference between personal faith and assembled faith, the faith of the individual and the faith of the community. And, finally, it must also be clear that the encounter with God in the assembly of the faithful sets up a tension between life in the world and life in the community of faith.

There are factors in modern society that make a sense of encounter with the transcendent in the liturgical assembly hard to come by. We have already seen how the lack of a sense of community in the secular world puts pressure on the liturgical assembly to provide that and thus takes energy away from this other task. Not only are worshiping assemblies taxed by the need to offer an experience of human, social community, but the utilitarian nature of much modern architecture often renders liturgical spaces devoid of any ability to conjure up a sense of the transcendent. Gothic architecture often worked to produce buildings which even when empty are able to summon a sense of the transcendent. Modern architecture can do this too if we insist on it. Liturgical worship requires an appreciation of, indeed, a near cult of silence, a quiet, peaceful assembly from which emerges prayer, music and preaching. But modern man lives with noise, a music that is defined by propulsive rhythms. Here too, though, the point is not rejection of contemporary music but a selective use of it, the cultivation of aspects of it that are more conducive to Christian worship.

The second lesson: it is arguable that Moses' assembly of the Hebrew people at the foot of Mount Sinai signals a significant development in Israelite faith beyond the initial faith of Abraham. The whole Abraham saga (Gn 11:10-25:11) is about the dynamics of personal faith. People today concerned about inclusiveness will often casually link Abraham and Sarah, but the biblical narrative is clear, Abraham's greatest spiritual struggle — the decision whether to sacrifice his only son Isaac — was a lone one in which he never consulted Sarah (Gn 22:1-19). But with the revelation to Moses on Sinai Israelite faith takes a significant step forward. Sinai and its commandments written in stone are the promulgation of a public faith. Obligations to God and neighbor are clearly written out and made incumbent upon all. What had been for Abraham a dimly perceived personal duty now became a clear and public obligation. Indeed, I cannot help but think the priestly editors of the Abraham saga probably took particular satisfaction in the thought that their Levitical code regarding ritual sacrifice (Lv 1-7) would make impossible Abraham's moral quandary, his initial thought of sacrificing Isaac. Those who enter the Hebrew (and Christian) assembly enter an area of general public accountability for their faith, a thing which makes retreat into private conscience a dubious maneuver. Religious rules when written down provide a common identity for a people. After Sinai, the Hebrew people could say while others sacrifice their children to Moloch, among us there is no such practice. Today there is much pressure to escape into personal faith. Some

Christian politicians do this by privatizing their faith. Here the contrast between Abraham's quandary and the revelation to Moses may be a lesson to learn from.

Finally, the third lesson is also difficult to achieve. We have already seen how the Hebrew sacred assembly was meant to be an alternative community, a counter culture. But it is important that we see this is also true of the Christian community. A strong expression of this is the use made of the language of alienation in the New Testament work called the First Letter of Peter. We hear it in the very first line of that work, the salutation or greeting: "Peter, an apostle of Jesus Christ, to the chosen exiles of the dispersion." Later, 2:11, we hear this theme invoked again: "Beloved, I beseech you as aliens and exiles to abstain from the passions of the flesh that wage war against the soul."

However, for the sake of balance, one must always be careful when invoking this "alienation" theme. By that I mean, Peter is not trying to teach that Christians should be some sort of sectarian cult, cut off from the world. Indeed, in the next sentence of the passage quoted Peter tells them to "maintain good conduct among the Gentiles" (2:12). And in the next sentence he lectures them on civil obedience: "Be subject for the Lord's sake to every human institution" (2:13). And thus we must be especially wary of sectarianism, the temptation to totally reject the world. The members of Qumran lived apart. And indeed, later on, in a chapter on the radical witness of the vowed life, we shall see that there is a place in Christian spirituality for retreat from the world. But at this point it is more important to see that while indeed the Church must be a counter culture — Catholics might well recall here the preface to one of the Masses in the revised post-Vatican II liturgy the phrase "a people set apart" — even so, it is important to be balanced about this thing. While we must preserve a tension between Christian culture and popular culture, one must also beware of taking a stance that totally rejects contemporary culture. But we must also be aware of factors in ourselves that make it difficult to maintain that balance today. This balance is not always easy to preserve these days. For example, it is arguable that Catholic

Christians in the USA once had something of a ghetto mentality, that is, they came from foreign lands often speaking a foreign language and these things were held against them, made their acculturation into American society more difficult. However, after 1950, the second and third generation of these immigrant Catholics achieved considerable acculturation in that they now found admission to colleges and jobs formerly the preserve of mainline Protestants. It is arguable however that this new found legitimacy makes Catholics loathe to take prophetic stances. On the other hand, the temptation for some Evangelical Christians seems to be precisely that of sectarianism, for not only have some created their own schools to preserve Christian values, but they in some cases created an alternative curriculum that denies the evidence of empirical science.

Further Reading

See the entry "Church" in John L. McKenzie's *Dictionary of the Bible* (Milwaukee, 1965).

See in *The New International Dictionary of New Testament Theology* (Eng. Trans., 1975) Vol. A-F, the entry "Church" by Lothar Coenen.

CHAPTER 3

The Origin of the Church

Some of you who know your Bible well might recall that more than once in the Bible Jesus talks about the Church making it clear that not only did he intended to found a Church but that in fact the Church was a going enterprise during his lifetime. For example, in Matthew 16:18, we hear Jesus say, "You are Peter and on this rock I will build my Church." And, later in that same Gospel, in Matthew 18:15-17, Jesus says,

> If your brother sins against you, go and tell him his fault between you and him alone. If he listens to you, you have won over your brother. If he does not listen, take one or two others along with you, so that "every fact may be established on the testimony of two or three witnesses." If he refuses to listen to them, tell the Church. If he refuses to listen even to the Church, then treat him as you would a Gentile or a tax collector.

However, the matter isn't all that easy. Many modern theologians and biblical scholars have been quick to challenge both the assertion that Jesus intended to found a Church and the use of these biblical texts to support such a claim. That is, most biblical scholars will point out that while the word "Church" appears abundantly in Acts of the Apostles and the Epistles of the New Testament, the word "Church" is very rare in the Gospels. Indeed, the word occurs only three times in the canonical Gospels, and those three times are all in one Gospel, the Gospel according to Matthew, indeed, in the two passages I just quoted to you. And thus some have argued that they suspect when in Matthew's Gospel we hear Jesus use the word "Church," it is an anachronism and evidence of Matthew's having put that word into Jesus' mouth. Moreover, these same scholars will be quick to point out that, when in the Gospels Jesus preaches, his theme is not the Church but the coming of the kingdom. Indeed, a certain Alfred Loisy, a Catholic biblical scholar at the beginning of the twentieth century quipped, "Jesus preached the coming of the kingdom, but it was the Church that showed up," (this is my translation; the original is in *L'Evangile et l'Eglise*, Part IV, Ch. III, p. 155: *Jesus annoncait le royaume, et c'est l'église qui est venue*). Loisy's book appeared in October of 1902. Many devout Catholics were less than amused by Loisy's quip. The book was condemned by the Archbishop of Paris in January of 1903 and then by the Vatican in December of 1903. Loisy wrote another book to try to explain away what offended the pious. This was no avail. In 1908, Loisy was excommunicated by the pope. But today Loisy's infamous quip can stand for a general attitude shared by many scholars namely that there is a great discontinuity between what Jesus aimed at doing and what his disciples did in his name after Jesus' death. They will insist the Church is the creation of Jesus' disciples and not his work. Now I can tell you I myself do not agree with those scholars and I will try to show you that there is cogent evidence that Jesus did indeed found the Church. But I think it is an important exercise for you and me to go over the arguments against Jesus' founding of the Church. It is important for two reasons. Those arguments appeal to many and thus they need answering. But also in listening to those arguments and answering them, you and I will learn a lot about both Jesus and the Church. So what I am going to do now is to review for you the theories of several very influential modern theologians about the origin of the Church.

The very first theory I want to look at is that of a German scholar from the eighteenth century, a man named Hermann Samuel Reimarus. Reimarus (1694-1768) was a professor of Semitic languages in the University of Wittenberg. He was not a devout Christian. But neither was he an atheist. Instead he was what we call a deist. He believed in God, a reasonable, rational God who created the universe. In contrast, Reimarus judged Christianity to be a fanatical, bizarre religion. Reimarus spent most of his life working on a massive critique of Christianity which he tentatively entitled *An Apology for the Rational Believers of God*. This work was never published during Reimarus' lifetime, probably because he suspected his work would run into violent opposition. But while his great opus was not published during Reimarus' lifetime, it did make a partial appearance in print after his death. Not long after Reimarus' death, a certain Gotthold Ephraim Lessing, librarian to the Duke of Brunswick and rebellious son of a Lutheran minister, discovered Reimarus' manuscript in the library of the Duke and decided to publish excerpts from it. These he published in several installments between 1774-1778 under the title *Wolfenbüttel Fragments*, Wolfenbüttel (literally, Wolf's Den) being the name of the Duke of Brunswick's estate that contained his library. The tenth of these fragments sets forth Reimarus' theory of the origin of the Church. Reimarus argues that the Church is the result of a self-conscious fraud on the part of Jesus' disciples. That is, Reimarus argued that Jesus was a wild-eyed religious fanatic, an apocalyptic preacher of the coming of the kingdom who amassed a considerable following but was put to death. Upon the death of Jesus, his disciples were reluctant to see the great movement Jesus had started come to an end. So they stole his body, made up the story of the resurrection and founded the Church as a means to continue and develop their own importance and authority.

The next theory about the origin of the Church I want to look at is also the product of a German scholar, though this time a German professor who though born in the nineteenth century lived well into the twentieth century. His name is Adolf von Harnack. Harnack (1851-1930) was indeed a devout Christian, but a devout Christian of a particular sort. That is, Harnack advocated a very individualistic view of Jesus's teaching. He set forth his views on Christianity in a famous series of public lectures which he gave at the University of Berlin in the year 1900. Those lectures were so well received that Harnack was quick to publish them as a book with the title *Das Wesen des Christentums* (1900). The title of Harnack's book translates literally as "The Essence of Christianity" but the English edition of his book carried the title: *What is Christianity?* (1901). Even so, the original title is more to the point because its implicit distinction between what is essential and what is superfluous is at the heart of Harnack's nut-in-the-shell theory of Christianity. That is, in his book Harnack argues that Jesus' original teaching can be summed up in two moral simplisms, two essential teachings: the Fatherhood of God and the brotherhood of man. The rest is all accretion, like the thick shell that grows around a nut. At the beginning of his book Harnack describes what he calls the Gospel of Jesus, "Individual religious life was what he wanted to kindle and what he did kindle; it is, as we shall see, his peculiar greatness to have led men to God, so that they may thenceforth live their own life with Him." Later, Harnack begins his treatment of "the Gospel in history" by insisting, "The inner circle of the disciples, the band of twelve whom Jesus had gathered around him, formed itself into a community. He himself founded no community in the sense of an organized union for divine worship — he was only the teacher and the disciples were the pupils." Harnack's book is in print to this day. It is a classic example of religious liberalism as freedom from dogma, tradition and rituals.

The next theologian whose theory I want to look at I have already mentioned. He is the French priest Alfred Loisy (1867-1940). Loisy read Harnack's book when it first appeared and disagreed with it. Loisy felt that Harnack failed to recognize the vital importance of the work of Jesus' disciples. And so Loisy wrote a book in which he tried to show how, even though Jesus himself never intended to found the Church, the Church is not a distortion of Jesus' mission, instead it was a necessary aid to, indeed, a perfection of Jesus's mission. Loisy's 1902 book *L'Evangile et L'Eglise* was in no small measure meant to be a rejoinder to Harnack's contention that the dogmas of the Church merely distort and misrepresent Jesus' teaching. Loisy argues that even if the Church was not the direct creation of

Jesus, the Church is that necessary thing that was needed to preserve the gospel tradition, the memory of Jesus. In other words, Loisy argues that even though it is true that Jesus never himself founded a Church, the fact that the disciples did is a great and good thing, indeed, a natural thing. For it is only natural that after the death of a great religious teacher his disciples preserve and develop his original ideas. For Loisy the Church is that necessary means that arose to preserve and elaborate Jesus' preaching.

But our survey is not ended. There is still one more important theory regarding the origin of the Church. Late in the twentieth century, a number of Catholic theologians arose who saw the origin of the Church not in Loisy's natural processes but rather as a graced response, the work of the Holy Spirit upon the faithful after Jesus' death and resurrection. The Swiss theologian Hans Küng (b. 1928) in his 1967 book *Die Kirche* (translated that same year into English as *The Church*) argued that "in the pre-Easter period, during his lifetime, *Jesus did not found a Church*"; nevertheless, "his preaching and ministry, *laid the foundations* for the emergence of a post-resurrection Church" (the emphases in both of these quotations are Küng's, not mine). "Not the words and instructions of Jesus in the time before Easter alone, but the action of God in resurrecting the crucified Christ and in pouring out the Spirit, turned the group of those who believed communally in the risen Jesus into a community."

But there are also some other twentieth century Catholic theologians who give even more of a role to the Holy Spirit. They radically historicize Jesus' contribution and instead so emphasize the work of the Holy Spirit as to make it not only decisive but a continuing principle of development. For example, the Brazilian Franciscan friar, Leonardo Boff (b. 1938), produced two important ecclesiological studies: *Ecclesiogenesis: The Base Communities Reinvent the Church* (1977, Eng. 1986) and *Church: Charism and Power* (1981, Eng. 1985). On the one hand, Boff seems traditional and positive with regard to the role of Jesus in founding the Church. Indeed, on p. 46 of his *Ecclesiogenesis* he says, "In faith we say that Jesus Christ founded the Church. However — and here is the problem — this statement is neither unambiguous nor simple." A few pages later he asserts, "The apostles embarking on mission have concretely founded the Church, and it perdures to the present day. They have taken up the elements that the historical Jesus had introduced, translated them for the new situation, and established in the light of the Holy Spirit the basic structures of the Church." And a few paragraphs later:

> If the Church was born of a decision of the apostles under the impulse of the Spirit, the power of community decision in the areas of discipline and dogma pertain to the essence of the Church. If the Church itself sprang from a decision, it will continue to live if Christians and men and women of faith in the risen Christ and his Spirit permanently renew this decision, and incarnate, enflesh the Church in the new situations with which they are confronted, be it in the Greek and medieval culture of yesterday or in the popular culture of today in Latin America.

The Flemish Dominican Edward Schillebeeckx (b. 1914) produced three works on ecclesiology: *Ministry: Leadership in the Community of Jesus Christ* (1980, Eng. 1981), *The Church with a Human Face* (1985, Eng. 1990) and *Church: The Human Story of God* (1989, Eng. 1990). On page 74 of *The Church with a Human Face*, Schillebeeckx radically discounts the importance of both Jesus and the Twelve:

> Apart from apostleship proper, the Christian communities did not receive any kind of Church order from the hands of Jesus when he still shared our earthly history. Furthermore, "the Twelve" were the symbol of the approaching eschatological community of God, which originally was not yet organized for a long-term earthly history.

Instead, Schillebeeckx sees the origin of the Church as an

institution in a complex of basically human motives but graced by the Spirit, inspired human decisions. Indeed, it could be argued, for Schillebeeckx the Holy Spirit is identical with the exigencies of human community because in the next paragraph he says:

> It is obvious that what developed spontaneously from the community of faith (as we would put it, in accordance with the sociological laws of group formation) was rightly and spontaneously experienced by the communities as a "gift of the Lord."

What are we to say about all these theories? Reimarus' stolen body thesis is not just dubious and misleading but it actually creates more problems than it solves. First, it has scant documentation in history. Reimarus quotes as the source for his theory Matthew 28:13 and as confirmation of it a passage from the second century Christian writer Justin Martyr and two passages from the writings of the third century Church historian Eusebius. No doubt Matthew 28:13 is the primary source for Reimarus' theory, for it describes the chief priests as bribing the Roman soldiers to claim "His disciples came by night and stole him away while we were asleep." However, there can be no doubt Matthew intends this slander to be patently ridiculous — how could the soldiers testify to what had happened while they were asleep! Moreover, exegetes often point to the fact that this story is unique to Matthew's Gospel and that in Mark's Gospel — the earliest Gospel — there is no such claim of a stolen body. And thus it seems apparent that Matthew 28:13 is a distinctly Matthean interpolation in the story of Jesus, an interpolation deriving from animosity between Jesus' disciples and the Jewish authorities which arose in the 80's, at least fifty years after the death and burial of Jesus. Indeed, Matthew's interpolation could be judged a nasty anti-semitism because he makes the chief priests look like idiots for suggesting this preposterous, downright laughable, ruse. As for the allegedly corroborative passages cited from Justin Martyr and Eusebius, scholars argue they are not examples of independent or collateral witnesses to Reimarus' claim.

Rather Justin and Eusebius are uncritically repeating what they read in Matthew 28:13. Finally, Reimarus' claim has found little or no support from modern scholarship. Even the most skeptical of modern exegetes — for example, Rudolf Bultmann — prefer to see the resurrection narratives as the product of self-delusion, innocent psychological projection, rather than self-conscious fraud. But we are not finished with the problems inherent in Reimarus' thesis. Yet another problem is that Reimarus' theory turns Jesus' disciples into not just scoundrels but creative religious geniuses — that scheming Galilean fishermen should have invented one of the great social institutions of the Western world! No doubt, in the case of Saint Paul we are dealing with a first rate religious mind and imagination but in the case of Peter and the other first-generation Christians we are dealing with much humbler material. I will say something about Paul's creative genius a little later.

As for the theories of Harnack, Loisy, Küng, Schillebeeckx and Boff: they all do a grave injustice to Jesus by failing to recognize that Jesus did a lot more than just preach to the crowds about the coming of the kingdom. Jesus did a lot more than just say or do things that later his disciples could use to form a community. Jesus did a lot more than just lay the foundations for the emergence of a post-resurrection Church. He himself was a powerful community organizer. During his public ministry he created a network of itinerant and domestic disciples. He worked hard to gather together what he liked to call his "little flock" (Lk 12:32; cf. Mk 6:34, 14:27; Mt 10:6, 15:24; Jn 21:15-17), a community of faith, hope and love that could challenge Israel (Mk 7:5-8, 8:15) and eventually even the world (Mk 13:10). Indeed, it is clear from the Gospels that to be a disciple of Christ meant more than just to be an individual follower of Christ. To be a true disciple of Christ one must assume a whole new pattern of relationships with others. Christian discipleship is not just a personal relationship to Jesus but participation in a pattern of relationships with others, the other disciples, the Jewish people and the world (Mk 10:29-30). Moreover, that Jesus had considerable ambition for this, his small flock, can be seen in the symbol of "the Twelve."

When considering the life and work of the prophet from

Nazareth one must give even-handed consideration to the fact that he was powerful not only with words but also with deeds, and, moreover, his deeds should not be limited to miracles. No doubt there is substantial witness to the tradition that Jesus of Nazareth practiced faith-healing. But there is also considerable evidence that he demonstrated what we today might want to call a penchant for symbolic acts but what is more properly understood as a penchant for performing prophetic actions. That is, going way back into the earliest traditions of Israel, prophets not only spoke powerful words but at times theatrically mimed their meaning by the use of dramatic parables in action. For example, the prophet Ahijah in 1 Kings 11:29-32 demonstrated God's judgment against Israel by tearing his cloak into twelve pieces; in Jeremiah 19 we read how that prophet took a potter's earthen flask and shattered it as a sign of God's impatience with Israel; in Ezekiel 4 that prophet symbolically "packs his bags." There is considerable evidence that Jesus of Nazareth, besides preaching and faith-healing, also employed symbolic actions to get across his message. Sometimes these actions are as simple and prosaic as "eating and drinking with sinners"; at other times they are more contrived and theatrical, for example, the cursing of a fig tree (Mk 11:12-14). With regard to his having established his own religious movement, a visible community meant to challenge and even replace the old Israelite community, the most important action to consider is Jesus' creation of the social instrument called the Twelve.

In the nineteenth century critics like F.D.E. Schleiermacher and F.C. Baur challenged the thesis that Jesus really chose twelve men to be his intimate companions and suggested instead that the concept of the Twelve came from the Church's patterning itself on the twelve-tribe model of the Old Testament. But modern exegetes such as Raymond Brown have argued persuasively that there is substantial evidence to suggest the concept is original to Jesus and the creation of the Twelve was an historical deed of his. Brown offers the following arguments: not only do the Gospels attribute the institution of the Twelve to Jesus himself, but the historical existence of this institution during the life of Jesus is also implicit in the story about the choice of Matthias in Acts 1:15-26;

and when Paul, in 1 Corinthians 15:5, claims that one of the first post-resurrection appearances was to the Twelve, he too witnesses to the fact that the Twelve must have been in existence before the end of Jesus' life. Brown also draws our attention to the fact that each of the four Gospels gives a list of the names of the Twelve; however, there are discrepancies among the lists, the names in the four lists do not precisely coincide. And thus Brown argues, if the Twelve were a literary or theological fiction created by the early Church the list would have exhibited a consistent uniformity. Instead, that there are discrepancies among these lists suggests that at the time of the composition of the Gospels, the names of the original list, with the exception of a few prominent ones, were becoming a vague memory.

As for the meaning of the twelve disciples of Jesus: the number twelve in the Jewish Scriptures primarily denotes the people of God in its totality; that is because in the Jewish Scriptures the Israelites of old are described as a tribal amphictiony, that is as a tribal confederation, each of the twelve tribes tracing its ancestry back to one common ancestor. In the time of the judges (see Judges 5) and before the consolidation of a unifying national consciousness, Israelite society was a loose association of tribes, held together by a common religion and common ancestry. According to the biblical account the tribal grouping of Israel originated with the twelve sons of the patriarch Jacob by his wives, Leah and Rachel, and concubines, Bilhah and Zilpah (see Gn 46:8-27; Ex 1:1-7). His sons' names were Reuben, Simeon, Levi, Judah, Dan, Naphtali, Gad, Asher, Issachar, Zebulun, Joseph, and Benjamin. (Let the reader beware: confusion sometimes arises because in the tribal lists in the OT, Joseph is usually divided into two tribes, which are named after his sons, Ephraim and Manasseh, but the number twelve is retained because the tribe of Levi, the priestly tribe is removed from the list in view of the fact it was given no land; the Levites were expected to live off of religious offerings.) With the advent of the united kingdom of Israel in the time of Saul, David and Solomon, the practical importance of the tribal units tended to disappear. But the idea of Israel as a tribal confederation of twelve clans remained long after its historic tribal confederation disappeared. For example, the organization of the monarchy left little room for the functions of tribal society, which was not much more than a memory during the monarchy. But, even so, consciousness of Israel's tribal origins remained, and the idea of Israel as a tribal confederation flourished as a powerful theological motif. We see this literary theme in several Old Testament works. Jeremiah 31 sees the restoration of Israel in terms of the return of the twelve tribes. In Ezekiel's vision of Israel as an ideal state (47:21-23) the land is redistributed among the twelve tribes. But it was it was in late Jewish apocalyptic literature, from the second century B.C. to A.D. 30, that this image got its greatest development. For example, the literary work called *The Testament of the Twelve Patriarchs*, presents what are supposed to be the final speeches of Jacob's twelve sons to their descendants. *The Testament of Moses* (3-4) predicts that the twelve tribes will have contact in their exile, while *The Testament of Benjamin* (9) pictures the twelve at the future temple. *The Testament of Abraham* (19) speaks of their judgment. Ben Sira prays that all may be gathered to their original inheritance (Sirach 36:11). The Qumran community of Jesus' time, steeped in eschatological expectation, was governed by a council of twelve representing the tribes (*Manual of Discipline* 8). *The Temple Scroll*, which describes a splendid, massive temple complex, has twelve gates in different courtyards and they are named after the sons of Jacob. *The War Scroll*, which describes the final battles, mentions the presence of the Twelve several times and says that their names were written on the great standard and on the shield of the prince of the congregation (cols. 2-3, 5). Historical self-consciousness of the twelve tribes survived in practical terms in Jesus' day in the custom of still identifying oneself with one of the historic tribes. For example, Jesus himself is often described as being from "the tribe of Judah" (Mt 1:2, 2:6, Heb 7:14, Rv 5:5); Saint Paul describes himself as being from the tribe of Benjamin (Rm 11:1): Luke in the Acts of the Apostles describes Barnabas as "from the tribe of Levi" (4:36).

Did Jesus get his idea of the Twelve from his reading of Ezekiel or the example of Qumran? We will probably never know for sure. What we do know is that there is plenty of evidence suggesting Jesus himself employed the image of the Twelve in the form of a public prophetic sign, a sort of parable in action, as a clear signal that he intended to assemble a new Israel. True, Jesus does once speak of the Twelve's future, saying in Matthew 19:28 and its parallel, Luke 22:30, "You will sit on thrones to judge the twelve tribes when the Son of Man sits on his thrown." But one must also see that, contrary to Schillebeeckx's claim, the Twelve were more than just a symbolic sign. There is considerable biblical evidence suggesting Jesus preached to the Twelve more intently and clearly than he did to the crowds (Mk 4:10-34; Mt 13:36), and that he trained the Twelve in ministry and sent them forth on mission (Mk 3:14-15, 6:7-13; Mt 10:5-16; Lk 9:1-6, 10:1-12). Moreover, it must be seen that it was these actions of Jesus in instructing and sending forth the Twelve on mission and not innovations by the early Christian community that established the idea of pastoral leadership for all time as the mission to gather a flock and provide for it. Indeed, a pointed example of how the original teaching of Jesus shaped the mission and ministry of the Church from the beginning is the idea of clergy compensation. When Jesus first sent out the Twelve he instructed them to take no money with them (Mk 6:8; Mt 10:9; and Lk 9:3). Instead, they were to live off the hospitality and free will offerings that would come from the people to whom they preached. There is evidence in the NT that strongly suggests this practice soon came in for abuse, that is, there soon arose Christian shepherds who at times fleeced the flock, took their money and ran (1 Th 2:5; 2 Cor 2:17). And thus Saint Paul came to the decision that he would forego any financial remuneration and instead fall back on the traditional rabbinic practice of being self-supporting (1 Th 2:9; 1 Cor 4:12; 1 Cor 9:3-12). Here is a clear example of how Paul's discerning moral intelligence, however shrewd, was not enough to supplant Jesus' bold and original instruction. For, to this day it is common throughout Christianity that Christian pastors are supported by their communities and not expected to support themselves. It is Jesus' original vision of how his disciples, the Church should function that has prevailed.

But this was not the only historic action on the part of Jesus that went into determining much of what we later call the

Church. For example, Harnack is wrong. Holy Communion is not an ecclesiastical sacrament, a later Hellenistic cult imposed upon Jesus' Gospel. It is of the very essence of his Gospel and Jesus instituted the practice. "Table fellowship" was a hallmark of his ministry from the beginning. All the Gospels are of one accord in claiming that Jesus early on developed a reputation for "eating and drinking with sinners" (Mk 2:16; Mt 9:11; Lk 5:30; Jn 2:1-11). Moreover, this was no casual social habit of Jesus. It was a prophetic strategy, a prophetic sign. Such fellowship was meant to be a holy communion. To be invited to sit at table with Jesus was to enter into a sacred fellowship. The same thing can be said of all the ecclesiastical sacraments. No doubt their ritual formulation came later and was a work of the Church, but all seven of the sacraments are rooted in precise historic actions or words of Jesus, prophetic signs of grace. For example, if in time the Christian community developed the practice of public and later private confession and absolution of sins, this too was but the heritage of Jesus' historic public ministry. For reconciliation, repentance and forgiveness, were principal features of Jesus' public ministry (see the references to repentance in Mk 1:5, 6:12; Lk 13:5, 15:7, 15:10, 15:19; Mt 3:2, 4:17, 11:20; and to forgiveness and reconciliation in Mk 2:5, 2:10, 11:25; Lk 5:20, 5:24, 7:42, 7:47, 11:4; Mt 6:12-15, 18:21-35; Jn 20:23).

Now as for the fate of the original community of believers that Jesus first gathered. It is true that at the time of Jesus' arrest, trial and execution, the small community of faith which he had assembled, the little flock made up of his disciples, scattered. But not long after his death, in response to encounters with the risen Christ and under the guidance of the Holy Spirit his community of disciples reassembled in Jerusalem with the intention of carrying on what Jesus had originally intended for them when he first gathered them together. Here is where I must say something about the Holy Spirit. Not only do Harnack, Loisy, Küng, Schillebeeckx and Boff do a grave injustice to Jesus by failing to recognize the historically momentous work he did in forming a community of disciples, the little flock that constituted the beginning of the Church, but Küng, Schillebeeckx and Boff also commit a serious error by misunderstanding the work of the Holy Spirit. The Holy Spirit is important but not as a principle independent of Jesus. Rather it is always "the Spirit of Jesus" (the phrase used in Ac 16:7; Rm 8:9; Gal 4:6; 1 P 1:11; Ph 1:19). Moreover, the promise of the Holy Spirit is not to supply new revelation but to provide recollection and insight that will lead us into the fullness of the revelation Jesus has already delivered. The classic expression of this idea is the words of Jesus in John 14:25-26 where there is a precise parallelism between the "all things" [*panta*] that the Spirit will teach and "all" [*panta*] the things that Jesus has already spoken to us: "These things I have spoken to you while I am still with you. But the Counselor, the Holy Spirit, whom the Father will send in my name, *he will teach you all things [panta], and bring to your remembrance all [panta] that I have said to you.*" The Holy Spirit will "teach," elaborate upon, instruct us about, give us further insight into, what Jesus has already "spoken." Finally, we do well to recall the warning: we must always test all spirits for there are many spirits abroad in the world and they are not all of Christ. See 1 John 4:1: "Do not trust every spirit but test the spirits to see whether they belong to God, because many false prophets have gone out into the world." Also, we must be humble and careful not to make overly ambitious claims about the work of the Spirit now and in our lives (2 Cor 13:5; Gal 6:4). For sure, the Spirit is still with us and active among us. But we would do well to keep in mind the words of the French Dominican Yves Congar on the very first page of his great work *I Believe in the Holy Spirit* (1979, 1980): "Generations of believers have reflected about faith before us and they have also experienced the Spirit. We seek an understanding of faith not alone, but with them." And thus we cannot exalt our contemporary experience over and against the past; today's Christians must exhibit a deep knowledge of and respect for the way the Spirit has worked in the past. We must be concerned to keep a deep continuity with the past. We today are not free to reshape the Church in any way we want so as to correspond with our experience alone.

Further Reading

Gerhard Lohfink, in his *Jesus and Community* (1982; trans. 1984), Chapter I, "Jesus and Israel," has a keen sense of the prophetic realism in Jesus' foundational actions regarding the Church.

Still valuable is Rudolf Schnackenburg's *The Church in the New Testament* (1965). See especially "The Post Paschal Assembly" and "The Outpouring of the Spirit" which is found on pages 12-17.

Two good summaries of the issue are Chapter 2, "Did Jesus Intend the Church?" in Ben Meyer's *The Church in Three Tenses* (1971), pp. 31-53 and Chapter III, "Jesus and the Church," in Miguel Garijo-Guembe's *Communion of the Saints* (1988; Eng. Trans. 1994).

CHAPTER 4

The Church and the Kingdom of God

In the south of Italy, in the year 1183, in the early hours of Easter Sunday, the abbot Joachim awoke from sleep to experience a profound insight. After weeks of intense and fruitless struggle to understand the Revelation to John, the final book of the New Testament, the abbot at last understood the meaning of what he had been reading. It suddenly appeared clear to him that "the beast" of Revelation 11:7 (and the "anti-Christ" of 1 Jn 2:18) had come in the person of the emperor Frederick Barbarossa. But Frederick would soon be defeated and then a utopia of the Holy Spirit would dawn — wars would cease, universal love would reign, a peaceable kingdom would be established here and now — a kingdom foreshadowing the kingdom of heaven (there are, indeed, in the Revelation to John two visions of the New Jerusalem, one celestial in 21:1-8 and the other terrestrial in 21:9-22:5). In the 1960's, in Latin America groups of Christians — pastors, theologians, and laity — came together motivated by a comparable vision of salvation erupting into history, into people's lives here and now. Taking inspiration, in part, from the Exodus account of the liberation of Israel from slavery in Egypt and from gospel passages such as Luke 4:18 where Jesus proclaims himself as sent "to proclaim release to the captives," these liberation theologians argued the Church must not just preach the consolation of heaven but work hard now to transform social and political structures so as to bring a measure of true freedom to suffering humankind now. Liberation theology insists that salvation is not to be viewed primarily in terms of life after death, or a judgment at the end of time, but in terms of working toward the realization of something of the kingdom of God now in a new social order. What is the kingdom of God? What place did it have in Jesus' preaching? To what degree is it realizable here and now on earth? And what is the Church's relationship to or role regarding the kingdom of God? These are questions we must address in this chapter.

The kingdom of God is a theme that appears most prominently in the later works that comprise what Christians call the Old Testament. That is, this theme has its origin in the experience of the people of Israel over a long period of time. In its earliest history, the Hebrews considered God their king (Dt 33:5; Jg 8:23). But even when Israel became a political monarchy with an earthly king they still acknowledged their God as eternally king in heaven. Such is the meaning of the acclamation in Psalm 99:1, "The Lord reigns; let the peoples tremble! He sits enthroned upon the cherubim; let the earth quake!" But Israel also knew that God's creation had become rebellious through sin and thus God's kingship or sovereign rule was not visibly and outwardly discernible on earth. And so they often prayed to their king reigning in heaven to make his authority felt on earth as in Psalm 108:5: "Be exalted, O God, above the heavens! Let thy glory be over all the earth!" But in later times, when Israel suffered a new exile in Babylon and the oppression of foreign nations, the hope for God's decisive intervention in world affairs took more precise and imaginative expression. The late prophetic works of the Old Testament contain powerful and graphic images of God's intervention. And thus the prophet Zechariah announced "Behold, a day of the Lord is coming" (Zc 14:1), a day when God will intervene decisively in human and cosmic history to assert his sovereignty and thus set things aright. Of that day the prophet said, "The Lord will become king over all the earth" (Zc 14:9). The prophet Isaiah elaborated more precisely: On that day God would right wrongs, punish the wicked, reward the just (Is 11:3-5) heal the sick, reconcile the outcast, restore right order, and create "new heavens and a new earth" (Is 65:17). This day of decisive intervention was called variously "the day of the Lord" (Is 13:6; Am 5:18-20) or the day of "judgment" (Dn 7:9-10; Ml 3:5). And its principal agent, a historic figure, was described variously as the Messiah, the Anointed One (Dn 9:25), or "one like a son of man" (Dn 7:13). When and how this day would come about, what form it would take, who the Messianic agent, the Anointed One, who "the son of man" to herald and initiate all this work of God soon became the subject of various explanations or imaginative speculations. These are called in the technical language of theology "eschatological speculation" from the Greek word *eschaton*, meaning, "end" or "end of time."

Eschatological speculation was particularly rife in Israel just before and during the lifetime of Jesus. Several literary expressions of it have come down to us. The kingdom of God was a popular theme in the contemporary Jewish literature of Jesus' time. For example, there are strong apocalyptic elements in a work called *The Testament of Moses*. This work was probably first written around 170 B.C. but revised sometime between A.D. 7 and 30. In it Moses, shortly before his death, speaks to Joshua and reveals to him the future history of Israel including Israel's fate at the end of time (T Mo, Ch. 10). *I Enoch*, a composition roughly contemporary with Jesus, contains a dream vision of the end time with a new Jerusalem replacing the old (I En 90:20-28).

The kingdom of God was not however just a literary theme. It also found expression in people's practical lives in the time of Jesus and in various forms. For example, the most pragmatic concept of the kingdom of God, how it would come about and what it would be, was held by a sect called the Zealots whom we know from the Jewish historian Josephus as well as the New Testament. The Zealot party in Jesus' time were devout Jews who were convinced that the promised Messiah or deliverer of Israel (and eventually the nations) would be a warrior-prince or political insurgent leader who would throw off Israel's yoke of foreign domination and inaugurate a reign of such political justice and material prosperity that would make Israel the envy or model even for the transformation of the world. The Pharisees and rabbinic Judaism on the other hand conceived of the promised kingdom of God as a spiritual and invisible kingdom to which righteous men could enter during this life by acts of piety, purity and devotion. An example of this is the common rabbinic phrase "to take upon oneself the yoke of the kingdom" (used several times in the classic work of Pharisaic piety, the *Mishnah*) which meant "to submit to the kingdom of God by prayer and observance of the law." Finally, there was a more daunting notion of the coming of the kingdom of God held by John the Baptist and the Essenes. John the Baptist's preaching, as recorded in the Gospels, includes an ominous day of judgment, indeed, of a universal conflagration, "the wrath to come" (Lk 3:7). And his vision of the Messiah is a fearsome one: "His winnowing fork is in his hand, to clear his threshing floor, and to gather he wheat into his granary, but the chaff he will burn with unquenchable fire" (Lk 3:17). The Essenes, a Jewish religious community in the Israel of Jesus' day, with whom we have come to identify the collection of literary works called the Dead Sea Scrolls, were extremely conscious of the end of days and regarded themselves as the last generation. They believed the end of days would involve an eschatological conflict both on the heavenly plane and the earthly plane. The battle of the spirits of light and darkness on the heavenly plane would be paralleled by the battle of the sons of light and the sons of darkness on earth. This battle is described in the so-called "War Scroll."

However, for our interests the most important fact is that there can be no doubt the kingdom of God was a paramount theme in the preaching of the historical Jesus. All three of the Synoptic Gospels claim the kingdom of God and repentance in preparation for it were the major themes of Jesus' initial preaching. In Mark 1:14-15, we are told: "Now after John was arrested, Jesus came into Galilee, preaching the gospel of God and saying, 'the time is fulfilled, and the kingdom of God is at hand; repent and believe in the Gospel.'" Matthew 4:17 is almost an exact parallel, and Luke 4:43 summarizes the original motive of Jesus' ministry as "I must proclaim the good news of the kingdom of God" (Lk 4:43).

But what did Jesus mean when he preached the kingdom

of God? No doubt Jesus at times preached of the kingdom of God as a future, indeed, end-time cataclysmic event. In each of the Synoptic Gospels there is what is called an eschatological discourse. Here is but a part of the eschatological discourse in Mark 13:24-27:

> But in those days, after that tribulation, the sun will be darkened, and the moon will not give its light, and the stars will be falling from heaven, and the powers in the heavens will be shaken. And then they will see the Son of man coming in clouds with great power and glory. And then he will send out the angels, and gather his elect from the four winds, from the ends of the earth to the ends of heaven. (cf. Mt 24:29-31 and Lk 21:25-28; Jl 2:10; Dn 7:13-14.)

But there are several other passages in the Gospels where Jesus speaks with a much more immediate sense of the kingdom of God, indeed passages that suggest the kingdom of God is not an entirely remote event in the future, at the end of time, rather it is very close at hand. We have already seen the Marcan summary of Jesus' preaching: "The time is fulfilled, and the kingdom of God is *at hand*" (Mk 1:15). But there is also Luke 10:8: "Whenever you enter a town and they receive you, eat what is set before you; heal the sick in it and say to them, 'The kingdom of God has come near to you.'" And in Mark 9:1 we read: "He also said to them, 'Truly, I say to you, there are some standing here who will not taste death before they see the kingdom of God come with power.'"

But there are still other Gospel passages that suggest the kingdom of God is not just an event at the end of time nor even just imminent, that is, about to happen, but instead it is already present among us, has in a sense already arrived for some. This sense of Jesus' proclamation of the kingdom of God is best seen in some accounts of his miracles.

Indeed, in considering Jesus' teaching about the reign of God we must also consider the importance of his miracles. For one of the things that clearly distinguishes Jesus' mission from that of John the Baptist is that while the Baptist was famous for his preaching we have no reason to believe he performed "mighty deeds." In contrast, miracles are a prominent and sententious part of Jesus' ministry. Indeed, it is interesting to see how, at times, Jesus made use of his miracles to point to, not just the imminence, but the immediate presence of the kingdom. For example, in Matthew 12:28 we hear Jesus say, "But if it is by the Spirit of God that I drive out demons, then the kingdom of God has come upon you." This has a parallel narrative in Luke 11:14:

> Now he was casting out a demon that was dumb; when the demon had gone out, the dumb man spoke, and the people marveled. But some of them said, "He casts out demons by Beelzebul, the prince of demons"; while others, to test him, sought from him a sign from heaven. But he, knowing their thoughts, said to them, "Every kingdom divided against itself is laid waste, and house falls upon house. And if Satan also is divided against himself, how will his kingdom stand…? But if it is by the finger of God that I cast out demons, then the kingdom of God has come upon you." (cf. Mt 12:28)

And then in Luke 17:20-21 we are told of Jesus:

> Being asked by the Pharisees when the kingdom of God was coming, he answered them, "The kingdom of God is not coming with signs to be observed; nor will they say, 'Lo, here it is!' or 'There!' for behold, the kingdom of God is in the midst of you."

Even greater insight into the nature and workings of the kingdom of God can be found by examining certain images which Jesus employed in his preaching about the kingdom. For, as Jesus said to his disciples: "To you has been given the secret of the kingdom of God, but for those outside everything is in parables" (Mk 4:11-12). Here we look at three images of the kingdom from the parables of Jesus, one from each of the Synoptic Gospels. In Mark 4:26-29 we read:

> And he said, "The kingdom of God is as if a man should scatter seed upon the ground, and should sleep and rise night and day, and the seed should sprout and grow, he knows not how. The earth produces of itself, first the blade, then the ear, then the full grain in the ear. But when the grain is ripe, at once he puts in the sickle, because the harvest is come."

In Luke 13:20, we find:

> And again he said, "To what shall I compare the kingdom of God? It is like leaven which a woman took and hid in three measures of meal, till it was all leavened."

There is yet another image of the kingdom offered in Matthew 13:31-32:

> Another parable he put before them, saying, "The kingdom of heaven is like a grain of mustard seed which a man took and sowed in his field; it is the smallest of all seeds, but when it has grown it is the greatest of shrubs and becomes a tree, so that the birds of the air come and make nests in its branches."

In each of these parables the kingdom of God is a small but powerful thing, it is initially hidden even, but eventually it grows into something great. All of this suggests that Jesus is teaching that the rule or reign of God is, rather than one event, a series of events in a process of planting, growth and harvest. That is, the kingdom of God has now begun to assert itself in his, Jesus', own person and work. The kingdom of God is breaking into this world even now, in small and discreet, often hidden ways. It is a dynamic reality which we can experience now even though its fulfillment, its final, consummate, universal realization, may be far in the future.

It is interesting to see how this same dynamic of the kingdom as not just an event at the end of time but as something that can take root and happen among people now if their hearts are open to it, continues as a theme in the preaching of the first generation of Christians. For example, Paul in his preaching seems to echo Jesus' own conception of the kingdom not as a onetime event but as a process. For, no doubt there are times when we hear Paul speak of the coming of the kingdom as a cataclysmic event signaling the end of this world, as in Romans 2:5-8:

> But by your hard and impenitent heart you are storing up wrath for yourself on the day of wrath when God's righteous judgment will be revealed. For he will render to every man according to his works: to those who by patience in well-doing seek for glory and honor and immortality, he will give eternal life; but for those who are factious and do not obey the truth, but obey wickedness, there will be wrath and fury.

In 1 Corinthians 15:22-26, Paul uses more comforting language:

> For just as in Adam all die, so too in Christ shall all be brought to life, but each one in proper order: Christ the first fruits, then at his coming, those who belong to Christ; then comes the end, when he hands over the kingdom to his God and Father, when he has destroyed every sovereignty and power. (cf. also 1 Th 4:16-17.)

But there are also passages wherein we hear Paul speak of the critical importance of the present time. In 2 Corinthians 6:2, he insists "now is the acceptable time, now is the day of salvation." Paul speaks as if Christians have already been saved in Romans 8:24, "For in hope we were saved." And in 1 Corinthians 15:2, "Through it you are also being saved." And in 2 Corinthians 5:17, it is clear we need not wait the dawn of a new heaven and a new earth for Paul insists "Whoever is in Christ is a new creation." In Romans 8:23, Paul's description of his converts as "the first fruits" is based on Jesus' parables of the growth of the kingdom and has implicit the image of "the harvest at the end of time." It is interesting how the Second Vatican Council (1962-1965), in its Dogmatic Constitution on the Church, *Lumen gentium* 5, used this same horticultural image to describe the Church as "the initial budding forth of the kingdom." But this is precisely the point at which we need to raise the question: What do all these biblical references imply about the Church? What is its relationship to the kingdom?

In response to such questions, the first thing that needs to be noted is that Scripture makes clear the kingdom is not present only in the preaching and actions of Jesus but also in the words and deeds of his disciples, for example, in the Twelve whom he sends forth to preach and to heal. If miraculous healings were part and parcel of Jesus' proclamation of the kingdom, so too were they an important part of the mission of his disciples. In Mark 6:7 we are told: "He summoned the Twelve and began to send them out two by two *and gave them authority over unclean spirits.*" And in Mark 6:12-13, we hear the result of this mission: "So they went off and preached repentance. They drove out many demons, and they anointed with oil many who were sick and cured them." Indeed, it is not hard to argue there is a special relationship between Jesus' disciples and the kingdom of God. For one thing, as we have already seen, they have a special, intimate, knowledge of the kingdom not given to others. Mark 4:11-12 says: "To you has been given the secret of the kingdom of God, but for those outside everything is in parables." Moreover, there is the astounding claim in Matthew 16:19, "I will give you the keys to the kingdom of heaven," which constitutes the Church the principal agent of the kingdom, helping to determine who will or will not be a part of the kingdom. The implication is that the acceptance or rejection of Jesus' disciples is a similar eschatological crisis as the acceptance or rejection of Jesus himself. This is certainly the import of such sayings as Mark 6:11: "And if any place will not receive you and they refuse to hear you, when you leave, shake off the dust that is on your feet for a testimony against them." Or Luke 10:16: "He who hears you, hears me, and he who rejects you rejects me" and its parallel (Mt 10:40). Thus we must recognize the crucial importance of the Church for the kingdom. Jesus' disciples are those who, because they have accepted the gospel of the kingdom in faith, now participate in the dynamic reality of that kingdom. Indeed, the Church may be called the people of the kingdom (and their principal historic churches basilicas from *basilea*, "kingdom," and thus "kingdom halls") because they have received it, witness to it and will be its principal heirs (Lk 6:20; Mt 5:3). More precisely, in a subjective sense the Church witnesses to the reality of the kingdom to the degree that its members themselves realize the fruits of the gospel. But in a more objective sense the Church also witnesses to the reality of the kingdom when, whether worthily or unworthily, it enacts or celebrates such prophetic signs as the Eucharist which is a foreshadowing of the banquet in the kingdom. Indeed one of Jesus' great signs that the mercy of God was at hand was that he ate and drank with sinners (Lk 7:34; Mt 11:19). And at the end of his life he made this into an eschatological sign when he said, "Amen I say to you I shall not drink again of the fruit of the vine until the day I drink it anew in the kingdom of God" (Mk 14:25).

Moreover, the witness of Jesus' disciples is particularly important because there is much in the world, in people, that resists the kingdom of God. Indeed, in the Gospels it is made clear to us that a certain spiritual blindness keeps some people from recognizing the reality of the kingdom of God even when dramatically confronted by evidence of its available presence even now. This seems to be the implication of John 3:2-3:

> This man [Nicodemus] came to Jesus by night and said to him, "Rabbi, we know that you are a teacher come from God; for no one can do these signs that you do, unless God is with him." Jesus answered him, "Truly, truly, I say to you, unless one is born anew, he cannot see the kingdom of God."

Indeed in Mark's Gospel such spiritual blindness prevents Jesus himself from working those miracles that make clear the kingdom of God is indeed breaking in now. Such is the reason given for Jesus' failure in his home town as seen in Mark 6:5-9: "So he was not able to perform any mighty deed there, apart from curing a few sick people by laying his hands on them. He was amazed at their lack of faith." Others are prevented from entering the kingdom because of their wealth. Indeed, the admonition in Mark 10:23, "How hard it will be for those who have riches to enter the kingdom of God!" may be an especially ominous statement in view of the affluence that characterizes modern industrialized societies. Finally, it appears that humility, a certain spiritual docility is required of all if any are to enter the kingdom of heaven: Mark 10:14-15, "Let the little children come to me; do not prevent them for the kingdom of God belongs to such as these." And thus we see again the importance of Jesus' disciples whose faith allows them not just to follow him but to give a credible witness to the kingdom, to keep alive the gospel vision of a new heaven and a new earth especially in the face of the failure of utopian schemes and political, social, industrial and technological revolutions that all too often bring only subtler forms of enslavement (even democracy contains the specter of the tyranny of the majority).

Some people will not be happy with the argument presented here for the intimate, if indeed partial, identification between the Church and the kingdom. Indeed, many modern theologians make a sharp distinction between the Church and the kingdom. For example, not just Protestant theologians such as Barth, Bultmann and Pannenberg but also Catholics such as Hans Küng see the Church's relationship to the kingdom as simply that of announcing it. But while I want to argue the Church has a much larger role than merely announcing the kingdom — it is not just a sign but an instrument of the kingdom, an eschatological phenomenon not just pointing to the end but making its reality felt here and now — one must also be wary of the all too emphatic, un-nuanced identification of the Church with the kingdom. This has indeed led to serious errors in the past when the Church was given an aura of sanctity and perfection inappropriate and indeed unverifiable. We must be wary of triumphal notions of the Church as a great power in the world. Some people lament the loss of Christendom, the fact that in the Middle Ages the Christian faith had grown to the point where it dominated most of Western society and culture. Such nostalgia needs to be tempered by the evidence that that situation of cultural dominance often really meant more the domination of the Church by the State. Here it is best if we examine more carefully Jesus' use of the image "the finger of God" in the passage quoted from Luke.

Matthew's version of this incident and pronouncement has Jesus using the expression "the spirit of God" rather than "the finger of God." Who knows which version, Matthew's or Luke's, more accurately reflects the speech of Jesus? Whatever the answer to that question, the expression "the finger of God" is especially revelatory. The expression "the finger of God" is a rare one in the Bible. It is used only twice in the entire Old Testament. In Exodus 31:18 it is used to describe the stone tablets given to Moses on Sinai which we are told were "written with the finger of God." In Exodus 8:19 we hear the magicians of Pharaoh say in response to Moses' having made gnats infest Egypt, "This is the finger of God." The much more common expression was a reference to "the hand of God" or "God's strong hand" (cf. Dt 3:24; Jos 4:24; 1 S 5:11; Jb 6:9, 12:6, 19:21; Ps 10:12; Ps 48:10; Ec 2:24; Is 8:11, 49:4) or, in the refrain "by a mighty hand and an outstretched arm" (Dt 4:34, 5:15, 7:19, 11:2). And thus Jesus' use of the expression "the finger of God" may be taken as a humble assertion. Jesus is not making grandiose claims for his work, he is not claiming that the mighty hand of God is in what he does, maybe it is only the finger of God, but it is no less than God who is at work in all this. So too we should be modest about our claims for the Church. Far from dominating or controlling society, the Church is probably at its best when it is a small but strategic minority helping to give direction to that larger secular culture, that is, when it functions like the biblical leaven in the dough.

Further Reading

Wolfhart Pannenberg's "The Kingdom of God and the Church" which is Chapter II in his *Theology and the Kingdom of God* (Philadelphia: Westminster, 1969), pp. 72-101, is a concise and intelligent analysis of the issues at hand.

John Fuellenbach's *The Kingdom of God: The Message of Jesus Today* (Maryknoll, New York: Orbis, 1995) is a comprehensive treatment of the theme.

CHAPTER 5

Models of the Church

While my principal job is teaching in a seminary and university, in addition to that job I go out on weekends and help pastorally at churches that want or need the assistance of a "supply priest" — that is, a priest to preside and preach at one of the Sunday Masses. A few years ago, there had been a change of pastor at a church where I was assisting on Sunday. On the first Sunday after the new pastor's arrival, I had yet to meet him. And so when I arrived at the church and encountered the director of religious education, I inquired whether she had met the new pastor. She was prompt to reply, yes, she had indeed met him, and she was quick to add with considerable emotion, "I can tell you now: he and I are working out of different models of the Church." I do not know whether this director of religious education had ever read Avery Dulles' *Models of the Church*. But even if she had not read it, I suspect her focus upon the different conceptions of the Church held by her and the new pastor probably owes something to that book and its author's way of thinking about the Church.

Avery Dulles is an American Jesuit and a cardinal of the Catholic Church. Moreover, Avery Dulles is a theologian whose published works constitute a significant contribution to contemporary theology. In his lifetime, Dulles has published no less than twenty-two books of theology and more than seven hundred articles. And Dulles is not only a prolific but an insightful theologian from whose writings I have learned much. However, of all Dulles' writings perhaps no one work has been so popular or influential as his *Models of the Church*. First published in 1974 and twice expanded by the author (1987, 2002), *Models of the Church* is still in print to this day, more than thirty years after its first appearance. And it has been available electronically as well as on paper. Dulles' book introduced a whole new way of thinking about the Church, a way that seems to have eclipsed a more traditional approach to understanding the Church. We need to consider carefully this work of Avery Dulles. All my quotations here are from the third edition.

The most recent or third edition of Dulles' *Models of the Church* consists of an introductory essay, thirteen chapters, and an appendix. In the introduction Dulles says his book is an exercise in "comparative ecclesiology" and that from the writings of a number of modern ecclesiologist he has "sifted out five major approaches, types" or what he prefers to call "models." In the second edition, he added yet another, a sixth, model of the Church as his final chapter, "The Church: Community of Disciples." And in this third edition he has added an appendix on "The Ecclesiology of John Paul II."

In Chapter I, "The Use of Models in Ecclesiology," Dulles begins by insisting the Church is a mystery and thus we cannot use ordinary concepts to consider it. And, he explains, this is why verbal images (that evoke mental pictures with emotional content) such as those that abound in the preaching of Jesus have always had a special place in our thinking about the Church. Indeed, Dulles insists "Among the positive tools that have been used to illuminate the mysteries of faith we must consider, in the first place, images" (p. 11). He goes on to show how "the Bible, when it seeks to illuminate the nature of the Church, speaks almost entirely through images" (p. 11). Moreover, he quotes a theological expert at the Second Vatican Council regarding that Council's preference for biblical images when speaking about the Church: "The theological value of the images has been stoutly affirmed by the Council" (p. 11). Dulles himself, however, is less than enthusiastic about the usefulness of biblical images for our understanding of the Church. He says no doubt, "images are immensely important for the life of the Church — for its preaching, its liturgy, and its general *esprit de corps*" (p. 14). But he raises serious doubt as to their probative or cognitive value in theology, saying the theologian knows "images are useful to a point and beyond that point they can become deceptive" (p. 15). For example, he argues: "It may follow, for instance, that the sheep (i.e., the faithful) hear the voice of their master (Christ), but it does not follow that the members of the Church grow wool" (p. 15). He also feels biblical images are of limited use today because they are so historically remote:

> To be fully effective, images must be deeply rooted in the corporate experience of the faithful. In times of rapid cultural change, such as our own, a crisis of images is to be expected. Many traditional images lose their full power. The contemporary crisis of faith is, I believe, in very large part a crisis of images. City dwellers in a twentieth century democracy feel ill at ease with many of the biblical images, since these are drawn from the life of a pastoral and patriarchal people of the ancient Near East. Many of us know very little from direct experience about lambs, wolves, sheep, vines, and grapes, or even about kings and patriarchs as they were in biblical times. There is need therefore to supplement these images with others that speak more directly to our contemporaries. (pp. 13-14).

And while he does know some modern theologians who have come up with "brilliant suggestions for new imagery" — he names three: Tillich, Teilhard de Chardin and Bonhoeffer — Dulles avers we would do better to avoid images and instead use models of the Church. Dulles shows how his notion of a theological model is derived not from architecture where a model is precisely accurate if it is a scaled reproduction. Rather Dulles derives his concept of a theological model from the "more schematic concept" of model which is in use in the "physical and social sciences" (p. 15). Indeed, Dulles claims that some models of the Church really are nothing more than an image of the Church employed "in a reflective and discriminative way" (p. 15) so as to produce a schematic conception of the Church that synthesizes what we known about the Church. Dulles then proceeds to spend the rest of his book showing us how certain models, certain schematic conceptions of the Church, have dominated thought about the Church in modern times.

In Chapter II, "The Church as Institution," Dulles introduces us to the first and earliest of the models of the Church which he treats, "the institutional vision of the Church" (p. 27) which considers the Church as essentially a social organization, a corporate entity, a structured society. He sees this model as having received initial expression in the Counter-Reformation writings of the Jesuit Robert Bellarmine (1542-1621) and quotes Bellarmine's affirmation that the Church is a society "as visible and palpable as the community of the Roman people, of the kingdom of France, or the Republic of Venice." He says this been the predominant model of the Church in Catholic thought right on up to Vatican Council I and, after that, in the thought of several popes — Leo XIII, Pius XI and Pius XII — or as he puts it "from about 1550 to 1950" (p. 34). While Dulles concedes a few positive values to this model, for example, it "has in recent centuries served to give Roman Catholics a strong sense of corporate identity" (p. 35), he is, for the most part, strongly critical of it. The institutional model, besides having "meager basis in scripture and in early Church tradition" (p. 35), "raises obstacles to creative and fruitful theology" (p. 36), is "ecumenically... sterile" (pp. 36-37) and "out of phase with the demands of the times" (p. 37). Finally, Dulles indicts it as fostering a view of the Church that is emphatically clerical, juridical and triumphal.

In Chapter III, "The Church as Mystical Communion," Dulles shows how another conceptual schema or model of the Church arose in the nineteenth century to challenge Bellarmine's model. In this model the focus is not on external structure but on the Church as "an inner communion of spiritual life (of faith, hope and charity)" (pp. 41-42); in other words, the Church is seen as primarily an intimate spiritual fellowship with God and each other. Dulles shows how this model of the Church has roots in theories about community and society originating in the works of the German sociologist Ferdinand Tönnies. Then he traces how Tönnies' theories were developed by both Protestant theologians such as Rudolph Sohm, Emil Brunner and Dietrich Bonhoeffer and by Catholic theologians such as Johann Adam Möhler. Then he shows how this model underwent even further development in the writings of such twentieth century Catholic theologians as Arnold Ademacher, the French Dominicans Yves Congar and Jérôme Hamer, and the Belgian Jesuit Émile Mersch. Moreover, Dulles shows how this model of the Church began to influence the teaching of the official Church as it first found expression in Pius XII's 1943 encyclical letter *Mystici corporis* and eventually in the theology of Vatican II. Dulles sees this model, with its emphasis upon inner communion in faith, hope and love, as a helpful antidote to the institutional model's view of the Church as a social organization, simply a community in the sociological sense.

In Chapter IV, "The Church as Sacrament," Dulles explores another modern view of the Church, this time one propagated by a group of twentieth century theologians — De Lubac, Rahner, Semmelroth, Schillebeeckx, Smulders and Groot and others influential in the work of the Second Vatican Council. This point of view insists the Church must be more than just an interior, spiritual fellowship but must be a sign and instrument of the intimate unity with God to which the world is called in Christ.

In Chapter V, "The Church as Herald," Dulles describes the radically "kerygmatic" view of the Church espoused by Swiss theologian Karl Barth (1886-1968). From the New Testament term "kerygma" which means apostolic proclamation, this model is rooted in Saint Paul and Luther and insists the Church's essential nature is not just that of a sign unto the nations but that of a herald announcing the gospel as a prophetic challenge to the world and even to the local congregation to repent and believe. Dulles notes Hans Küng as one of the people influenced by Barth's conception.

In Chapter VI, "The Church as Servant," Dulles treats of a movement in twentieth century theology which he identifies seminally with the French Jesuit Teilhard de Chardin and the German Lutheran pastor, Dietrich Bonhoeffer. Then he notes theologians influenced by their thought: Anglican bishop John A.T. Robinson and Notre Dame professor Richard McBrien. This model sees the Church's task as that of identifying with and encouraging the world rather than challenging it, for this model claims to see God already at work in the world.

In Chapter VII, "The Church and Eschatology" he shows how these five models of the Church which have shaped thought about the Church in the last four hundred years also can condition and, indeed, have shaped our concept of the Church's relationship to the Kingdom of God. In Chapter VIII, "The True Church," Dulles shows how these models affect our understanding of the marks of the Church: one, holy, catholic and apostolic. In Chapter IX, "The Church and the Churches" he shows how these models affect our conception of Church unity. Dulles demonstrates the effects of models on related yet other themes in Chapter X, "Ecclesiology and Ministry," and in Chapter XI, "The Church and Revelation." In Chapter XII, "The Evaluation of Models" Dulles cautions us about some limitations regarding the use of models for thinking about the Church. Though each model embodies a genuine insight into the nature of the Church, models are not easily put together. In fact, they tend to be not just analytic but paradigmatic and mutually exclusive visions of the Church. And so he gives guidelines "to support a reconciling approach" (p. 185) that will recognize the value in each but he does caution that the one model which can never be taken as primary is the institutional model.

In Chapter XIII, added in 1987, Dulles introduces his own model of the Church as community of disciples. He claims to have found inspiration for this model from a remark in the very first encyclical of Pope John Paul II. But in his development of this theme he shows himself indebted to the work of Catholic exegetes such as Raymond Brown, Karl Schelkle and Gerhard Lohfink. The emphasis here is upon community: "For the successful transmission of Christian faith, it is highly important for the neophyte to find a welcoming community of faith with responsible leaders who are mature disciples" (p. 209). "There is a need for communities in which people can experience a full Christian environment" (p. 210).

It is not difficult to understand the popularity of Dulles' book. No doubt one of the things that makes Dulles' book so attractive to readers, especially students of theology, is the fact that his method enables him to survey and sum up a great deal of intellectual history in a very small book. *Models of the Church* is a comprehensive survey, an invaluable synopsis, of much of Christian thought on the Church in the last five hundred years. Moreover, his use of models provides clear conceptual tools allowing him to give concise descriptions of elaborate theories and whole movements of thought. Thus Dulles' method is extremely helpful to students who want to understand how certain thinkers and their ideas have influenced modern thought on the nature and function of the Church.

But Dulles' method yet can be criticized and in several ways. For example, to achieve such clarity of outline Dulles often resorts, if not to caricature, at least to painting with a very broad brush. He himself admits as much when, in the introduction, he says:

> While picking out what is dominant in a given author's work at a certain stage of his career, or in a certain discussion, I am consciously leaving out things, the same author may have said at another time and in another context. Thus, when I use Karl Barth to exemplify the kerygmatic approach to ecclesiology, I am quite aware that some of his later work could be used also to illustrate certain other approaches. (pp. 11-12)

And thus one cannot help but wonder if at times Dulles is giving us not so much models of the Church but stereotypes. Another example of this might be Dulles's treatment of Robert Bellarmine. Is it foolish to think a more careful investigation into Bellarmine's ecclesiology would reveal a more nuanced concept of the Church? For example, surely Bellarmine's emphatic realism about the Church constituting a visible community is a well-considered response to Calvin's radically spiritual view of the Church as an *ecclesia abscondita,* that is, Calvin's claim the true Church is known only to God.

Another problem is Dulles's conflicted attitude toward the institutional aspect of the Church. While he indicts in uncompromising terms what he calls "the exaggerated institutionalism" (p. 37) that he insists characterized Catholicism from 1550 to 1950, he concedes that the institutional model does possess some genuine values: "Although there are exaggerations in this theology, we do not wish to be understood as suggesting that every position taken by the institutionalists was wrong" (p. 29). But the problem is that Dulles will not allow the institutionalists to take a public position in theological debate. In the 1975 first edition, while claiming "there is nothing to prevent a given theologian from building his own personal theology on one or another of the paradigms in the traditions" (p. 196), Dulles denied such a place to the institutional model: "One of the five models, I believe, cannot properly be taken as primary — and this is the institutional model" (p. 189). In the 1987 second edition, while admitting, "I may have been somewhat too severe on the institutional model" (p. 196), Dulles's prohibition of the institutional approach is unrelenting, for he completes this sentence with an even more forceful stricture: "I continue to believe that, in the light of Scripture and Catholic tradition, and especially in the perspectives of Vatican II, the institutional aspect of the Church should not be treated as primary" (p. 196).

Also one cannot help but wonder if Dulles's championing of models in ecclesiology has not set us an impossible task; for, while Dulles insists no single model is sufficient and we must take care to cull from each model what is valuable, he often refers to the character of models or types as being "radically different visions of the Church" (p. 15), "irreducibly distinct models" (p. 28). And, in Chapter XII, he reminds us that "All five models... to some extent come into conflict with each other. They suggest different priorities and even lead to mutually antithetical assertions" (p. 194). He gives "two general working principles... to support a reconciling approach" (p. 185). But are these enough to mitigate the phenomenon he describes: "Certain kinds of persons will be spontaneously drawn to certain models" (p. 184)?

But the most serious criticism of Dulles's championing of models of the Church is its displacement of biblical images.

There are several problems with Dulles' decision to give preference in theology to models of the Church over biblical images. First, it introduces an unhealthy divide between liturgy and theology. While biblical images of the Church can be relegated to secondary importance in the library or classroom, they have a central place in the worship assembly. There they cannot be avoided. No doubt, in those Christian assemblies that do not use a lectionary (a systematic and cyclical arrangement of Bible readings for worship services), the preacher may conveniently choose not to employ readings from the Bible that refer to the Church by resorting to antique conceptions or quaintly rural language such as in references to lambs, wolves, sheep, vines, grapes, *et cetera*. But in the Catholic Church where a lectionary cycle is employed so as to expose the congregation to a wide range of Scripture, these images cannot be avoided. Every Catholic congregation will inevitably hear Jesus say, "I am the good shepherd." Catholic congregations sometimes repeat again and again as a responsorial psalm refrain, "The Lord is my shepherd." They will hear Jesus say, "You are the salt of the earth, you are the light of the world," "I am the vine, you are the branches." Moreover, even in the liturgy these images cannot be allowed to remain merely emotive; biblical images of the Church have an intellectual content that needs to be explored, set forth, not just in the scholar's study and in books of exegesis but also in a chapel, in homilies and sermons from the pulpit. The congregation needs to know what, indeed, is the nature of the relationship between sheep and shepherd. They need to be alerted to the fact that the herd instinct operates powerfully among us to this day. They should be challenged to ask themselves: Who indeed is my shepherd? Whose voice have I been following? No doubt Dulles is right in claiming that members of the Church, unlike a flock of sheep, do not grow wool. Nevertheless, they can be fleeced by faulty theological constructs as well as by unworthy pastors, both of which, while claiming to yield lucid revelations, conceal as much as they reveal. And so the validity of the image stands. Similarly, when a congregation sings Jean Greif's hymn "We are the Light of the World," if those words are not to be an idle boast, then that congregation needs to be taught from whence comes this light and what are the dangers of its fading. Moreover, it is not just the liturgical assembly that needs to wrestle with these images but also the theologian. But, once again, here Dulles causes difficulties.

No doubt, Dulles often insists the Bible and Tradition must be reference points for the theologian. Indeed, he claims that a model of the Church will validate itself precisely according to how well it accounts for the witness of Scripture and Tradition. But, in fact, Dulles, for all his insistence that Scripture and Tradition are important to the theologian, gives paramount importance to contemporary experience. For example, in Chapter XII, "The Evaluation of Models," while he lists as his first two criteria for evaluating models "basis in Scripture" and "basis in Christian Tradition" (p. 191), these are severely attenuated in his fifth criterion, "Correspondence with the religious experience of men today":

> In recent years there has been a revolt against making either the Bible or Tradition a decisive norm apart from the experience of believers themselves. Granted the tremendous cultural shifts that have been taking place, it is to be expected that men today will approach the Christian message from a new point of view. Some models, much honored in the past, may prove to be excessively bound up with the concerns and dominant images of a culture not our own. (p. 192)

Dulles is absolutely right: all models are culturally conditioned. But, it could well be argued that biblical images, precisely because of their cultural conditioning, represent a unique experience of enduring importance that cannot be dismissed as merely cultural baggage. Quite the contrary, they must be seen as in some sense normative. They are not just the earliest expression of the corporate character of Christian faith. They contain the first lessons of the Christian community in what it means to be Church. Moreover, they are basic lessons of enduring value. They may be supplemented, but they must never be allowed to be overshadowed, much less superseded, by contemporary experience. In fact, our immediate experience needs to be measured against the original experiences embodied in biblical images. In particular, as regards the demands of contemporaneity, biblical images of the Church represent the corporate experience of the Church of the past and thus an important check against an oppressive modernity, that is, the inappropriate absolutizing of contemporary experience. An informed, educated, Christian clergy and laity ought to be familiar with several of the classic biblical images of the Church. Indeed, true empowerment of the laity is to educate them as well as their pastors, to acquaint them with the basic biblical images of the Church and how these images function so that they in turn can judge wisely when theologians come along with models that insist the Church must be this or the Church ought to be that. Contemporary theologians, perhaps even more so than contemporary congregations, need the chastening effect of exposure to biblical images.

And so in this book I give no further consideration to models of the Church. Instead, in the next several chapters I will attempt to wrestle with several important images of the Church from the Bible. There is no way we could explore all the biblical images. American scholar Paul Minear in his *Images of the Church in the New Testament* (1960) identified no less than ninety-six images. Thus we must be selective. I have selected these five because of their importance in the history of Christian thought. In Chapter 6, we shall explore an image of the Church which, arguably, comes from the very preaching and teaching of Jesus himself and continues to structure the Christian assembly to this day: the pastoral image of the Church as "Sheep with Shepherd." In Chapter 7, we shall focus upon two images from the preaching of the apostles. The first, the image of the People of God, is found originally in the First Letter of Peter and it is probably the most popular image today. The second, that of the Church as "the Body of Christ" was Saint Paul's favorite image of the Church and as such it has had a considerable influence upon Christian thought about the Church throughout the Church's history. In Chapter 8, we shall look at an image of the Church which had great currency in the Patristic Era — the Church as Holy Mother, a mother who tends and feeds her children. This image too was long a favorite but in the twentieth century it fell into neglect. The reason for its neglect will in itself be quite instructive. With the exception of the Petrine image of the Church as "People of God" each of these classic images of the Church might well be judged as decidedly dated today, that is, remote from our experience. But, as I said earlier, I believe each is based upon a universal experience which, once disclosed, will be seen to have great meaning for us even today. Moreover, there are no antinomies here, that is, no redoubtable antitheses. The Church is at once Sheep with a Shepherd, the People of God, the Body of Christ, and a Mother with Children, for each is but a partial view, a revealing glimpse of a multifaceted and ever-wondrous thing.

Further Reading

Another elementary but much more positive introduction to this theme is Chapter 4, "Theological Models" in D. and J. Carmody's *Bonded in Christ's Love: Being a Member of the Church: An Introduction to Ecclesiology* (New York: Paulist Press, 1986), pages 105-127.

Important treatments of this subject and examples of Dulles' influence are Chapter 6, "The Use of Models in Ecclesiology," and Chapter 7, "Two Models for the Future Church" in John Fullenbach's *Church: Community for the Kingdom* (2002), pages 108-166 and 167-207.

CHAPTER 6

A Biblical Image of the Church:
Jesus' Sheep with Shepherd

This chapter is given over to our consideration of one particular image of the Church, an image of the Church that has its origin in the preaching and teaching of Jesus himself. The image I refer to is that of "Sheep with Shepherd." My choice of this image needs little defense. I chose this image for two reasons, both because of its indisputable historical importance and its current problematic status. "Sheep with Shepherd" is possibly the most abundant image of the Church in the New Testament. It is found not only in all four Gospels but also in Acts, several of the Pauline epistles, Hebrews, 1 Peter and the Book of Revelation. Moreover, from the beginning of the Christian movement this image of sheep with shepherd has shaped the very character of the Church, the Christian assembly, as not merely a casual and amorphous gathering of people, a crowd, but an organized indeed strategic and disciplined assembly (the strategic character of the Christian assembly will be treated in the section on mission). And thus it is no aesthetic caprice or theatrical indulgence that long ago it became traditional for the principal pastoral leaders in the Catholic Church, bishops, to carry a shepherd's staff as a symbol of their office. Moreover, in almost all Christian assemblies today we can observe the distinction between "pastor" and "congregation," English words that are derived from Latin and Greek originals meaning, shepherd and flock.

But, despite its venerable antiquity, today, "Sheep with

Shepherd" is a highly problematic image. This is due to its ability to both attract and repulse: attract some and repulse others. I cannot help but think most people are deeply offended at the suggestion that as followers of Christ they are a herd of dumb animals who must be led, even corralled. This reaction is especially so for members of modern democratic societies wherein general education has achieved a high level. On the other hand, I feel equally certain that even in modern democratic societies there is yet a small but appreciable number of Christians who find this image rather attractive. Some probably take a great deal of satisfaction and pleasure from this image because they see in it a precise depiction of their own talents and objectives, that is, they are convinced they themselves would make good leaders and they know precisely the direction in which "the flock" should be going. I hope to show that while there is some measure of truth in these two opposing reactions, both of these responses are little more than superficial reactions to the image of Sheep with Shepherd, reactions that can only be tempered by a deeper understanding of this image. Moreover, a deeper understanding of this image is neither an idle task nor an exercise in obscure scholarship; rather the deeper meaning of this image, far from being arcane, antique and alien to us, addresses some pressing problems in today's contemporary society and Church. What we shall do here is first acquaint ourselves with the vast usage made of this image in the New Testament. No doubt, most readers have heard almost all the passages I shall quote, but I doubt there are many who have ever heard these passages strung together in a way that might allow us to appreciate how strongly and richly developed an image this is. Then as an aid to our understanding what we have just read, I will say something about sheep and shepherd in biblical times, that is, I shall attempt to describe the reality that informs the image. Finally, we shall attempt to clarify something of the meaning of this image for the Church both historically and in our time.

In the earliest Gospel, the Gospel according to Mark, we find this image used only twice. The first time the narrator uses the image of sheep without a shepherd to describe Jesus' reaction to the crowds that come to see him. In Mark 6:34, we hear it said of Jesus: "As he landed he saw a great throng, and he had compassion on them, because they were like sheep without a shepherd; and he began to teach them many things." But later, in Mark 14:27, we hear the image from the lips of Jesus himself when at the beginning of the Passion narrative we are told: "And Jesus said to them, 'You will all fall away; for it is written: "I will strike the shepherd, and the sheep will be scattered."'"

The image appears much more frequently in Matthew's Gospel. There we find approximate echoes of its use in Mark. That is, in Matthew 9:36 we find the narrator telling us, "When he saw the crowds, he had compassion for them, because they were harassed and helpless, like sheep without a shepherd." And, as in Mark, in Matthew too at the beginning of the passion narrative (26:31-32), we hear Jesus say, "You will all fall away because of me this night; for it is written, 'I will strike the shepherd, and the sheep of the flock will be scattered.'" But in Matthew there are also several more fleeting invocations of this image. In Matthew 7:15, we hear Jesus say, "Beware of false prophets, who come to you in sheep's clothing, but inwardly are ravenous wolves." In Matthew 10:5-6, Jesus instructs the Twelve: "Go nowhere among the Gentiles, and enter no town of the Samaritans, but go rather to the lost sheep of the house of Israel." A similar sentiment is expressed in Matthew 15:21-24:

> And Jesus went from there and withdrew to the region of Tyre and Sidon. And behold, a Canaanite woman from that region came out and cried, "Have mercy on me, O Lord, Son of David; my daughter is severely possessed by a demon." But he did not answer her a word. And his disciples came and begged him, saying, "Send her away, for she is crying after us." He answered, "I was sent only to the lost sheep of the house of Israel."

In Matthew 12:11-12, the image of a sheep is used to teach a moral lesson: "He said to them, 'What man of you, if he has one sheep and it falls into a pit on the sabbath, will not take hold of it and lift it out? How much more valuable a person is than a sheep.'" And in Matthew 25:31ff. it is used as an image of eschatological judgment:

> When the Son of Man comes in his glory, and all the angels with him, he will sit on his glorious throne. Before him will be gathered all the nations, and he will separate them one from another as a shepherd separates the sheep from the goats, and he will place the sheep at his right hand, but the goats at the left.

But the most extended use of the image is in Matthew's version of the parable of the one lost sheep (Mt 18:12-14):

> What do you think? If a man has a hundred sheep, and one of them has gone astray, does he not leave the ninety-nine on the hills and go in search of the one that went astray? And if he finds it, truly, I say to you, he rejoices over it more than over the ninety-nine that never went astray. So it is not the will of my Father that one of these little ones should perish.

In Luke's Gospel there is a quick passing reference to the image of Sheep with Shepherd when in Luke 12:32, we hear Jesus say, "Fear not, little flock, for it is your Father's good pleasure to give you the kingdom." But then there is also Luke's version in 15:4-7 of the extended parable of the one lost sheep:

> What man of you, having a hundred sheep, if he has lost one of them, does not leave the ninety-nine in the wilderness, and go after the one which is lost, until he finds it? And when he has found it, he lays it on his shoulders rejoicing. And when he comes home, he calls together his friends and his neighbors, saying to them, "Rejoice with me, for I have found my sheep which was lost." Just so, I tell you, there will be more joy in heaven over one sinner who repents than over ninety-nine righteous persons who need no repentance.

In the Gospel according to John, this image of Sheep with Shepherd is used twice. One time it is used as a fleeting though highly suggestive image. In John 21:15-17, in a passage recounting a post-resurrection appearance of Jesus to his disciples, we hear it said:

> When they had finished breakfast, Jesus said to Simon Peter, "Simon, son of John, do you love me more than these?" He said to him, "Yes, Lord; you know that I love you." He said to him, "Feed my lambs." A second time he said to him, "Simon, son of John, do you love me?" He said to him, "Yes, Lord, you know that I love you." He said to him, "Tend my sheep." He said to him the third time, "Simon, son of John, do you love me?" Peter was grieved because he said to him the third time, "Do you love me?" And he said to him, "Lord, you know everything; you know that I love you." Jesus said to him, "Feed my sheep."

But much earlier in John's Gospel, in John 10:1-16, this image is used by Jesus in a very long and developed passage wherein Jesus portrays himself as the good shepherd in contrast to several examples of bad shepherding:

> "Truly, truly, I say to you, he who does not enter the sheepfold by the door but climbs in by another way — that man is a thief and a robber; but he who enters by the door is the shepherd of the sheep. To him the gatekeeper opens; the sheep hear his voice, and he calls his own sheep by name and leads them out. When he has brought out all his own, he goes before them, and the sheep follow him, for they know his voice. A stranger they will not follow, but they will flee from him, for they do not know the voice of strangers." This figure Jesus used with them, but they did not understand what he was saying to them.
>
> So Jesus said to them, "Truly, truly, I say to you, I am the door of the sheep. All who came before me are thieves and robbers; but the sheep did not heed them.

I am the door; if any one enters by me, he will be saved, and will go in and out and find pasture. The thief comes only to steal and kill and destroy; I came that they may have life, and have it abundantly. I am the good shepherd. The good shepherd lays down his life for the sheep. He who is a hireling and not a shepherd, whose own the sheep are not, sees the wolf coming and leaves the sheep and flees; and the wolf snatches them and scatters them. He flees because he is a hireling and cares nothing for the sheep. I am the good shepherd; I know my own and my own know me, as the Father knows me and I know the Father; and I lay down my life for the sheep. And I have other sheep that are not of this fold; I must bring them also, and they will heed my voice. So there shall be one flock, one shepherd."

In the rest of the New Testament, this image of Sheep with Shepherd appears several times and for multiple purposes. In 1 Corinthians 9:7 it is used to justify clergy compensation: "Who tends a flock without getting some of the milk?" In Hebrews 13:20, it is employed as part of a blessing: "Now may the God of peace who brought again from the dead our Lord Jesus, the great shepherd of the sheep by the blood of the eternal covenant, equip you with everything good." In 1 Peter 2:25, it is used for moral correction: "For you were straying like sheep, but have now returned to the Shepherd and Guardian of your souls." In Revelation 7:17 it is used for a vision of heaven: "For the Lamb in the midst of the throne will be their shepherd, and he will guide them to springs of living water." But more concretely this image is used in the New Testament to give precise outline to the Christian assembly. For example in Acts 20:28-29, Paul is portrayed as using it to address an assembly of elders or presbyters of the Church at Ephesus so as to outline for them their duties:

Take heed to yourselves and to all the flock, in which the Holy Spirit has made you guardians, to feed the Church of the Lord which he obtained with his own blood. I know that after my departure fierce wolves will come in among you, not sparing the flock; and from among

your own selves will arise men speaking perverse things,
to draw away the disciples after them.

And so is Peter similarly portrayed (1 P 5:1-4):

> So I exhort the elders among you, as a fellow elder and
> witness of the sufferings of Christ as well as a partaker
> in the glory that is to be revealed. Tend the flock of God
> that is your charge, not by constraint but willingly, not
> for shameful gain but eagerly, not as domineering over
> those in your charge but being examples to the flock.
> And when the Chief Shepherd is manifested you will
> obtain the unfading crown of glory.

To begin to understand the meaning of this image, it would
be good to point out that it is not original to Jesus or to his disciples, Christians. No, it is a derived term, derived from the Old
Testament where it is developed to illustrate not only God's own
care for his people (as in Psalm 23:1, "The Lord is my shepherd.")
but his use of human agents to provide leadership for his people.
In Psalm 77:20, it says: "Thou didst lead thy people like a flock
by the hand of Moses and Aaron." In Numbers 27:17, when
Moses invests Joshua with authority, he gives as his motivation:
"That the congregation of the Lord may not be as sheep which
have no shepherd." And in 2 Samuel 5:2, God says to Samuel,
"You shall be shepherd of my people Israel." But we also need
to know more precisely about sheep and shepherding in Bible
times, the reality behind this OT and NT image.

The sheep is by nature a timid and defenseless animal.
It has neither the speed nor the strength to protect itself from
predators. Because of its wary nature, the sheep is easily fright-
ened and will often react in a self-defeating manner. For example,
at the approach of a predator (in the Israel of Jesus' day: bears,
wolves, jackals, wild dogs, hyenas and occasionally lions),
the sheep, if alone, would, instead of running, often become
petrified with fear, lie down and shiver. If in a flock, the sheep
at the approach of a predator would readily scatter, or worse,
pile up against an obstruction causing some to be injured or

even smothered. While sheep are naturally gregarious, tending to group and feed together, nonetheless, individual sheep will at times wander off from the herd, often inadvertently, that is, while eating. Also when in quest of food, a sheep would at times get itself in difficult situations — wedged between rocks or enmeshed in thickets — situations from which it could not extricate itself. These characteristics lend the impression that sheep are stupid animals. However, other aspects of their behavior witness to a certain measure of intelligence: for example, sheep have a well-developed sense of weather; in bad weather they naturally seek shelter, and in hot weather they readily hunt for shade. Also they forage easily for themselves, that is, they recognize good pasturage and will readily go to it. And this should serve as a warning to pastors: while one sheep might occasionally get distracted and wander off, if many wander off it is probably a sign of poor pasturage — inane homilies, insipid music, indifferent liturgies.

We must also say something about goats here because usually sheep and goats were herded together. The Israelites raised sheep principally for their wool and not as food (but when slaughtered every part of the animal was used). They raised goats for their milk, a large portion of which was used to make cheese. Moreover, they could be grazed together because while the sheep normally grazed on grass the goats went for heartier fare such as brush and twigs. But there were difficulties because of their differing temperaments: while sheep tend to be passive and defenseless, goats are aggressive and agile. And goats have voracious appetites. Indeed, in ancient Israel, it was especially important that goats be controlled lest their aggressive grazing lead to soil erosion. Also the goat's overbearing temper required that the shepherd keep close watch over the flock so that the goats would not harm the sheep.

As for the shepherd: while the nature of sheep and goats did not change over the centuries, the nature of shepherding did. Initially Israel was a nomadic society but after the conquest of Canaan, the Hebrews settled down into homes and an agricultural economy. Eventually, by Jesus' time, shepherding had become less a personal or family occupation and more a specialized occupation done by hired hands. And thus when we consider a biblical reference to sheep and shepherding we must be careful to discern whether this is an image of the nomadic shepherd, the village shepherd or the hired hand. The shepherd's duties were many: to protect the herd from wild beasts, thieves and bad weather, to bring them to forage and water. The latter was often the biggest challenge: moving a large flock from one pasture to another, the shepherd had to be concerned not only about direction but pace. That is, he had to be especially careful the flock did not move too fast (note Jacob's advice to Esau in Gn 33:13-14), so as to tire pregnant ewes or lambs too small to keep up such a pace.

As for the theological interpretation of those passages employing the image of Sheep with Shepherd, the first thing I must caution is the need for balance, balance in assessing the image of both sheep and shepherd. For example, it is perhaps arguable that in the past Catholics and Protestants both have tended to interpret the role of the shepherd in an unbalanced way. That is, it is arguable that at times some expressions of Protestant thought seem to take refuge in a "Jesus and me" spirituality that refuses to acknowledge any earthly pastoral authority. On the other hand, Catholic Christianity is open to the accusation that at times it so emphasizes the authority of earthly pastors as to obviate the need for a personal relationship with Christ. The biblical image of Sheep with Shepherd, however, when accurately understood, forestalls such simplistic outlines. All shepherding, whether in the nomadic days of ancient Israel or in the comparative urbanization of Jesus' time, was a cooperative venture. Even the shepherd with a very small flock was assisted by members of his family — Jesse by his son David in 1 Samuel 17:15, 20 and Reuel by his daughters in Exodus 2:16-18. Indeed, the very reason that Jesus can claim that the good shepherd leaves the ninety-nine in the field to go after the one lost sheep is that the good shepherd never leaves his flock untended, there are co-pastors, other shepherds who will watch the herd while the chief shepherd goes after the one that has strayed. And thus it is reasonable to insist even today that all pastoral ministry is co-operative. And, while, no doubt, the image of the Sheep with Shepherd does place him over the herd — his height allowed him to see further — and sometimes even places him over and against the flock — his staff, the symbol of authority was used to point the right way — he would never beat the sheep. Only if a sheep was lodged in a thicket or a tight spot did the shepherd use the crook of his staff to pull the sheep to safety. More often, he led by his voice (whistling and clicking, and calling to them) than by his staff. Shepherds in Israel never used dogs to herd their sheep. Indeed, his work was more gentle care: examining the sheep for disease or injuries, gently laying his staff upon them as he counted them. Moreover, any who would lead the flock of Christ should acquaint themselves with those biblical passages that indict the failures of shepherds. Both Old and New Testaments are replete with prophetic critiques of bad shepherding, of shepherds who lord it over their flock or even fleece the sheep. The most famous is probably Ezekiel 34:1-4:

> The word of the Lord came to me: "Son of man, prophesy against the shepherds of Israel, prophesy, and say to them, even to the shepherds, 'Thus says the Lord God: "Ho, shepherds of Israel who have been feeding yourselves! Should not shepherds feed the sheep? The weak you have not strengthened, the sick you have not healed, the crippled you have not bound up, the strayed you have not brought back, the lost you have not sought, and with force and harshness you have ruled them."'"

But what remains to be seen is that we must exercise the same careful balance when interpreting the nature of the flock in this image as well as the role of the shepherd. We must be balanced and not naively idealize the flock. Though it is true the sheep are not entirely dumb animals, nevertheless, they are not easily kept together. And they are often totally unaware of the danger that lurks on the borders of the flock. When Jesus says, "My sheep hear my voice, they will not respond to another's call," he is saying the sheep are not dumb. Moreover, while the parable in John describes the shepherd as walking ahead of the sheep, in fact, in the shepherding of Jesus' day, the shepherd more often kept up a rear guard. That is, the sheep know where the green grass is and they naturally migrate in that direction. The shepherd therefore often walked behind so as to look for the stragglers. Nevertheless, there were also problems in the herd; the danger was not just external — from predators outside, but also from bullies inside. Indeed, the eschatological image of Jesus' separating the sheep from the goats makes it clear to us that the Church is a mixed herd. Not all are meek fluffy sheep, tender little lambs; there are also bullying goats in the herd, also large rams, which, if not carefully watched and restrained, will trample on the others. Indeed, it is interesting to note that, while Ezekiel's indictment of the shepherds is well known and often quoted, rarely is any reference ever made to Ezekiel's equally indicting lament over the sheep of Israel. In Ezekiel 34:17-24, we read:

> As for you, my flock, thus says the Lord God: Behold, I judge between sheep and sheep, rams and he-goats. Is it not enough for you to feed on the good pasture, that you must tread down with your feet the rest of your pasture; and to drink of clear water, that you must foul the rest with your feet? And must my sheep eat what you have trodden with your feet, and drink what you have fouled with your feet? Therefore, thus says the Lord God to them: Behold, I, I myself will judge between the fat sheep and the lean sheep. Because you push with side and shoulder, and thrust at all the weak with your horns, till you have scattered them abroad, I will save my flock, they shall no longer be a prey; and I will judge between sheep and sheep.

When I consider the history of the Catholic Church in the last forty years I cannot help but ask: Is this image of strong sheep who bully the weak not applicable to aggressive, agenda-driven, ideologues of both left and right, who have been an all-too prominent feature of the post-Vatican II Church? I think especially of theologians who raise their voice over that of the shepherds of the flock so as to appeal directly to the sheep whom they are convinced need new direction, theologians who seek to give alternative teaching to that of the Church's principal pastors.

In conclusion I call the reader's attention to two things. First, the conceptual analysis of the image of Sheep with Shepherd which we have undertaken brings to light the basic elements and dynamics that characterize every Christian assembly, the smallest local congregation and the relationship between congregations that is the universal Church, the Church spread across the earth. This analysis makes us aware of certain factors and dynamics that deserve our constant vigilance and attention. It reveals a structure and dynamics with roots in the religious experience of ancient Israel focused upon, endorsed and amplified by Jesus himself. In this regard, how misleading are the claims of Edward Schillebeeckx, "The Christian communities did not receive any kind of Church order from the hands of Jesus" (*The Church with a Human Face*, 1990, p. 74). Or only with time did the Church begin to "take on institutional aspects" (Schillebeeckx's *Church: The Human Story of God*, 1990, p. 156). The structure of the Christian assembly was given by the Lord. But the other thing I would note is the importance of this image as a critical tool for reflection not just on the Church but also the world. Despite the prominence of democracy and education, there is much in contemporary experience that suggests the herd instinct among human beings is as powerful today, perhaps even more so, as in any time in the past. Human beings still need and look for direction from others. In today's complex world, we are perhaps more than ever aware that by ourselves we cannot find the way, and thus more than ever we turn to experts to advise us. Moreover, modern technological society is quite ready to supply this need. Some might argue there is an information overload that supplies us with all too many, ready sources for direction: the self-help section of bookstores, television gurus, or the spectacle of mass media and a relentless hucksterism that tries to tell people what they should wear, what they should eat, what they should think.

Today even theology appears to have become a fashion industry! If the herd instinct plagues the human community today, then this image of Sheep with Shepherd, far from being a quaint product of the past, can serve as a critical tool for assessing all such situations, in the world as well as in the Church.

Further Reading

Paul Minear's *Images of the Church in the New Testament* (Philadelphia, 1960) is still a valuable introduction and general survey of this theme of images of the Church.

Another, shorter, general introduction to the concept of images of the Church is Chapter 5 in George H. Tavard's *The Church, Community of Salvation: An Ecumenical Ecclesiology* (Collegeville, Minnesota: Liturgical Press, 1992), pages 79-94.

A more thorough exposition of this image of "Sheep with Shepherd" with attention to its Old Testament precedents and its post-New Testament, historical developments is my essay "Sheep and Shepherd: An Ancient Image of the Church and a Contemporary Challenge," which appeared in the Roman theological journal *Gregorianum* 82 (2001), 51-85.

W. Philip Keller's *A Shepherd Looks at Psalm 23* (Grand Rapids, 1970).

CHAPTER 7

More Biblical Images of the Church: People of God and Body of Christ

In this chapter we consider two images of the Church which offer an appreciably different perspective on the Church from that afforded us by the image of Sheep with Shepherd. The first image, People of God, has, like Jesus' Sheep with Shepherd, a literary background in the Old Testament. But unlike the image of Sheep with Shepherd which today meets with bewilderment or even consternation, this image of the People of God is not only attractive to many of our contemporaries but it often summons forth considerable enthusiasm. The second image we shall examine in this chapter — Body of Christ — is interesting precisely because it is not traditional. By that I mean, unlike Sheep with Shepherd and People of God, images which have Old Testament literary backgrounds, the image of the Church as the Body of Christ appears to have a secular background. That is, its theological development appears to be the result of considerable creative adaptation on the part of Saint Paul.

The image of the Church as the People of God has deep roots in the Old Testament. The precise phrase "people of God" does not occur often in the OT. Indeed, there are but two uses of it. In Judges 20:2 we find a reference to "the assembly of the people of God." And in 2 Samuel 14:13, we hear asked, "Why then have you planned such a thing against the people of God?" Nevertheless, the concept of Israel as God's people is implicit in several other very common expressions such as "my people" (Ex 5:1), "the people of the Lord" (Nb 16:41, Dt 27:9), or "Thy people Israel" (Dt 21:8, 26:15). Moreover, there are certain classic passages in the OT where the concept is not only explicit but also clearly developed. For example, in the historical narrative of Deuteronomy 7:6-8, it is made clear to us that while in ordinary parlance a people is a group of men and women bound together by ties of common blood, speech, moral and social standards, as well as by a common history and mutual solidarity, what makes Israel the people of God is not those things but rather their special relationship to God, moreover, a relationship freely, indeed, arbitrarily begun by God:

> For you are a people holy to the Lord your God; the Lord your God has chosen you to be a people for his own possession, out of all the peoples that are on the face of the earth. It was not because you were more in number than any other people that the Lord set his love upon you and chose you, for you were the fewest of all peoples; but it is because the Lord loves you, and is keeping the oath which he swore to your fathers, that the Lord has brought you out with a mighty hand, and redeemed you from the house of bondage, from the hand of Pharaoh king of Egypt.

This same theme finds equally explicit but more cultic expression in a passage from the late prophet Ezekiel 37:26-27:

> I will make a covenant of peace with them; it shall be an everlasting covenant with them; and I will bless them and multiply them, and will set my sanctuary in the midst of them forevermore. My dwelling place shall be with them; and I will be their God, and they shall be my people.

But for our interests the truly remarkable thing is that we find, in the classic writings of the early Christian movement as preserved in the New Testament, this exclusive and honored title of Israel, its divine election as God's people, is now appropriated and applied to the flock of Christ, the community of the disciples of Christ. It is interesting to see how this shift was made. Paul makes use of Old Testament quotations of God's making a new covenant, another covenant after the Sinai covenant, that will issue in a holier people. For example in Romans 9:22-26, Paul strings together a few passages from the prophet Hosea (1:10, 2:23) to show the Roman Christians how it was prophesied that they who are not all Jews (the Christian community at Rome included many Gentiles) have become the new people of God:

> As indeed he says in Hosea, "Those who were not my people I will call 'my people,' and her who was not beloved I will call 'my beloved.'" "And in the very place where it was said to them, 'You are not my people,' they will be called 'sons of the living God.'"

In a similar fashion the author of the Epistle to the Hebrews, in Chapter 8 of that work, teaches that "Christ has obtained a ministry which is as much more excellent than the old as the covenant he mediates is better" (vs. 6) and thus in him is fulfilled the prophecy of Jeremiah 31:31-33: "The days will come, says the Lord, when I will establish a new covenant with the house of Israel.... This is the covenant I will make with the house of Israel after those days, says the Lord: I will put my laws into their minds, and write them on their hearts, and I will be their God, and they shall be my people."

Even the boldest and most direct statement of this theme, indeed, the only place in the New Testament wherein the Church is expressly called "the People of God," 1 Peter 2:9-10, is but a pastiche of Old Testament phrases, titles of Israel taken from Isaiah 43:20, Exodus 19:6, and Deuteronomy 7:6-9. Some exegetes have argued this letter is really not in epistolary style and instead is probably a baptismal catechesis. For our purposes, if this is true then this makes its teaching even clearer as Peter says to these newly baptized Christians:

> But you are a chosen race, a royal priesthood, a holy nation, God's own people, that you may declare the

wonderful deeds of him who called you out of darkness
into his marvelous light. Once you were no people but
now you are God's people; once you had not received
mercy but now you have received mercy.

This New Testament image of the Church as the People
of God will gain considerable currency in the patristic era. For
example, "the people [of God]" is a common reference found in
the work called, *The Shepherd of Hermas* (ca. 125?), in the writings
of the early Christian apologist Justin Martyr (ca. 100-ca. 165), in
Irenaeus, the bishop of Lyons (ca. 130-ca. 200), in the theologian
Hippolytus of Rome (ca. 170-ca. 236) and the exegete Origen of
Alexandria (ca. 185-ca. 254). In Latin Christianity, the Church is
often referred to as "the people [of God]," for example, in the
works of Cyprian the bishop of Carthage (d. 258) and Tertullian
(ca. 160-ca. 225). In those works, however, it is most often simply
an image, an expression, an idea not greatly developed. Its first
elaboration as an idea can be found in the writings of the great
Church father Augustine the bishop of Hippo (354-430), especially
in his work called *Explanations of the Psalms*. The image of the
Church as the People of God was, nevertheless, only one of several
images employed by these writers. Moreover, it was eventually
eclipsed by a preference in the Middle Ages for the image of the
Church as the Body of Christ. But in more recent times, the twentieth century, this image of the Church as the People of God has
come in for a great revival of interest among both Catholic and
Protestant scholars. It is important that we know precisely why
and how this image has come back into favor.

Among Protestant scholars, interest in the image of the
Church as the People of God arose in the nineteenth century as an
ecumenical concern, that is, as a concern to find some principle
for understanding the Church, some image for understanding
the nature of the Church, that might appeal beyond denomina-
tional differences. For example, as early as 1838, "People of God"
is a theme in Frederick Denison Maurice's *The Kingdom of Christ*,
a discussion of the causes and cures of divisions within the Christian Church. In 1912, the Anglican scholar, H.F. Hamilton came

out with a two-volume work entitled *The People of God*. In 1941, the Norwegian Nils Alstrup Dahl's *Das Volk Gottes* appeared. It is an exhaustive study of the term in the Old Testament. In 1950, Albrecht Oepke, of the University of Leipzig, produced his comprehensive study *The New People of God*. Paul Minear's *Images of the Church in the New Testament* (1960) was a study occasioned by a commission that came out of the World Council of Churches at its meeting in Lund, Sweden in 1952. After that meeting, the WCC's "Faith and Order Commission on Christ and the Church" asked Minear and some other scholars to study this image. Thus one of the largest chapters in Minear's book (Ch. III) is given over to this theme.

Catholic interest in the image of the Church as the People of God was spurred more by the concern of some theologians that their Church was burdened by authoritarian clericalism. And so, they wanted to explore an image of the Church that might be more inclusive, an image that would feature all the baptized and not just the clergy. The Benedictine monk, Dom Anscar Vonier, in his 1937 *The People of God,* contrasted the terms "Church" and "People of God" and argued "the Church" focuses upon what is sacramental and cultic while "People of God" refers to the spiritual life of the community. In 1940, Dominican theologian Mannes Koster published his *Ekklesiologie im Werden* wherein he argued for the primary and fundamental importance of People of God as not just an image but the "only clear and non-metaphorical objective designation of the Church" (p. 143). Lucien Cerfaux in his 1942 work *The Church in the Theology of Saint Paul* argued against traditional scholarship that it was "People of God" rather than "Body of Christ" that functioned as Paul's fundamental tool for defining the Church. This movement in Catholic scholarship found dramatic expression in the formal statements made by the Second Vatican Council (1962-1965). Many scholars have observed it is "People of God" that functions as the dominant image of the Church in those conciliar statements. For example, not only is "People of God" the title and theme of the second chapter of that Council's Dogmatic Constitution on the Church, *Lumen gentium*, but the image is used extensively in several other documents, for example, in Vatican II's Decree on the Laity, Decree on Ecumenism, Decree on Religious Life, Pastoral Constitution on the Church in the Modern World.

However, for all the contemporary enthusiasm for this image of the Church as the People of God, there are yet several problems that attend this image. For example, when ancient Israel's title "People of God" is appropriated by the Church, no matter how respectfully and carefully the transition is explained, it can produce a tension, even anger and resentment, on the part of devout Jews. Secondly, the German Jesuit theologian Karl Rahner has made clear the considerable ambiguity of this image. That is, he has argued convincingly that the People of God is not truly identical with the Church; indeed, Rahner insists there is a sense in which the whole human race can be called the People of God. Finally, voices have been raised insisting that the image of the Church as the People of God needs completion by the image of the Church as the Body of Christ. For example, shortly after the close of the Second Vatican Council, the French Dominican theologian Yves Congar criticized Lucien Cerfaux's insistence upon the primacy of "the People of God" and insisted that "St. Paul never contented himself with adding the attribute, the Body of Christ to the concept of the People of God, just as he had received it from Judaism. He introduced the idea of the Body of Christ as the essential concept in treating of the Church" (in *The Church and Mankind*, Concilium Vol. I, p. 36). And so it is important that we here also look into this other image of the Church so as to see how it "corrects" or gives more precision to, fills out, the image of the Church as the People of God.

The physical body of Christ was important to the early Church because in the doctrine of the incarnation it insisted that Jesus was at once fully human and fully divine, that is, it insisted that he had a normal human body. And thus we can find both a literal reference to the physical body of Jesus as in Mark 15:43, "Joseph of Arimathea... went to Pilate, and asked for the body of Jesus (*soma tou Iesou*)," and a profoundly theological reference to the physical body of Jesus as in Hebrews 10:10, which claims: "We have been sanctified through the offering of the body of Jesus Christ (*somatos Iesou Christou*) once for all." But an equally important concept of early Christianity is its belief in the sacramental body of Christ. Early Christian tradition insisted that Jesus in his last meal with his disciples identified the bread of that meal as "my body" (1 Cor 11:24; Mk 14:22; Mt 26:26, Lk 22:19). But besides the theological importance given to the natural body of Jesus and the sacramental body of Christ, there is also discernible in the Pauline writings yet another more mystical theological reference to the body of Christ, a metaphorical meaning by which the people who make up the Church are seen as the Body of Christ (*soma Christou*). However, even here the means by which they make up the Body of Christ is cast in discernibly different ways.

There is considerable controversy regarding the origin of Paul's image of the Church as "the Body of Christ." Some have argued that its origin is Jewish. Discernible in the Old Testament is a portrayal of certain characters, for example, Adam and Jacob, as personifications of a larger group, Adam as the father of humankind, Jacob as personifying Israel. It could well be argued this concept of personified corporate identity is observable in the moral use that Paul makes in his first reference to this image. Paul's First Letter to the Corinthians was written to his largest and most successful mission. But the Church at Corinth was not only Paul's most successful missionary effort; it also produced some of his most significant pastoral challenges. For example, Corinth was a port city and sailors coming into port often sought fleshy entertainment, and thus in Corinth prostitution was a major industry. I draw the reader's attention to this because this is the background of Paul's first use of this image of the Body of Christ in 1 Corinthians 6:15-20:

> Do you not know that your bodies are members of Christ? Shall I therefore take the members of Christ and make them members of a prostitute? Never! Do you not know that he who joins himself to a prostitute becomes

one body with her? For, as it is written, "The two shall become one." But he who is united to the Lord becomes one spirit with him. Shun immorality. Every other sin which a man commits is outside the body; but the immoral man sins against his own body. Do you not know that your body is a temple of the Holy Spirit within you, which you have from God? You are not your own; you were bought with a price. So glorify God in your body.

Paul is saying: you Christians are the hands, and feet, eyes and ears of Christ in this world. You are no longer radical individuals but rather are now participants in the corporate life of Christ. This moral meaning of the image of the Church as the Body of Christ is an important corrective to the vague, not to say, indiscriminate, inclusiveness provided by the image of the Church as the People of God.

But sexual immorality was not the only problem in the Church at Corinth. The Church at Corinth was highly charismatic, that is, the gifts of the Holy Spirit not only abounded there but also, in some cases, found dramatic expression there. And here Paul seems to employ a more Stoic notion of the body politic to remedy this situation.

That is, not only were there gifted teachers, and preachers, counselors or spiritual directors in that community, but there were also some spectacular gifts of healing, miracles, and speaking in tongues (see 1 Cor 12:8-10). It is apparent from the First Letter to the Corinthians that this great manifestation and variety of gifts was making for some disorder in the community. It is not all that clear as to what is the nature of the tensions that have arisen. Later there is some suggestion that speaking in tongues was causing confusion by its dominance of the worship assembly and that prophecy too was problematic, at least in the sense of too many prophets with too many messages. But it seems that this abundance of gifts was causing tensions maybe even divisions or rivalries in the community. And thus in Chapter 12 of First Corinthians, Saint Paul lectures that community at length on mutual respect for each of these gifted members and moreover the importance of cooperation. He does this by developing at length the image of the Church as the Body of Christ. We shall examine 1 Corinthians 12 carefully, considering one by one Paul's development of this image. First he simply introduces the analogy:

> For just as the body is one and has many members, and all the members of the body, though many, are one body, so it is with Christ. For by one Spirit we were all baptized into one body — Jews or Greeks, slaves or free — and all were made to drink of one Spirit. (1 Cor 12:12-13)

Then he goes into a deeper development of the image in a way that suggests some of the gifted were overemphasizing the importance of their own specific gift for the rest of the community. In 1 Corinthians 12:14-21, Saint Paul seems to be saying, even if a particular gift is important, it cannot claim exclusive importance:

> For the body does not consist of one member but of many. If the foot should say, "Because I am not a hand, I do not belong to the body," that would not make it any less a part of the body. And if the ear should say, "Because I am not an eye, I do not belong to the body," that would not make it any less a part of the body. If the whole body were an eye, where would be the hearing? If the whole body were an ear, where would be the sense of smell? But as it is, God arranged the organs in the body, each one of them, as he chose. If all were a single organ, where would the body be? As it is, there are many parts, yet one body. The eye cannot say to the hand, "I have no need of you," nor again the head to the feet, "I have no need of you."

In the next section Paul seems to address another kind of discord, namely, it seems that some of the gifted not only were overemphasizing the importance of their particular gift, but were looking down upon other members of the community who apparently had much less impressive gifts. To do this Paul, in 1 Corinthians 12:22-26, daringly employs even a reference to the genital or excretal parts of the body:

The parts of the body which seem to be weaker are indispensable, and those parts of the body which we think less honorable we invest with the greater honor, and our un-presentable parts are treated with greater modesty, which our more presentable parts do not require. But God has so adjusted the body, giving the greater honor to the inferior parts, that there may be no discord in the body, but that the members may have the same care for one another. If one member suffers, all suffer together; if one member is honored, all rejoice together.

There are many ways in which Paul's meaning here can be translated in terms of our own contemporary experience. For example, while brilliant theologians and prophetic preachers are indeed a great gift to the Christian community, something to be celebrated with applause and honor, the assembly should not forget the fundamental importance of the gifts of those whose talents are comparatively less spectacular, the ministry of ushers, sacristans and sextons who set up for and make inviting, or clean up after the church meeting. But there is yet another point Paul wants to make by use of this image of the Church as the Body of Christ. Next, in 1 Corinthians 12:27-28, he introduces the concept of hierarchy, namely the concept of a pecking order or grades of authority in the community:

Now you are the body of Christ and individually members of it. And God has appointed in the Church first apostles, second prophets, third teachers, then workers of miracles, then healers, helpers, administrators, speakers in various kinds of tongues.

This concept of hierarchy is most controversial today and we shall treat it at length in Part II of this our study in the section dealing with Christian ministries. But even at this point we can understand something of Paul's meaning if we note what exegetes have said about the possibly pagan, that is, Hellenistic origin of Paul's image of the Church as the Body of Christ.

We have already seen how Paul's use of this image may have been in part influenced by traditional Jewish modes of thinking.

But at this point we must recall: Saint Paul had a diverse cultural background. A Jew born and raised in the Hellenistic *diaspora*, that is, outside of Palestine, in the town of Tarsus in the Roman province of Cilicia, Paul's thought and writing at times discloses not only his Jewish (Pharisaic) heritage but also his acquaintance with Hellenistic culture. For example, while Jesus in his preaching often employs imagery from the agricultural life of rural Palestine, Paul often uses the language of Greek athleticism. And so we should not be surprised to find that some exegetes have argued Paul's use of this image of the Church as the Body of Christ, while it may have some roots in the Jewish concept of corporate identify, also discloses deep roots in Hellenistic thought, that is, in the world of ideas that was the political-speculative tradition in the ancient pagan societies of Greece and Rome. Paul's home town was a cosmopolitan city and Paul had had a cosmopolitan education wherein he may well have been introduced to the Stoic concept of the body politic, that is, a political concept regarding the organization of the political state as analogous to that of the coordinating function of the human limbs with hand and eye and heart. This political image is called "the body politic." This secular, political concept is found as early as Aristotle's *Politics* 5.2.7. Moreover, it was a standard theme in Stoic philosophy of Paul's time (see Cicero's *Philippic Orations* 8.5.15, Seneca's *Epistolae Morale* 95.52). There is an especially intriguing expression of this political concept in Plutarch's *Moralia* 426A:

> Is there not often in this world of ours a single body (*soma hen*) composed of disparate bodies, such as an assembly (*ekklesia*) or an army or a chorus, each one of which happens to have a faculty of living, thinking, and learning…?

Some have found the association here of the two Greek words, *soma* with *ekklesia*, as particularly striking. But other scholars caution this analogy however striking is only superficial. Paul's use of the image of a corporate body of which Christ is the head or principle of living and thinking, etc., does not really correspond to the Stoic notion of a political assembly as a union of autonomous entities. These critics may be right, but such a distinction should not be allowed to obscure the great value the body politic image serves. The image of the body politic makes clear whatever the constituent elements — eyes, ears, legs, hands — every body needs a head, no body is complete without one. Louis Bouyer, in his *The Church of God* (Franciscan Herald Press, 1982, pp. 177-178), claims the biblical witness makes it clear: "It remains a constant, basic principle of the People. Whatever the title of the providential individual on whom it is centered, the People will exist as a People only around a king, a priest, a prophet, a 'father.'" After the Second Vatican Council, some theologians made use of the image of the Church as the Body of Christ in a Marxist or populist, not to say libertarian, fashion that seems to obscure the relevance of any head, for example, Leonardo Boff's *Ecclesiogenesis: The Base Communities Reinvent the Church* (1986). This is very misleading. The image of the Church as the People of God implies leadership. For example, note how while the First Letter of Peter begins with the one precise and clear evocation of the theme of the Church as the People of God (1 P 2:9-10), it ends with an invocation of the theme of the Church as Sheep with Shepherd. More precisely, Chapter 5, the final chapter of this letter and a sort of peroration, begins with the words (verses 1-2): "So I exhort the elders among you, as a fellow elder and a witness of the sufferings of Christ as well as a partaker in the glory that is to be revealed. Tend the flock of God that is your charge." One image does not exclude the other, in fact, one complements the other. The image of the Church as the People of God needs completion by the image of the Church as the Body of Christ, not just a mystic body, but also a politic one.

Further Reading

Yves Congar's essay, "The Church: The People of God," (pages 11-37) in *The Church and Mankind*, which is Dogma Vol. 1 in the series called "Concilium" (Paulist Press, 1965).

Chapter 9, "The Body of Christ," 85-92 in Geoffrey Preston's *Faces of the Church: Meditations on a Mystery and Its Images* (Eerdmans, 1997).

CHAPTER 8

An Image of the Church from Three North African Theologians

One could argue that both verbal and visual images have an emotive form as well as an intellectual content and that we tend to respond more quickly to an image's emotive form than to its intellectual content. If this is true, then it is important that we critically examine why we are so spontaneously attracted or repulsed by a particular image of the Church. The image we consider in this chapter has a particularly strong ability to either attract or repulse. The image of the Church as Mother is an ancient and venerable one and indeed it was a common one right on up to the last century. Even in my childhood it was not uncommon for me to hear a preacher make reference to "Holy Mother Church." Moreover, when such a reference was made I think there were many in the congregation who took a certain comfort from it. In the latter half of the twentieth century, however, the image of the Church as Mother underwent a precipitous decline into disuse and even outright disfavor. The principal reason for this appears to be the claim that it lends itself to authoritarianism. Brazilian theologian, Leonardo Boff, in Chapter 1 of his *The Church, Charism and Power: Liberation Theology and the Institutional Church* (1981, Eng. 1985), took strong objection to it and for precisely that reason. There is also the possibility that nowadays to speak of the Church as Mother might be judged by some feminists as one more instance of idealization of woman in a restrictive, traditional role. And so it is at some risk that I dare probe the meaning of this currently despised and neglected image. But I feel it is worth doing and for several reasons. First, it has had such an important place in the history of Christian thought. Secondly, the fact that this image is found only "in germ" in the New Testament and is principally a development of later, patristic, theology, makes this image an important example of fruitful as well as imaginative development in theology if not outright innovation. Thirdly, its geographical provenance is intriguing. That is, the image of the Church as Mother is the product of three North African theologians. No doubt, all three are Latin writers from Roman North Africa, what was called at that time Africa Proconsularis. Nevertheless, it is not impossible that the attractiveness of this image to these three theologians was due to something characteristic of indigenous North African culture rather than imported Roman civilization. Peter Brown, in his *Augustine of Hippo: A Biography* (2nd ed, 2000, Chapter 19), describes North Africa as, if not a matriarchal society, yet "a land which, to judge from Monica [Augustine's mother], had a fair share of formidable mothers." And thus it could be argued the development of this image of the Church serves as an example of inculturation of the gospel, an example of how local culture can bring out otherwise latent themes in the gospel. Finally and perhaps most importantly, I think the reader will see that this image of the Church as Mother, despite its ability to repulse some, still holds some important lessons for all of us today, clergy and laity alike, regarding some basic requirements for effective membership in the Church.

And so what I would like to do here is a three-part study. First, we shall look at the biblical background of this image. Second, we shall look at its development by these three North African theologians. Finally, I shall try to indicate what I see as some of its value even to this day.

Unlike an image such as "flock of sheep" which is well-developed in the New Testament itself and indeed can arguably be attributed to Jesus himself, the image of the Church as Mother is not well developed in the New Testament and, indeed, can only be found there in germ, as it were, that is, in brief, incidental, more or less undeveloped, even as a fleeting idea in the preaching of Jesus and Paul. No doubt this is the reason why this image got no significant notice in Paul Minear's comprehensive work *Images of the Church*. There are two New Testament passages, however, where the ground work is prepared for the later development of this image of the Church. In the Gospel according to Matthew 23:37-39, we hear Jesus say: "O Jerusalem, Jerusalem, killing the prophets and stoning those who are sent to you! How often would I have gathered your children together as a hen gathers her brood under her wings, and you would not!" It is a quaint image for a man to use and yet it is very suggestive of Jesus' mission. For one thing he uses the concept of gathering. Also, it is at one with the image we have already seen of Jesus' mission as a judgment against the old Israel, that is, in its image of Israel's having rejected prophetic voices in the past. Saint Paul in his Epistle to the Galatians 4:25-26 is yet another source for this concept. There, in an extended allegory, he develops a striking image:

> It is written that Abraham had two sons, one by a slave and one by a free woman. But the son of the slave was born according to the flesh, the son of the free woman through promise. Now this is an allegory: these two women are two covenants. One is from Mount Sinai, bearing children for slavery; she is Hagar. Now Hagar is Mount Sinai in Arabia; she corresponds to the present Jerusalem, for she is in slavery with her children. But the Jerusalem above is free and she is our mother.

There is an important literary background to both Jesus' and Paul's use of this imagistic language. Jesus' language has as its literary precedent a passage from the prophet Isaiah (66:10-13) in which Isaiah employs the imaginative personification of Jerusalem as woman and nursing mother:

> Rejoice with Jerusalem and be glad because of her, all you who love her; exult with her, all you who were mourning over her! Oh, that you may suck fully of the

milk of her comfort. That you may nurse with delight at
her abundant breasts! For thus says the Lord: Lo, I will
spread prosperity over her like a river, and the wealth
of the nations like an overflowing torrent. As nurslings,
you shall be carried in her arms, and fondled in her lap.
As a mother comforts her son, so will I comfort you; in
Jerusalem you shall find your comfort.

As for Paul's image of Jerusalem as a mother, many exegetes
believe Paul's image in Galatians 4:26 is a self-conscious allusion
to Psalm 87:1-5, where we find a similar apocalyptic vision of
Jerusalem as a mother to the nations:

On the holy mountain is his city cherished by the Lord.
The Lord prefers the gates of Zion to all Jacob's dwell-
ings. Of you are told glorious things, O city of God!
"Babylon and Egypt I will count among those who know
me; Philistia, Tyre, Ethiopia, these will be her children
and Zion shall be called 'Mother' for all shall be her
children."

Now that we have seen something of the biblical background
to this image of the Church, we need to look at the precise
development of this image. In this regard the work of three
Latin-speaking theologians of North Africa in the early history
of the Christian movement is of pivotal importance. For in their
writings we find the next significant development of this image
of the Church as Mother.

The first is Quintus Septimus Florens Tertullianus (ca. 160-
ca. 225), known simply to us as Tertullian. Born and brought up
in the great metropolitan center of Carthage (near modern Tunis,
Tunisia on the north coast of Africa) as a pagan, Tertullian converted to Christianity in mid-life. Educated as a rhetorician and
lawyer, he was especially well-equipped to become an apologist
for his new-found faith. Several times in his writings he employs
the image of the Church as Mother. For example, in the opening
words of his *Exhortation to Martyrdom* — his encouragement to
imprisoned Christians awaiting martyrdom — Tertullian self-

consciously echoes the words of Isaiah about the bountifulness of Jerusalem as a providing mother when he says:

> Blessed martyrs designate, along with the provision which our lady mother the Church from her bountiful breasts, and each brother out of his private means, makes for your bodily wants in prison, accept also from me some contribution to your spiritual sustenance; for it is not good that the flesh be feasted and the spirit starve. (Ch. I, vs. 1)

This image gains even more strength when Tertullian, in an exhortation this time to candidates for baptism, refers to the assembly of the faithful, the community of faith not as the house of the Lord but as the house of your mother: *family name*

> Therefore, blessed ones, whom the grace of God awaits, when you ascend from that most sacred font of your new birth, and spread your hands [in prayer] for the first time in the house of your mother together with your brethren, ask from the Father, ask from the Lord, that His own specialties of grace and distribution of gifts may be supplied to you. (*De baptismo* XX)

Finally, in his commentary on the Lord's Prayer, Tertullian uses the image of the Church as Mother in its most sententious form. That is, in Chapter 2 of his *Treatise on Prayer* Tertullian argues for the supernatural character of the Church as no mere human configuration or mere social convention when he claims that the maternity of the Church is implicit in the Trinitarian relation of the Father and the Son:

> Nor is even our mother the Church passed by, if, that is, in the Father and the Son is recognized the mother, from whom arises the name both of Father and of Son. (*De oratione* 2)

This aggrandizement of the Church via the image of Mother is carried even further by another North African theologian,

Cyprian of Carthage (d. 258). Cyprian too was a pagan rhetorician converted to Christianity, but Cyprian, unlike Tertullian,
went on to become bishop of Carthage, more precisely bishop of
what was in his day the largest Christian community in North
Africa. While Tertullian emphasized the idea that the Church
is a caring parent, a mother who nurtures and feeds her child,
Cyprian went further to depict her as a great matriarchal figure
presiding over her large and extended family, her many children
throughout the world. Indeed, in his treatise *On the Unity of the
Church*, Cyprian combines the image of the prolific maternity
of the Church along with other New Testament themes such as
Jesus' disciples being light for the world and the Isaian vision
of the overflowing torrent from Jerusalem. With this he is able
to produce an awesome image of the Church as the principal
vehicle for the salvation of the world:

> And the Church forms a unity, however far she spreads
> and multiplies by the progeny of her fecundity.... Our
> Lord's Church is radiant with light and pours her rays
> over the whole world; but it is one and the same light
> which is spread everywhere, and the unity of her body
> suffers no division. She spreads her branches in gener-
> ous growth over all the earth, she extends her abundant
> streams even further; yet one is the head-spring, one the
> source, one the mother who is prolific in her offspring,
> generation after generation: of her womb are we born,
> of her milk are we fed, of her Spirit our souls draw their
> life-breath. (*De unitate* 5)

And, like Saint Paul, Cyprian also celebrates the spotlessness
of the bride of Christ, the Church. But Cyprian spells out more
clearly the role of the Church. And if Tertullian saw the maternity of the Church implicit in the Lord's Prayer, in the relation
between Father and Son, and thus gave a sort of Trinitarian
foundation to the Church, Cyprian goes further and insists that
there is no access to the Father except through the Mother:

> The spouse of Christ cannot be defiled, she is inviolate
> and chaste; she knows one home alone, in all modesty
> she keeps faithfully to one only couch. It is she who
> rescues us for God, she who seals for the kingdom the
> sons whom she has borne. Whoever breaks with the
> Church and enters on an adulterous union cuts himself
> off from the promises made to the Church. And he who
> has turned his back on the Church of Christ shall not
> come to the rewards of Christ: he is an alien, a worldling,
> an enemy. You cannot have God for your Father if you
> have not the Church for your Mother. (*De unitate* 6)

For some readers these passages from Cyprian will prove especially distasteful, that is, they will appear as inappropriate aggrandizement of the Church. However, that reader would do well to be patient, because, in the writings of the next North African theologian that we survey, Cyprian's extravagance is redressed or at least balanced.

Augustine of Hippo (354-430) was born in Thagaste, a hill town of coastal North Africa, about 150 miles west of Carthage, near the modern Souk Ahras in Algeria. Augustine was born of a pagan father and a Christian mother. His mother was a very devout Christian and so she provided her child with a Christian education. But as he grew older he wandered from his mother's faith. As a young man he went off to Carthage to study rhetoric with the aim of becoming a lawyer. However, Augustine soon gave up legal studies, took a mistress, and began literary pursuits. For nine years he was associated with a bizarre religious cult called Manicheism. Then he went to Rome to teach rhetoric. From there he moved to Milan where he came under the influence of the bishop Ambrose. Augustine underwent a conversion. He returned to Africa, where he first became an ascetic, then a priest and finally the bishop of a town about 60 miles north of his birthplace of Thagaste. This town was called in Augustine's time Hippo Regius, the Roman name for a Mediterranean seaport town, near the modern Annaba in Algeria.

Several times in his writings as priest and bishop, we find Augustine having recourse to the image of the Church as Mother. Most often he does it in a way that echoes the image as first set forth by Tertullian and Cyprian of Carthage. For example, in his Sermon on Matthew 6, "The Lord's Prayer," Augustine, probably taking his cue from Tertullian's commentary on the same prayer, says: "We had a father and mother on earth, that we might be born to labor and death; but we have found other parents, God our Father, and the Church our Mother, by whom we are born into life eternal." And in the very first paragraph of his "On the Creed: A Sermon to the Catechumens" Augustine tells these neophytes: "For have you now merely heard that God is Almighty? But you begin to have him for your Father when you have been born by the Church as your Mother." However Augustine's true originality with this image is to be found in his debate with the Donatists.

It was while he was bishop of Hippo that Augustine got into a literary debate with a certain Petilian, one of the spiritual leaders of a puritanical and schismatic Christian movement called Donatism. The Donatists made much use of passages from Scripture that could be used to support their puritanical approach. One such favorite passage was from the Revelation to John (Rv 21:10-11, 27). It is a vision of the Church as the spotless bride of Christ:

> And in the Spirit he [one of the seven angels who minister before God's throne] carried me away to a great, high mountain, and showed me the holy city Jerusalem coming down out of heaven from God having the glory of God... nothing unclean shall enter it.

In contrast, Augustine insisted this is an eschatological image of the Church, that is, an image of the Church triumphant at the end of time. And instead Augustine develops the image of Mother Church while on this earth as a plain and humble *hausfrau*. We see this image most dramatically in a work of Augustine's called his *Answer to Petilian* (Bk II, ch. 5). There Augustine, aware of the power and wealth of the Donatist Church and the intellectual and political acumen of its leaders, develops a picture of Mother

Church as the comparatively humble and plain *hausfrau* whose beauty is perhaps not obvious to all but is real nonetheless because it arises from an inter-relational, interpersonal relationship:

> Do you, therefore, holy scions of our one Catholic mother, beware with all the watchfulness of which you are capable, in due submission to the Lord, of the example of crime and error such as this. With however great light of learning and of reputation he may shine, however he may boast himself to be a precious stone, who endeavors to lead you after him, remember always that brave woman who alone is lovely to her husband, whom holy Scripture portrays to us in the last chapter of the book of Proverbs, is more precious than any precious stones. (*Contra petilianus*, Bk II, Ch 5)

But, if we want to truly appreciate this image of the Church as Mother, it is important that we go back to the Bible and trace another New Testament motif and that is the image of the disciples of Jesus as children. It is interesting how Jesus is portrayed in the Gospels as at times addressing his adult male disciples, the Twelve, as children. This is especially prominent in John's Gospel. There, in Jesus' last discourse to his disciples before his passion and death he says, in John 13:33, "Little children, yet a little while I am with you. You will seek me; and as I said to the Jews so now I say to you, 'Where I am going you cannot come.'" And then in his first post-resurrection appearance to the disciples on the shore of the sea of Tiberias, in John 21:4, Jesus says, "Children, have you any fish?" In Mark 10:24, we hear Jesus say to the Twelve, "Children, how hard it is for those who trust in riches to enter the kingdom of God!" And the figure of a child as innocently impressionable, trusting, is used several times by Jesus in the Gospels. Matthew 18:3, "Truly, I say to you, unless you turn and become like children, you will never enter the kingdom of heaven." Mark 10:15, "Let the children come to me, do not hinder them; for to such belongs the kingdom of God." Luke 10:21, "I thank thee, Father, Lord of heaven and earth, that thou hast hidden these things from the wise and understanding

and revealed them to babes." But it can also be used of childish
willfulness as in Luke 7:31-32:

> To what then shall I compare the men of this generation,
> and what are they like? They are like children sitting in
> the market place and calling to one another, "We piped
> to you, and you did not dance; we wailed, and you did
> not weep." (See its parallel in Mt 11:16-17.)

We can see a comparable use of the parent/child image
in the epistles of Paul. In 1 Thessalonians 2:7, "We were gentle
among you like a mother caring for her children"; Romans 8:16,
"we are all children of God"; Galatians 4:19, "My dear children."
But even more dramatically in 1 Corinthians 3:1-3:

> But I, brethren, could not address you as spiritual men,
> but as men of the flesh, as babes in Christ. I fed you
> with milk, not solid food; for you were not ready for it;
> and even yet you are not ready, for you are still of the
> flesh.

Indeed, Saint Paul makes great use of the image of growing up
later in this same letter when in 1 Corinthians 13:11, he says,
"When I was a child, I spoke like child, I thought like a child,
I reasoned like a child; when I became a man, I gave up childish ways."

Indeed, the way this theme is repeated in other New Testament letters can lead us to believe that maturity in the ways
of faith, hope and love was a major challenge for many early
Christians. For example, this sentiment is echoed in Ephesians
4:13-15:

> Until we all attain to the unity of the faith and of the
> knowledge of the Son of God, to mature manhood, to
> the measure of the stature of the fullness of Christ; so
> that we may no longer be children, tossed to and from
> and carried about with every wind of doctrine, by the
> cunning of men, by their craftiness in deceitful wiles.
> Rather speaking the truth in love, we are to grow up in
> every way into him who is the head, into Christ.

And then look at Hebrews 5:11-14:

> For though by this time you ought to be teachers, you
> need some one to teach you again the first principles
> of God's words. You need milk, not food; for every one
> who lives on milk is unskilled in the word of righteous-
> ness, for he is a child. But solid food is for the mature,
> for those who have their faculties trained by practice to
> distinguish good from evil.

And so this image of the Church as a Mother with children
is a humbling image. That is, it serves to remind the Christian
community that many of us are still "babes in the woods" as regards the Christian life. It serves to remind us that when it comes
to faith, hope and love, some of us have a long way to grow. But
it also encourages us to remain close to the Church to try to be
open to its teaching, to be willing to learn, to attend Church services regularly, so as to hear all the Gospel read aloud, reflected
upon and preached to us, to listen attentively to the readings,
to keep close to the sacraments, to try everything in Mother's
cupboard — all the sacraments, as well as religious exercises
such as retreats, prayer groups, ecclesial movements, reading the
lives of the saints, reading theology or spiritual writers, trying
various forms of prayer. But in this regard it should be noted:
this maternity of the Church should not be seen exclusively
in clerical terms. That is, it is the whole Church that nurtures
faith, hope and love. This begins with parents, continues with
catechists, and other laity who also prove the maternal character
of the Church when they lead prayer groups or take on other
forms of spiritual, charitable and educational leadership.

It could be argued this image of Mother Church also entails
something of a warning about not abusing this parental role.
All three of the Synoptic Gospels record Jesus' warning: "Whoever causes one of these little ones who believe in me to sin, it
would be better for him if a great millstone were hung round
his neck and he were thrown into the sea" (Mk 9:42, with parallels Mt 11:16; Lk 7:32). And thus the image of Mother Church is
a challenge not just to those of us today who fear the spectre of

authoritarianism but also to those today (both lay and clerical) who want to assume roles of authority or responsible leadership in the Church.

Finally, I think it is worth considering the words of NT scholar Raymond Brown on the use and abuse of this image of the Church. Brown in his *The Churches the Apostles Left Behind* (New York: Paulist Press, 1984, pages 53-54) says:

> In my own Church, before the Second Vatican Council one heard frequently the language of "mother Church." Admittedly that imagery smacked of over-supervision and of a maternalism that reduced everyone to a child status, or at times to a childish status. In part, such weakness explains why the imagery is no longer very popular; yet no real replacement has been found. Post-Vatican II references to "the institutional Church" often embody the misunderstanding that there are two Churches of which one is non-institutional. The Church is by nature social and implicitly institutional. Those who "opt out of the institutional Church" may continue with private religion, but they are no longer in the Church as it exists on this earth.... But even when references to "the institutional Church" do not involve such a misunderstanding, they scarcely reflect warmth or passionate admiration.... For all its defects, "mother Church" was both personal and familial; and even when a mother overdoes her role, she can be loved by her children.

Further Reading

There are classic historical studies of this theme such as Joseph C. Plumpe's *Mater Ecclesia: An Inquiry into the Concept of the Church as Mother in Early Christianity* (Washington, D.C., 1943) and Stanislaus Grabowski's *The Church: An Introduction to the Theology of St. Augustine* (St. Louis, 1957). But an important summary treatment is the entry "Mother, Church as" in Christopher O'Donnell's *Ecclesia: A Theological Encyclopedia of the Church* (Collegeville, Minnesota: Liturgical Press, 1996). Another noteworthy study is Henri de Lubac's *The Motherhood of the Church* translated by S. Englund (San Francisco: Ignatius Press, 1982).

In witness to the fact that this image is not totally out of circulation today, it should be noted that in some recent theological literature the image of the Church as Mother is evoked for ecumenical considerations. For example, it appears in the title of Carl Braaten's *Mother Church: Ecclesiology and Ecumenism* (Minneapolis: Fortress Press, 1998) and Lucas Vischer's essay "The Church — Mother of the Believers" in *Toward the Future of Reformed Theology: Tasks, Topics, Traditions* edited by D. Willis and M. Welker (Grand Rapids: Eerdmans, 1999, pp. 262-282). But it also has received more precise theological treatment in John Klenig's "Mother Zion — Mother Church" in *Lutheran Theological Journal*, August 28, 1994, pp. 50-57.

CHAPTER 9

Introduction to the Essential Attributes
of the Church

On this coming Sunday many a Christian will stand up in
a church or worshiping assembly and publicly profess along with
everyone there his or her faith. On this Sunday as on many another Sunday, the assembled believers will recite from an ancient
and venerable text popularly called the Nicene Creed. There is
much scholarly debate as to the precise origin of this creedal
statement. All scholars agree that in large measure the text that
we currently have is the product of a meeting of bishops called
the Council of Nicea which was held in 325. More precisely, that
Council produced a tri-partite profession of faith in Father, Son
and Holy Spirit. And because that Council spent most of its time
defending the orthodox Christian faith against the claims of the
Arians regarding the relationship between God the Father, and
Jesus as his Son, the creed they drafted made important statements regarding God the Father and Jesus Christ his Son but
said nothing much about the Holy Spirit. Indeed, that creed
ended with the simple profession of belief "in the Holy Spirit."
However, at the Council of Chalcedon in 451, Nicea's creedal
statement was presented with an expanded article on the Holy
Spirit. And this expanded creedal statement was called "The
Creed of the Council of Constantinople," a Council which had
been held in AD 381. This expanded creed added some important
phrases to the two sections on the Father and the Son, a much
more extended statement about the Holy Spirit, and assertions
of belief regarding the Church, baptism, the resurrection of the

dead, and eternal life.

There is much scholarly debate as to the origin of these expansions. That is, many scholars question whether those additions really came from the Council of Constantinople in 381. But regardless of its origin, this sometimes-called "Nicene-Constantino-politan Creed" soon became accepted throughout East and West as the standard of Christian orthodoxy and as such it is still used to this day. And for our interests it is the assertion regarding the Church that is especially important. The statement reads, "We believe in one, holy, catholic, and apostolic Church." Any modern theological study of the Church needs to include a treatment of these four adjectives in their application to the Church. The reasons for this are two. First, as in my defense of our treatment of biblical images of the Church, here too we have an example of an element in liturgical worship that should not be ignored by theology. More precisely, since so many Christians do indeed publicly profess and with some regularity their belief in "one, holy, catholic and apostolic Church" it is important that theologians help us try to understand what indeed is being professed, what precisely it is that these people who recite this formula are saying. It is important to make sense of that statement, to try to make it as intelligible as possible if for no other reason than that the faithful should know what they are professing. Secondly, even for those who do not attend a worship-assembly that employs the so-called Nicene-Constantinopolitan Creed with its affirmation of "one, holy, catholic and apostolic Church" these four adjectives remain important. For example, of these four adjectives, three of them refer to important biblical concepts. That is, the concepts of Church unity, holiness and apostolicity are gospel ideals. They are Christian values with their origin in the New Testament. And even the adjective "catholic," though it is not found in the New Testament, is still an ancient, venerable, important word in Christian thought and history as well as an important contemporary issue. Witness how worship assemblies in the Reformation tradition still profess their faith in a Church that is "catholic." How and why this is so deserves explanation and we can all learn from that explanation.

But even if I have convinced the reader of the importance of our treating these four adjectives, there is yet another issue we must face. And that is the viability of these four creedal affirmations in a skeptical world. While a devout Christian might accept these terms precisely because of their prominence in the Bible or Church history, outsiders — that is, non-believers — relying upon reason alone, will find these assertions especially problematic if not downright risible. These four adjectives — one, holy, catholic, and apostolic — do not easily or readily disclose their meaning. Indeed, for many today these four adjectives when applied to the Church raise more questions that they answer. For example, when one claims to believe "in one, holy, catholic and apostolic Church," a skeptic might easily challenge that assertion by asking: "Indeed, which one?" This question being an indirect reference to the fact that Christianity might well appear to many observers as outstanding among religions for its rabid sectarianism. Or when we profess our faith in a Church that is holy, a reasonable person, recalling recent disclosures of sexual and financial wrongdoings by both clergy and laity, could well offer the challenge: "Do you never read the newspapers? It seems to me the Church harbors as many sinners as any other human organization." And as for the adjectives "catholic" and "apostolic," there is a tension between the use of the word "catholic" to refer to one historic manifestation of Church, that is, catholic is not only an essential attribute of the Church but also a confessional designation. The adjective "apostolic" is also capable of extremely differing interpretations. And this raises yet another problem attendant upon the use of these four adjectives to describe the Church: they have always been somewhat contentious, that is, they have not been simply descriptive adjectives but value judgments.

From the very beginning of Christian thought, these adjectives were often used not just to describe the essential character of the Church itself but they were also used to define the distinguishing features, signs of the true Church, against false representations. For example, though we do not find the adjective "apostolic" in the New Testament, biblical scholars are united in the conviction that the noun "apostles" is used in the New Testament with increasing sententiousness, that is, implying not only a value to be preserved but a judgment regarding legitimacy. More precisely, consider how those referred to in Mark 3:16 as simply "the twelve" become in Matthew 10:2 "the twelve apostles." In Acts 2:42, Luke reports how the earliest community of Christ's disciples at Jerusalem "devoted themselves to the apostles' teaching." In 2 Corinthians 11:3, we hear Paul denounce "false apostles." Revelation 2:2 contains a similar value judgment when it speaks of "those who call themselves apostles but are not." Two early Church fathers, Irenaeus of Lyons (ca. 130-ca. 200) and Tertullian (ca. 160-ca. 225), noting how the New Testament writings made much of the apostles and their prominent role in the founding and leadership of the earliest Christian communities, both made much use of the term "apostolic" as a means of critiquing the legitimacy of Gnostic sects and their idiosyncratic interpretations of the Christian faith. Irenaeus does this in his *Against Heresies* 3.2, as does Tertullian in his *The Prescription of Heretics*. The adjective "catholic" has an even more pronounced character as a term of judgment. Two North African bishops, Optatus of Milevis (370) and Augustine of Hippo (354-430), seized upon the term "catholic" as applied to the Church and used it as an effective tool allowing them to critique the claims of the powerful Donatist sect of their day. Optatus did this in Book I of his *Against Parmenian;* Augustine in his *On True Religion*.

However, one could argue that with the general adoption of the Nicene-Constantinopolitan Creed as an element in liturgy, the marks became more doctrinal than apologetic. For example, Saint Thomas Aquinas treats of the four marks of the Church in his *Catechetical Instruction on the Creed*. This is not a collection of university classroom lectures. Rather these were sermon-conferences given outside the classroom, in the Dominican priory church at Naples, during Lent of 1273 to a general audience of university students and the lay faithful of Naples. In Article 9 he treats of the four marks. Aquinas does not make reference to the historic background of each note. For example, in his treatment of "the unity of the Church" he makes a very general statement that "various heretics have founded various sects" with no reference to any in particular. And the rest of his treatment is entirely made up of his quotation of passages from Scripture which emphasize the spiritual reasons for the unity which should characterize the Church. Or he gives such moral exhortation as "this is a true love when the members are solicitous for one another and sympathetic towards each other." But not long after Aquinas things began to change.

Soon other theologians came along who not only denounced the moral failures of the clergy but proposed a doctrine of the Church quite different from the traditional doctrine. For example, the Englishman John Wycliffe (ca. 1330-84), a fellow and master and warden of Oxford University did this in a series of theological works, viz., his treatises *On the Church, On the Truth of Scripture,* and *On the Power of the Pope* (1377-8). Another university professor, priest and popular preacher, John Hus (ca. 1372-1414) from the University of Prague in Bohemia (today the Czech Republic), not only gave violent sermons denouncing the morals of the clergy but published a theological tract *De Ecclesia* (1413) heavily influenced by Wycliffe and equally unstinting in its denunciation of the legitimacy of the contemporary Church. These theological challenges prompted responses from scholastic theologians such as John of Ragusa (his *Tractatus de Ecclesia* of 1431 was a direct attack upon Hus) and John of Torquemada (in his *Summa de Ecclesia* of 1436) to compose defenses of the Church based upon the four notes. German reformers Martin Luther (1483-1546) and his colleague Philip Melanchthon (1497-1560) offered an even greater challenge. Melanchthon was a fervent disciple of Luther whose teachings, originally set forth in polemical tracts, Melanchthon was able to recast into a more rational and systematic form in a work entitled, *Loci communes* (1521). When Melanchthon wrote the Augsburg Confession (1530), the official standard of Lutheran faith, in Article VII he acknowledged only two notes: that is, the Augsburg Confession defines the true Church as "the assembly of all believers in whose presence the gospel is preached in its authenticity, and the holy sacraments publicly administered according to the gospel." But later, Luther, in his *On the Councils and Churches* (1539), added five more to the two in the Augsburg Confession. And two years later, in his polemical work *Against Hans Worst* (1541), Luther added still more notes. The Genevan reformer John Calvin (1509-64), in his treatment of the Church in his *Institutes of the Christian Religion* Book IV (Chapter 1, Articles 1 and 2), begins his treatment of the Church by giving a nod to the four classic creedal attributes. But he goes on to give special place to the two criteria proposed in the Augsburg Confession. After the death of the South German reformer Zwingli in 1531, a certain Martin Bucer (1491-1551) became leader of the Reformed Churches in Switzerland and southern Germany. But in 1549 he went to England where he became a theology professor at Cambridge University (holding a chair endowed by the crown) and thus influenced the Reformation in England. For example, in treating of the notes or marks of the Church, Bucer added "disciplined" as the third mark in addition to the Lutheran two. And many followed Bucer's lead. In Chapter 18 of the first Scots Confession of 1560 authored by John Knox and some colleagues, "ecclesiastical discipline" is the third mark. So too in the 1561 Belgic (Dutch) Confession's article 29, entitled "The Marks of the True Church," ecclesiastical discipline appears as an added mark.

The *Catechism of the Council of Trent* kept to the four creedal notes (Part I, ch. 10). So did Polish Cardinal Stanislaus Hosius (1504-79) in his *Confessio Catholicae Fidei Christiana* of 1553, a work in which he argued against the Protestant Reformers that the true Church could be recognized by the four marks of the creed. But other Catholic apologists added to the four classical marks. Italian Dominican Friar Dominic Gravina (1593-1643), theologian at Naples, built his arguments around six marks of the Church. Hungarian Cardinal Peter Pazmany (1570-1637), a convert from Protestantism, in his comprehensive apologetic *Guide to Truth* (1613) argued seven. Francisco de Suarez (1548-1617) set forth eight and Robert Bellarmine (1542-1621) marshaled fifteen notes. A record seems to have been reached with Tommaso Bozio

(1548-1610). Bozio, one of the founding members of the Oratory of Saint Philip Neri, listed no less than a hundred notes in his great apologetical work of 1591, *De signis ecclesiae*. While eventually most Catholic theologians settled down to the classical four, as late as the mid-twentieth century, theologians such as Ludwig Ott in his *Fundamentals of Catholic Dogma* (1952) taught that there were seven properties or essential attributes of the Church: alongside the four creedal ones he added indefectibility, infallibility, and visibility.

In the latter half of the twentieth century, however, due to the influence of the ecumenical movement and especially the Second Vatican Council (1962-1965) there have been several important attempts to rethink the whole issue of the marks of the Church and their use. Here I have selected works by four theologians that I believe are particularly deserving of our consideration. I have chosen these four because of their precise focus upon the marks, innovative treatment, and finally, availability in English for our readers.

Swiss theologian Hans Küng published in 1967 his *Die Kirche* which was translated that very same year as *The Church*. Küng's book is divided into five parts. The fourth part, Section D, is entitled "The Dimensions of the Church." And that is where he treats of the four creedal marks. Küng had been a theological expert at the Second Vatican Council but his book begins on a note of regret that that Council did not go further in its pursuit of doctrinal revision and reconciliation with the Reformation and the modern world. Küng then announces this is precisely what he seeks to do in this book. Later, when we treat of the individual notes, we shall note the peculiar character of Küng's rethinking of the notes. But, for now, we can be satisfied with a general description of Küng's concept of the marks and the way in which he treats them. But that we might understand what he is trying to improve upon, and in view of the fact that the next three authors also address in one manner or another the teaching of the Second Vatican Council, I will begin here with a brief overview of the treatment of the marks at Vatican II.

The Second Vatican Council cited the four marks in Article 8, Paragraph 2 of its Dogmatic Constitution on the Church: "This is the unique Church of Christ which in the Creed we avow as one, holy, catholic and apostolic." But it did not treat of them programmatically and uniformly. Instead, they are addressed occasionally and the treatment varies in length. For example, unity which is mentioned in passing in the Dogmatic Constitution on the Church is treated at length in the Council's Decree on Ecumenism. But there is a consistent approach to the marks. An effort is always made to treat them in a doctrinal rather than an apologetic much less a polemical fashion. For example, referring to the catholicity of the Church, the Council says in Article 23, Paragraph 6 of its Dogmatic Constitution on the Church: "This variety of local Churches with one common aspiration is particularly splendid evidence of the catholicity of the undivided Church."

So too Hans Küng begins his treatment of the four classical marks of the Church with a lament for the polemical use made of them in the recent past. Secondly, he argues there really is no essential conflict between the classic four marks and the Lutheran or Reformation two marks (p. 267); indeed, they should be seen as complementary (p. 268). Then he tackles the problem of the intelligibility of the four classic marks especially as regards the witness of the Church to the world. On page 269, Küng puts this task this way:

> What is truly decisive is not the formal presence of certain characteristics, but their use and practice. The word of the Gospel must truly be preached, heard and followed, the sacraments must really be used; oneness, holiness, catholicity and apostolicity must be lived by living men in a living Church, and the *notae Ecclesiae* must become in one way or another *notae Christianorum*. To bring about the living realization of its own signs is a big enough task for each Church, whichever of them it places most emphasis on.

The work of the next theologian we consider has been

influenced both by the work of the Second Vatican Council and Hans Küng. In 1975, Jürgen Moltmann (b. 1926), a theologian at Tubingen University in Germany, published his *Kirche in Der Kraft des Geistes* (Eng. trans., *The Church in the Power of the Spirit*, 1977). Moltmann's is a comprehensive ecclesiology which includes an extended treatment of "The Marks of the Church" (the concluding Part VII of the book). Moltmann not only cites both the Second Vatican Council and Küng, but his treatment of the marks concurs with both of them. For example, not only does he too eschew the apologetic much less polemical use of the marks but he too shows how the four classical creedal adjectives can be readily reconciled with the Reformation's two marks, insisting Luther's marks are not meant to replace the traditional four but rather when taken together make for "a mutual complementing" (p. 341). Moreover, Moltmann too wants to see the marks as not just addressing the inner nature of the Church but also as a challenge for believers. Moltmann too wants to see the marks as a task to be done and a witness to the world. But it is important to see the original element in Moltmann's treatment of the marks of the Church: his strongly christological focus and his emphatically eschatological view. Moltmann's *The Church in the Power of the Spirit* is often seen as the third volume in something of a trilogy of dogmatic works, the first being *The Crucified Christ* and the second *The Theology of Hope*. Here the subtitle of Moltmann's book is important: "A Contribution to Messianic Eschatology." Moltmann's originality lies in his emphatically eschatological view of the four classical marks whereby he gives them a contemporary urgency, as part of the task of proclaiming the nearness of the kingdom: "The Church's unity is its unity in freedom. The Church's holiness is its holiness in poverty. The Church's apostolicity bears the sign of the cross, and its catholicity is linked with its part as support for the oppressed" (p. 341).

Another German theologian who has treated the marks of the Church is Johann Auer (1910-1989). Auer was a priest of the Regensburg diocese in the Bavarian or southern part of

Germany. He taught at Bonn University 1950 to 1968 and at the University of Regensburg from 1968 until his death in 1989. During that time he taught a number of Catholic theologians, among them Joseph Ratzinger who became Pope Benedict XVI. Auer's ecclesiology is entitled *The Church: The Universal Sacrament of Salvation* (1983; Eng. 1993). This book is but one volume in his nine-volume systematic theology. The final section of this book is a treatment of "The Marks or Essential Attributes of the Apostolic Church." On the very first page of that section, Auer states clearly: "Our intention in concluding this chapter on manifestations of the Church's being, life, and activity with a discussion of its marks or essential characteristics is dogmatic, not apologetic.... Our goal in this section is not to prove that our Church is the true Church, but to reach a deeper understanding of the Church itself" (p. 345). Auer achieves this mostly by his biblicism, that is, he always begins with Scripture, and then a dogmatic method by which he sees each note as primarily an inner quality, an "inner dimension" (p. 350).

The American Jesuit Francis A. Sullivan taught systematic theology at Rome's Gregorian University for thirty-six years, 1956 to 1992. In 1988 he published a book-length study called, *The Church We Believe In: One, Holy, Catholic and Apostolic*. Ecumenical concern shaped this book too, but Sullivan also wanted to rework the four notes "paying special attention to the teaching of the Second Vatican Council" (p. 4). While Sullivan sketches the origin and development of each note, much of Sullivan's book is taken up with his criticism of Post-Vatican II interpretations of the Vatican II documents. Indeed, much space is given over to Sullivan's refutation of interpretations of Vatican II by the Vatican's Congregation for the Doctrine of the Faith. Sullivan's arguments here are always intelligent but some readers — especially those who are not Catholic — might find them too narrowly insular.

What can I say of these four modern treatments of the marks of the Church? While there is much to be learned from each of these treatments, there are also some elements in each that give pause. For example, it seems to me that the existentialism of both Küng's and Moltmann's approaches places far too much emphasis upon the work to be done and not enough on the innate sense of these attributes. While it is important to emphasize the dynamic character of the marks as something to be worked at, the New Testament makes it clear that they are gift as well as goal, an essential reality as well as an eschatological sign. While I do not want to claim these attributes are "inalienable signs of the true Church," they did always have something of a probative character. More precisely, they always served as criteria by which we might discern the genuine ecclesial character of Christian assemblies that call themselves Church. These attributes are not just goals or ideals to be worked at, they are essential attributes. As for Auer, his treatments are in some cases too cursory. For example, his treatment of apostolicity: no doubt, this is one of the most difficult marks because of the radically different approach by Catholic and Protestant, but it still needs more work. And as for Sullivan's arguments: though they are always intelligent, some readers, especially non-Catholic readers will perhaps find them too narrowly confessional, too much taken up with internecine strife among Catholic theologians trying to give precision to the teachings of Vatican II. Finally, in all the works I have surveyed here the marks or essential attributes of the Church are all treated as an inter-confessional dialogue, when in fact most human beings have some idea of what unity is, what holiness is. Moreover, the world also has some ideas about catholicity and apostolicity. And in fact those ideas provide a common ground on which to begin one's exploration. And so what I shall try to do in the next four chapters is to give treatments of these four marks that try to address more specifically the biblical and early historical developments of these four terms in the belief that this is the best way to avoid the extreme character given to them in the modern, Reformation and post-Reformation periods. That is, as a student of Christian thought and an aspiring biblical theologian, I shall try hard to retrieve the original biblical meaning of the terms "one, holy and apostolic" and the historic sense of the term "catholic" as it might have been recognizable in the late fourth century, more

precisely, in the time shortly after the Council of Constantinople's inclusion of "catholic" in its creedal affirmation of the
character of the Church. And while I am determined to avoid
polemics, I think that the biblical evidence will make clear it is
not entirely possible to avoid the probative use of these terms.
That is, as I already noted above, some of them — namely, apostolic and catholic — have an apologetic character in their very
origin that cannot be entirely avoided. Unity and holiness are
also not merely hidden properties that can only be the object
of a leap of faith. It is right to say the four marks are objects of
faith but Christian faith should never be simply blind faith, there
must always be some empirical motive of credibility — that was
the point of Jesus' miracles. They were the criteria upon which
one might resolve any ambiguity that might have attended his
words and deeds. No doubt even Jesus' words and deeds could
be evaluated ambiguously, but those who put their faith in him
were not blindly trusting, they were responding to ambiguous
but recognizable criteria — his words rang true, his deeds were
a genuine blessing. While no doubt Protestants insist on a less
visible unity dependent on inner faith in Christ, this cannot be
allowed to be an excuse for a more visible and concrete expression of unity.

Finally, over the centuries these four adjectives were variously called *notae, argumenta, signa, proprietates, conditiones, car-
acteres, insignia, criteria praerogativae*, that is, notes, arguments,
signs, properties, conditions, characters, insignia, criteria. Moreover, Küng uses the term "dimensions" and Auer follows him on
this point. While each of these terms can be justified and I have
employed a number of them in this chapter, I have decided to use
the phrase "essential attributes" to express my conviction that
historical circumstances can at times obscure the fundamental
truth of the essential inner nature of the Church.

Further Reading

Two articles from reference works written from a Catholic perspective: "Notes of the Church" in *Ecclesia: A Theological Encyclopedia of the Church* by Christopher O'Donnell (Collegeville, Minn., 1996), pp. 331-332, and "Marks of the Church" by G. Thils in *The New Catholic Encyclopedia* (second edition, 2003), Vol. 9, Mab-Mor, pages 189-191.

Gordon Lathrop and Timothy Weingert's *Christian Assembly: Marks of the Church in a Pluralistic Age* (Minneapolis: Augsburg Fortress, 2004). This is written from a Lutheran perspective by a Church historian and a liturgist.

Christian Link and Lisa Dahl's "The Notae Ecclesiae: A Reformed Perspective" in *Toward the Future of Reformed Theology* (Grand Rapids, 1999), pp. 239-261.

The Unity of the Church

The origin of this note or mark or characteristic of the Church is clearly and emphatically biblical. There are several passages from the New Testament that make it clear how important was the value of Christian unity for the writers of the works that comprise the New Testament. For example, the Gospel according to John portrays Jesus in his last meeting with his disciples as praying for the unity of his followers. Chapters 13–17 of John's Gospel are an account of Jesus' last supper with his disciples. Much of the narrative in those chapters is given over to a lengthy discourse which Jesus delivers to his disciples. But that long discourse concludes with a lengthy prayer which Jesus addresses to his Father in heaven. The content of that prayer is dictated by the circumstances in which Jesus finds himself, namely Jesus knows his death is imminent. And so he is concerned about the fate of his disciples after his death when they will be "on their own," as it were. And so he prays to the Father that divine guidance be given to the disciples. It is arguable that Jesus in this prayer is concerned about two potential threats to his disciples, one external and one internal. Jesus' first petition is for God's protection of his disciples against fierce opposition from "the world." But Jesus' next petition is for the unity of his disciples: "And now I am no more in the world, and I am coming to thee. Holy Father, keep them in thy name, which thou hast given me, that they may be one, even as we are one" (Jn 17:11).

And, indeed, as though it was a confirmation of Jesus' final prayer with his disciples, the earliest portrait of a Christian community describes that community as distinguishable precisely because of its marvelous unity. In Acts 4:32, Luke the evangelist and historian of the earliest Christian community at Jerusalem says of that community, "Now the community of those who believed were of one heart and soul, and no one said that any of the things which he possessed was his own, but they had everything in common." Note how perfect and complete this unity is: it is a unity not just of mind and heart but even unity of possessions. Indeed, some commentators have described this unity regarding possessions as "early Christian communism." That expression is misleading. That is, it would be better to refer to it as Christian "communitarianism." For communism as a social-political system has historically entailed the communality or sharing of material goods by means of political coercion; by means of political force material goods are taken from the rich and given to the poor. In contrast to such politically enforced "sharing" of goods, Luke, just a few verses later, in Acts 4:34, makes clear the voluntary nature of this communal sharing that distinguished the first Christian community at Jerusalem: "There was not a needy person among them, for as many as were possessors of lands or houses sold them, and brought the proceeds of what was sold and laid it at the apostles' feet; and distribution was made to each as any had need."

Other New Testament passages supply us with a theological rationale for this wondrous bond of unity. In 1 Corinthians 10:17 we hear Saint Paul give a highly spiritual reason for this marvelous unity, using the language of sacramental communion, that is, a vivid reference to the Christian Lord's Supper Service which from early on became the principal Christian form of worship: "Because there is one bread, we who are many are one body, for we all partake of the same loaf." And thus Paul suggests that participation in the Lord's Supper is at once an expression of as well as the cause of Christian unity. In another passage Paul locates the rationale for Christian unity in the rite of baptism: "For as many of you as were baptized in Christ have put on Christ. There is neither Jew nor Greek, there is neither slave nor free, there is neither male nor female;

for you are all one in Christ" (Gal 3:27-28). In the Epistle to the Ephesians 4:1-6, we hear yet another appeal to unity but this time it is phrased with reference not to any one religious element such as sacramental communion, sharing in the Lord's Supper or baptism in Christ, but to a wide range of elements in their common religious heritage that should make Christians one:

> I therefore, a prisoner for the Lord, beg you to lead a life worthy of the calling to which you have been called, with all lowliness and meekness, with patience, forbearing one another in love, eager to maintain the unity of the Spirit in the bond of peace. There is one body and one Spirit, just as you were called to the one hope that belongs to your call, one Lord, one faith, one baptism, one God and Father of us all, who is above all and through all and in all.

And so we should not be surprised to find in the epistles of Paul not just rationales for unity but strong exhortations to unity. For example, in Paul's First Letter to the Church at Corinth 1:10, we hear him say, "I appeal to you, brethren, by the name of our Lord Jesus Christ, that all of you agree that there be no dissensions among you, but that you be united in the same mind and the same judgment." In his Epistle to the Church at Rome 15:5, Saint Paul prays, "May the God of steadfastness and encouragement grant you to live in such harmony with one another, in accord with Christ Jesus, that together you may with one voice glorify the God and Father of our Lord Jesus Christ."

However, there is also considerable evidence in the New Testament that suggests, while Christian unity was indeed a highly prized value and indeed at times not just vehemently urged but even marvelously demonstrated, unity among the disciples of Christ was also at times a highly threatened value, indeed a value that needed to be worked at, prayed for and requiring great self-discipline.

For example, it is important to see that while Luke in the

Acts of the Apostles claims to give dramatic evidence of the unity of the Christian community at Jerusalem, at the same time, he himself tempers that portrait of perfect unity with more than one equally dramatic, indeed, sobering qualification. More precisely, in Acts 5:1, he describes the treachery of Ananias and Sapphira, a Christian couple, who were less than honest about their generosity. That is, they sold a piece of property and made a gesture of generously giving all the proceeds of the sale to the community, but in fact held some of it back. In his next chapter Luke supplies us with yet another example of how the sharing in the community at Jerusalem was less than perfect when in Acts 6:1 he describes how "the Hellenists murmured against the Hebrews because their widows were neglected in the daily distribution." This verse seems to witness to the phenomenon of ethnic loyalties and linguistic traditions causing divisions in the community at Jerusalem. The ethnic diversity of this new community of faith, the Church at Jerusalem, brings with it as many challenges as benefits. But threats to unity are not just a Lucan theme. The portrait of the Christian community in the Pauline epistles also witnesses to tension and divisions that worked against Christian unity.

Paul's letters, while containing profound theological reflections on the basic dynamic of Christian unity and several appeals for the preservation of or efforts toward unity, also give vivid reference to practical disunity not just regarding the sharing of material goods but even the content of faith itself. Sometimes the disunity seems to come from too much adherence to certain personalities, the preaching of particular preachers. This is certainly the impression we get from 1 Corinthians 1:10-15, when Paul says:

> I appeal to you, brethren, by the name of our Lord Jesus Christ, that all of you agree that there be no dissensions among you, but that you be united in the same mind and the same judgment. For it has been reported to me by Chloe's people that there is quarreling among you, my brethren. What I mean is that each one of you says, "I belong to Paul," or "I belong to Apollos," or "I belong

> to Cephas," or "I belong to Christ." Is Christ divided?
> Was Paul crucified for you? Or were you baptized in the
> name of Paul? I am thankful that I baptized none of you
> except Crispus and Gaius lest any one should say that
> you were baptized in my name.

Much exegetical scholarship has been spent on trying to identify clearly who are the groups to which Paul refers here. It seems that after Paul left Corinth, other Christian missionaries came representing other outlooks on the Christian faith than that represented by Paul. For example, most scholars agree that the Apollos referred to was a Jewish Christian from the great city of Alexandria. Acts 18:24-25 describes him as "a Jew... a native of Alexandria... an eloquent man, well versed in the scriptures... [who] spoke and taught accurately the things concerning Jesus." Apollos' native city of Alexandria was famed for its intellectual culture, one expression of which was the exegetical method of a Jewish scholar there named Philo of Alexandria. It could be that the preaching of Apollos reflected the learned and pious exegetical method of Philo and thus appealed to the better educated in the Christian community at Corinth. The "Cephas" mentioned is a reference to the apostle Peter to whom Jesus gave the sobriquet, "the Rock." Cephas is the Greek word for rock. It is doubtful that Peter himself came to preach at Corinth. It is much more likely that this group was the result of Jewish Christians from Palestine or Syria who boasted of their attachment to the teaching of Peter. Many scholars conjecture that the Pauline group was the majority of the faithful, poor freedmen and slaves, who, in reaction to the boast of these other groups to be followers of Apollos or Peter, now boasted of their loyalty to Paul's preaching. There has been even greater controversy over the identification of the group which apparently seems to claim Christ himself as its leader. Here there are at least three possible positions. First there are those scholars who claim there was no such group, rather this is Paul indulging himself in outrageous irony or rhetoric or wry humor, that is, suggesting that if various groups are going to be formed by boasting of allegiance to some great preacher, it is only logical there ought to be some group that could boast its allegiance is only to the very voice of Christ himself. Then there are those scholars who argue that this is a reference to a precise group in the Corinthian Church. They argue this "Christ party" was made up of mystics who rejected all human teachers and pretended to be guided by revelations received directly from Christ through charismatic gifts. In this sense, this group is probably the charismatics to whom Paul offers the following retort in his Second Letter to the Church at Corinth 10:7: "If anyone is confident that he is Christ's, let him remind himself that as he is Christ's, so are we." Finally, there is yet another group of scholars that claims the "Christ party" were not mystics but rather people who actually did hear the preaching of the historical Jesus! As support for this idea, those same scholars cite 2 Corinthians 11:13 as Paul's pointed indictment of the Christ party's leaders: "For such men are false apostles, deceitful workmen, disguising themselves as *apostles of Christ*." Whatever the precise facts may be this is a clear indication that factionalism developed in earliest Christianity because of the people's identification or idolization of one particular preacher over another.

However, there are other passages in Paul that make it clear it was not just adherence to particular personalities that made for divisions in the Christian community, but also adherence to particular doctrines. Note this passage from Galatians 1:6-7: "I am astonished that you are so quickly deserting him who called you in the grace of Christ and turning to a different gospel – not that there is another gospel, but there are some who trouble you and want to pervert the gospel of Christ."

Nor is it just the Pauline communities that are afflicted with false doctrines. When Paul writes to the Church at Rome he says in Romans 16:17: "I appeal to you, brethren, to take note of those who create dissension and difficulties, in opposition to the doctrine which you have been taught." Galatians and Romans are both relatively early works of the New Testament. Most scholars date Galatians to A.D. 54-55 and Romans to A.D. 57-58.

Several later New Testament works witness to the continuing and growing problem of disunity. For example, many scholars dispute the genuine Pauline authorship of 2 Timothy, but whether it is genuinely Pauline or not, it witnesses to a continuing problem that of idiosyncratic teachers who cause divisions in the community of faith. 2 Timothy 2:14-18 reads:

> Avoid disputing about words, which does no good but only ruins the hearers. Do your best to present yourself to God as one approved, a workman who has no need to be ashamed, rightly handling the word of truth. Avoid such godless chatter, for it will lead people into more and more ungodliness, and their talk will eat its way like gangrene. Among them are Hymenaeus and Philetus, who have swerved from the truth by holding that the resurrection is past already. They are upsetting the faith of some.

Two late works of the New Testament, 2 Peter and the Epistle of Jude echo each other's concern. 2 Peter 2:1-2: "But false prophets also arose among the people, just as there will be false teachers among you, who will secretly bring in destructive heresies, even denying the Master who brought them." In Jude 3-4 we read:

> Beloved, being very eager to write to you of our common salvation, I found it necessary to write appealing to you to contend for the faith which was once for all delivered to the saints. For admission has been secretly gained by some who long ago were designated for this condemnation, ungodly persons who pervert the grace of our God into licentiousness and deny our only Master and Lord, Jesus Christ.

However, there is a passage in the First Letter to the Corinthians that is even more important for us to examine because of its historic influence in supplying us with technical language to describe divisions and dissensions in the community of faith. In 1 Corinthians 11:19: "When you assemble as a Church, I hear

that there are divisions (*schismata*) among you; and I partly believe it, for there must be factions (*haeresis*) among you in order
that those who are genuine among you may be recognized." In
the quotation above I have put in parentheses a transliteration
of the original Greek of two words which Paul uses to describe
divisions and factions in the Church at Corinth. They will in the
later history of Christian thought become the terms, "schism"
and "heresy." Our English word "schism" comes from the Greek
schisma, meaning split, rent, divided. In the New Testament it
refers to divisions and quarrels of all kinds which had developed
in the Church. Later, the word will come to be used solely for
divisions of a lasting nature which had developed in the Church
not over questions of doctrine but because of disagreements over
questions of discipline. Our English word "heresy" comes from
the Greek *haeresis* which, in its original sense, meant choice or
preference – hence opinion or party. In the Acts of the Apostles
it is often used to refer to Jewish sects such as the party of the
Pharisees (15:5) or the party of the Sadducees (5:17). It is not
unfair to call these two groups sects for the Pharisees and the
Sadducees differed not only according to customs or rituals but
also doctrinally as in their dispute over the resurrection of the
dead (see Ac 23:6-8). In Acts 24:14, Paul is portrayed as using the
term "heresy" to protest that the Christian Church is not a sect
but a "way." When divisions begin to emerge in the Church (1
Cor 11:49), Paul protests, considering heresies as the fruits of
sin (Gal 5:20; Titus 3:10). In 2 Peter 2:1, we find the sense which
was to be generally used in the Church: an error which leads to
perversion of the faith and corruption of the Christian life.

What now can one conclude regarding the New Testament
witness to unity, diversity and divisions among the disciples of
Christ?

First, one should be careful not to confuse unity with
uniformity. Alongside the passages from St. Paul wherein he
urges unity, it is possible to cite other passages in which St.
Paul appears to defend a legitimate diversity in services to and
maybe even expression of the Christian faith. For example in 1
Corinthians 12:3-11, he says:

> Therefore I want you to understand that no one speaking by the Spirit of God ever says, "Jesus be cursed!" and no one can say, "Jesus is Lord" except by the Holy Spirit. Now there are varieties of gifts, but the same Spirit; and there are varieties of service, but the same Lord; and there are varieties of working, but it is the same God who inspires them all in every one. To each is given the manifestation of the Spirit for the common good. To one is given through the Spirit the utterance of wisdom, and to another the utterance of knowledge according to the same Spirit.

Also we should be careful about assigning blame for disunity. While Apollos' style of preaching may have been appreciably different from Paul's there is much that suggests it was not Apollos himself, but his followers who fomented division at Corinth. Indeed, Paul has only good words for Apollos. In 1 Corinthians 3:5-6, he sees their ministries as complementary rather than conflicting: "What then is Apollos? What is Paul? Servants through whom you believed, as the Lord assigned to each. I planted, Apollos watered, but God gave the growth." In 1 Corinthians 16:12, Paul says, "As for our brother Apollos, I strongly urged him to visit you with the other brethren." In Titus 3:13, Paul urges others to help Apollos: "Do your best to speed Zenas the lawyer and Apollos on their way; see that they lack nothing."

However, while diversity, ethnic and cultural as well as in talents and style, may lead to a rich and desirable variety, diversity also can pose serious challenges to unity. For example, in Part II of this book, in a chapter on the mission of the Church we shall see how the history of the Christian missions shows inculturation is not easy and sometimes it can lead to doctrinal deviation. Indeed, it appears there is always the temptation to trade the universality of the Church for something merely local. And thus on the one hand while we must be careful and not make of everything that divides Christians today an insurmountable obstacle — some of it may simply be legitimate and acceptable cultural variations on the one theme of Christ among us — on the other hand, we must also be ready to acknowledge that much of the divisions among Christians are due, not to legitimate diversity, but to sin, to immaturity in the faith.

Another attitude we must consider is the fact that in 1 Corinthians 11:19, there is a certain note of pragmatic resignation in Paul's assertion "there must be factions among you in order that those who are genuine among you may be recognized." In this sense, one could argue that we will probably have to resign ourselves to the thought that there will always be divisions among us. And, indeed, there are passages in the New Testament that seem to suggest an awareness that Christian unity will always be more an ideal that a reality. In Ephesians 4:13-14, it seems apparent that doctrinal disputation is a sign of immaturity in the faith, which for some Christians will always be a factor: "until we all attain to the unity of the faith and of the knowledge of the Son of God, to mature manhood, to the measure of the stature of the fullness of Christ; so that we many no longer be children, tossed to and fro and carried about with every wind of doctrine, by the cunning of men."

But we must also be wary of that sort of quietism or resignation that despairs of Christian unity and instead tries to comfort itself with the pious thought that unity is ultimately a gift from God. Yes, ultimately, it will be a gift of God but meanwhile we cannot afford to do nothing. Indeed, one should not allow such qualifications to diminish the urgency of Christian unity. None of these qualifications should be allowed to obscure the fact that Christian unity is seen in the NT as an invaluable prophetic sign that sets Christians apart from the world and indeed should make Christianity attractive and believable, because it shows that Christianity is truly of God. Look at the words of Jesus in the prayer of John 17:20-23:

> I do not pray for these only [the twelve in the room with him], but also for those who believe in me through their word, that they may all be one; even as thou, Father, art in me, and I in them, that they also may be one in us, so that the world may believe that thou hast sent me.

To sum up the New Testament teaching on the unity of the Church, the assembly of believers, we can say, the restoration of Church unity cannot await the end of time, because the Church in her unity should and must be a sign of grace in time, in our time, within history. In other words, disunity among Christians appreciably undermines Christian witness to the world and renders ineffectual the witness of the Church as a sign of the unity to which God in Christ is calling all humankind. Christianity, if it is more than just one among many religions, ought to be distinguishable from the other religions precisely by the absence of sectarian hate and strife among its members. This is clearly the message of Jesus in John 13:35, "By this all men will know that you are my disciples, if you have love for one another." And "love of the brethren" appears as a major theme in the very first document of the Christian movement. In 1 Thessalonians 4:9, we hear St. Paul say, "But concerning love of the brethren you have no need to have any one write to you, for you yourselves have been taught by God to love one another."

However, in fact, the Church has suffered greatly from disunity particularly in the second millennium of Christian history. During the first thousand years there were indeed heretical and schismatic movements that arose. These were for the most part localized ruptures such as Donatism in North Africa or Priscillianism in Spain. Moreover, they all came to an end. But in the second millennium decisive divisions arose: first the split between East and West. Then the problem of reform gave rise to charismatic figures who pursued Church reform to the point of leading separatist movements: at first John Hus but eventually Luther, Calvin, Zwingli, and the English Reformers. In the wake of this followed rabid sectarianism, mutually indicting views of the gospel, indeed, wars of religion in which Christians killed each other. Right up into modern times, division of the Churches has continued though with less violence. For example, in the late nineteenth century the Polish National Catholic Church arose. But the nineteenth century also brought the beginning of a turn of events. Ecumenism or cooperation among the Christian denominations to work toward some form of unity began in the nineteenth century in no small measure due to the concerns of missionaries acutely aware of the scandal of various missionaries working among the same peoples but often presenting significantly varying, at times even mutually indicting, versions of the Gospel. Various organizations arose to promote cooperation among the Churches; most prominent was the creation of an organization called the World Council of Churches. The WCC has since produced several important statements.

As a practical and modern response to Christian disunity one might look at the WCC's so-called "Toronto Statement of 1950" and the statement on "Baptism, Eucharist and Ministry" issued by the 1982 meeting of the WCC's Faith and Order Commission. At its Toronto conference in 1950 a statement was issued among which was the recognition that in Churches other than one's own there are elements of the true Church, but that some of these ecclesial assemblies were in some measure incomplete, not having all the essential elements that go into making up a Church. Vatican II in its Decree on Ecumenism adopted a similar position. In 1982, the WCC's Faith and Order Commission met in Lima, Peru, and produced a statement called "Baptism, Eucharist and Ministry," seeing these three as essential elements that go into making up a Church. The conceptions set forth in these statements seem to hold the possibility for not just future dialogue but genuine steps toward mutual recognition that will make for genuine unity.

Further Reading

The Second Vatican Council's Decree on Ecumenism (*Unitatis redintegratio*).

In Rene Latourelle's *Christ and the Church: Signs of Salvation* (Alba House, 1972), Chapter V: "The Paradox and Tensions of Unity," which is to be found on pages 133-161.

CHAPTER 11

The Holiness of the Church

On this Sunday morning many a Christian congregation, at one point in its worship service, will stand and profess its faith in a Church that is holy. But to insist that the Christian assembly, the Church, is holy is to make a claim which today certainly challenges, even severely strains, the credibility of not just outsiders, atheists or adherents of other religions, but even of many of the most fervent Christians. What I mean by that is: one need only read the newspapers to see evidence that the Church or certainly its members and ministers, that is both laity and clergy, are guilty of all kinds of malfeasance, of what they themselves would judge to be serious sin. Recently, such news reporting has featured the sexual transgressions of one element in the Catholic clergy. But long before that the news media have reported the moral malfeasance of both clergy and laity, Protestant as well as Catholic, taking expression in a variety of manner not just sexual but financial, murder as well as fraud. Moreover, we all know that every Christian congregation contains within it a number of unfaithful spouses, corrupt politicians, unscrupulous merchants, *et cetera*. How can anyone call this assembly holy?

In this chapter we are going to examine the reasons why it ever came about that holiness might be attributed to the Church and its members. We shall look first at a simple, dictionary definition of holiness. But then we shall examine the biblical evidence, next the witness of a great theologian and teacher of the faith, Augustine of Hippo, and finally we shall see something of the treatment of this theme in modern theology.

The *Oxford English Dictionary* offers two definitions of "holy" when that word is used as an adjective, that is, when it is used to describe a thing. One definition focuses upon moral perfection: something is called holy if it is "free from all contamination of sin and evil, morally and spiritually perfect and unsullied, possessing the infinite moral perfection which Christianity attributes to the divine character." But then it offers another definition, this time one that focuses upon not moral perfection but religious consecration or dedication: something is called holy if it is "kept or regarded as inviolate from ordinary use, and appropriated or set apart for religious use or observance; consecrated, dedicated, sacred." It could well be argued this definition is an example of how the Christian tradition has tutored the mind of the Western world. For, when we look at the use of the adjective "holy" in the Bible (in Hebrew, *kadosh*, in Greek, *hagios*), we see a similar distinction.

In the Bible, holiness as moral perfection is attributed primarily and indeed supremely to God. Indeed, in the OT, holiness is the principal attribute of God. We read in Leviticus 19:2, "I the Lord your God am holy," and in Leviticus 21:8, "I the Lord, who sanctify you, am holy." And in Joshua 24:19 it is written, "The Lord... is a holy God." In fact holiness is the God of Israel's most distinguishing characteristic according to Exodus 15:11, "Who is like Thee, O Lord, among the gods? Who is like Thee, majestic in holiness?" So too in 1 Samuel 2:2 we find the exclusive assertion: "There is none holy like the Lord." Indeed, in Isaiah 6:3, the threefold attribution of holiness to the God of Israel — "Holy, holy, holy is the Lord of Hosts" — is meant to emphasize the plenary character of God's holiness. The holiness of the God of Israel is celebrated in the psalms: Psalm 22:3, "Yet Thou art holy"; Psalm 77:13, "Thy way, O God, is holy"; Psalm 99:3 and 5 "Holy is He"; and Psalm 99:9, "For the Lord our God is Holy." Throughout the Old Testament the preferred title for God is "the Holy One of Israel." Thus is it found in the psalms: Psalm 71:11, "O Holy One of Israel"; Psalm 78:41 and 89:18: "The Holy One of Israel." This is the favorite title for God in Isaiah (1:4, 5:19, 5:24, 10:20, 12:6, 17:7, 29:19, 30:11, 30:15, 31:1, 37:23). And it is used in Jeremiah 50:29,

51:5, and Ezekiel 39:7, as well as in Hosea 11:9, 12: "the Holy One." So too do we find it in Habbakuk 3:3 and Proverbs 9:10 and 30:3 and in 2 Kings 19:21. As for a definition of this holiness which so characterizes the God of Israel, the moral content of the idea of God's holiness is embodied in several concepts such as goodness, righteousness (as moral judgment) and truth. Psalm 25:8, "Good and upright is the Lord"; Psalm 27:13, "The goodness of the Lord"; Psalm 89:4, "Righteousness and justice are the foundation of thy throne"; Psalm 7:11, "God is a righteous judge"; Psalm 11:7, "For the Lord is righteous." Exodus 34:6 talks about the Lord "abounding... in truth." Moreover, God is not only infinitely perfect in terms of wisdom, power, goodness, justice and truth, but he also exhibits a justice and mercy in human affairs that is amazing, that is, rarely found among human beings. Nevertheless, the Israelite people themselves are also expected to exhibit moral holiness. Goodness, uprightness, and truth are also expected of God's people, of those to whom he has drawn close. For example, Leviticus 19:2, "Say to all the congregation of Israel, You shall be holy; for I the Lord your God am holy." Elsewhere we find such moral injunctions as Deuteronomy 6:18, "You shall do what is right and good"; Psalm 34:14, "Depart from evil and do good"; Isaiah 1:17, "Learn to do good, seek justice." And indeed the Israelites are castigated by the prophets when goodness, righteousness and justice are not found among them, as in Hosea 4:1-2: "Hear the word of the Lord, O people of Israel; for the Lord has a controversy with the inhabitants of the land. There is no faithfulness or kindness, and no knowledge of God in the land; there is swearing, lying, killing, stealing, and committing adultery; they break all bounds and murder follows murder."

But there is also a sense in which holiness is attributed to Israel regardless of any subjective moral goodness in its people but rather simply to anything or anyone related to the God of Israel, that is, by analogy, to anything and anyone associated with him. In this derivative, secondary sense the concept of holiness, the title "holy," is applied to the priests of Israel, as in 2 Chronicles 23:6 where we read: "Let no one enter the house of

the Lord except the priests and ministering Levites; they may
enter, for they are holy, but all the people shall keep the charge
of the Lord." Even the vestments worn by the priests are called
"holy garments" as in Exodus 28:2, 4; 29:28; 31:10; 35:21; 39:1,
41; 40:13. The temple where they serve is called "holy," the inner
sanctum of the temple is called "the holy of holies" (Ex 26:33,
34), the gifts sacrificed in the temple are called "holy" (Ex 28:8;
Lv 22:10, 14, 15, 16), the oil of anointing is "holy" (Ex 30:21, Nb
32:25, Ps 89:20), the Sabbath is a holy day (Ex 35:2). And, moreover, the Hebrew people are holy (Dt 14:2), "For you are a holy
people to the Lord your God" (cf. Dt 28:9, 22:3), Israel is a holy
nation (Ex 19:6), the assemblies of God's people (Ex 12:16) or
their convocations are holy (Lv 23:3, 4, 7, 8, 21, 24, 27, 35, 36, 37).
The importance of this latter, objective holiness or what some
call "cultic holiness" cannot be underestimated. Israel is a holy
people not because it exhibits an extraordinary degree of moral
perfection but rather because God has drawn close to the people
of Israel, they belong to him by election and covenant, they are
the people who, despite all their personal and even *national*
failings, are the vehicle by means of which God has chosen to
reveal himself to the world.

When we turn to the New Testament we see a similar phenomenon. In the New Testament, God too is referred to as holy.
In John 17:11, Jesus addresses God as "Holy Father." And then
there are several places in the New Testament where we find
holiness attributed to Jesus. In Mark 1:23-24, we hear a demon
whom Jesus is exorcizing, ask, "What have you to do with us,
Jesus of Nazareth? I know who you are — the Holy One of God."
There is a precise parallel in Luke 4:34. While there is no precise
parallel in Matthew or John, that is, no comparable narrative of
the cure of a demoniac wherein the demon says, "I know who
you are, the Holy One of God," even so in John 6:67-69, we hear
Peter make the same profession of faith: "We have come to be-
lieve and are convinced that you are the Holy One of God." In
Acts 3:14, Peter refers to Jesus as "the Holy and Righteous One."
In Acts 4:27 and 29, we hear a gathering of Christians refer to
Jesus in their prayer to God as "thy holy servant Jesus." Also,

holiness is often attributed to God's Spirit as in Mark 1:8, "He will baptize you in the Holy Spirit."

Moreover, in the New Testament, the "new Israel," that is, the disciples of Jesus, are also exhorted to holiness. Jesus in Matthew 4:48 echoes the teaching in Leviticus 19:2, indeed emphasizing the need for an extraordinary measure of goodness, when he says, "You, therefore, must be *perfect*, as your heavenly Father is perfect." And in 1 Peter 1:14-16: "As obedient children, do not be conformed to the passions of your former ignorance, but as he who called you is holy, *be holy yourselves* in all your conduct; since it is written, 'You shall be holy, for I am holy.'" In 1 John 3:3, we are told: "Everyone who has this hope based on him makes himself pure, as he is pure." And Jesus in Matthew 5:20 says, "For I tell you, unless your righteousness exceeds that of the scribes and Pharisees, you will never enter the kingdom of heaven." In the earliest literary work of the Christian movement, the First Letter to the Thessalonians 3:13, we hear Paul invoke the theme of the importance of holiness in a prayer that the Lord "may establish your hearts unblamable in holiness before our God and Father, at the coming of our Lord Jesus with all his saints."

However, there is also a sense in the New Testament of how the disciples of Christ possess a certain holiness which is more objective, more formal, than their own personal moral integrity. We can see something of this in the fact that throughout the New Testament epistles and the Acts of the Apostles and in the Book of Revelation, the common phrase used to refer to Christians is "the holy ones." For example, the word "saints" is often used in the opening salutation of New Testament epistles: in Ephesians 1:1, "to the saints who are at Ephesus"; in Philippians 1:1, "to all the saints in Christ Jesus who are in Philippi"; in Colossians 1:2, "to the saints and faithful brethren in Christ at Colossae." In Hebrews 13:24, "Greetings to all your leaders and to all the holy ones." But the term "holy ones" or "saints" is not just used in salutations, it also abounds as a general descriptive of Christians everywhere: in Acts 9:13 we find a reference to "the saints at Jerusalem"; in Acts 9:32, we hear recounted how "as

Peter went here and there among them all, he came down to
the saints who lived at Lydda"; Acts 26:10 talks of the "saints in
prison" at Jerusalem; Romans 15:26 also speaks of "the saints
at Jerusalem." In 1 Corinthians 16:1 we read, "Now in regard to
the collection for the holy ones, you also should do as I ordered
the Churches of Galatia." In 1 Peter 1:15, "as he who called you
is holy, be holy yourselves in all your conduct." The First Epistle
of Peter, the second chapter, we hear Christian described as
"a holy priesthood" (2:5), and then "a holy nation" (2:9). In the
Epistle to the Ephesians 2:21, we are told Christians constitute
a "holy temple."

    And yet, what must also be seen is that precisely in these
very same works that call Christians "saints" we hear depreca-
tions of their sinfulness. In Ephesians 4:18, Paul laments, "many,
as I have told you and now tell you even in tears, conduct themselves as enemies of the cross of Christ," and in Ephesians 6:12,
he describes the Christian life as a "struggle." In Philippians 1:15,
he is more pointed in his indictment: "some preach Christ from
envy and rivalry." In Colossians 3:9, we hear him urge his readers to "stop lying to one another." In the opening salutation of
First Corinthians there is a phrase that goes far toward explaining
this disjunction between the title "holy ones" or "saints" given to
the Christians at Ephesus, Philippi and Colossae and their faults
which Paul deprecates. In 1 Corinthians 1:2, Paul sends greetings
"to the Church of God which is at Corinth, to those who have been
sanctified by Christ Jesus, saints by calling." The NAB renders
this: "to you who have been sanctified in Christ Jesus, called to be
holy." The "sanctification" referred to is most probably a reference
to their baptism in Christ whose fruits have yet to fully appear. In
the First Letter to the Thessalonians several references are made to
other formal elements that objectively render Christians "holy" in
the sense of consecration. For example, the "election" referred to
in 1 Thessalonians 1:4, "For we know brethren beloved by God,
that he has chosen you," and in 1 Thessalonians 2:13, "the word
of God, which is at work in you believers."

    What are we to make of all this biblical evidence for the use
of the idea of holiness as applied to God and human beings?

The first thing we must see is that while holiness is attributed to both the people of the Old Covenant and the New, in neither case is this a perfect holiness. God alone is perfectly holy: Revelation 15:4, "For thou alone art holy." Among his people there are varying measures of holiness and in fact at times there are profound moral failures. In the Old Testament both Moses (Ex 2:12, Nb 20:12 and 27:12-14) and David (2 S 11) sin against God, and the people of Israel are constantly castigated especially in the prophetic literature for their sins. The situation is similar in the New Testament. Complete, utter, sinlessness is attributed to Jesus alone: Hebrews 4:15, "[Jesus] was in all points tempted as we are, yet without sin." 1 Peter 2:22: "Jesus committed no sin, nor was guile found in his mouth." 1 John 3:5: "In him there is no sin." But as for human beings, the followers of Christ, Paul says in Romans 3:23: "all have sinned and fallen short of the glory of God." And in 1 John 1:8: "If we say that we have no sin, we deceive ourselves, and the truth is not in us." Moreover, the Gospels provide precise examples of the sinfulness of Christ's disciples. Among Jesus' inner circle there are two glaring occasions of sin, the betrayal by Judas (Mk 14:10-11, 43-46) and later by Peter (Mk 14:66-72). Of course even here one must make allowances for repentance — Moses, David and Peter all repented. But we must also recall Romans 5:20: "where sin increased, grace abounded all the more."

We must also learn to make the distinction between objective and subjective holiness. That is, we must be careful not to compromise the idea that the Bible makes clear: While the fidelity of God's people to the covenant is often compromised, God's fidelity and presence to his people is a constant. And so in affirming the holiness of the Church, we are really affirming the fidelity of God to the covenant in Jesus Christ. In other words, Jesus' promise — "Where two or three are gathered in my name" (Mt 18:20) — still holds true despite the greatest failings of his disciples. We too should be willing to admit that the holy is a power far beyond the human realm and that it can assert its presence despite serious human failings. When we profess our belief in a Church that is holy, we are affirming the integrity of the Church's teaching, its sacraments and its ministries and not the probity of the lives of the Church's members or ministers. This distinction is implicit in Jesus' teaching in Matthew 23:2-3: "The scribes and the Pharisees sit on Moses' seat; so practice and observe whatever they tell you, but not what they do; for they preach but do not practice." Objectively, the scribes and the Pharisees are legitimate religious authorities and thus their teaching is worthy of respect, but subjectively they themselves are not good examples of the practice of what they have been teaching and preaching. With regard to this distinction between objective and subjective holiness — the holiness of the Church's teachings, sacraments and ministries despite the unworthiness and even infidelities of both its members and ministers — there is much to be learned from a confrontation in the early history of the Church, more precisely, the response of Augustine, bishop of Hippo, to the Donatist schism in North Africa.

In the year 311 at Carthage, the great seaport city on the north central coast of Africa (near modern Tunis in Tunisia), its bishop Mensuius died. Soon after the death of Mensuius, his archdeacon, a man named Caecilian, was elected bishop to succeed him. But a short time after Caecilian's consecration, there arose strong opposition to the legitimacy of his ministry from a group of Church leaders in the neighboring western province of Numidia (modern-day Algeria). Indeed, these Numidian bishops called into question the very validity of Caecilian's episcopal consecration because they claimed to have discovered that one of the three required co-consecrators at that ceremony, one Felix of Apthungi (El Homma du Djerd, Tunisia), had been a *traditor* during the persecution of Christians by the Emperor Diocletian (303-305). We get our modern English word "traitor" from the Latin word *traditor*. The Latin word *traditor* comes from the verb "to hand over" and it was used to refer to those Christians who had complied with the February 23, 303, imperial edict which demanded the confiscation and burning of Christian books, that is, the Bible. Some Christian clergy in North Africa handed over their Church books as a simple expediency, a way of avoiding martyrdom. But other Christians in North Africa saw this as unforgivable collaboration with the enemy and especially heinous since there were indeed at that very same time other Christians, brave martyrs, who chose to die rather than collaborate with the government agents in this persecution. Disagreement over this issue was to end up in a major Church schism in North Africa, that is, a separatist Church arose centered precisely in the province of Numidia. This separatist, rigorist movement came to be called Donatism after a man named Donatus who later became the Donatist bishop in Carthage and then, for thirty years, the movement's principal leader, a charismatic and articulate spokesman. Throughout the fourth century, from its beginning in 311 to the ordination of Augustine of Hippo as a priest in 391, Donatism grew to become a major force in North African society such that it posed a severe challenge to the life and work of the great North African theologian. For example, Augustine himself came under moral censure from the Donatists. In the year 395, on the eve of his episcopal consecration a rumor went round which seems to have had its source in Donatist circles that Augustine during his time as a priest had seduced a man's wife. When this was brought to the attention of Megalius of Calama the chief bishop, that is, primate of Numidia, Megalius considered withdrawing from the ceremony (he would have been the principal co-consecrator), and, indeed, Megalius' withdrawal would have prevented Augustine's episcopal consecration.

Some modern Church historians have argued that the origin of the Donatist schism was not entirely theological. That is, they argue it was due in large measure to ethnic and social enmity between, on the one hand, the native Berber population of Numidia who were largely of the laboring class and, on the other hand, the "foreign" Roman population of Carthage and its environs among whom were many patrician land owners. Whatever its ethnic and social origins, the Donatist schism did serve to raise some important theological issues. To what degree does the subjective immorality of a Christian minister affect the validity, effectiveness of his (or somewhat anachronistically, her) ministry. Indeed, these historical events help to raise the question of the holiness of the Church, and not just of its leaders but of all its members and the very institution itself. In response to the Donatists, Augustine honed two theological principles. These are the idea of the Church as a *corpus permixtum*, that is, a thoroughly mixed community where saints and sinners, good and evil are often found closely enmeshed, and the idea of the sacraments functioning *ex opere operato*, that is, that the efficacy of the sacraments, their holy character, is not dependent upon the subjective worthiness of the officiant or minister but rather their holiness resides in their very celebration, that is, "in the deed done." We can understand these concepts more clearly by examining Augustine's anti-Donatist writings.

Augustine's debate with the Donatists was in large degree a Bible battle, a Scripture war, that is, Donatist rigorism or puritanism was based on certain biblical passages that suggested the purity of the individual Christian and the Church, passages such as 1 John 3:9, "No one who is begotten of God commits sin" (in Augustine's *Correction of the Donatists* Ch IX, paragraph 40) or 2 Corinthians 11:2, "I betrothed you to Christ to present you as a pure bride to her one husband" (in his *Against Petilian*, Bk 3, ch 4). They also invoked images of purification as in John 15:1, "I am the true vine, and my Father is the vine grower. He takes away every branch in me that does not bear fruit" (in *On Baptism* Bk I, ch 28). In response, Augustine knew the Bible as well as, perhaps better than, his Donatist challengers and thus he was able to marshal several biblical passages in answer to their claims. For example, Augustine pointed out that, in Revelation 21, the vision of the Church as a pure bride come down out of heaven is an eschatological vision. In response to Donatist emphasis upon the importance of pruning the vine, Augustine makes much use of the parable in Matthew 13:24-30:

> Another parable he put before them, saying, "The kingdom of heaven may be compared to a man who sowed

good seed in his field; but while men were sleeping, his
enemy came and sowed weeds among the wheat, and
went away. So when the plants came up and bore grain,
then the weeds appeared also. And the servants of the
householder came and said to him, 'Sir, did you not sow
good seed in your field? How then has it weeds?' He said
to them, 'An enemy has done this.' The servants said
to him, 'Then do you want us to go and gather them?'
But he said, 'No; lest in gathering the weeds you root
up the wheat along with them. Let both grow together
until harvest; and at harvest time I will tell the reapers,
Gather the weeds first and bind them in bundles to be
burned, but gather the wheat into my barn.'"

Anyone who has ever done any form of gardening can
appreciate this image, for when seeds in a flower or vegetable
garden first sprout it is difficult to distinguish this first growth
or plant buds from the weeds that also sprout with them. In
Augustine's considerable use of this image (*On Baptism* Book 4,
chapters 9, 12, 13, 14, in his *Against Petilian* Bk 2, ch 26 and 39, Bk
3, ch 4) he likens the Church as a mixed garden. For Augustine
the meaning of this parable is that at this time the Church which
is the initial budding forth of the kingdom of heaven consists of
both good and bad. And to try to weed out the bad now would
be a serious mistake. Judgments as to who are the good and who
are the bad must await the divine wisdom and judgment to be
exercised at the harvest time, that is, at the end of time. In this
interpretation the reference to bundles to be burned is a pointed
reference to the fires of hell. In a similar way but with emphasis
upon God as the judge, Augustine also made use of Matthew
25:31-46, with its image of the Son of Man who at the end of time
will separate the sheep from the goats. And thus Augustine is
able to explain the co-existence of good and bad in the Christian
community, the Church.

But it is also important to see the arguments Augustine uses
in response to the moral rigorism of the Donatists to explain the
worthiness or unworthiness of Christian clergy, of pastors and

ministers. In his *Seven Books On Baptism, Against the Donatists*, Augustine pounds home his argument with several variations and repetitions. Augustine's principal argument is that the will of God is not frustrated by the unworthiness of the human instruments he employs; moreover, it is Christ who is the chief or true shepherd and it is he who is really feeding the sheep and not the hired hand. Augustine begins this theme in Book IV of his treatise on Baptism. After having treated at length the image of the Church as a mixed garden of "tares and wheat" in Book IV, ch 12, he says:

> When baptism is given in the words of the gospel, however great be the perverseness of understanding on the part of either him through whom, or of him to whom it is given, the sacrament itself is holy in itself on account of Him whose sacrament it is. And if anyone, receiving it at the hands of a misguided man, yet does not receive the perversity of the minister, but only the holiness of the mystery.

This theme is repeated with variations numerous times throughout this treatise *On Baptism*. For example, we see the same point made again in Book V, ch 13: "Baptism is as valid at the hands of a contemptible man as it was when given by an apostle; it is recognized as the baptism neither of this man nor of that, but of Christ." In Book V, ch 21, he reiterates this conviction saying: "Baptism is holy in itself, because it is of God; and whether it be given or whether it be received by men of such like character, it cannot be polluted by any perversity of theirs." In Book VI, ch 44: "I do not allow... that because the man himself is worse than a heathen, that is, than a Gentile and a pagan, therefore whatever the sacrament contains that is Christ's is mingled with his vices and character, and perishes through the corruption of such admixture." And finally it returns in Book VII, ch 53: "It makes no difference in respect to the genuineness of the sacrament within the Catholic Church itself, whether certain persons celebrate it in truth or in deceit."

Moreover, this same theme abounds in Augustine's *Three*

Books in Answer to the Letters of Petilian (ca. 354-ca. 420), the
Donatist bishop of Cirta (modern day Ksantina, Algeria). In Bk
I, ch 6 of his answers to the letters of Petilian, Augustine says:
"Whether a man receives the sacrament of baptism from a faithful or a faithless minister, his whole hope is in Christ." Bk II, ch
5: "The believer is born not from the barrenness of the minister,
but from the fruitfulness of the word." Bk II, ch 6: "When a man
preaches the word of God, or administers the sacraments of God
he does not, if he is a bad man, preach or minister out of his own
treasure." Bk II, ch 7:

> And if it so happens that certain ministers, being deceit-
> ful workers, seeking their own, not the things which are
> Jesus Christ's, proclaiming the gospel not in purity, and
> preaching Christ out of contention and envy, are to be
> called dead because of their unrighteousness, yet the
> sacrament of the living God does not die even in one
> that is dead.

What must be seen is that, even here, Augustine bases his theological argument on a biblical foundation.

I said above that when in his treatise *On Baptism* Augustine
introduces his argument regarding the validity of sacraments
celebrated by unworthy ministers, he prefaced it by a lengthy
treatment of the tares and the wheat. But more proximately, he
invoked yet another image, that of vessels of precious metal
versus vessels of wood taken from 2 Timothy 2:14-20:

> Remind them of this, and charge them before the Lord to
> avoid disputing about words, which does not good, but
> only ruins the hearers. Do your best to present yourself
> to God as one approved, a workman who has no need to
> be ashamed, rightly handling the word of truth. Avoid
> such godless chatter, for it will lead people into more
> and more ungodliness, and their talk will eat its way
> like gangrene. Among them are Hymenaeus and Phil-
> etus, who have swerved from the truth by holding that
> the resurrection is past already. They are upsetting the

faith of some. But God's firm foundation stands, bearing this seal: "The Lord know those who are his," and, "Let every one who names the name of the Lord depart from iniquity." In a great house there are not only vessels of gold and silver but also of wood and earthenware.

It is the image in that final line, the first half of verse 20 that Augustine makes much use of. It is a typically Pauline expression which Paul uses in Romans 9:21-23:

Has the potter no right over the clay, to make out of the same lump one vessel for beauty and another for menial use? What if God, desiring to show his wrath and to make known his power, has endured with much patience the vessels of wrath made for destruction, in order to make known the riches of his glory for the vessels of mercy, which he has prepared beforehand for glory.

It is an ancient image used often in the Old Testament to portray God as a potter (Is 29:16, 45:9, 64:8, Jr 18:6, Ws 15:7). Augustine makes particularly telling use of this image when developing his theme in *On Baptism*, Bk IV, ch 13:

I ask, how could those vessels which the large house contains not to honor, but to dishonor, administer what is holy for the sanctifying of men within the great house itself, unless because that holiness of the sacrament cannot be polluted even by the unclean.

He returns to this image once again in *On Baptism*, Bk VII, ch 52 and in his *Against Petilian*, Bk III, ch 2 in a lengthy passage that makes use of all three of his preferred images for the question of sin in the Church:

For if you cling most firmly to what I urge on you with all my might, that every one is cursed who places his trust in man, so that none should make his boast of man, then you will in no wise desert the threshing-floor of the Lord on account of the chaff which either is now being dispersed beneath the blast of the wind of pride, or will be separated by the final winnowing; nor will you fly from the great house on account of the vessels made to dishonor; nor will you quit the net through the breaches made in it because of the bad fish which are to be separated on the shore; nor will you leave the good pastures of unity, because of the goats which are to be placed on the left when the Good Shepherd shall divide the flock.

Augustine's theology of the holiness of the Church exerted tremendous influence on Christian thought down through the centuries such that I can quote an eloquent expression of Augustinian theology taken from Martin Luther's *Lectures on Galatians* of 1535 in referring to his greatest enemy, the object of much of his wrath:

Although the city of Rome is worse than Sodom and Gomorrah, nevertheless there remain in it Baptism, the Sacrament, the voice and text of the Gospel, the Sacred Scriptures, the ministries, the name of Christ, and the name of God.... For Baptism, the Gospel, etc. do not become unholy because I am defiled and unholy and have a false understanding of them. On the contrary, they remain holy and exactly what they were, regardless of whether they are among the godly or the ungodly; men can neither defile them nor hallow them.

In the twentieth century, however, the holiness of the Church has come in for considerable theological reevaluation and by several outstanding Catholic theologians. An example of this is Jesuit Karl Rahner's essay "The Church of Sinners" which was first published in 1947 as an essay in the theological journal *Stimmen der Zeit* (an English translation appeared in 1967 in Rahner's *Theological Investigations,* Vol. VI, 253-269). Then there is Swiss theologian Hans Urs von Balthasar's essay, *Casta Meretrix,* the title of which is Latin for "chaste whore," a sensational and provocative image of the Church which von Balthasar derives from an early and controversial Church writer, Origen of Alexandria (ca. 185-ca. 254). This essay first

148

A GUIDE TO THE CHURCH

appeared in 1961 in a collection of von Balthasar's essays which is available in English translation today as *Explorations in Theology*, Vol. II (Ignatius Press, 1991, pages 193-288). Another reevaluation is the chapter, "The Church is Holy," in Hans Küng's *Die Kirche* (1967, English translation, *The Church*, that same year). The most balanced of these treatments is Rahner's. Von Balthasar and Küng are less compromising in their indictment of the Church as sinful. As for von Balthasar: Origen's mixed metaphor for the Church as "chaste whore" is essentially a gross slander. An unfaithful wife might well be indicted as a sinner but it is abusive to label her a whore. And yet with considerable and characteristic erudition von Balthasar champions Origen's slander by marshalling a host of obscure references (Gregory of Elvira, Zeno of Verona, Odo of Cheriton, Anselm of Laon, Geroh of Reichersberg, Rupert of Deutz) dubious sources (quotations from Pseudo-Ambrose, Pseudo-Rufinus, Pseudo-Chrysostom) and disputed attributions — "a famous sermon of St. Augustine, which Hugo Rahner regards as genuine but Dom Morin ascribes to St. Caesarius." Along the way he employs discredited exegesis (Mary Magdalen as a reformed prostitute), makes at least one revealing admission: "St. Bernard would never call the Church a whore," and indulges in extreme language: "There is something about the essential form of the Church (and this is not her most inconspicuous feature) that is reminiscent of sin, conditioned by sin, something that in present context always means infidelity and fornication." Küng with less pedantry but as much a penchant for extreme statements insists "there is an evil at work here [in the Church] which is far greater than the failures of individual human beings, a force which can only be described as demonic," "it is human beings, not God, not the Lord, not the Spirit, who make up the Church," "the Church is a sinful Church — the effect not of God or Christ or the Holy Spirit, of course, but of its sinful members." And, in contrast to the traditional, creedal image of the Church as *communio sanctorum* (communion of saints), Küng insists "the Church is a dismal *communio peccatorum* (communion of sinners)." True, later, toward the end of his chapter, Küng tries to balance these earlier statements with more positive ones, insisting there is a legitimate sense in which the Church can be considered holy, and that despite human failings God does work through the Church. But to some readers these will appear disjunctive from the earlier statements and such readers might well conclude the co-existence of good and evil in the Church needs more judicious, more balanced formulation. This is, moreover, a balance and care observable in one of Küng's principal sources. Küng probably got the phrase *communio peccatorum* from Karl Barth who in his *Church Dogmatics*, Vol. 4, Part 2 (1955, English translation 1958), uses this expression when treating of the holiness of the Church. But there, Barth, as soon as he evokes this negative image, is quick to qualify it and qualify it decisively:

> They are still the *communio peccatorum*, members of the race of Adam, participant in the transgression and fall and misery of all men. But, in spite of this, and in triumph over it, they are already distinguished from all other men, constituting in fact and on behalf of the world the *communio sanctorum*.

Further Reading

Two chapters in René Latourelle's *Christ and the Church: Signs of Salvation* (Staten Island, N.Y.: ST PAULS/Alba House, 1972) are devoted to "The Paradox of Sin and Holiness in the Church." These are Chapter VII and VIII which comprise pages 211-264.

Chapter X, "A Pilgrim Church," in Miguel Garijo-Guembe's *Communion of the Saints: Foundation, Nature and Structure of the Church* (Collegeville, Minnesota: The Liturgical Press, 1994), pages 124-130.

In Jürgen Moltmann's *The Church in the Power of the Spirit* translated by M. Kohl (San Francisco: Harper and Row, 1977), Chapter VII, part 4, "Holiness in Poverty," 352-357.

Louis Bouyer's *The Church of God* translated by C.U. Quinn
(Franciscan Herald Press, 1982), Chapter 11, "The Spouse and
the Betrothed of Christ," in particular pages 491-509.

CHAPTER 12

The Church's Catholic Character

This coming Sunday many a Christian will stand up in a building called a church or in the midst of an assembly of Christians
gathered in a public place, whether built for Christian worship
or not, and at one point in the Sunday worship service, that man
or woman, along with the rest of the assembled believers will
profess their faith in a Church that is not only "one" and "holy"
but also "catholic." We have already wrestled with the terms
"one" and "holy" to try to understand what they have meant
historically in the Christian tradition. Now we must examine
this term "catholic."

One of the very first things we must note about this word
is its peculiarly problematic character. For example, of the four
marks or notes of the Church, this one is not biblical in origin.
We have seen how the idea that the Church is one and holy are
claims deeply rooted in the New Testament, those literary works
that date from the earliest period in Christian history and which
have been universally recognized by Christians as foundational
documents representing essential Christian self-understanding.
Moreover, when we examine the claim that the Church is apostolic we shall see that it too is biblical in origin. But in the New
Testament this term "catholic" as an adjective applied to the
Church is nowhere to be found. This fact will be a serious obstacle for those Christians who maintain a *sola scriptura* attitude,
who insist everything must be grounded in the Bible. But I ask
them to exercise special patience for the following reason.

The second thing that the reader should know is that, de-

A GUIDE TO THE CHURCH

spite the fact that this term "catholic" is not biblical in origin, in Christian history it soon became a very important theological concept tied up with Christian self-identity. That is, from early on Christian pastoral leaders and Christian speculative theologians found this word "catholic" very helpful in discussing both the Church and its faith. Indeed, it soon became an adjective applied not only to the Church but also to many other Christian things. Moreover, it eventually came to have use not just as an adjective but as a noun. That is, the term "catholic" can be used as a descriptive adjective for the Church and as a noun referring to a general attitude in theology, catholicism. Indeed, this is another aspect of its problematic character. This is because, though it has great antiquity and appears in classic creedal formulas that no Christian assembly wants to reject, even so, because of historical circumstances it is a word often associated with one particular and often exclusive current in the Christian tradition.

Yet a final thing the reader should know by way of preface for our treatment of this note or essential attribute of the Church is that the term is not just antique but has been a fertile idea in modern times. In the past few decades there have appeared several significant studies of this term. Just to name a few prominent or notable ones, Orthodox scholar John Meyendorff published in 1983 his *Catholicity and the Church*. Soon after there appeared Avery Dulles' *The Catholicity of the Church* (1985), a densely written, carefully reasoned, ecumenically sensitive work. Some Catholics will find Hans Küng's treatment of it in his *The Church* (1967) polemical, perhaps even mean-spirited. Monika Helwig has treated the term at length and in a pastoral fashion in her *Understanding Catholicism* (1981) and in her entry "Catholicism" in *The New Dictionary of Theology* (1987). Paul Tillich in his *The Protestant Era* (1948) introduced his concept of "the Protestant principle" as tempering extremes of Catholic sacramentalism. In Volume III of his *Systematic Theology* (University of Chicago, 1963), Paul Tillich sets forth the theme of uniting "catholic substance" and "protestant principle." And Jaroslav Pelikan in his *Obedient Rebels: Catholic Substance and Protestant Principle* (1964) carried this idea further. Here, however, our treatment of this term is much more limited; for we aim at simply acquainting the reader with information that can help us to understand the origin of this term and something of its historical development in the early history of Christian thought. More precisely, the information assembled here aims to help us understand something of its meaning for those who heard it invoked at the Council of Chalcedon in 451 when they read what was then called the Creed of Constantinople but which we call today the Nicene Creed or the Nicene-Constantinopolitan Creed. That creed with its profession of faith in a Church that is one, holy, catholic, and apostolic soon went on to become the test of orthodoxy in the Church of both east and west and still serves as such for many Christian assemblies to this day. Despite this limited range of our study here, in a concluding section, I will suggest some things about the practical use of the term "catholic" today.

We have already noted that this term is not biblical but rather has its origin in classical Greek language and thought. In this regard, I think it is most helpful to begin by looking at the meaning of this word in classical Greek. The first thing we should note in this regard is that etymologically, that is, in terms of word-origins, our English word "catholic" is derived from the Greek word *katholikos*. *Katholikos*, in turn, is a composite word derived from the prepositional phrase *kath'holon*, that is, the first part of this word, *kata*, is a preposition meaning "according to." Students of the Greek New Testament will recognize this preposition immediately because it is the preposition used in the title of the four canonical Gospels. That is, students of the Greek New Testament are used to seeing the Gospels according to Matthew, Mark, Luke and John referred to as *kata Matthaion, kata Markon, kata Loukan, kata Ioannen*. But in the Greek word *katholikos* the prefix *kata* prefaces or stands before, not an author's name as in the Gospel titles, but a noun, *holon*, which is the origin of our English word, "whole." And thus the Greek word, *katholikos*, means "according to the whole." In this regard it is important to see the very careful definition of the term *holon* or "whole" given by Aristotle in Book 5 of his *Metaphysics*. There the great Greek philosopher says:

> A "whole [*holon*]" means (1) that from which are absent
> none of the parts of which it is said to be naturally
> a whole, and (2) that which so contains the things it
> contains that they form a unity; and this in two senses
> – either as being each severally one single thing, or as
> making up the unity between them. For what is said of
> the whole [according to, toward the whole, *kathoolou*]
> and wholly [*holos*], as if it were [in itself] a whole [*holon*]
> is so universal [*katholou*] because it contains many, inas-
> much as it is predicated of each and all together are one,
> as each [is one].... Wholeness is in fact a kind of oneness.
> Again (3) [whole] can be said of quantity, quantitative
> things that have spatial extension, that is, things that
> have a beginning, a middle and an end, those to which
> the position [*thesis*] does not make a difference are called
> totals [*pan*], and those to which it does wholes [*holon*].

And thus the Greek word *katholikos* from which we derive our
English word "catholic" means basically "wholeness," inclusiv-
ity in the sense of a thing that has all that it should have, all its
constituent parts.

Now that we have discovered what the secular Greek term
"catholic" basically meant, we are going to survey how that term
has been used by Christian pastors and thinkers.

Here probably the best thing to do is to begin by looking
at the one New Testament usage of a derivative of this classical
Greek word. This occurs in the Acts of the Apostles 4:18. This
passage is part of a narrative that tells of an incident in the earliest history of the Christian movement, an incident that occurred
to two leaders of the earliest Christian Church at Jerusalem, the
apostles Peter and John. In Chapter 3 of the Acts of the Apostles
we are told how one day Peter and John were preaching Jesus
in the very precincts of the temple, more precisely in the portico
called "Solomon's Portico." In Chapter 4 we are told how Peter
and John were arrested by the temple guard at that same time,
after the end of their preaching and then were brought before
the Sanhedrin, the supreme council of Israel made up of the
leading men but headed up or presided over by the high priest,

in this case Annas. Peter and John came off with only a stern admonition which is described in Acts 4:18, in these words: "So they called them and charged them not to speak or teach at all in the name of Jesus." A form of the word *katholikos* is used in the phrase "not at all," *kath'olou me.*

The first important historic use of this term "catholic" with reference to the Church is found in the eighth chapter, the second verse of the *Letter to the Church at Smyrna* authored by Ignatius, the bishop of Antioch about the year 107. Ignatius lived approximately from A.D. 35 to 107. He was probably of Syrian origin. Not much is known of his life. There is speculation that he was a convert from paganism and that he knew some of the apostles perhaps Peter who, according to Paul in Galatians 2:11, spent some time at Antioch in the 50's when Ignatius would have been a young man. But what we know best about Ignatius is how his life ended. About the year 107, Ignatius was arrested for his profession of the Christian faith and his prominent leadership in the Christian community at Antioch. He was quickly dispatched to Rome under the armed guard of ten Roman soldiers. At Rome he was probably fed to lions in one of the spectacles at one of the city's great arenas of which the building called the Colosseum is the principal remaining witness. But for our interest and history's the more important thing is that on his road to martyrdom he was received en route at Smyrna with great honor by the bishop of that city, a man by the name of Polycarp. Moreover, while at Smyrna, Ignatius was visited by representatives of the Churches of Ephesus, Magnesia, and Tralles. Later when he continued his journey to martyrdom he wrote back "thank you" letters to the Church at Smyrna and the other churches that had sent people to visit him there. It is in his *Letter to the Church at Smyrna* that he used the word "catholic" as applied to the Church. I quote it to you in the fuller context of chapter 8:

> Flee from schism as the source of mischief. You should
> all follow the bishop as Jesus Christ did the Father. Fol-
> low too the presbytery as you would the apostles; and
> respect the deacons as you would God's law. Nobody

must do anything that has to do with the Church without the bishop's approval. You should regard the Eucharist as valid which is celebrated by the bishop or by someone he authorizes. Where the bishop is present, there let the congregation gather, just as where Jesus Christ is, there is the Catholic Church. Without the bishop's supervision, no baptisms or love feasts are permitted. On the other hand, whatever he approves pleases God as well. In that way everything you do will be on the safe side and valid.

The second oldest reference we have to a Christian pastor's use of this term "catholic" as applied to the Church is in a work called *The Martyrdom of Polycarp*, the same Polycarp who hosted Ignatius at Smyrna. Polycarp, whose dates are traditionally given as ca. 69–ca. 155, was the bishop of Smyrna and has been described as the leading Christian figure in Roman Asia in the middle of the second century. A staunch defender of orthodoxy, he devoted much of his energy to combating such heretics as the Marcionites and the Valentinians. Marcion was a theologian, a native of Sinope in Pontus, who came to Rome about the year 140 and in the next few years worked out a religious system and organized his followers. His central thesis was that the Christian Gospel was wholly a Gospel of love to the absolute exclusion of law. This caused him to reject the Old Testament completely and to exalt Paul as the only one to have understood the radical contrast between law and grace. Marcion had considerable success in the spread of his doctrines. Valentinus was a native of Egypt who also came to Rome where he lived from about the years 136 to 165 and developed his systematic theology and a large following. He claimed that he had been taught by one Theodas, a pupil of Saint Paul. His theology seems to have pitted the visible material world against a spiritual world.

The Martyrdom of Polycarp is a letter in twenty chapters written by another Marcion (not the founder of the heretical movement). This letter was sent from the Church of Smyrna to the Church of Philomelium as an account of the martyrdom of not just Bishop Polycarp but also of several Christians at Smyrna. This is the earliest literary account outside the Bible of a Christian martyrdom (Acts of the Apostles 7:54-60 recounts the martyrdom of Stephen). In this letter, the word "catholic" is applied to the Church several times. For example, it is used in the opening salutation, "The Church of God which sojourns in Smyrna, to the Church of God which sojourns in Philomelium, and to all the sojournings of the Holy Catholic Church (*hagias kai katholikes ekklesias*) in every place." In Chapter 7, Polycarp's arrest by the "police and cavalry" is described. They came to his home on a Friday evening about supper time. In his conversation with them it became obvious they meant to take him away. But Polycarp asked if they would give him some time to pray and meanwhile he would see to it that they would be served food and drink. Chapter 8 begins with the words, "Now when he had at last finished his prayer, after remembering all who had ever even come his way, both small and great, high and low, and the whole Catholic Church throughout the world (*kata ten oikoumene katholikes ekklesias*), the hour came for departure." Chapter 15 describes Polycarp's death; he was burned at the stake. And Chapter 16 concludes with the tribute, vs. 2, "And of the elect was he indeed one, the wonderful martyr, Polycarp, who in our days was an apostolic and prophetic teacher, bishop of the Catholic Church in Smyrna." Chapter 19 concludes with a reference to "our Lord Jesus Christ, the Savior of our souls, and Governor of our bodies, and the Shepherd *of the Catholic Church throughout the world*" (*kata ten oikoumene katholikes ekklesias*).

 ⌐Clement of Alexandria (ca. 150-ca. 215), an Athenian by birth, a convert to Christianity and educated at Alexandria became head of the Catechetical School of Alexandria. One of his most important literary works is called the *Stromata*. The word means literally "carpets" but it is used figuratively to suggest a multicolored patchwork cloth or bag, suggesting our modern literary form called the miscellany, that is, a collection of various thoughts. This is appropriate for Clement because while his was a probative intellect he had not the gift for strict logical arrangement of his thought. This work consists of eight "books." In the passage that I quote here "the later heresies" he refers to are examples of a movement in second century Christianity called Gnosticism. This word Gnosticism is derived from the Greek word *gnosis* meaning knowledge and points to one of the central characteristics of the movement, the importance it placed upon the revealed knowledge of God which came from either a special secret source or from a direct revelation bestowed by God on the founder of the sect. This has an ecclesial theme because for Clement true *gnosis* or true knowledge of the Christian faith rests on an ecclesial basis. We see this especially in Book 7. In his *Stromata*, 7.17.107, he teaches that the Church differs in its unity and in its antiquity from the heresies:

> Such being the case, it is evident, from the high antiquity and perfect truth of the Church, that these later heresies, and those yet subsequent to them in time, were new inventions falsified [from the truth]. From what has been said, then, it is my opinion that the true Church, that which is really ancient, is one, and that in it those who according to God's purpose are just, are enrolled.... We agree that both in substance and in seeming, both in origin and in development, the primitive and Catholic Church is the only one, agreeing as it does in the unity of one faith.

Another important passage witnessing to the use of the term "catholic" to describe the Christian assembly comes from Eusebius's *Ecclesiastical History*, one of the principal sources for our knowledge of the history of Christianity from the Apostolic age to the conversion of Constantine. Eusebius (ca. 260-ca. 340) trained at the theological school at Caesarea in Palestine and in 315 he became the bishop of the Church there. Of his many writings the most celebrated is his *Ecclesiastical History*. He worked on it for many years. It seems it received its final form in about the year 323. There in 5.16.9, Eusebius describes the teaching of one Montanus as "blasphemy against the Catholic Church, the whole Church spread out under heaven." It seems that Montanus was originally a priest of the oriental ecstatic cult of Cybele, a fertility goddess, but he converted to Christianity. Shortly after his conversion, around the year 172 he entered into an ecstatic state and began prophesying in the region of Phrygia, now in central Turkey, proclaiming that he was the embodiment of the Holy Spirit and announcing that the Heavenly Jerusalem would soon descend on the village of Pepuza in Phrygia. He soon became the leader of a group of similar ecstatics who exhibited not only enraptured seizures but also speaking in strange tongues. Because he was convinced that the world would soon end, he preached a rigorist morality meant to purify Christians and detach them from their material desires.

The next example that we shall look at is the use of the word "catholic" by Cyril of Jerusalem (ca. 315-386). We do not have a great deal of detail about his personal life. It seems he was a Palestinian, probably born and raised in Caesarea by Christian parents. He became a deacon and presbyter of the Church at Jerusalem. And around 349, he became bishop of Jerusalem. One of his duties as bishop of Jerusalem was to give formal instruction to catechumens, a technical term used to refer to adult Christians being prepared for baptism on Saturday evening, the vigil of Easter Sunday. The form for their instruction was a lengthy discourse on the articles of the creed to which these baptismal candidates would make their profession of faith before immersion in the waters of baptism. These discourses were given after the Sunday services of the Sundays leading up to Easter, the Sundays of Lent. Twenty-three of Cyril's catechetical instructions were long ago collected together in a literary work called *The Catechetical Lectures*. The lecture that most interests us is the 18th which carries the title, "On the words, and in one holy catholic Church, and in the resurrection of the flesh, and the life everlasting." These words refer to the final codicils in the baptismal creed of the Church at Jerusalem. Scholars have conjectured that because of its topic this lecture must have been given on the night of Good Friday, or in the early hours of the morning of the "Great Sabbath" in the year 347 or 348 in the great basilica or Church of the Resurrection, built by Constantine on the site of the Holy Sepulcher.

In his 18th Catechetical Discourse, paragraph 23, Cyril sets forth a rather long and complicated definition of what we mean when we say the Church is catholic:

> The Church is called catholic because it has spread over the whole world, from one end to the other; because it proclaims comprehensively and without defect all the doctrines of faith which we must know, about the visible and the invisible, about heavenly and earthly things; because it brings the whole human race, princes and subjects, the educated and the uneducated, to the right worship of God; and finally, quite in general, because like a doctor it heals all sins which have been committed with the soul or the body; it also possesses every kind of virtue, whatever it may be called, in action and words and every kind of spiritual gift.

A little later, in paragraph 26 of this lecture, we hear Cyril say: "And if ever you are sojourning in any city, inquire not simply where the Lord's house is — for the sects of the profane also attempt to call their own dens, houses of the Lord — nor merely where the Church is, but where is the Catholic Church. For this is the peculiar name of the holy body the mother of us all."

Another author to be considered is Pacian, bishop of Barcelona during the fourth century. During his time as bishop Pacian received a challenging letter from one Sympronian, a member of a rigorist schismatic group in Spain called the Novatianists after the founder of this movement, one Novatian. Novatian had been a presbyter of the Church at Rome in the previous century. But when Cornelius was elected pope in 251, Novatian joined a rigorist party in the Church at Rome that objected to Cornelius because they considered him too lenient toward Christians who had compromised their faith during the Decian persecution of 250. In fact this rigorist group insisted such people should be banned from the Church forever. Soon this group arranged for Novatian's consecration as rival bishop, anti-pope, to Cornelius. Novatian was martyred under Valerian in 257-258 but the movement he had headed continued to grow in various parts of the empire, including Spain. Apparently Sympronian's letter to Pacian requested explanations of the use of the term "catholic," of penitential practice and of repentance generally. Pacian responded but it seems Sympronian, not satisfied with Pacian's answers, sent a further challenging letter to which Pacian responded once again, only to be rebuffed once more. This final rebuff occasioned a veritable treatise against Novatianism on Pacian's part. However, for our interests, Pacian's most important point was made in his first letter wherein he explains the meaning of the word "catholic":

> And yet, my brother, do not be troubled. "Christian" is my first name, and "Catholic" is my surname. The former term designates me; the latter distinguishes me from others. By one I am given sanction; by the other I am signified. And if, lastly, we must give an explanation of the word "Catholic" and extract it from the Greek by a Latin interpretation, "Catholic" means "one in every place" or perhaps, as our learned men think, it is said to mean "obedience in all things" — that is, in all the commandments of God, whence the Apostle states, "If you are obedient in all things." And again, "For just as by the disobedience of one man many were made sinners, so I declare, by the attention of one many will be made righteous." Therefore the person who is a Catholic, this same one is obedient. And the person who is obedient, this same one is Christian. Thus, the Catholic is a Christian. Wherefore, our people, when they are designated as Catholics, are separated by this appellation from any heretical name.

The translation here does not do justice to Pacian's stylistic genius. For example, the letter is most famous for Pacian's lapidary phrasing of his answer to Sympronian's request for an explanation of the term "catholic." Pacian's reply is, *Christianus mihi nomen est, catholicus vero cognomen,* that is, "My name is Christian, my surname is Catholic."

Augustine of Hippo (354-430) represents yet another important witness to the use of this term "catholic" as applied to the Church. Augustine's *On True Religion* was written at the end of the year 390 just before his ordination as a priest. It is addressed to Romanianus, a longtime friend of Augustine's whom he had long ago led to become a Manichean. But this time Augustine is trying to lead Romanianus away from Manicheism into the Christian faith. Manicheism is named for its originator, one Mani. Mani was born in Babylonia in A.D. 216 of Jewish Christian parents. As a young man he styled himself "Apostle of Jesus Christ" and presented himself as completing the work of Christ by bringing people into a fuller light, by teaching a strong dualism between darkness and light, spirit and matter. Not only did Mani present himself as an "Apostle of Jesus Christ" but his followers consistently referred to themselves as Christians, indeed as belonging to the only authentic form of Christianity. Against such an exclusive claim Augustine, in his treatise *On True Religion* 7.12, asserts regarding the adjective "catholic":

> We must remain true to the Christian faith and to the community of that Church which is catholic and which is called the Catholic Church as well by its opponents as by all the members of it. Whether they intend to or not, even heretics and schismatics, if they are talking not among themselves but to outsiders, can only refer to one Church as catholic, namely the Catholic Church. They can only make themselves clear by giving it that name by which it is known the world over.

In 396 or 397, Augustine produced a treatise *Against Mani's Epistle Called "The Fundamentals."* In writing this work, Augustine was responding to a text of Mani's in which Mani had summarized the fundamentals of his own teachings. In Ch. 4, section 5, of this work, Augustine sets forth a list of catholic fundamentals, suggesting what he feels are the elements that make a Church catholic:

> For in the Catholic Church... there are many other things
> which most justly keep me in her bosom. The consent
> of peoples and nations keeps me in the Church; so does
> her authority, inaugurated by miracles, nourished by
> hope, enlarged by love, established by age. The succes-
> sion of priests keeps me, beginning from the very seat
> of the Apostle Peter, to whom the Lord, after His resur-
> rection, gave it in charge to feed His sheep, down to the
> present episcopate. And, so lastly, does the name itself
> of Catholic, which, not without reason, amid so many
> heresies, the Church has thus retained; so that though all
> heretics wish to be called Catholics, yet when a stranger
> asks where the Catholic Church meets, no heretic will
> venture to point to his own chapel or house.

The last author whom we survey is Vincent of Lérins,
a learned monk from the island of Lérins who died before 450.
"Lérins" was the ancient name of two islands off the southern
coast of France (today near Cannes, the modern film festival
city). The two islands are now called Saint Honorat because in
the year 410, Saint Honoratus (ca. 350-429) founded an abbey on
these islands. That abbey soon produced several famous scholars
and bishops, among them Hilary of Arles, Caesarius of Arles, and
Vincent of Lérins. Vincent's great claim to fame is a literary work
which he chose to call the *Commonitoria*, a Latin word meaning
"things to be remembered." In that work, he makes considerable use of the adjective "catholic." We find him referring to not
only "the Catholic Church" (paragraph 6), but also "the Catholic
faith" (4), the "Catholic interpretation" of the Bible (5), a "Catholic
Christian" (7), "Catholic doctrine" (21), "Catholic priesthood"
(71), "Catholic consent" (73). However, Vincent's *Commonitoria*, is
most famous for its lapidary definition of catholicity. The English
word "lapidary" refers to a cutter, polisher, or engraver of precious
stones. As an adjective it means "of or relating to precious stones
or the art of cutting them," or "having the elegance and precision
associated with inscriptions on monumental stone." Vincent's
literary skill enabled him to produce a lapidary definition of the
Catholic faith as "that which has been believed everywhere, al-

ways and by everyone." The Latin being "*quod ubique, quod semper, quod ab omnibus creditum est.*" Here I give it in the larger context of the passage in which it appears, paragraph 6:

> Within the Catholic Church itself, great care must be taken that we hold on to that which has been believed everywhere at all times by all the faithful. This is what is truly and properly "catholic" as the very force and meaning of the name indicates, that is, it includes everything universally. This will be the case if we follow universality, antiquity, consent. We shall follow universality in this way if we confess that to be the one true faith that is confessed by the whole Church throughout the world; antiquity, if we never depart from the meaning that our forefathers declared sacrosanct; finally, consent, if in its very age we hold to the decisions and convictions of all, or almost all, the bishops and teachers.

It should be obvious from this our historical survey that, without doubt the simplest meaning of the term "catholic" is "universal" in the sense of geographical comprehensiveness. With almost all of the authors we have surveyed the primary meaning of this term "the Catholic Church" is the whole Church in the sense of the aggregate of all the local churches, what we heard Eusebius describe as "the whole Church spread out under heaven." And no doubt this is dictated by the fact that most often the divisions in the early Church, initially at least, were from small splinter groups and thus the contrast between the universal Church and small sects is a ready to hand and helpful one. And no doubt this is the basic meaning that many Christians today will insist upon. We see it in those hymnals or service books where there is an asterisk beside the word catholic in the creed and a footnote indicating the term means universal. However, it should also be apparent that there is as well a decisive movement in the use of this term toward a more sententious meaning that implies not just spatial or geographical inclusiveness but also doctrinal wholeness or integrity and moral comprehensiveness. For example, while Ignatius of Antioch's use of the phrase "the Catholic Church" can be taken as simply a reference to the spatial and geographical comprehensiveness of the Church spread across the earth, it is obvious that in this very same passage Ignatius sees certain things such as the ordered ministries of bishops, presbyters and deacons and Eucharists "celebrated by the bishop or by someone he authorizes" as constitutive elements of true Church assemblies, primary and elemental things that make for catholicity.

Moreover, I think it must be seen that among all these witnesses, Cyril's is the most important because his definition of catholicity is not based primarily upon drawing a distinction between the teaching of the great Church and that of various sects or heresies. No, Cyril's is purely catechetical. This is a much more comprehensive and elaborate notion of what it means to be catholic. To be sure, Cyril begins with the simplest meaning of catholicity, the sense of spatial or geographical inclusiveness. In this regard he says the Church can be understood as catholic, integral, fully inclusive, in that it consists of all the believers, all the Christian worshiping assemblies spread across the earth. However, he goes on to add yet another note of catholicity, namely, a doctrinal integrity, doctrinal inclusiveness, what he calls "all the doctrines of the faith." Next, he adds yet another meaning to the word "catholic." This time it is what might best be called a moral inclusiveness, the Gospel's ability to address all human beings in all situations, the rich and the poor, the educated and uneducated. But there is yet a fourth meaning Cyril proposes and that is the Church is able to not just address the human condition in all its variety but it also has a great variety of means, indeed, all the means necessary to remedy that condition. When Cyril describes this as "every kind of spiritual gift" he is probably referring to various forms of prayer and various acts of charity, for example, the seven acts of mercy. It is probably at one with the image of Mother Church as having a cupboard with everything we might need for nourishment and amendment.

Two other things that should be said about this our survey: first, not all these witnesses are probative; for example, Vincent of Lérins' definition of catholicity is indeed lapidary but it is also seriously misleading. There are very few doctrines or traditions that could meet the criteria of having been held "always, everywhere and by everyone." Moreover, sometimes the truth is held by the embattled few, as during the Arian crisis. And French Jesuit theologian Henri de Lubac, in his 1947 work *Catholicisme: les aspects sociaux du dogme* (Catholicism: the Social Aspects of Dogma) translated by L. Sheppard and E. Englund as *Catholicism: Christ and the Common Destiny of Man* (San Francisco: Ignatius Press, 1988), makes this point with an accomplished literary style equal to that of Vincent of Lérins:

> The Church is not Catholic because she is spread abroad over the whole of the earth and can reckon on a large number of members. She was already Catholic on the morning of Pentecost, when all her members could be contained in a small room, as she was when the Arian waves seemed on the point of swamping her; she would still be Catholic if tomorrow apostasy on a vast scale deprived her of almost all the faithful. For fundamentally Catholicity has nothing to do with geography or statistics. If it is true that it should be displayed over all the earth and be manifest to all, yet its nature is not material but spiritual. Like sanctity, Catholicity is primarily an intrinsic feature of the Church. (pp. 48-49)

Further Reading

John Meyendorff's *Catholicity and the Church* (Crestwood, NY: St. Vladimir's Seminary Press, 1983).

In Jürgen Moltmann's *The Church in the Power of the Spirit* translated by M. Kohl (San Francisco: Harper & Row, 1977), Chapter VII, Part 3, "Catholicity and Partisanship," which is to be found on pages 347-352.

In Francis Sullivan's *The Church We Believe In: One, Holy, Catholic, and Apostolic* (Mahwah, NJ: Paulist Press. 1988), Chapter 5, "The Catholic Unity of the People of God," which is on pages 84-108.

CHAPTER 13

A Church that is Apostolic

Even though the school of theology at which I teach is a Catholic seminary, in this seminary we have given an honored place to a fine piece of art from the Protestant Reformation. As one enters the foyer of our seminary library, one can see through the glass wall into the library staff room where hangs on the wall facing the entrance thirteen woodcut engravings by artist Andreas Kaufmann of Nuremberg and renowned printer Henricus Hondius of Amsterdam. These engravings are dated 1607 and depict Paul among the apostles, that is, the artist has taken the early Church legend that each of the Twelve had contributed a line in the composition of the so-called Apostles' Creed, and depicted each of the Twelve standing above a subscript of a line from that creed and Paul above a quotation of one of his principal doctrinal themes, Philippians 1:21, "For me to live is Christ, and to die is gain." This is faithful to Paul of Tarsus who, though he was not one of the original Twelve called by Jesus, never ceased to insist that he too had been called to be an apostle and thus should be given equal status with them.

The word "apostolic" is an adjective used to indicate that something is closely related to the apostles. From early on in the history of the Christian movement this word "apostolic" became very important, for everyone wanted to be able to claim that their teaching, their traditions, their Christian assembly was ultimately and profoundly related to the apostles, the Twelve original disciples of Jesus, his handpicked, inner-circle along with Paul of Tarsus, the self-styled "apostle to the Gentiles" (Rm 11:13). Why and how Christian assemblies came to attach so much importance to their relationship to the apostles and how they, to this day, demonstrate that relationship is the theme of this chapter. What we shall do here is to look first at the biblical origin of the terms "apostle" and "apostolic" and then at their development in the early Church.

These two words, "apostle" and "apostolic," are derived from the classical, Attic Greek verb *apostellein* meaning "to send." That verb, "to send," is found commonly in classical Greek literature. And we have three modern English words that are derived from it. Our word "post" as in the question, "Has the post arrived yet?" refers to objects, letters and packages which are being or have been *sent*, delivered from a distance. Then there is the verb "to post," which designates the act of sending something, and, finally, there is the adjective "postal" as used, for example, in the phrase, "The US Postal Service." All three of these words are derived from Greek verb *apostellein*, to send. While this verb, "to send" is found commonly in classical Greek literature, the adjective *apostolike* and the noun *apostelos* occur only rarely in Greek or Hellenistic literature, and when they do occur there they do not have the meaning these words have in the Christian tradition. For example, the noun, *apostolos*, is found only once in the writings of the fifth century B.C. Greek historian Herodotus. In the Ionic Greek of Herodotus' *The Histories* I.21.38, it is used of a personal envoy, a messenger who comes with terms of peace. As for the rest of classical Greek literature, there too its occurrence is extremely rare and when it does occur it most often refers to a fleet of ships, in a few cases an admiral, at other times it refers to an export license. The noun *apostolos* is equally rare in the literature of Hellenistic Judaism. It is totally absent from the writings of the Jewish philosopher and exegete Philo of Alexandria (ca. 20 B.C.-ca. A.D. 50) and appears only once in the works of the Jewish historian Josephus (ca. 37-ca. 100). Likewise, it is used only once in the Septuagint, the Greek translation of the Jewish Scriptures, in 1 Kings 14:6. But in the small corpus of works that comprise the New Testament, the word "apostle" appears no less than 79 times. And the adjective "apostolic" appears countless times in the writings of the early Christian era after the composition of the New Testament. Indeed in the patristic period the term "apostolic" comes to be applied to many things. In addition to the apostolic Church we find references to apostolic preaching, apostolic teaching, apostolic tradition. In order to understand something of what the word "apostolic" meant when it was inserted alongside the word "Church" in the creed we now recite on Sunday, what I shall do here is to treat first of the use of the noun "apostle/apostles" in the New Testament and then of the adjective "apostolic" in the writings of the early Church fathers.

In three of our Gospels, the word "apostle/apostles" is used sparingly, that is, it occurs but once in Matthew, Mark and John. In Mark 6:30 we read, "The apostles returned to Jesus and told him all that they had done and taught." Matthew 10:2 begins, "The names of the twelve apostles are these...." In John 13:16, we hear Jesus say, "Truly, truly I say to you, a slave is not greater than his master, nor is an apostle great than the one who sent him." On the other hand, the word "apostles" is used six times in the Gospel according to Luke. In Luke 6:13 we are told "... and when it was day, he called his disciples [*mathetas*], and chose from them twelve [*dodeka*], whom he named apostles [*apostolous*]." In Luke 9:10, "On their return the apostles told him what they had done." In Luke 11:49 we hear Jesus say, "The wisdom of God said, 'I will send them prophets and apostles.'" And in 17:5: "The apostles said to the Lord, 'Increase our faith!'" And in the Acts of the Apostles, the companion volume to Luke's Gospel, the word "apostles" is used 29 times. There are too many to be quoted here but I offer a representative sampling. In Acts 1:2 it is said of Jesus' ascension: "He was taken up, after he had given commandment through the Holy Spirit to the apostles whom he had chosen." In Acts 1:25, the Eleven, seeking to fulfill the place left by Judas, pray that God reveal to them the one whom God has chosen "to take the place in this ministry and apostleship." In Acts 2:42, we are told that the brethren at Jerusalem "devoted themselves to the apostles' teaching." Acts 5:12 states, "Many signs and wonders were done among the people by the hands of the apostles." In Acts 6:1: "These they set before the apostles, and they prayed and laid their hands upon them." In Acts 8:1 we read how after the stoning of Stephen, "a great persecution arose against the Church in Jerusalem; and they were all scattered throughout the region of Judea and Samaria, except the apostles." Acts 8:14 says, "Now when the apostles at Jerusalem heard that Samaria had received the word of God they sent to them Peter and John." Acts 8:18 states, "the Spirit was given through the laying on of the apostles' hands." Beginning with Acts 15:2, we hear constant reference to decisions made by "the apostles and the elders" [*apostolon kai presbuteron*] at Jerusalem (cf. Acts 15:4, 6, 22, 23; 16:4).

When we look at the Pauline literature of the New Testament, the first thing that impresses us is how often Paul applies the title of "apostle" to himself. Indeed, Paul employs the word "apostle" to identify himself in the opening salutation of almost all of his letters: Romans 1:1, "Paul a servant of Jesus Christ, called to be an apostle." 1 Corinthians 1:1 reads, "Paul, called by the will of God to be an apostle of Christ Jesus." 2 Corinthians 1:1 says, "Paul, an apostle of Christ Jesus by the will of God." Galatians 1:1 has, "Paul an apostle — not from men nor through man, but through Jesus Christ and God the Father." Ephesians 1:1: "Paul, an apostle of Christ Jesus by the will of God." Colossians 1:1, "Paul, an apostle of Christ Jesus by the will of God." 1 Timothy 1:1: "Paul, an apostle of Christ Jesus by the command of God our Savior and of Christ Jesus our hope." 2 Timothy 1:1: "Paul, an apostle of Christ Jesus by the will of God according to the promise of the life which is in Christ." Titus 1:1, "Paul, a servant of God and an apostle of Jesus Christ." And even when it is not used in the opening salutation it finds expression elsewhere, for example, in 1 Thessalonians 2:8, "Nor did we seek glory from men, whether from you or from others, though we might have made demands as apostles of Christ." In the latter quotation, the plural "we" includes Paul along with Silvanus and Timothy whom he mentions in the opening salutation of that letter, and this is helpful to note because one of the things that must be seen is that in addition to the Twelve whom Paul acknowledges as "those who were apostles before me" (Galatians 1:17), Paul also uses the term "apostle" with reference to others besides the Twelve and himself.

In Romans 16:7 he says, "Greet Andronicus and Junias, my kinsmen and my fellow prisoners; they are men of note among the apostles." This is the RSV translation. The New RSV uses inclusive language at this point because many modern scholars argue that Junias is the name of a woman. In 2 Corinthians 8:23, Paul says, "As for Titus, he is my partner and fellow worker in your service; and as for our brethren, they are messengers of the Churches (*apostoloi ekklesion*), the glory of Christ." It is interesting how the translators of the Revised Standard Version have chosen to translate *apostoloi* in this passage as "messengers" rather than as "apostles." Yet another passage in which Saint Paul uses the word *apostolos* to refer to Church workers is in Philippians 2:25, "I have thought it necessary to send to you Epaphroditus my brother and fellow worker and fellow soldier, and your messenger and minister to my need." Here once again the translators of the RSV have chosen to render *apostolon* as "messenger" rather than literally as "apostle." It could be that they felt Epaphroditus is functioning not as a preacher of the Gospel but indeed simply as a messenger. But one cannot help but wonder if Paul is intentionally nuancing the term "apostle" to show how though he himself is an apostle of the Lord there are others who are apostles of the churches. If so, this leads to our next observation.

The Pauline corpus also witnesses to a considerable controversy as to who deserves this title "apostle" and thus to several distinctions, not to say incriminating variations of this term. We have already seen the possible novelty in the term "apostles of the churches." But now we shall see Paul's use of such innovative terms as the indicting "pseudo apostles" and the sarcastic "super apostles" and his limitation of the title "apostles of Christ." The Second Letter of Paul to the Church at Corinth makes it clear that other preachers in addition to Paul had visited Corinth and moreover these other preachers had proven as effective and maybe even more eloquent and popular than Paul. And so Paul becomes somewhat defensive, saying in 2 Corinthians 11:5-6, "I think that I am not in the least inferior to these superlative apostles (*hyperlion apostoloi*). Even if I am unskilled in speaking, I am not in knowledge." And, in fact, a few verses later, in 2 Corinthians 11:12-13, he becomes accusatory using the term "pseudo apostles" to describe such: "And what I do I will continue to do, in order to undermine the claim of those who would like to claim that in their boasted mission they work on the same terms as we do. For such men are false apostles (*pseudapostoloi*), deceitful workmen, disguising themselves as apostles of Christ." Indeed, it is possible to argue that such challenges lead Paul to modify his once liberally inclusive use of the term "apostle." In Paul's earliest surviving literary work, 1 Thessalonians 2:6, he casually applied the term "apostle" not just to himself but also to his companions, Silvanus and Timothy, saying "nor did we seek glory from men, whether from you or from others, though we might have made demands as apostles of Christ (*Christou apostoloi*)." But in later letters he seems to keep the title solely to himself. For example, in the opening salutation of his First Letter to the Corinthians he says, "Paul, called by the will of God to be an apostle of Christ Jesus, and our brother Sosthenes." And he begins his Second Letter to the Corinthians with the words, "Paul an apostle of Christ Jesus by the will of God, and Timothy our brother." Is he now choosing to distance Sosthenes and Timothy from the title of "apostle of Christ"? Anyway, Paul's hypersensitivity about his own apostolicity does not end with his seeking to reserve to himself the title, but he also seeks to identify himself with a special group in the Church. While Paul seems to use the term "apostle" quite generally at times to mean anyone who has been sent whether by Christ or a Church, there is at least one passage wherein he appears to be dealing with a much more delimited notion of what an apostle is. It could be that already in Paul's time there is a growing sense of the special character of that unique witness to Christ which can be given by those who had quite literally seen the historical Jesus of Nazareth. But Paul finesses that claim by suggesting that to have seen the risen Christ is even more important than to have witnessed the historical Jesus of Nazareth. In 1 Corinthians 9:1 Paul says, "Am I not free? Am I not an apostle? Have I not seen Jesus our Lord?" Later in that same epistle (1 Cor 15:7-10), Paul elaborates on this claim: "Then he appeared to James, then to all the apostles. Last of all, as to one untimely born, he appeared also to me. For I am the least of the apostles, unfit to be called an apostle, because I persecuted the Church of God. But by the grace of God I am what I am."

Finally we should note the use of the term "apostle" in the non-Pauline letters and the Johannine literature of the New Testament. The word "apostle" is used in the epistles of Peter in a fashion similar to Paul's. The First Epistle of Peter begins with the words, "Peter, an apostle of Jesus Christ." The Second Epistle opens with the salutation, "Simon Peter, a servant and apostle of Jesus Christ." 2 Peter 3:1 compares the apostles with the Old Testament prophets: "This is now the second letter that I have written to you, beloved, and in both of them I have aroused your sincere mind by way of reminder; that you should remember the predictions of the holy prophets and the commandment of the Lord and Savior through your apostles." Also consider that in Hebrews 3:1 the word "apostle" is applied to Jesus, "Therefore, holy brethren, who share in a heavenly call, consider Jesus, the apostle and high priest of our confession." And though the word "apostle" appears only once in the Gospel of John and nowhere in the Johannine epistles it is used significantly in two places in the Book of Revelation. In 2:2, Jesus tells the angel of the Church of Ephesus, "I know your works, your toil and your patient endurance, and how you cannot bear evil men but have tested those who call themselves apostles but are not." And then there is a reference in the vision of the heavenly Jerusalem in Revelation 21:14, "And the wall of the city had twelve foundations, and on them the twelve names of the twelve apostles of the Lamb."

What are we to make of all this evidence? First, there can be no doubt that occasionally in the New Testament the term "apostle" is used in a very general sense to designate anyone with a message, that is, not just the Twelve and Paul but Timothy, Silvanus, Epaphroditus, Junias and Andronicus, Jesus even. And no doubt even to this day while acknowledging the fundamental importance of Paul and the Twelve Apostles, nevertheless we still refer to original preachers of the faith to foreign lands as apostles to those lands: Patrick as the apostle of Ireland, Boniface of Germany, Cyril and Methodius apostles to the Slavs. Nevertheless, there is also in the New Testament a noticeable narrowing of the term "apostle" to designate a very limited and historic group. More precisely, look at the requirements set forth in Acts 1:21-23 for the selection of a replacement for Judas: "So one of the men who have accompanied us during all the time that the Lord Jesus went in and out among us, beginning from the baptism of John until the day when he was taken up from us — one of these men must become with us a witness to his resurrection." And thus according to these criteria Paul's claim to having been a witness to the resurrection in his encounter with Jesus on the road to Damascus would not qualify him for the title of "apostle", which is never given Paul in the Acts of the Apostles. No doubt this narrowing of the definition of an apostle was a response to the fact that not a few of those who were claiming the title were spreading false teachings. But what must also be seen is that in the Acts of the Apostles not only is the title of "apostle" limited to the Twelve but the Twelve function now not so much as missionaries but as the corporate leadership of the Church headquartered at Jerusalem. Indeed, the apostles seem to become institutionalized, making corporate decisions for the whole community. When a crisis arose among the disciples of Christ at Jerusalem, we are told in Acts 6:2-3:

> The twelve summoned the body of the disciples and said, "It is not right that we should give up preaching the word of God to serve tables. Therefore, brethren, pick out from among you seven men of good repute, full of the Spirit of wisdom, whom we may appoint to this duty."

But not only do the apostles summon the disciples at Jerusalem and give direction to them but they also exercise oversight of the growing Christian mission and, indeed supply certain ministries that apparently only the apostles can provide as in Acts 8:14-16:

> Now when the apostles at Jerusalem heard that Samaria had received the word of God, they sent to them Peter and John, who came down and prayed for them that they might receive the Holy Spirit; for it had not yet fallen on any of them, but they had only been baptized in the name of the Lord Jesus.

When disagreement threatens to tear apart the Christian community at Antioch, that community turns to the "apostles and elders" in Jerusalem for a resolution of the issue. Of this we are told in Acts 15:1-2:

> But some men came down from Judea and were teaching the brethren, "Unless you are circumcised according to the custom of Moses, you cannot be saved." And when Paul and Barnabas had no small dissension and debate with them, Paul and Barnabas and some of the others were appointed to go up to Jerusalem to the apostles and the elders about this question.

Moreover, when "the apostles and elders" make a decision they invoke the authority of none less than the Holy Spirit as the motivator of their decision. For example, in response to the conflict at Antioch, the apostles and elders at Jerusalem send a letter saying in Acts 15:28, "For it has seemed good to the Holy Spirit and to us." And Paul himself when asserting his authority as an apostle over and against other ministries in 1 Corinthians 14:37, invests his directives with a similar awesome weight: "If anyone thinks that he is a prophet or spiritual person, he should recognize that what I am writing to you is a commandment."

We see this institutionalized character of the apostles even more when we look at the post-biblical literature of the early

Church, the literature from the so-called sub-apostolic period, the period after the death of the last apostle and the initial preaching of the Gospel. In this regard, we do well to look first at a work called the *First Letter of Clement to the Church at Corinth*.

This was written from Rome in the early '90's, that is, just about the time of the last written work of the New Testament, the Book of Revelation. The author, one Clement, appears to be one of the principal leaders of the Church at Rome, perhaps even its chief overseer (*episkopos*). In this letter he writes to the Church at Corinth attempting to intervene in a conflict that is dividing the community there. The occasion of the letter is internal strife in the Church at Corinth. More precisely what some have described as "sedition against presbyters," that is, the rejection of presiding elders. That a Roman Church leader would presume to intervene in the affairs of the Church at Corinth can be explained with regard to the fact that Paul, who had founded the Christian community at Corinth, spent his final days in Rome and thus perhaps Church leaders at Rome would feel a special solicitude for that particular sister Church. However, it should be noted that when Clement writes to Corinth he calls to their attention not simply the historic legacy of Paul at Rome but also that of Peter. In 1 Clement 4, he has been writing about Old Testament leaders whose authority was challenged out of jealousy. Then in 1 Clement 5:1-6 he says:

> But, to cease from the example of old time, let us come to those who contended in the days nearest to us; let us take the noble examples of our own generation. Through jealousy and envy the greatest and most righteous pillars of the Church were persecuted and contended unto death. Let us set before our eyes the good apostles: Peter, who because of unrighteous jealousy suffered not one or two but many trials, and having thus given his testimony went to the glorious place which was his due. Through jealousy and strife Paul showed the way to the prize of endurance.

> Indeed, this passage contains the first mention of apostles,

"good apostles" (*agathous apostolous*). One cannot help but wonder if here Clement is doing something similar to what we saw Paul did in 1 Corinthians with the terms "pseudo apostles" and "super apostles." That is, does Clement's language here suggest there it was the jealousy of "bad apostles" that sought to undermine the leadership of both Peter and Paul? But for our interests the more important reference in this letter occurs in 1 Clement 42:1-4 where Clement treats of the way in which the witness of the apostles was passed on:

> The apostles received the Gospel for us from the Lord Jesus Christ. Jesus the Christ was sent from God. The Christ therefore is from God and the apostles from the Christ. In both ways, then, they were in accordance with the appointed order of God's will. Having therefore received their commands, and being fully assured by the resurrection of our Lord Jesus Christ, and with faith confirmed by the word of God, they went forth in the assurance of the Holy Spirit preaching the good news that the Kingdom of God is coming. They preached from district to district, and from city to city, and they appointed their first converts, testing them by the Spirit, to be bishops and deacons of the future believers.

In 1 Clement 44:1-3, the author goes on to add:

> Our apostles also knew through our Lord Jesus Christ that there would be strife for the title of bishop. For this cause, therefore, since they had received perfect foreknowledge, they appointed those who have been already mentioned, and afterwards added the codicil that if they should fall asleep, other approved men should succeed to their ministry. We consider therefore that it is not just to remove from their ministry those who were appointed by them, or later on by other eminent men, with the consent of the whole Church, and have ministered to the flock of Christ without blame, humbly, peaceably, and disinterestedly, and for many years have received a universally favorable testimony.

This is what is called the concept of apostolic succession in ministry, which is given classic expression in a somewhat later figure. The more important witness for our interests is that of Irenaeus of Lyons who makes much of the idea of an apostolic Church.

Irenaeus is an interesting figure for many reasons. For one, he has a link with the first generation of Jesus' disciples. That is, he was born in Asia Minor about the year 144, probably at Smyrna, and in a letter Irenaeus tells us that in his early youth he had listened to sermons by the bishop of Smyrna, Polycarp, who had personally known and learned from the apostle John and others who had seen Jesus of Nazareth. Though born and raised in Smyrna, Irenaeus moved to southern France and when we encounter him he is a presbyter of the Church of Lyons and battling a contemporary religious movement which historians have come to call "gnosticism." This word "gnosticism" is from the Greek word *gnosis* which means "knowledge." And this refers to the fact that in the first century of the Christian era, there arose certain men who claimed to have *special knowledge* about salvation in Christ, knowledge which they had derived from either secret sources or divine inspiration, further knowledge than was provided us by the Jewish scripture or the literature that was then being read in Christian assemblies as Christian scripture. For example, the three principal Christian Gnostics we know of are Valentinus, Basilides and Marcion. Basilides was a Greek theologian who taught at Alexandria, Egypt ca. 125-150 A.D. He claimed his special knowledge was derived from St. Peter and St. Matthias. Valentinus, a brilliant teacher and orator, was an Egyptian who taught philosophy at Rome from ca. 136 to ca. 165. His teaching was a strange mixture of Christianity and Platonic and Pythagorean philosophy along with Hellenistic religious myths. However, his disciples insisted the novelties in Valentinus' version of Christianity came from a very reliable source, one Theodis, a pupil of St. Paul, under whom Valentinus had studied. Marcion claimed his source of special knowledge was none other than the Holy Spirit himself. In response to these Gnostic claims, Irenaeus wrote his *Against Heresies*. It appears to have been written over several years during the papacy of Eleutherus at Rome which was 174-189.

Irenaeus in the preface to his *Against Heresies* points out how the fact that these Gnostic teachers boasted of secret sources made them particularly difficult to refute:

> Inasmuch as certain men have set the truth aside, and bring in lying words and vain genealogies, which, as the apostle says, "minister questions rather than godly edifying which is in faith" [1 Tm 1:4], and by means of their craftily-constructed plausibilities draw away the minds of the inexperienced and take them captive.... Error, indeed, is never set forth in its naked deformity, lest, being thus exposed, it should at once be detected. But it is craftily decked out in an attractive dress, so as, by its outward form, to make it appear to the inexperienced (ridiculous as the expression may seem) more true than the truth itself. A clever imitation in glass casts contempt, as it were, on that precious jewel the emerald (which is most highly esteemed by some), unless it come under the eye of one able to test and expose the counterfeit.

In response to such a situation Irenaeus advised his readers to trust only those Christian teachers who can historically demonstrate the pedigree of their teaching authority, who can trace their lineage:

> It is within the power of all, therefore, in every Church who may wish to see the truth, to contemplate clearly the tradition of the apostles manifested throughout the whole world, and we are in a position to reckon up those who were by the apostles instituted bishops in the Churches, and the succession of these men to our own times: those who were by the apostles neither taught nor knew of anything like what these heretics rave about. For if the apostles had known hidden mysteries, which they were in the habit of imparting to "the perfect," apart and privily from the rest, they would have delivered them

especially to those to whom they were also committing the Churches themselves. For they were desirous that these men should be perfect and blameless in all things, whom also they were leaving behind as their successors, delivering up their own place of government to these men. (III.3.1)

And then in the very next paragraph as illustration he says:

Since, however, it would be very tedious, in such a volume as this, to reckon up the successions of all the churches, we do put to confusion all those who, in whatever manner, whether by an evil self-pleasing, by vainglory, or by blindness and perverse opinion, assemble in unauthorized meetings; we do this, I say, by indicating that tradition derived from the apostles, of the very great, the very ancient, and universally known Church founded and organized at Rome by the two most glorious apostles, Peter and Paul; as also by pointing out the faith preached to men, which, comes down to our time by means of the successions of the bishops.

However, we must also consider the witness of Tertullian because he introduces a further nuance into this concept of apostolicity, not so much historical succession in ministry but continuity in doctrine or thought.

Quintus Septimus Florens Tertullianus (ca. 155-230), known to us today simply as Tertullian, was born in Carthage in Roman North Africa of a pagan family but he converted to Christianity in middle age and became an ardent, enthusiastic Christian. There is debate as to whether he was a professional lawyer, but there can be no doubt he was an accomplished rhetorician with a considerable knowledge of the terms and procedures of Roman law. He employed these in his apologetic defense of Christianity. We see something of this in the very title of the literary work of his which concerns us here. In the year 258, he produced a work called *De praescriptione hereticorum*, in English, *The Prescription of Heretics*. The "prescription" in the title is a technical legal term for what we would call today a demurrer or formal objection. Tertullian like Clement and Irenaeus invokes the memory of the historic preaching of the apostles and their founding of various churches. In Chapter XX he says of the Eleven:

> Having... chosen Matthias by lot as the twelfth, into the place of Judas, they obtained the promised power of the Holy Spirit for the gift of miracles and of utterance; and after first bearing witness to the faith in Jesus Christ throughout Judea, and founding churches there, they next went forth in to the world and preached the same doctrine of the same faith to the nations. They then in like manner founded churches in every city, from which all the other churches, one after another, derived the tradition of the faith, and the seeds of doctrine, and are every day deriving them, that they may become churches. Indeed, it is on this account only that they will be able to deem themselves apostolic, as being the offspring of apostolic churches. Every sort of thing must necessarily revert to its original for its classification. Therefore the churches, although they are so many and so great, comprise but the one primitive Church, founded by the apostles, from which they all spring. In this way all are primitive and all are apostolic.

But notice how there is no reference to authoritative teachers, simply to authoritative churches and doctrine. The emphasis upon apostolic doctrine is made even clearer in the very next chapter of Tertullian's *The Prescription of Heretics*, Chapter XXI:

> Now what that was which they preached — in other words, what it was which Christ revealed to them — can be proved in no other way than by those very churches which the apostles founded in person, by declaring the Gospel to them directly themselves, both *viva voce* as the phrase is, and subsequently by their epistles. If, then, these things are so, it is in the same degree manifest that all doctrine which agrees with the apostolic churches — those moulds and original sources of the faith must

be reckoned for truth, as undoubtedly containing that which the (said) churches received from the apostles, the apostles from Christ, Christ from God. Whereas all doctrine must be prejudged as false which savors of contrariety to the truth of the churches and apostles of Christ and God, it remains, then, that we demonstrate whether this doctrine of ours, of which we have now given the rules, has its origin in the tradition of the apostles, and whether all other doctrines do not *ipso facto* proceed from falsehood. We hold communion with the apostolic churches because our doctrine is in no respect different from theirs. ~~our doctrine is the same as their~~

These two methods of explaining how a Church is apostolic still divide Christian assemblies to this day. The Catholic and Orthodox insist on apostolic succession in ministry while those Christian assemblies that stem from the Protestant Reformation insist on apostolic succession in doctrine.

Further Reading

John J. Burkhard's *Apostolicity Then and Now: An Ecumenical Church in a Postmodern World* (Liturgical Press, 2004).

Joseph Ratzinger's "The Key Question in the Catholic-Protestant Dialogue: Tradition and *Successio Apostolica*," in *Principles of Catholic Theology* (San Francisco: Ignatius Press, 1987), pp. 239-284.

In Walter Kasper's *Leadership in the Church* translated by B. McNeil (New York: Crossroad, 2003), Chapter 4, "The Apostolic Succession: An Ecumenical Problem," 114-143.

CHAPTER 14

The Church is a Communion

That the Church is a communion is a major theme in modern ecclesiology or theology of the Church. But this theme has deep biblical and historical roots.

Our English word "communion" is derived from the Latin *communio* which in turn was the Latin Vulgate word used to translate a New Testament Greek word *koinonia* where it means "sharing or participation."

No doubt for most people today this word "communion" has primarily a sacramental, indeed, Eucharistic meaning. And, no doubt, in the New Testament this is indeed one of its principal meanings. For example, in the First Letter to the Church at Corinth 10:16, Paul uses the word *koinonia* to refer to sacramental communion in the Eucharist:

> The cup of blessing which we bless, is it not a participation [*koinonia*] in the blood of Christ? The bread which we break, is it not a participation [*koinonia*] in the body of Christ?

But that the word "communion" can also refer to kinds of sharing other than the sacramental may be seen from another familiar usage. No doubt, many people have heard the phrase from the Apostles' Creed, "We believe in the Holy Spirit, the Holy Catholic Church, *the communion of saints,* the forgiveness of sins, the resurrection of the body, and life everlasting." Indeed, in the New Testament, *koinonia/communio* is used to refer to several other kinds of sharing besides the Eucharist. For example, there is the sharing of material things as when Paul, in Romans 15:26, uses the word *koinonia* to refer to financial assistance provided by one Christian community for another: "For Macedonia and Achaia have been pleased to make some contribution [*koinonia*] for the poor among the saints at Jerusalem." In Galatians 6:6, Paul uses *koinonia* in its verbal form to express not charitable assistance but the thoughtful remuneration or reward of a catechist by his or her catechumen: "Let him who is taught the word share [*koinoneito*] all good things with him who teaches."

Then there are those times in the New Testament when "communion" is used to refer to social fellowship. For example, in Acts 2:42, it is used in a very general sense to describe the common life in general of the first Christian community in Jerusalem: "And they devoted themselves to the apostles' teaching and fellowship [*koinonia*], to the breaking of bread and the prayers." As to precisely what forms this fellowship or social sharing could take we have the example of Galatians 2:9. In this passage it is not financial assistance but approval and encouragement that are shared among the brethren, as Paul tells us how "James and Cephas and John, who were reputed to be pillars, gave to me and Barnabas the right hand of fellowship [*koinonias*]."

However, in addition to material and social sharing, there are also several different forms of spiritual sharing. In the Epistle to the Philippians 3:8-10, it is the trials and tribulations of life that are seen as a sort of mystical sharing in the sufferings of Christ to which Paul gives particularly eloquent expression:

> Indeed I count everything as loss because of the surpassing worth of knowing Christ Jesus my Lord. For his sake I have suffered the loss of all things and count them as refuse in order that I may gain Christ and be found in him, not having a righteousness of my own, based on law, but that which is through faith in Christ, the righteousness from God that depends on faith; that I may know him and the power of his resurrection, and may share [*koinonia*] his sufferings, becoming like him in his death.

In the concluding line of the Second Letter to the Corinthians 13:14, it is communion with the Holy Spirit: "The grace of the Lord Jesus Christ and the love of God and the fellowship [*koinonia*] of the Holy Spirit be with you all." The phrase here, "the fellowship of the Holy Spirit," is most probably a reference to the common baptism which they all share.

In 1 John 1:3, it is communion with the Father and the Son: "That which we have seen and heard we proclaim also to you, so that you may have fellowship [*koinonian*] with us; and our fellowship [*koinonia*] is with the Father and with his Son Jesus Christ."

But there is yet another thing which we must see regarding the communion — spiritual, material and social — that is set forth in the New Testament. And that is the fact that it has what I would like to call certain parameters. There is both the extent and the limits of communion and fellowship in the New Testament. Paradoxically, these parameters are at once both larger than we might imagine and yet at the same time Christian fellowship is not without its inherent or essential limitations. As already suggested in the introduction to this chapter, there are New Testament passages which suggest that the bonds of communion and fellowship go beyond this world to include the dead. But what also must be seen is that Christian communion and fellowship even in this world has its limits, that is, fellowship can be both transgressed and lost. And, moreover, fellowship in Christ or in the Holy Spirit necessarily excludes certain other fellowships.

The limits of communion and fellowship in the New Testament are seen in two sets of passages, one dealing with moral behavior, the other with admission to the Table of the Lord, the Eucharist.

The passages regarding moral behavior make it clear that communion with Christ excludes other types of fellowship, for example, with prostitutes as in 1 Corinthians 6:15-18:

Do you not know that your bodies are members of Christ? Shall I therefore take the members of Christ and make them members of a prostitute? Never! Do you not know that he who joins himself to a prostitute becomes

> one body with her? For, as it is written, "The two shall
> become one." But he who is united to the Lord becomes
> one spirit with him. Shun immorality.

And indeed it is such teaching that leads effectively to a doctrine
of excommunication. We see this in Paul's First Letter to the
Church at Corinth. In 1 Corinthians 5:1-5, Paul addresses a current moral problem in that community, an incidence of incest:

> It is actually reported that there is immorality among
> you, and of a kind that is not found even among pagans;
> for a man is living with his father's wife. And you are
> arrogant! Ought you not rather to mourn? Let him who
> has done this be removed from among you.
>
> For though absent in body I am present in spirit, and
> as if present, I have already pronounced judgment in the
> name of the Lord Jesus on the man who has done such
> a thing. When you are assembled, and my spirit is pres-
> ent, with the power of our Lord Jesus, you are to deliver
> this man to Satan for the destruction of the flesh that his
> spirit may be saved in the day of the Lord Jesus.

Some commentators have suggested that because no mention
at all is made of the woman's husband, the problem here is not
just incest but perhaps even murder. Two paragraphs later Paul
makes it clear that his action in excommunicating that fellow
was neither a one time thing nor just permitted to him, to Paul,
an apostle alone; rather it is a duty upon the whole community
to pass judgment on the worthiness of its members. For as he
says in 1 Corinthians 5:9-13:

> I wrote you in my letter not to associate with immoral
> men; not at all meaning the immoral of this world, or the
> greedy and robbers, or idolaters, since then you would
> need to go out of the world. But rather I wrote to you not
> to associate with any one who bears the name of brother
> if he is guilty of immorality or greed, or is an idolater,
> reviler, drunkard, or robber — not even to eat with such
> a one. For what have I to do with judging outsiders? Is

it not those inside the Church whom you are to judge? God judges those outside. "Drive out the wicked person from among you."

Later in this same letter to the Corinthians, Paul addresses yet another pastoral problem in the Church at Corinth that touches upon the doctrine of communion, fellowship, *koinonia*. In 1 Corinthians 11:27-29, he warns against casual communion in the Eucharist:

> Whoever, therefore, eats the bread or drinks the cup of the Lord in an unworthy manner will be guilty of profaning the body and blood of the Lord. Let a man examine himself, and so eat of the bread and drink of the cup. For any one who eats and drinks without discerning the body eats and drinks judgment upon himself.

As for the question of the extent of fellowship and communion, Catholic Christianity has long insisted that the spiritual communion of Christians goes far beyond the grave. For example, Chapter VII of the Second Vatican Council's Dogmatic Constitution on the Church, *Lumen gentium*, is entitled, "The Eschatological Nature of the Pilgrim Church and Her Union with the Heavenly Church." The Council Fathers opted for the image of the Church as a pilgrim precisely because it conveys the idea of the Church as a work in progress which will only attain its perfection in the glory of heaven. Thus, while the kingdom of heaven has indeed been inaugurated, it has yet to reach its full realization which will only be at the end of time. But meanwhile "Christ, having been lifted up from the earth, is drawing all men to himself." And one of the ways he does this is by drawing us into a communion that includes both the living and the dead. The Council in article 49 of *Lumen gentium* expresses this in these words:

> When the Lord comes in His majesty and all the angels with Him (cf. Mt 25:31), death will be destroyed and all things will be subject to Him (cf. 1 Cor 15:26-27). Mean-

while some of His disciples are exiles on earth. Some have finished with this life and are being purified. Others are in glory, beholding "clearly God Himself triune and one, as He is."

But in various ways and degrees we all partake in the same love for God and neighbor, and all sing the same hymn of glory to our God. For all who belong to Christ, having His Spirit, form one Church, and cleave together in Him (cf. Eph 4:16). Therefore the union of the wayfarers with the brethren who have gone to sleep in the peace of Christ is not in the least interrupted. On the contrary, according to the perennial faith of the Church, it is strengthened through the exchanging of spiritual goods.

As for the concept of our communion with the saints in heaven: devotion to the saints and their agency in the lives of the brethren on earth is perhaps best understood in terms of the biblical teaching about good example and salutary imitation. Saint Paul several times recommends imitation. Sometimes he recommends imitation of himself as in Philippians 3:17, "Brethren, join in imitating me, and mark those who so live as you have an example in us." In 1 Thessalonians 1:5-7 he celebrates not only the example set by himself and the Lord but also encourages his converts to set a good example for others to imitate:

> You know what kind of men we proved to be among you for your sake. And you became imitators of us and of the Lord, for you received the word in much affliction, with joy inspired by the Holy Spirit; so that you became an example to all the believers in Macedonia and Achaia.

But the author of the Epistle to the Hebrews gives the example of the model provided us by the dead, for we are told in Hebrews 13:7: "Remember your leaders, those who spoke to you the word of God; consider the outcome of their life, and imitate their faith." And he follows up his directive in Hebrews 12:14, "Strive for peace with all men, and for the holiness without which no one will see the Lord," with a vision of the heavenly communion into which a Christian's baptism initiates us; for it has permitted us entry not just into the assembly of the faithful here on earth:

> But you have come to Mount Zion and to the city of the living God, the heavenly Jerusalem, and to innumerable angels in festal gathering, and to the assembly of *the firstborn who are enrolled in heaven,* and to a judge who is God of all, and to *the spirits of just men made perfect,* and to Jesus, the mediator of a new covenant, and to the sprinkled blood that speaks more graciously than the blood of Abel (Heb 12:22-24).

And surely this is a powerful and readily understandable way in which saints' lives do indeed inspire moral behavior. For example, Christian lawyers do well to study and imitate the moral probity of Saint Thomas More and moreover this is precisely the agency ascribed to the Blessed Virgin Mary in the liturgy when the collect prayer on her feast says, "May we imitate the life of the Blessed Virgin Mary." The dead do indeed continue to influence the lives of the living, and the living certainly do honor to the dead when they cultivate their memory by sincere imitation of their heroic lives. This is a sort of divine economy, a communion in such spiritual goods as "example" and "praise," goods that enrich the lives of all in the Church.

As for the intercession of the saints, in Jn 2:5, Mary intercedes with her Son on behalf of the married couple at whose wedding banquet the wine has run out. In 1 Cor 9, Paul urges the Corinthians to be generous to the poor in Macedonia, promising them that if they are generous, then those poor, whom he calls "the saints" (v. 12), will, in turn, pray for the Corinthians. In Rv 5:8 there is a reference to "the prayers of the saints" in heaven. And Rv 8:3-4 describes "the prayers of all the saints" in heaven as rising like incense before the throne of God.

And as for prayer and sacrifices for the dead, Augustine of Hippo's treatise *On Faith, Hope and Love,* is an *enchiridion* or handbook of the Christian faith written in 421-422 at the request of a layman named Laurentius. In Chapters 68-69 Augustine treats of a passage from Paul's First Letter to the Church at Corinth (3:10-15). Paul is talking about the "house of the Lord," that is the Christian community at Corinth which he founded, and of how after he himself laid the foundation other preachers have come and built upon it. After warning them, "Let each man take care how he builds upon it" in 1 Corinthians 3:12-15, Paul develops the Old Testament image of the last day as a fiery day of judgment:

> Now if any one builds on the foundation with gold, silver, precious stones, wood, hay, stubble — each man's work will become manifest; for the Day will disclose it, because it will be revealed with fire, and the fire will test what sort of work each one has done. If the work which any man has built on the foundation survives, he will receive a reward. If any man's work is burned up, he will suffer loss, though he himself will be saved, but only as through fire.

Augustine claims to find in this passage a distinction between the fire of judgment and the fire of purgation. And because of that Catholic tradition has long made use of this passage to support the idea of purgatory and prayers for the dead. Augustine in his *On the Care of the Dead*, written in 422 shortly after the completion of his handbook *On Faith, Hope and Love*, treats specifically of prayers for the dead. Moreover, it is interesting how a modern Protestant theologian, Paul Tillich, treats of this same idea in his systematic theology, suggesting how it might be an example of combining Catholic substance with Protestant principle. More precisely, in Paul Tillich's *Systematic Theology*, Volume III (Chicago, 1963), in the final section which is Part V, "History and the Kingdom of God," there is an essay entitled, "The Kingdom of God as the End of History." There, after treating of the individual person and his or her eternal destiny, Tillich insists there is a dynamic between universal and individual fulfillment. Therein he says:

> The Catholic doctrine which recommends prayer and
> sacrifice for the deceased is a powerful expression of
> belief in the unity of individual and universal destiny in
> Eternal Life. This element of truth should not be forgot-
> ten because of the many superstitions and abuses in the
> practical carrying out of the idea. (p. 418)

In conclusion, regarding our treatment here of the theme
of the Church as a communion: no doubt some of the above
quoted biblical passages need careful analysis before we can
understand and apply them to the contemporary situation of
the Church. For example, the doctrine of excommunication has
been at times abused. It is perhaps not so well known but the
fact is the concept of excommunication is not peculiar to Catholic Christianity but found strong expression in the teachings
of the Protestant Reformers. In Part Four of Calvin's *Institutes*,
Chapter 12 is entitled, "The Discipline of the Church: Its Chief
Use in Censures and Excommunication," and in the Dordrecht
Confession of April 21, 1631, a statement produced by a Dutch
Mennonite Conference held at Dordrecht, Holland, Article 16
is entitled "Of the Ecclesiastical Ban or Separation from the
Church," Article 17, "Of Shunning the Separated." All religious
traditions and most secular organizations provide some measure
for the expulsion of members for serious infractions. However,
in modern times most Protestant congregations have abandoned
excommunication. And even in the Catholic Church where there
is still a provision for it, in the most recent edition of the Code
of Canon Law (1983), excommunication is seen as principally
a "medicinal" procedure. That is, it is not the equivalent of dam-
nation. Moreover, in danger of death any priest even if deprived
of the faculties for hearing confessions can absolve from every
sin and excommunication (see article 1463 of the *Catechism of the
Catholic Church*). Thus it is best that all recognize the doctrine
of excommunication is a last, desperate measure and was never
intended as an ordinary means of discipline. Indeed, the current
Code of Canon Law cautions "a legislator is not to establish
censures, especially excommunication, except with the greatest

moderation and only for more serious offenses" (Canon 1318). In this regard it is worth considering once again the procedure advised by the Lord himself in Matthew 18:15-17:

> If your brother sins against you, go and tell him his fault, between you and him alone. If he listens to you, you have gained your brother. But if he does not listen, take one or two others along with you, that every word may be confirmed by the evidence of two or three witnesses. If he refuses to listen to them, tell it to the Church; and if he refuses to listen even to the Church, let him be to you as a Gentile and a tax collector.

Further Reading

Communio Sanctorum: The Church as the Communion of Saints; Bilateral working group of the German National Bishops' Conference and the Church Leadership of the United Evangelical Lutheran Church of Germany (Liturgical Press, 2005).

In Walter Kasper's *Theology and Church* (New York: Crossroad, 1989), Chapter VIII, "The Church as Communion: Reflections on the Guiding Ecclesiological Idea of the Second Vatican Council," 148-165.

In Jerome Hamer's *The Church is a Communion* (NY: Sheed and Ward, 1964), Part Three, "Communion in Itself and in its Various Modes of Expression," 159-213.

Philip Esler's *New Testament Theology: Communion and Community* (Augsburg Fortress, 2005).

Part II

THE CHURCH: ITS MISSION AND MINISTRIES

CHAPTER 15

The Mission of the Church:
Its Origin and Content

Our English word "mission" is derived from the classical Latin *missus,* which is the past participle of the verb *mittere* meaning "to send." In Middle Latin the word *missio* meant "task assigned." It seems the theological use of the word *missio* or mission first appeared in the writings of Ignatius of Loyola (ca. 1491-1556), the founder of that religious order popularly known as the Jesuits, and in the writings of Ignatius' successor in leadership of the Jesuits, one James Laynez (1512-65), the second Jesuit general. Loyola and Laynez both used the word *missio* or "mission" to describe the strategic assignment of Jesuits. But, it could be argued from the Bible that long before the Jesuits thought of using the word "mission" to describe, strategically, the task of their members, both the theme and method of strategic mission had arisen in Scripture, indeed both arose from Jesus himself. For example, in Matthew's Gospel there are two accounts of Jesus sending forth his disciples, his inner circle of "the Twelve" on strategic missions. The first reference is in Matthew 10:5-6, where we read: "These twelve Jesus sent out, charging them, 'Go nowhere among the gentiles, and enter no town of the Samaritans, but go rather to the lost sheep of the house of Israel.'" However, later in the Gospel according to Matthew, we hear Jesus assign yet another strategic but more extensive mission. In Matthew 28:18-20 we read:

> And Jesus came and said to them, "All authority in
> heaven and on earth has been given to me. Go therefore
> and make disciples of all nations, baptizing them in the
> name of the Father and of the Son and of the Holy Spirit,
> teaching them to observe all that I have commanded you;
> and lo, I am with you always, to the close of the age."

This passage from Matthew (note its parallels in Mk 16:15-16 and Lk 24:46-49) has become known as "The Great Missionary Mandate." Those who quote the Great Commission of Matthew 28:18-20 are correct in that it is certainly one of the sources of the mission of the Church. However, thoughtful people in the Church (exegetes and theologians) have found other reasons besides this one Bible passage, this one saying of Jesus as the foundation for the Church's mission.

An exegete might argue that this dramatic expression of mission in Christianity, this dynamic character of the Church whereby it has historically mounted huge efforts to spread itself abroad, can be explained by more than just a recourse to the words of Jesus in the New Testament. That is, a biblical scholar might argue that the missionary character of the Church resides not simply in the historic mandate of the Resurrected Christ but in the very nature of God himself as revealed in the Bible, the Old as well as New Testament. A student of the Bible could point to evidence that suggests the God of the Bible is a "sending God." For example, in Exodus 3:10 we hear God say to Moses, "I will send you to Pharaoh to lead my people, the Israelites, out of Egypt." In Isaiah 6:8, we hear the prophet remark, "Then I heard the voice of the Lord saying: 'Whom shall I send? Who will go for us?' 'Here I am, I said; Send me.'" In Luke 1:26, we are told, "The angel Gabriel was sent by God." In John 1:6, "There was a man named John sent by God." In John 20:21, Jesus tells his disciples, "As the Father has sent me, so I send you." Luke 10:1 describes how "the Lord appointed a further seventy-two and sent them in pairs." In John 14:36, Jesus speaks of "The Paraclete, the Holy Spirit whom the Father will send in my name." And Saint Paul in Romans 10:15 asks, "But how shall they preach unless they are sent?" And thus we see the God of the Bible has sent Moses, Isaiah, Gabriel, John the Baptist, Jesus, the Twelve, and a host of others most of whom we have not mentioned. From this one can conclude this is indeed a sending God, expansive in his very nature. He sends messengers, prophets, leaders, angels, his Son, their Spirit to his people and finally us into the world. Indeed, the closer the God of the Bible calls someone to himself, the farther he sends that person out. And thus one can reason that the Church, like its Maker, is innately ex-centric, outward bound, searching out, explorative, spreading itself abroad, so as to be as inclusive as possible, in-gathering, collecting and saving everything and everyone.

Dogmatic theologians, however, go even further and use Trinitarian theology to ferret out more and deeper implications regarding this image of the God of the Bible as expansive, inclusive, inviting, sending out even further those whom he calls ever nearer to himself. In Trinitarian theology, dogmatic theologians insist that Absolute Being (God) is different from Contingent Being (us) in that Absolute Being is relational in its very nature. Contingent beings like you and me, though we have the capacity for relating intimately with others, can often be isolated individuals. Indeed, most human beings appear to be inveterate individuals trapped within their subjectivity, struggling to relate to God and each other, always looking for community outside the self. But the doctrine of the Trinity insists God is pre-eminently personal, indeed, "communal" by nature, because there is a richness of mutuality and relationship within the one Absolute Being. These real relationships within God are called Father, Son and Holy Spirit. A dogmatic theologian would argue these relationships in the Trinity imply a justice, fellowship, wholeness and harmony of life pre-eminent within the Godhead. And thus the work or goal of the Church which claims to be an expression of the activity of God in redeeming this world should itself have the character of action towards justice, fellowship, wholeness and harmony of life.

So far, in this chapter we have been concerned to introduce the concept of the Church's mission and to speculate about the source of that idea. But now it is important that we treat more

fully of the content, goal or aim of that mission. It is obvious
from the very words of the great missionary mandate in Matthew 28:18-20 that the principal aim of the Christian mission
is to "make disciples of all nations." Our English word "disciple" comes from the Latin word *discipulus* meaning "pupil"
or "learner." Early in the history of the Church this Latin word
was used to translate the New Testament Greek word *mathetes*
which at its root means "learner" or "apprentice." The disciple,
as an adherent and follower of Jesus is a prominent figure in each
of the four Gospels. Indeed, the noun is used 261 times in the
Gospels and Acts of the Apostles. And, besides this noun, there
is a rich disciple-related vocabulary in the New Testament that
includes also the verbal form *matheteuein*, "to make disciples,"
and such cognate words as *summathetes*, "fellow disciples."
And so it is no exaggeration to say we are dealing here with
a major element of the Christian faith whose origin is rooted in
the historic ministry of Jesus himself. Now, while many cultures
exhibit the master/disciple, teacher/pupil relationship — Jewish
rabbis had disciples, Socrates had pupils — it is apparent that
discipleship to Jesus, while analogous to these other forms of
teacher/student or master/disciple relationships, has a peculiar
intensity. For example, Jesus appears to have demanded a much
more complete personal surrender to himself than any rabbinic
master or philosophical pedagogue demanded of his pupils or
disciples. Discipleship to Jesus entailed not just a separation
from family (Mt 10:27: "He who loves father or mother more
than me is not worthy of me") and livelihood or occupation (Lk
5:11: "They left everything and followed him"; also Mt 10:37), but
even an abandoning of the most sacred of family responsibilities (Mt 8:21-22: "Another of the disciples said to him, 'Lord, let
me first go and bury my father.' But Jesus said to him, 'Follow
me, and leave the dead to bury their own dead.'"). Moreover,
Jesus' call demands, not just a radical readjustment of social
responsibilities and material wealth (Lk 14:23), but also a radical personal conversion, a denial of self (Mk 8:34: "If any man
would come after me let him deny himself"; see also Mt 16:24;
Lk 9:23). All these make for what a modern disciple, Dietrich

Bonhoeffer, has aptly called *The Cost of Discipleship* (the title of his 1937 literary work).

But what must also be seen is that discipleship to Jesus meant not just radical personal allegiance to him but also initiation into a community of faith. The invitation to follow Jesus meant to enter into communion, intimate identity and unity, not only with the Master but with the rest of his disciples, to "love one another; even as I have loved you" (Jn 13:34). Indeed, Jesus taught that love of the brethren should be the most distinguishing mark of his disciples (Jn 13:35): "By this all men will know that you are my disciples, if you have love for one another." This love of the brethren includes not just the sharing of goods (Lk 6:30 and Lk 14:12-13) but also spiritual sharing. When Jesus' disciples pray, they say "*Our* Father" (Mt 6:9, *pater hemon*), not "*My* Father." Moreover, Jesus promises "Where two or three are gathered together in my name, there I am in your midst." This love includes not just companionship — Jesus sends his disciples forth two by two (Mk 6:7: "He... began to send them out two by two," and Lk 10:1: "He sent them on ahead of him, two by two," cf. Mk 11:1, 14:13; Mt 21:1), but correction and accountability. His disciples not only correct each other, and call each other to account (Mt 18:15: "If your brother sins against you, go and tell him his fault") but they forgive each other (Lk 17:3 "If your brother sins, rebuke him; and if he repents, forgive him"). And such forgiveness must know no end (Mt 18:21-22; Lk 17:4; Mk 11:25).

But there is yet a third distinctive character to Christian discipleship. For true discipleship to Jesus also includes the mandate to testimony, witness and proclamation (Mk 6:7-13; Lk 10:2-12). But what must be seen here is that this witness to the world cannot be just verbal — preaching and teaching are not enough; a true disciple of Christ witnesses also with good deeds. Jesus sends forth his disciples not only to preach with words but also to witness with impressive deeds, with the power to exorcise, that is, to heal human infirmities, to confirm his doctrine with miracles (Mt 10:1; Lk 10:1-20) to give a powerful sign that with the proclamation of the Gospel of Christ there begins the redemption not just of sinners but of this world, its restoration to a unity of purpose with the divine will. This means the mission of the Church is not completed by personal conversion and the establishment of a community of faith. There is yet another task that remains and that is a witness to the world that includes an attempt at the very transformation of society.

There are several biblical passages that witness to this. For example, in Luke 4:17-18 Jesus is portrayed as applying to himself the words of Isaiah: "The Spirit of the Lord is upon me, because he has anointed me to bring glad tidings to the poor. He has sent me to proclaim liberty to captives and recovery of sight to the blind, to let the oppressed go free." Jesus' words here should not be overly spiritualized so as to imply that it is only the poor in spirit whom he addresses or that he promises only a spiritual liberation or that the captivity and blindness he refers to are only spiritual. Indeed, if one looks carefully at the life and ministry of Jesus, one will quickly recognize that Jesus did not just preach and teach. He also healed, reconciled, raised up and set free the people whom he encountered (Mk 1:39). This means that the Church which is the prolongation of Jesus' presence, the Church which is now the Body of Christ in this world must beware of presenting an overly spiritualized Gospel, that is, one that offers spiritual comfort but no real concrete, existential relief. In our chapter on "the Church and the kingdom," we saw how Jesus did not simply preach preparation for the near coming of the kingdom tomorrow, but rather he insisted that the kingdom is now already breaking in upon us in at times very dramatic ways. Especially instructive in this regard is the story of Jesus' healing of the Gerasene demoniac in Mark 5:1-17:

> They came to the other side of the sea, to the country of the Gerasenes. And when he had come out of the boat, there met him out of the tombs a man with an unclean spirit, who lived among the tombs; and no one could bind him any more, even with a chain; for he had often been bound with fetters and chains, but the chains he wrenched apart, and the fetters he broke in pieces; and

no one had the strength to subdue him. Night and day among the tombs and on the mountains he was always crying out, and bruising himself with stones. And when he saw Jesus from afar, he ran and worshiped him and crying out with a loud voice, he said, "What have you to do with me, Jesus, Son of the Most High God? I adjure you by God, do not torment me." For he had said to him, "Come out of the man, you unclean spirit!" And Jesus asked him, "What is your name?" He replied, "My name is Legion; for we are many." And he begged him eagerly not to send them out of the country. Now a great herd of swine was feeding there on the hillside; and they begged him, "Send us to the swine, let us enter them." So he gave them leave. And the unclean spirits came out, and entered the swine; and the herd, numbering about two thousand, rushed down the steep bank into the sea and were drowned in the sea.

The herdsmen fled, and told it in the city and in the country. And people came to see what it was that had happened. And they came to Jesus, and saw the demoniac sitting there, clothed and in his right mind, the man who had had the legion; and they were afraid. And those who had seen told what had happened to the demoniac and to the swine. And they began to beg Jesus to depart from their neighborhood.

It is not difficult to understand why the people in that region "began to beg Jesus to depart from their neighborhood" for he had just ruined someone's livelihood, someone's flourishing economic enterprise. That is, this herd of about two thousand pigs represented a substantial investment. But the sense of this Gospel reading is that it cannot be "business as usual" when Jesus comes through a town. If the Gerasene demoniac's healing had to come at the cost of the destruction of a dubious economy, then so be it. I say "dubious economy" because pig farming would have been looked upon by devout Jews with the same attitude that today we regard the drug trade. But the point I am trying to make is that witness to the Gospel of Christ will at times entail challenges to the economic and social status quo, challenges that might be in some measure revolutionary. I think anyone who looks at the history of the Christian mission will see that the Church has never simply preached faith, hope and love to the peoples it sought to evangelize. It has also undertaken for these same peoples education efforts (the founding of schools), provision for health care (the creation of medical dispensaries, the teaching of sanitation methods), and even economic development (instruction in planting methods and systems of irrigation) that could work to transform their individual lives and indeed their whole culture or society.

And thus, we can sum up the arguments so far as implying that a truly balanced notion of the mission of the Church must include three things: a direct appeal to each human heart (the conversion of individual lives), the creation of a community of faith, and an effective witness to the world that aims at its transformation. But there are some further things that need to be said about these three goals.

As for repentance or the conversion of hearts: this is a formidable, perhaps never-ending task because every human being must be saved from his or her radical preoccupation with self, and blindness to the reality of eternal life. There is an egocentricity that corrupts all human efforts, even the most noble. The Gospel saves us from that by making clear to us the importance of two significant others in our lives: God and our neighbor. The Gospel helps us overcome this egocentricity by making us adore someone other than ourselves, namely God. But this kind of conversion is not easily achieved, and rarely, if ever, is it perfectly achieved. In one sense discipleship to Jesus is broadly inclusive. No doubt, Jesus called people into fellowship with him and each other regardless of social, religious, and ethnic background or gender. However, there are discernible varying degrees of discipleship to Jesus. In this regard, the saying "many are called, but few are chosen" (Mt 22:14) is perhaps revelatory. More precisely, in some cases discipleship to Jesus was based upon a personal call, indeed a summons to discipleship (Mk 1:16-20, 2:13f.; Lk 9:59-62). But there are also some instances of persons volunteering their allegiance and discipleship to Jesus (Lk 9:57ff). Certainly the "large crowd" of disciples referred to in Luke 6:17, 19:37 and John 6:60, suggests a number larger than would be gathered by personal invitation. Also we must take account of the fact that some of Jesus' disciples, though initially attracted to him and his teaching eventually decided to drop out (Mk 12:22; Jn 6:66), some, though personally instructed by him, denied him and at least one betrayed him (Mk 14:12). In the early Church we find imperfectly instructed disciples like the eloquent preacher Apollos who had never even heard of Christian baptism (Acts 19:1-5) or other preachers who preach out of such dubious motives as personal profit (1 Th 2:5; 2 Cor 2:17) or even envy or rivalry (Ph 1:15). This initial broad inclusiveness of the invitation to Christian discipleship followed by increasing challenges to fidelity makes for some amazing ironies. For example, while the Gospels supply us with no accounts of the direct call of women disciples, the apparently voluntary discipleship of these women proved more enduring than that of the men Jesus personally recruited; for the number of women who followed Jesus all the way to the cross and stayed with him till he died far exceeded the number of male disciples. In John 19:25-26 the ratio is three women to one male. The contrast appears even greater in Mark 15:40-41 and Matthew 27:55-56.

As for the second task, integration into a community of faith: one can argue that initiation into the community of faith, that is Christian discipleship, includes more than just the fraternal support, correction and forgiveness we have already mentioned. What is also required is a regular, even programmatic, Christian assembly, programmatic structures for the public celebration of both word and sacraments. That is, provision must be made for exposition of the whole Gospel and not just its partial appropriation and at some point this regular and programmatic Christian assembly must give a clear sign that it is more than just a Bible study but a profound communion, it must demonstrate the kind of dramatically significant "table fellowship" that later theology will come to call *eucharistia*. Let me elaborate these two points.

As for a regular even programmatic Christian assembly, it is important that we recognize that the Christian life is not complete with personal conversion to the Lord; it is not enough simply to read the Scriptures on one's own each day and pray by oneself to the Lord. Such laudable and pious practices when pursued independently of the larger Christian community can lead to a dangerously myopic view of one's self and the Word of salvation. Thus it is important that the individual be confronted periodically and methodically by the preached word, that is, provision must be made so that he or she can gather periodically and regularly with the rest of the community, with the rest of the Body of Christ, to hear all the major themes of Scripture publicly proclaimed, read aloud in the presence of all, and authoritatively addressed (preached upon by people who themselves have undergone a formal preparation both intellectual and spiritual, part of which preparation is a sufficient knowledge of the apostolic preaching). But these preachers must also employ a schedule of biblical readings that will expose the congregation to and maybe even force the preacher to address all the major themes of the Gospel, that is, the full Gospel, the cross as well as the resurrection, the cost of discipleship as well as the general invitation, Jesus' warnings and admonitions as well as his blessings and promises. We can observe this programmatic character even in the Jewish synagogue assembly of Jesus' time. For example, in Luke 4:16-20, we are told the story of how during Jesus' public ministry he returned to his home town of Nazareth and on the Sabbath day attended the local synagogue. Verse 17 informs us that when Jesus stood up to read "there was given to him the book of the prophet Isaiah." This is a reference to the fact that in all synagogues of the day there was a set program of readings. Jesus had not determined ahead of time to read from Isaiah, the text was handed to him as the assigned reading for the day. Early in its history the Church developed a comparable schedule of readings which is the forerunner of the lectionary employed by many Lutheran, Anglican, Methodist, Presbyterian, Orthodox and Catholic Christians today. Such an institutional structure, far from being a denial of freedom, works to protect the individual and the congregation from the demagoguery of preachers who emphasize one Gospel theme to the neglect of another.

As for the concept of "table fellowship" as obligatory memorial: Jesus was powerful not only in word but also in deed. And among his significant deeds were not just healing miracles but also prophetic signs. An especially important prophetic sign was his eating and drinking with sinners. This eating and drinking with sinners took many different forms in his public ministry — the multiplication of loaves on a Galilean hillside, his dining with the tax collector Zacchaeus, with the tax collector Levi (Mk 2:14-15), with Simon the leper (Mk 14:3), eating the Passover with his disciples (Mk 14:14). Indeed, it was so prominent a part of his ministry that it became a tag for identifying him as in "The Son of Man came eating and drinking" (Mt 11:19; cf. Lk 7:34). But it would be naïve to interpret this as evidence that Jesus was a *bon vivant;* rather the evidence strongly suggests he employed these meals as a teaching device, a prophetic parable in action, a truly potent, and as much real as figurative, sign of the eternal banquet that is the kingdom. For example, see the extended parables of the great banquet in Luke 14 and Matthew 22. Moreover, there is considerable evidence that at Jesus' final meal with his disciples this becomes a mandate. And thus at some point in the worship service of a Christian assembly, the Scripture readings must be put aside and the preaching stop so that the assembly can break bread and share wine not only in memory of Christ but as a visible expression, however humble, of the eschatological banquet.

Finally, as for the idea that the Church's mission consists not only of efforts toward personal conversion and the creation of a community of faith but also of effective witness in the world to the reality of the kingdom, we must see there is a logical order to these three constituent parts of the Church's mission. One way of teaching this is to point out that, as with Jesus, in the mission of the Church, action toward justice usually follows upon the preaching as a confirmation of the truth of the former. For example, in the account of the healing of a paralytic in Mark 2:1-12 (parallels

Lk 5:17-26; Mt 9:1-8), Jesus' first response to the man is to tell him, "My son, your sins are forgiven" (verse 5). It is only when Jesus' authority to do such is challenged that Jesus goes on to physically heal the man. And his language makes clear that the healing is a demonstration of his spiritual power: "That you may know that the Son of Man has authority on earth to forgive sins" — he said to the paralytic — "I say to you, rise, take up your pallet and go home" (verses 10-11)). And thus I want to insist here that the content of the Church's mission consists of three things: personal conversion, establishment of community, and transformation of society. Moreover, while they should be pursued simultaneously, there is yet something of a logical priority to these tasks at least in terms of effectiveness.

However, what has happened in modern times is that human means for technological, agricultural, industrial and social development and progress have attained such effectiveness that they now threaten the delicate balance that ought to exist between the evangelical and social elements in the proclamation of the Gospel. Indeed, we have come to a point where some Christians are convinced that the Gospel can best function as the rationale for a political or social liberation which has no identifiably religious content. It was precisely this situation which Pope Paul VI addressed when he said in his Apostolic Exhortation of December 8, 1975, *Evangelii nuntiandi,* article 18:

> For the Church, evangelizing means bringing the Good News into all the strata of humanity, and through its influence transforming all humanity from within and making it new: "Now I am making the whole of creation new" (Rv 21:5). But there is no new humanity if there are not first of all new persons renewed by Baptism and by lives lived according to the Gospel. The purpose of evangelization is therefore precisely this interior change; and if it had to be expressed in one sentence the best way of stating it would be to say that the Church evangelizes when she seeks to convert, solely through the divine power of the Message she proclaims, both the personal and collective consciences of people, the activities in

which they engage, and the lives and concrete milieux
which are theirs.

This means it must be seen: Christianity brings to the world's
often only feeble and dimly perceived struggle for justice,
peace and dignity, a unique vision (the parousia) and unique
means (the sacraments). Attempts at social development, work
for justice apart from this primary conversion will always be
superficial and ultimately self-defeating wrestling with the
secondary external manifestations of enslavement which are
poverty, injustice, *et cetera*. The problem with some liberation
theology is that it makes the Gospel a servant for direct social
or political programs or aims. But we must remember Jesus was
not a political revolutionary. Isaiah's description of the peaceful
ministry of the suffering servant, "a bruised reed he will not
break, and a dimly burning wick he will not quench" (Is 42:1-4)
is aptly applied by Matthew to describe the peaceful ministry
of Jesus (Mt 12:19-20). His is a peaceful if true revolution. While
Christianity promises human fulfillment and works hard toward
achieving that goal, it does not guarantee its final realization in
this world. In fact, it could be argued that in large measure Christianity is not problem-solving. It is not the ultimate panacea for
every human ill. The Christian God is not some great Buffered
Aspirin in the sky; rather Christianity has more traditionally
been problem-recognizing and accepting — for example, the
unwanted pregnancy. At times Christianity teaches us how to
make a virtue of living with problems that both God and nature
seem to pose as unsolvable.

Finally, one must also have a realistic view of the goals of
the Christian mission. The Church's mission will never be easily
fulfilled. It will always encounter the opposition of sinful men.
As the Gospel says, "They loved the darkness more" (Jn 3:19).
Something within us, namely sin, does not want us to be free,
does not want to enter the light of day. Something within us
holds on desperately and dearly to enslavement. In Luke 10:10,
we hear Jesus say: "If the people of any town you enter do not
welcome you, go into its streets and say, 'We shake the dust of

this town from our feet as testimony against you.'" But even here one must be careful. True Jesus says in Mark 16:15-18, "Go into the whole world and proclaim the gospel to every creature. Whoever believes and is baptized will be saved; whoever does not believe will be condemned." But the point here is not that the non-baptized are necessarily condemned to hell but rather that when the Gospel is adequately presented it is irresistible Good News to which one cannot help but respond affirmatively. Thus a negative response is an ambiguous sign pointing to one of two possible causes. Indifference to the Gospel message may be due to closed-mindedness and hardness of heart, spiritual deafness on the part of the audience. But it also might be due to inadequate preaching or unconvincing witness to the Gospel.

Whatever its precise origin, this missionary character of the Christian faith has left a dramatic mark on Christian and indeed world history. That is, Christian missionaries have for almost two thousand years gone forth and preached the Gospel in every land on earth and often greatly transformed the lands and cultures they have encountered. Indeed, one could make the argument that one of the things that distinguish Christianity from other religions is this, its emphatically missionary character. For example, a landmark in the study of the Christian missions is Kenneth Scott Latourette's seven-volume *A History of the Expansion of Christianity.* Latourette published this mammoth work in the years 1937–1945. To this day it stands as a masterly study. Indeed, some might argue it is the major work in the history of the missions, covering six continents, twenty centuries, and all the historic expressions of the Christian faith, Catholic, Protestant, Orthodox, Evangelical. There is no comparable study of Buddhist, Hindu, Jewish, Muslim missions. Moreover, one might argue this is not simply a scholarly lacuna. These other religions do, indeed, see themselves as having a responsibility toward the world. And each certainly has a claim to being a world religion. Nevertheless, it is arguable that Latourette's study witnesses to not just Christianity's greater expansion but, as we shall see in a later chapter, a greater degree of inculturation. In some cases, the reason for this difference is perhaps readily discernible. For example, the Old Testament theme of "the pilgrimage of the nations" to Zion to worship there the one true God (Ps 68, Ps 86:9; Is 60:3, 5-6, 11; Zc 8:22-23), no doubt, worked to mitigate the missionary impulse in Judaism.

It is interesting to see how the notion of a well-thought-out mission is now used in secular society. Often today hospitals, schools, corporations even, have "mission statements" posted in public places so as to remind everyone, management, employees, customers, visitors, what are the goals and objectives of this particular institution whose services they have employed or whose service ranks they have entered. This self-conscious spelling-out of an institution's goal or task is an effective way of giving clear direction and focus, clarity of focus and expectations to a large group of people, not only the employees of the corporation but even more importantly those they serve. It could be argued this admirable and effective practice owes something to Christianity.

Further Reading

Avery Dulles' essay on the Church's mission and its current state, though written many years ago, is very perceptive and still valuable: "Rethinking the Mission of the Church" which is Chapter I in his *The Resilient Church* (Doubleday, 1977), pp. 9-27.

See in Lesslie Newbigin's *The Open Secret: An Introduction to the Theology of Mission* (Revised edition: Wm. B. Eerdmans, 1995), Chapter 3 "The Mission of the Triune God" and Chapter 8, "Mission as Action for God's Justice."

Karl Rahner's "The Mission of the Church and the Humanizing of the World" in *Doctrine and Life* 21 (1971): 171-178; 231-242.

CHAPTER 16

The Home Mission: Biblical Portraits

In no small measure the concept of the Christian mission that is held by most people today has its source in the cinematic portrayal of the Christian foreign missions.

Because of such films as "The Keys of the Kingdom" (1944) about a Scottish missionary in China, "Black Narcissus" (1947) about Anglican nuns in the Himalayas, "Hawaii" (1966) about New England missionaries in Polynesia, "Damien: the Leper Priest" (1980) about a Belgian missionary on Molokai, "The Mission" (1986) about Jesuit missionaries among the Guarani Indians of Paraguay, "Black Robe" (1991) about a French Jesuit missionary in Canada, we have come to visualize the Christian missionary as a brave soul journeying off to exotic lands. And, no doubt, there is a measure of truth in this image. A significant, perhaps the most prominent, part of the Christian mission is comprised of such "professional" missionaries who at no small risk of their lives and through personal sacrifices of discomfort and dislocation ventured forth to bring the Christian faith to distant shores. The problem with this Hollywood portrayal of the Christian mission however, is that it ignores the fact that the Christian mission is carried on not just by professional missionaries in exotic foreign lands but also by average Christians who do not go far from their own home. Indeed, in traditional theology of the missions not only have we been taught to distinguish the mission *ad gentes* from the mission *ad intra*, that is, "foreign missions" from "home missions," but it is important that we also be able to distinguish between formal mission and casual evangelization.

In order to make these lessons clear, I want to focus in this chapter upon three figures from the New Testament work called Luke-Acts, that is, the Gospel according to Luke and its companion volume, the Acts of the Apostles. Luke was always known as something of a portraitist, that is, with a few words he can often conjure up a very precise and impressive portrait for our imagination. In the Gospel according to Luke, besides the portraits of the great central figures, for example, Jesus and John the Baptist, Luke also renders vivid portraits of "little people," attendant, relatively minor figures, characters in secondary roles like Jairus the synagogue official who knelt before Jesus in the midst of a crowd to request the healing of his daughter (Lk 8:40-56) or Zacchaeus the tax collector at Jericho who literally went out on a limb to see Jesus and then invited Jesus to his home (Lk 19). These verbal portraits of relatively minor figures are so vividly rendered that they remain etched in our memories. Similarly, while Luke in the Acts of the Apostles centers upon and features the work of two great apostles, Peter and Paul, at the same time, he also sets forth small but vivid portraits of other people, secondary figures, who were active and effective in the spread of the Gospel, at work in the mission of the Church. In the next chapter we shall examine at length the missionary journeys of Saint Paul. In a later chapter we shall do the same for the image of Peter in the New Testament and its implications for ministry. But at this time I want to focus upon portraits of comparatively minor figures in the history of the Christian mission as presented in Luke-Acts. The three figures I want to treat of here and their significance for understanding the Christian mission are conveyed by the following descriptive headings: the "personal propaganda" of Anna the prophetess, the "casual evangelization" of Philip the evangelist, and the "hospitality and instruction" of a husband and wife catechetical team, Prisca and Aquila. Each of these figures can stand as a model for imitation in the task of the Church's mission today in the world but even more so at home.

The second chapter of the Gospel according to Luke contains a narrative of Joseph and Mary's bringing the new born

Jesus to the Jerusalem temple for purification rites. There they run into an old woman of which Luke 2:36-38 tells us:

> And there was a prophetess, Anna, the daughter of Pha-
> nuel, of the tribe of Asher; she was of a great age, having
> lived with her husband seven years from her virginity
> and as a widow till she was eighty-four. She did not
> depart from the temple, worshiping with fasting and
> prayer night and day. And coming up at that very hour
> she gave thanks to God, and spoke of him to all who
> were looking for the redemption of Jerusalem.

The phrase "from her virginity" is a quaint expression for "from the day of her marriage." But New Testament scholar Raymond Brown — in his *Birth of the Messiah* (1977), pp. 466-468 — goes into a more detailed and insightful analysis of this Lucan portrait. He says of this passage:

> To what extent are the details that Luke tells us about
> Anna symbolic? The Anawim features are hard to evalu-
> ate: Luke may be creating a type of Anawim piety, or he
> may be giving us a woman who was remembered by
> the Jerusalem Christian Anawim precisely because she
> was a saintly model of their ideals. The exact details of
> her age and her genealogy may be signs of historical
> memory. Much depends on how literally Luke means
> the statement: "She never left the Temple courts; day
> and night she worshiped God...." What is of particular
> interest is the emphasis on Annas' widowhood of 84
> years. To what extent has this aspect of Annas' portrait
> been painted in light of an ideal of widowhood that Luke
> knew in the Pauline Churches? Luke mentions widows
> more than all the other Gospels combined, and there
> is an awareness of their special place in Christianity in
> Acts 6:1 and 9:39, 41. The most detailed description of
> Christian widows is in 1 Timothy 5:3-16, many features
> of which match Luke's description of Anna.

I have quoted Brown at length because he argues there are elements here that suggest we might indeed be hearing some details about an actual historical person, but no doubt that person has also been somewhat stylized. I feel that both of these elements, history and stylization, make for an important lesson regarding the Church's mission. As for the historical element: the word "Anawim" which Brown uses to identify this woman is the plural form of an Old Testament Hebrew word meaning "the afflicted and poor." While it may have originally designated the materially poor, it also came to be used as a designation of the pious and oppressed poor who see in God their only hope, "the poor of God." But Brown speculates that it might in this context refer to a class or group within the earliest Christian community at Jerusalem. But of more interest to us is the stylized element. When we read that Anna "spoke of him [Jesus] to all who were looking for the redemption of Jerusalem," we must not think this refers to a one time utterance then and there. The verb is in the imperfect and thus implies "she kept speaking" as to imply she spread abroad the word about the child. Nor does this mean Anna was simply a talkative old lady. Rather the language here is a technical expression for an element of the Christian mission, namely, personal propaganda. Nor should we underestimate the importance of this form of propaganda. For example, the Church of Rome was not founded by Peter and Paul. They were late arrivals. When they came to Rome there was already a flourishing Christian community there. The seed of faith had been first planted there and the community of faith at Rome grew, no doubt, and in no small measure because of the personal witness of Jewish-Christian travelers, converted Roman soldiers, Syrian merchants, Greek sailors, who witnessed to their faith verbally in Roman synagogues, markets and taverns.

The next person we shall look at is Philip the evangelist. There are two different figures in the New Testament among Jesus' disciples called Philip. Prominent in the Gospel according to John is Philip, one of the Twelve. In the first chapter of John's Gospel we are told that Andrew, the brother of Simon Peter, was one of two disciples of John the Baptist who became intrigued with Jesus. After one day of listening to Jesus, Andrew goes home and tells his brother Simon, "We have found the Messiah!" Then Andrew brings Simon to Jesus who gives him the name Peter. Then in John 1:43-45 we read:

> The next day Jesus decided to go to Galilee. And he found he found Philip and said to him, "Follow me." Now Philip was from Bethsaida, the city of Andrew and Peter. Philip found Nathanael, and said to him "We have found him of whom Moses in the law and also the prophets wrote."

This is not the Philip about whom we are concerned. We first hear of our Philip in Acts 6:1-6 which recounts a story about the earliest Christian community in Jerusalem after the death and resurrection of Jesus. It tells of a controversy that developed when the Hellenist widows were being ignored in the daily distribution of the bread. The apostles decide the only solution for this is to appoint seven men who will have responsibility for such charitable activity. Our Philip was one of the Seven chosen to assist the apostles. But the Acts of the Apostles never shows him doing that. Instead, in Chapter 8 of Acts, sometimes called "The Acts of Philip," we are told how Philip was among those who were forced to leave Jerusalem when a great persecution of Christians arose, one dramatic expression of which was the martyrdom of one of the other Seven, Stephen. The first of Philip's exploits recounted is of how Philip first fled north of Jerusalem to Samaria where he started to proclaim Christ. Acts 8:9-25, tells of Philip's encounter there in Samaria with one Simon the magician who though converted tried to buy his way into the ministry. This is an incident we shall treat of later in Chapter 18 of this book in our chapter on the Church and other religions, for there is another episode of Philip's missionary effort that is more central to our interests here. Next, Philip goes south of Jerusalem and there we are told of an incident that happened on the road that goes down from Jerusalem to Gaza. Acts 8:27-38 tells of Philip's casual encounter with an Ethiopian eunuch. I quote it here in its entirety:

> And behold, an Ethiopian, a eunuch, a minister of Can-
> dace the queen of the Ethiopians, in charge of all her
> treasure, had come to Jerusalem to worship and was re-
> turning; seated in his chariot, he was reading the prophet
> Isaiah. And the Spirit said to Philip, "Go up and join this
> chariot." So Philip ran to him, and heard him reading
> Isaiah the prophet, and asked, "Do you understand what
> you are reading?" And he said, "How can I, unless some
> one guides me?" And he invited Philip to come up and
> sit with him. Now the passage of the scripture which he
> was reading was this: "As a sheep led to the slaughter
> or a lamb before its shearer is dumb, so he opens not his
> mouth. In his humiliation justice was denied him. Who
> can describe his generation? For his life is taken up from
> the earth." And the eunuch said to Philip, "About whom,
> pray, does the prophet say this, about himself or about
> someone else?" Then Philip opened his mouth, and be-
> ginning with this scripture he told him the good news of
> Jesus. And as they went along the road they came to some
> water, and the eunuch said, "See, here is water! What is
> to prevent my being baptized?" And he commanded the
> chariot to stop, and they both went down into the water,
> Philip and the eunuch, and he baptized him.

This passage is filled with even more drama than Philip's meeting with that other exotic, Simon the magician. Simon may have
been into gross superstition, but Philip's evangelization of this
eunuch is even more remarkable, for this eunuch is a pariah, an
object of social ostracism by Jew and Gentile alike. The castration
of males was severely frowned upon not only in Jewish society
but also in Hellenistic culture. Indeed, in the Old Testament
eunuchs were proscribed from ever entering the community of
Israel (Dt 23:2), and thus we have in Acts a poignant portrayal
of ostracism: As interested as this eunuch might be in Israelite
worship, he would stand forever in the court of the Gentiles, he
could never be admitted directly into the temple. Moreover, even
for the Gentiles, that is, the Hellenistic audience, this eunuch is
an image of loathing and disgust. Castration had practical side
effects, not just loss of facial hair but also increase in weight

accompanied by atrophy of the muscles, and a high-pitched voice, and loss of bladder control with the resultant smell of uncontrolled urination. This made him an object of social ridicule and avoidance, social ostracism. That Philip is willing to jump into the chariot and sit beside this man would have amazed both a Jewish and a Hellenistic audience. What Philip does is comparable to those people who dared to break the "color line" in segregationist America of the 1950's or apartheid South Africa. And thus we have here a powerful image of the Gospel going into all sectors of society, perhaps even a fulfillment of the prophecy in Is 56:3-5. Philip is not so much an example of personal propaganda as he is a sterling example of casual evangelization. By that I mean Philip, like Anna the prophetess had no missionary mandate, no missionary plan. Unlike Paul and Barnabas who in Acts 13:2-3 are portrayed as being sent forth on mission by a local Church and sponsored by them, Philip is not sent by a Christian community. Rather circumstances beyond his control — the persecution of Christians that started with the martyrdom of Stephen — forced him to abandon his charitable ministry at Jerusalem and to become, instead, an enthusiastic but purely casual evangelist.

Prisca and Aquila are mentioned no less than five times in the New Testament. We are going to look at all of those passages in order to get a full picture of them. They are first mentioned in the Acts of the Apostles in Chapter 18. There we are told how, during Saint Paul's second great missionary journey, after his relative lack of success in preaching the Gospel in Athens, he went to the Greek city of Corinth. There he will have much more success. Indeed, he will stay in Corinth two years and in that time he will have great success, establishing the largest of his churches. Acts 18:1-3 describes Paul's arrival at Corinth in these terms:

> After this he left Athens and went to Corinth. And he found a Jew named Aquila, a native of Pontus, lately come from Italy with his wife Priscilla, because Claudius had commanded all the Jews to leave Rome. And he went to see them; and because he was of the same trade he

stayed with them, and they worked, for by trade they were tent-makers.

The next time they appear in Scripture, is in this same Chapter 18 of Acts. But this time they are living in the city of Ephesus. In Acts 18:24-26, we are told:

> Now a Jew named Apollos, a native of Alexandria, came to Ephesus. He was an eloquent man, well versed in the scriptures. He had been instructed in the way of the Lord; and being fervent in spirit, he spoke and taught accurately the things concerning Jesus, though he knew only the baptism of John. He began to speak boldly in the synagogue; but when Priscilla and Aquila heard him, they took him aside and expounded to him, the way of God more accurately.

The next three references to Prisca and Aquila are three small passing references in the Pauline Corpus. Brief as they are they are still revelatory. It was the habit of Paul often at the end of his letters to greet several people. In 1 Corinthians 16:19 Paul tells the Corinthians: "The Churches of Asia send greetings. Aquila and Prisca, together with the church in their house, send you hearty greetings in the Lord." At the end of the Epistle to the Romans, Chapter 16:3-5, we hear Paul say, "Greet Prisca and Aquila, my fellow workers in Christ Jesus, who risked their necks for my life, to whom not only I but all the churches of the Gentiles give thanks; greet also the church in their house." Finally, in 2 Timothy 4:19, we find: "Greet Prisca and Aquila, and the household of Onesiphorus."

From these small passages exegetes have claimed to discern great implications. For example, many exegetes argue it is fairly reasonable to conclude that Prisca and Aquila were a prosperous, maybe even wealthy, couple. Two things suggest this. For one thing, they move about a great deal, they can afford to travel. Secondly, wherever they travel, they seem to have spacious accommodations, for not only do they have enough room to offer hospitality to Paul but they also host a "house church." In those early days of Christian history, the Christian community, a small and often persecuted minority, had no public worship spaces. So those Christians who had large enough homes hosted a congregation of worshipers on Sundays. Besides their being people of means, however, some other exegetes have argued that there is telltale evidence here of an even further drama. That is, Paul when he refers to the couple always uses Prisca's formal name while Luke uses the diminutive, more affectionate and familiar, form Priscilla. Also, Paul in his Letter to the Romans uses a strange pattern of mentioning the wife's name before the husband's. From this some have argued that Prisca was not just a wealthy woman but had married beneath her station. William Barclay has pointed out that there is a cemetery, a catacomb, in Rome bearing the name of Priscilla. It is located on the Salarian Road in the northeast part of Rome. That cemetery was the burial ground of the ancient family of the Acilii, who gave Rome a consul, Acilius Glabrio, in A.D. 91. Moreover, the inscriptions in the tombs of that cemetery give ample evidence that Prisca and Priscilla were common names of the Acilii. And thus it could be that Aquila had been a freedman of the family of the Acilii, a former slave. If that is true, then the marriage of Prisca and Aquila is an early example of the Christian faith breaking through the barriers of caste and station in Roman society. Some feminist theologians have gone so far with this social drama as to argue that if indeed Prisca was the principal source of this couple's wealth and a high society matron, it could well be that when Christians gathered in Prisca and Aquila's home for Sunday worship, it was she and not her husband who presided over their house church and thus she may well have been the one who broke the bread and shared the word at the Sunday Eucharist (I address this opinion later in my chapter on "Women and Ministry"). Such feminists may also be aware of the fact that even before them the great historian of the early Church, Adolf von Harnack, long ago speculated that Prisca was not only an influential woman in the Roman Church but was probably also the author of the Epistle to the Hebrews! I myself when I once visited the Church of Santa Prisca on Rome's Aventine Hill and saw the painting over the high altar of Prisca being blessed by Saint Paul was led to muse that painting could easily be interpreted as Paul's ordination of Prisca. But these arguments are probably more an object lesson in how it is all too easy to over-interpret biblical passages and garner from them arguments far beyond the author's original intention.

On the other hand, it is more reasonable to argue that Luke has taken a real, historical Christian couple and sought to portray them as a model of a Christian ideal. That is, this couple is friendly, hospitable, and generous with their wealth. And the subject of wealth here is not a mere side issue. It can be a legitimate ministry. We should not be surprised to find that wealthy people played such an important part in the early Church. Jesus in his ministry preached the importance of generosity. And there is evidence that his own ministry was supported in part by the generosity of the wealthy. Luke 8:1-3 claims that Jesus and the Twelve were accompanied by a group of wealthy women who supported them out of their means. Mark 14:15 and Luke 22:12 suggest some wealthy patron provided in the high rent district of Jerusalem "a large upper room furnished" for Jesus to celebrate his final Passover feast with his disciples. When Jesus instructed his disciples to carry no money or provisions, he taught them to expect hospitality (Mk 6:8, Mt 10:9, and Lk 9:3). Hospitality will become a major Christian virtue, e.g., Romans 12:13: "Contribute to the needs of the saints, practice hospitality"; 1 Timothy 5:10: "[A Christian widow] must be well attested for her good deeds, as one who has brought up her children, shown hospitality"; Hebrews 13:2: "Do not neglect to show hospitality to strangers, for thereby some have entertained angels unaware." But there is yet another important lesson here.

The Lucan portrait of Prisca and Aquila also illustrates another important element in the Christian mission. Evangelization, the proclamation of the Gospel, is but the first step in the Christian mission; initial conversion is not enough. It must be followed up by proper instruction in the faith and formal admission to the community of faith. Prisca and Aquila's instruction of Apollos is a particularly dramatic example of this. Apollos (a name probably abbreviated from Apollonius, some suggest Apollodorus or Apollonides) was a Jewish Christian from Alexandria, in its day one of the great cultural centers of the Western world. Apollos possessed great skill in Greek rhetoric and may even have been a student of the great Jewish scholar Philo of Alexandria. Despite all this learning and eloquence, his own Christian formation was seriously incomplete. "He knew only the baptism of John." This story of Prisca and Aquila taking Apollos aside and instructing him and baptizing him is also a message about the importance of observing right order in the community of faith. We have already seen in our chapter on the idea of the mission Avery Dulles' stress upon the importance of initiation into the wider community of faith with its observances. In Acts itself, Luke puts much emphasis upon right order and sacramental observances. In Chapter 8, in his description of the ministry of Philip the evangelist, Luke is careful to point out the sequence of the rites of initiation. Philip baptizes, but then the Jerusalem community sends apostolic figures to confirm those who have been baptized:

> Now when the apostles at Jerusalem heard that Samaria had received the word of God, they sent to them Peter and John, who came down and prayed for them that they might receive the Holy Spirit; for it had not yet fallen on any of them, but they had only been baptized in the name of the Lord Jesus. (Ac 8:14-16)

The passage I have quoted and the interpretation I have given to it would, no doubt, be labeled by Ernst Käsemann as an example of "early Catholicism." But that does not undermine its logical importance. A significant part of the Christian mission consists of those men and women who, like Prisca and Aquila, take the time to instruct beginners in the faith, even opening their homes to strangers to host prayer groups and Bible studies and give assistance to apostles. A significant part of the Christian mission is undertaken by those men and women who, like Philip, boldly seize the opportunity to reach out to the socially marginalized, or who, like Anna, give personal witness to their faith before a hopeful if still unbelieving world.

Further Reading

Kilian McDonnell's "Evangelization and the Experience of Initiation in the Early Church" in *John Paul II and the New Evangelization* edited by Ralph Martin (2nd edition, Servant Publications, 2006), pages 86-100.

Robert S. Rivers' *From Maintenance to Mission: Evangelization and the Revitalization of the Parish* (Paulist Press, 2005).

CHAPTER 17

The Foreign Mission:
Paul's Inculturation of the Gospel

In our last chapter, Chapter 16, we learned something about the mission of the Church by studying portraits of some relatively minor figures in the New Testament. We learned from them how all Christians should be involved in the mission of the Church and that they need not go far from home to do this, that, indeed, there is need for a home mission. But there are still some other important lessons to be learned about the Church's mission. And here it is an awesome figure from the New Testament who can best instruct us. Paul of Tarsus made not only individual converts but he founded entire churches. Moreover, he not only instructed people in the faith but he translated an originally Semitic Gospel into the thought categories of the major cultures of the Western world, so that the Christian faith could indeed become a world religion. Saint Paul is one of the towering figures in the early history of Christianity and, indeed, a giant whose influence remains a constant throughout Christian history. However, the reader should also know that at times Paul's influence has been exaggerated. For example, there have been and still are those who go so far as to insist that Christianity, the Christian faith even, is more the creation of Paul than of Jesus. I consider this a gross overstatement. But that you might get a proper perspective on Paul's achievement and take the true measure of the man so as to see his importance for the theology of the Christian mission, what I shall do here is to first present a sketch of his life, the most significant part of which was his Christian missionary effort. And then I shall attempt to analyze and evaluate his mission effort.

In Acts 22:3 Paul is recorded as having said, "I am a Jew, born at Tarsus in Cilicia, but brought up in this city [Jerusalem] at the feet of Gamaliel, and educated according to the strict manner of the law of our fathers." It seems that Paul was born in the first decade of the Christian era, sometime between 5 and 10 A.D. The Tarsus Paul refers to as his place of birth was a city situated close to the Mediterranean Sea at the foot of the Taurus Mountains, on the road leading over high passes from Asia Minor to Syria. In Acts 21:39, he is described as having boasted he was "a citizen of no mean town." In this he was quite right. Tarsus, besides being the capital city of the region and Roman province of Cilicia, was also a very cosmopolitan city, a center of Hellenistic culture, philosophy and education. Stoic and Epicurean philosophers taught there. His letters reveal he knew Greek and could write it well; also there are traces of the rhetoric of Stoic diatribe in Paul's writings. Another bit of evidence of his dual cultural heritage is his dual name, Saul/Paul and the fact that he had Roman citizenship. However, as we shall see there is considerable debate as to the relevance and importance of his acquaintance with Hellenistic culture. And to some degree this is appropriate because even though he was born in a Hellenistic city, Paul emphasizes that he was born of a Jewish family and brought up in Jerusalem. Of his Jewishness, the line, "at the feet of Gamaliel, educated according to the strict manner of the law of our fathers," is especially telling. This Gamaliel is referred to in rabbinical sources as "Gamaliel the Elder" or Gamaliel I to distinguish him from his grandson, another learned rabbi, Gamaliel II. And in those same sources he is given the honorific title of Rabban and is regarded as one of the great teachers of the law. Paul probably studied under him for the usual three or four years. From this it is not unreasonable to conclude that Paul was not only a Pharisee, strictly conscientious in his observance of Jewish law, but most probably a student for the rabbinate, maybe even himself a rabbi. Indeed, in Acts 7:58, more than a simple participant in the stoning of Stephen, Paul appears to have been one of the principal agents for the rabbinic council of Jerusalem in its attack upon Christians.

However, in about the year 35 A.D., that is, when Paul was about twenty-five to thirty years of age, he underwent a dramatic conversion to Christianity. We are given four accounts of this conversion in the New Testament: three in Acts (9:1-9, 22:1-11, 26:1-18) and Paul's own in Galatians 1:11-23. These narratives differ and some of the differences are quite telling. For example, Acts 9 tells with great detail of Paul's leaving Jerusalem to chase Christians who fled Jerusalem for Damascus. But on the road to Damascus Paul has a vision of Christ so dramatic it leaves Paul physically shaken. He takes refuge with Christians in Damascus. Paul's own narrative in Galatians agrees with Acts in insisting that his conversion "came through a revelation of Jesus Christ" (Gal 1:12), but it adds such interesting details as "I went away into Arabia" (Gal 1:17). The Arabia Paul refers to is most probably a reference to the Nabataen desert kingdom southeast of Jerusalem, in the Transjordan. It seems Paul spent three years there with Christian families during which time he was instructed in the Christian faith. But about the year 38 or 39, it seems Paul went back to Damascus and began to preach Jesus in the synagogues there. This incurred the murderous rage of the Jews; indeed, Paul had to be lowered over the city walls in a basket by night in order to escape to safety. From Damascus he went to Jerusalem. It seems that when Paul first arrived in Jerusalem ca. 40 A.D. as a newly-converted Christian, a prominent man in the Christian community at Jerusalem, a certain Barnabas, the surname of one Joseph, a Levite of Cyprus, first mentioned in Acts 4:3 as selling his property and giving the money for the disposal of the apostles, quickly befriended Paul and advanced Paul's cause. It seems that initially, at least, Paul received some measure of acceptance among the Christians in Jerusalem. But Paul's forceful evangelical efforts among Greek-speaking Jews in Jerusalem only caused trouble. And so the Christian community quickly ushered him out of the city, judging Paul's efforts as only counterproductive. And thus about the year 40 A.D., Paul quit Jerusalem and went back to his hometown of Tarsus. It appears that for the next few years he may have returned to his craft of tent-making (Acts 18:3), discouraged that he could not win the confidence of his fellow believers. In about the year 43 or 44, however, he was rescued from oblivion when recruited by the same Barnabas he first encountered in Jerusalem in Acts 4:3, now functioning as a representative of the Christian community of Jerusalem sent to help organize the fast-growing Christian Church in Syrian Antioch. Barnabas now brought Paul to Syrian Antioch where he secured for him a position as a teacher or catechist in the Christian community there where Paul seems to have functioned as Barnabas' right-hand man.

In about the year 45, Barnabas and Paul, along with Barnabas' cousin, John Mark, were sent off by the Church at Antioch, on a missionary journey. Even though it appears Barnabas was the leader and Paul his assistant, this missionary journey is now regarded as Paul's first great missionary journey. It lasted about three years. They sailed from Syrian Antioch southwestward to Salamis on the east coast of the island of Cyprus. Then they made their way on foot westward across the island to the seacoast town of Paphos, preaching all the way in the Jewish synagogues. From Paphos, Paul and his companions took a boat on a northwestward course and sailed to Perga in Pamphylia. At Perga in Pamphylia John Mark left them and returned to Jerusalem. From Perga, Paul and Barnabas journeyed on foot northward to Antioch in Pisida and then eastward to the Lyconian cities of Derbe and Lystra. Then they quickly retraced their steps northwestward to Pisidian Antioch and then southward down to Perga from which they sailed back to Syrian Antioch, their starting point and home base.

When they returned to Antioch, Paul and Barnabas were there only a short while when Judaizers arrived and began to preach that circumcision was necessary for salvation — a very sensitive point for non-circumcised Gentiles! This led to a dis-

pute between the Judaizers on the one hand and Paul and Barnabas on the other. Most of the converts Paul and Barnabas had
made on their missionary journey had been Gentiles. Thus the
Antiochene Church decided to send Paul, Barnabas and some
others to Jerusalem to consult Peter, James, the apostles and elders there. This conference or as it is often called "the Jerusalem
Council" took place around 48 or 49. The one issue that held the
day was that of circumcision or the observance of Mosaic legislation. Peter decided against circumcision and the observance of
the Mosaic Law. And thus Paul felt vindicated. However, Paul
had not been back long in Antioch before Peter himself arrived.
At first both of them ate with Gentile Christians. But Peter soon
yielded to criticism from Jewish Christians and began to separate
himself from the Gentile Christians. Paul challenged Peter and
accused him of being inconsistent, dishonest and unfair.

No sooner was this affair ended but Paul suggested to
Barnabas that they should go back to the Lyconian cities they
had evangelized to see how things were going. This beginning
of the second of Paul's great missionary journeys was marred by
dissension: Paul refused to take Barnabas' cousin John Mark with
him. And so Barnabas refused to go. Paul then chose another
man to accompany him, one Silas/Silvanus (as with Saul/Paul
here too we find a double name, the Jewish Silas and its Hellenistic equivalent Silvanus). This time they took the overland route
and traveled northwest along the southern coast of Asia Minor
to Derbe and Lystra once again. At Lystra Paul recruited another
companion for his missionary work: Timothy. Reaching Troas on
the eastern shore of the Aegean Sea, Paul wanted to sail northeast into the Black Sea and into Asia, but was prevented from
doing so by a vision in which Paul was told to go to Macedonia
(Ac 16:7-10). In response Paul passed over the Aegean Sea and
landed at Neapolis, the port city of Philippi. With this decision
Paul left behind the Middle East and brought his missionary
expedition onto European soil. Paul, Silas and Timothy now
traveled southwestward down the Greek peninsula founding
Christian communities at Philippi, Thessalonica and Beroea.
From Beroea, Paul left behind both Silas and Timothy and

with the assistance of native guides sailed to Athens. There he preached in the synagogues, dialogued with Epicurean and Stoic philosophers and even made an appearance at the Areopagus. The word "Areopagus" comes from the Greek Ares, the name of the Greek god of war. The Areopagus was the name given to a small hill northwest of the Acropolis, in front of the colonnade at the market place which had long ago become a renowned public meeting place in Athens. Paul in an appearance at the Areopagus presented a high-minded argument or apologetic for faith in the one God of Creation and his authoritative agent, Jesus Christ (Ac 17:22-31). However, the speech seems to have had little or no effect on his audience that day for we have no evidence of Paul having founded a church at Athens. From Athens Paul went to Corinth and during a two year residence (ca. 50-51) he experienced great success and founded the largest and most famous of his churches. It was probably early during this Corinthian stay, in 50 A.D. that Paul wrote the New Testament work we call First Thessalonians, the earliest surviving document of the Christian movement. Eventually, when Paul left Corinth he had decided to return to Syrian Antioch, the starting point for this his second great missionary journey. He sailed first about seven miles down the coast below Corinth to Cenchreae, Corinth's port city. From there he took a ship bound eastward to Ephesus. He remained but a short while in Ephesus and then took a boat southeast to Caesarea Maritima, the principal port of Palestine. From there he traveled by land to Jerusalem to relate to the Church leaders there the account of his missionary efforts. From Jerusalem Paul traveled northward by land up to Syrian Antioch.

Paul stayed in Antioch for well over a year, probably from 53-54. Then in the spring of 54 he traveled by land once again to the Lyconian cities of Derbe and Lystra, through Pisidian Antioch to Ephesus. This large and important city, the capital city of the proconsular province of Asia, became the center of his missionary activity for the next two and a half years. From Ephesus, a wealthy city, the chief port and market center of Asia with a population in New Testament times of about 250,000, Paul wrote his epistles to the Galatians, the Philippians and probably as many as three epistles to the Church at Corinth (although we have only two in the New Testament). Paul's success in building up the Church at Ephesus was so great that he made many enemies there and had to leave. He next spent several weeks revisiting his earlier missionary establishments in Troas, Philippi, Thessalonica, Beroea, Corinth and Cenchrae. Deciding to end this missionary journey, Paul, in about the spring of 56, sailed eastward to Miletus where, not daring to go back to Ephesus, he summoned the leaders of the Church at Ephesus for a conference. From Miletus Paul and his companions sailed to Tyre, the port city of Phoenicia. And then they traveled by land to Jerusalem to report to the Church leaders there. It was during this visit to Jerusalem in the spring of 56 that Paul was arrested by the Roman occupiers. It seems that his success as a Christian missionary had stirred up the animosity of the Jerusalem Jews. Paul, however, insisted upon his rights as a Roman citizen that he be allowed to appeal his case to Rome. And thus probably in the year 58 he was sent to Rome where he spent two years in jail or under house arrest (probably 58-59), and was eventually martyred under Nero ca. 64-65.

One cannot underestimate the importance of Paul's great missionary journeys. They are the first evidence we have for a strategic, comprehensive and methodic Christian mission. As for the strategic character of Paul's mission: all previous efforts had been casual and occasional. In Chapter 16 we saw the importance of such limited missionary efforts as the personal propaganda of Anna the prophetess, the casual even opportunistic evangelization of Philip the evangelist, and the occasional hospitality and catechetical instruction offered by Prisca and Aquila. All these mission efforts were spontaneous, casual and occasional. Paul's missionary efforts follow a self-conscious and logical geographical itinerary. He is out to conquer the world. True, like Jesus before him, Paul too preaches in towns and villages but he is headed for the big cities, Corinth, Athens and ultimately Rome. Indeed, some scholars interpret a passage from one of Paul's letters (Rm 15:24, 28) as indicating he intended to go as far as Spain.

As for the comprehensive character of Paul's mission: Paul is not satisfied to make individual converts, he is intent upon building community, establishing Christian assemblies and equipping them with the means to right worship, effective pastoral care and catechetical instruction. For example, Paul encourages recognition and respect for authority in the local Christian assembly (see 1 Th 5:12-13, 1 Cor 16:15-16). At Corinth, Paul lays down rules for charismatics who speak in tongues no one understands and has equally firm rules for the many prophetic voices in the assembly who all want to be heard (see 1 Cor 14). But it is not just order that concerns him. Paul is also concerned about proper religious observances, for example, proper observance of the Lord's Supper service. In 1 Corinthians 11 he gives instructions for liturgical assemblies. Indeed, in verses 17-34, he shows himself a bold liturgical reformer for he discourages casual communion and instead encourages examination of conscience before communion and replaces the agape with long sermons. (For an illustration of the dangers of long sermons see Acts 20:7-11.)

As for the methodic character of Paul's mission efforts: what is perhaps most remarkable about Paul's missionary efforts is his talent for acculturation, his ability to translate the Gospel into another language not just linguistically but culturally. Because Paul was a man of two cultures, diaspora Jew educated at Jerusalem, he was well equipped to translate the preaching of Jesus into Hellenistic terms. He is quick to adapt and incorporate elements of Hellenistic culture in his preaching of the Gospel. A simple example can be seen by contrasting the preaching method of Jesus with that of Paul. In his preaching, Jesus employed illustrations and images that reflected the agrarian life of rural Galilee. Jesus drew similes from sheep with shepherds, wheat in the fields, wine-making, a grain of mustard seed, a woman baking bread. In stark contrast, Paul draws his images from Roman and Hellenistic urban culture. For example, in 1 Corinthians 9:24-27 he employs the language of Greek athleticism:

> Do you not know that in a race all the runners compete, but only one receives the prize? So run that you

> may obtain it. Every athlete exercises self-control in all
> things. They do it to receive a perishable wreath, but we
> an imperishable. Well, I do not run aimlessly, I do not
> box as one beating the air; but I pommel my body and
> subdue it, lest after preaching to others I myself should
> be disqualified.

He also uses political terminology as in his invocation of such concepts as "partisanship" (Ph 1:17) and "citizenship" (Ph 3:20). He uses the language of the Roman law courts as in Galatians 3:15 where he talks of changing a will, or the language of "guardians" and "trustees" in Galatians 4:1-2. Paul makes use of many terms and concepts from the Stoicism of Greco-Roman philosophers such as Epictetus and Seneca. Examples of this abound in his letters, as when he speaks of "nature" (*physis*) in Romans 2:4, or "freedom" (*eleutheria*) in Galatians 5:1, 13, or "conscience" (*syneidesis*) (1 Cor 8:7, 10, 12; 1 Cor 10:25-29; 2 Cor 5:11, and Rm 2:15), or the Stoic idea of "self-sufficiency" (*autarchia*) in 2 Corinthians 9:8.

How daring a tactic such translation and accommodation to a foreign culture can be is observable in Paul's use of the language of "metamorphosis." Metamorphosis was a theme prominent in Hellenistic mythology (see Homer's *Iliad* 2.319, Ovid's *Metamorphoses*, Apuleius' *Golden Ass*). Paul uses this language of dramatic change several times and to varying effects. For example, in 2 Corinthians 3:18 Paul uses the language of metamorphosis to speak of our "transformation in Christ." In Romans 12:2 he uses it to express the radical conversion of life and manners required by the Gospel: "Do not be conformed to this world, but be transformed (*metamorphousthe*) by the renewal of your mind." In Philippians 3:21 he speaks of "the Lord Jesus Christ, who will change (*metaschematisei*) our lowly body to be like his glorious body." While Mark and Matthew seem to follow Paul in this regard — both Mark 9:2 and Matthew 17:2 say of Jesus on the mountain before Peter, James and John "he was transfigured (*metamorphothe*) before them" — Luke in his narration of the transfiguration of Christ does not. Apparently,

Luke felt the language of metamorphosis was all too common in classical paganism and thus should be avoided. And so in Luke 9:29, it is said of Jesus "the appearance of his countenance was altered (*heteron*)," not transfigured.

However, besides his translation of the Gospel into Hellenistic terms, Paul was equally bold in discarding what he felt was cultural baggage from the Gospel's Semitic roots, cultural baggage that would only encumber the Gospel's reception and growth on foreign soil. The two most obvious examples of this are Paul's decision to abrogate the Jewish dietary laws (Rm 14) and to abandon the custom of circumcising males (Gal 5:1-6).

No doubt, it is because of such daring language and such bold measures that some scholars have talked of Paul's "Hellenized" Gospel and even exalted him over Jesus as the real creator of the Christian faith. But this is precisely the point at which we must see that for all of Paul's daring and innovative moves to translate the Gospel so that it might take root on foreign soil, there is yet another aspect of his mission effort that we must examine and that is his profoundly conservative traditionalism regarding the core of the Gospel message. For example, note Paul's words in 1 Corinthians 11:2, "I commend you because you remember me in everything and maintain the traditions even as I have delivered them to you." The traditions to which Paul refers here are in part certain dogmatic formulas such as those in 1 Corinthians 15:3-5:

> For I delivered to you as of first importance what I also received, that Christ died for our sins in accordance with the scriptures, that he was buried, that he was raised on the third day in accordance with the scriptures, and that he appeared to Cephas, then to the twelve.

Another example of this is the language of tradition which Paul employs in 1 Corinthians 11:23ff.: "For I received from the Lord what I also delivered to you, that the Lord Jesus on the night when he was betrayed took bread, and when he had given thanks, he broke it, and said 'This is my body which is for you. Do this in remembrance of me.'"

Where did Paul get such dogmatic formulas? It is daring to speculate about what Paul learned in those years that he spent "in Arabia" after his dramatic conversion on the road to Damascus. It could be that the dogmatic formulas which he quotes in his letters were first learned there. But this is not the only characteristic of Paul's traditionalism. There is also the use he makes of early Christian hymns such as the one he quotes in Philippians 2:6-11:

> [Jesus], though he was in the form of God, did not count equality with God a thing to be grasped, but emptied himself, and became obedient unto death, even death on a cross. Therefore God has highly exalted him and bestowed on him the name which is above every name, that at the name of Jesus every knee should bend, in heaven and on earth and under the earth, and every tongue confess that Jesus Christ is Lord, to the glory of God the Father.

I have quoted this passage in the prose paragraph form in which it appears in the Bible I am using; however, I have seen it at times arranged in "strophic" form, that is, in a way that brings out the rhythmic quality of the lines in a poem. This is because most scholars agree these words are a piece of poetry, the lyrics of a hymn. Moreover, most scholars agree these lyrics are not Paul's own, rather Paul here is quoting a popular Jewish-Christian liturgical hymn which he probably first encountered in the time after his conversion but before he began his missionary journeys. But it is more than just a hymn; it is a hymnic confession, a well-conceived doctrinal confession of faith expressing the faith of Christian assemblies other than Paul's own, other than the ones he established. And thus Paul is once again the bearer and transmitter of an older and common doctrinal tradition. He is disseminating the communal faith of Christians and not his own theories.

There is one thing more that we must note about the Christian mission as witnessed to by Paul. And that is the fact that Paul's great missionary efforts have not been without criticism. Paul's missionary work, for all of its success and the brilliance of its strategy, has not been beyond reproach. Indeed, it has in modern times been indicted for being all too spiritual, that is, without a significant social agenda especially as regards a great social scourge of the time, the phenomenon of slavery in Hellenistic culture and indeed in the entire ancient world, even in Israel. It seems true that Jesus, for dramatic effect, made use of the language of slavery, as in Mark 10:44 where he says to the Twelve, "Whoever wants to be first must be slave of all." The word is *doulos* (slave) not *diakonos* (servant) which Jesus uses elsewhere. Or in John 8:34, where Jesus warns, "Everyone who sins is a slave to sin." And some who heard him reacted strongly to such language, as in John 8:33 where they say, "We are Abraham's descendants... and have never been slaves of anyone." No doubt, Paul in a similar manner uses the language of slavery to express dramatically the paradox of the Christian's liberation from sin but now radical indebtedness to God. For example, in Romans 6:18, "Freed from sin, you have become slaves of righteousness." Or in Romans 6:22, "But now that you have been freed from sin and have become slaves of God." These are understandable and acceptable, if shocking, images of a spiritual transformation. But elsewhere in his letters Paul addresses the fact of social slavery in what for some is an all too pacific, resigned, accepting attitude. For example, in 1 Corinthians 7:17, 20-22:

> Let every one lead the life which the Lord has assigned to him and in which God has called him. This is my rule in all the churches.... Every one should remain in the state in which he was called. Were you a slave when called? Never mind. Make use of your present condition instead. For he who was called in the Lord as a slave is a freedman of the Lord. Likewise he who was free when called is a slave of Christ.

In the secondary Pauline literature, that is, the letters attributed to Paul but whose authenticity many modern exegetes question, this attitude perdures. For example, Ephesians 6:5-9 appears a little more even handed, that is, it admonishes the masters as well as the slaves:

> Slaves, be obedient to those who are your earthly masters, with fear and trembling, in singleness of heart, as to Christ; not in the way of eye-service, as men-pleasers, but as servants of Christ, doing the will of God from the heart, rendering service with a good will as to the Lord and not to men, knowing that whatever good anyone does, he will receive the same again from the Lord whether he is a slave or free. Masters, do the same to them, and forbear threatening, knowing that he who is both their Master and yours is in heaven, and that there is no partiality in him.

And then there is Colossians 3:22: "Slaves, obey your human masters in everything, not only when being watched, as currying favor, but in simplicity of heart, fearing the Lord," and 1 Timothy 6:1: "Those who are under the yoke of slavery must regard their masters as worthy of full respect."

Two things can be said in defense of Paul. First, we must bear in mind the dangerous situation in which Paul preached. Christianity was a small fledgling movement amid a strongly hostile environment. Jesus himself had suffered a slave's form of execution precisely because he appeared to some to be inciting rebellion. Paul had to be careful not to use the Christian religion to exacerbate the situation by inciting open rebellion. Moreover, there is evidence that Paul when he could safely do so was quick to seek freedom for a slave. In this regard one should read Paul's Letter to Philemon, the smallest literary work in the NT. In this letter Paul reveals to a Christian named Philemon that while Paul was under house arrest at Rome he met a runaway slave named Onesimus who came under Paul's influence and was converted. Now Paul is sending Onesimus back to his master, but Paul skillfully and gently challenges Philemon to realize that the relationship between Philemon and his returning slave must change because the two are now brothers in Christ: "Perhaps this is why he was parted from you for a while, that you might have him back for ever, no longer as a slave but more than a slave, as a beloved brother" (vs. 15-16).

Further Reading

Read in Lesslie Newbigin's *The Open Secret: an Introduction to the Theology of Mission* (Wm. B. Eerdmans, Revised Edition, 1995), Chapter 9, "Church Growth, Conversion, and Culture."

In Donald Bloesch's *The Church: Sacraments, Worship, Ministry, Mission* (Downers Grove, IL: Intervarsity, 2002), Chapter 12, "The Gospel in a Syncretistic Age," 235-251.

In Miguel Garijo-Guembe's *Communion of the Saints: Foundation, Nature, and Structure of the Church* (Collegeville, MN: The Liturgical Press, 1994), Chapter XIV, "The Mission and Task of the Church," 233-251.

CHAPTER 18

The Church and Other Religions

Thus far we have been exploring the Church's mission to the world, the origin of that mission and the historic character and end or aim of that mission. But there is yet another aspect of the Church's mission that we have yet to broach. And that is the fact that the world is not without religion. Quite the contrary; the world exhibits in its history a wide variety of beliefs and faith systems. Indeed, some anthropologists would argue that if ancient history is any indication, human beings are innately religious, that is, atheism is a relatively modern phenomenon. Primitive peoples always acknowledged some kind of transcendent religious presence, the operation of some kind of spiritual power or powers beyond just the natural powers of earth and sky. And in more recent times, the past three thousand years, religious traditions have arisen and produced significant bodies of literature that have shaped civilizations and continue to shape people's lives to this day. What should be the attitude of Christians, the disciples of Christ, toward these other religions is the subject of this chapter.

There are several New Testament passages that witness to the encounter of Christian faith with other religions. And they make a helpful starting point for an answer to the question we have posed. Here we shall examine those passages. We begin by examining those passages that witness to the encounter between Christianity and Judaism. This encounter started with the public ministry of Jesus and continued with the work of his disciples after his death and resurrection.

Luke presents Jesus as having been raised in a religiously observant Jewish family. For example, Luke 3:41 says, "Each year his parents went to Jerusalem for the feast of Passover." And all four Gospels portray Jesus in his public ministry as adhering to a certain measure of regular religious observance. The assertion in Luke 4:16 that Jesus "went according to his custom into the synagogue on the Sabbath day" is at one with the other Gospel witness (for example, Mk 1:21, 3:1, 6:2). As for temple observance, while the Synoptic Gospels telescope Jesus' public ministry into one year culminating in his Passover visit to the temple, John's Gospel suggests the public ministry was almost three years and entailed Jesus' visiting the temple for all the major feasts. But there are yet tensions in his relationships with his co-religionists stemming from a perceived independence on Jesus' part regarding some traditional Jewish disciplines or observances. For example, there seems to have been considerable tension between Jesus and members of the Jewish sect called the Pharisees. The Pharisees were strict observant Jews following the letter of the law. Jesus, apparently, was less observant, more flexible in his attitude toward the law. Mark 7:1-6 is a classic example of this:

> Now when the Pharisees gathered together to him, with some of the scribes, who had come from Jerusalem, they saw that some of his disciples ate with hands defiled, that is, unwashed. (For the Pharisees, and all the Jews, do not eat unless they purify themselves; and there are many other traditions which they observe, the washing of cups and pots and vessels of bronze.) And the Pharisees and the scribes asked him, "Why do your disciples not live according to the tradition of the elders, but eat with hands defiled?"

In Matthew the tension between Jesus and the Pharisees reaches a high point. See for example Chapter 23, Jesus' long diatribe against the scribes, the Jewish intellectuals of his day, and the Pharisees, the pious lay spirituality movement of the day. It consists of a series of seven "woes" each beginning with the warning, "Woe to you, scribes and Pharisees, you hypocrites." And there follows one indictment after another, mostly of the moral obtuseness or the self-serving religious rigorism of these strict observant Jews. And then comes the final indictment, "You are the children of those who murdered the prophets" (Mt 23:29). In the Gospel according to John, there is a comparable indictment of the Pharisees (8:12-59) and even their demonization: "You are of your father the devil, and your will is to do your father's desires" (Jn 8:44).

Then there is Jesus' relationship to the temple priests. All four of the passion narratives in the Gospels present the temple priests as principal opponents to Jesus. For example, in Mark 14:1 we hear it said: "The chief priests and the scribes were seeking how to arrest him by stealth, and kill him." In Mark 14:43, it is servants of the chief priests who are sent to arrest Jesus. Mark 14:53-64 describes Jesus' trial before "the chief priests and the elders and the scribes" with the high priest leading the interrogation of Jesus. And in Mark 15:1-5 Jesus is brought before Pilate for trial and we are told: "The chief priests accused him of many things."

We must also consider Jesus' relationship to the Jewish people in general. While Jesus had no problem attracting crowds, those in the crowd had various motives, some purely adventitious. Moreover, in the end the crowd proved fickle. For example, there is the portrayal of the Jewish people's part in the death of Jesus as seen in Matthew's Gospel. While Mark 15:11 portrays them as stirred up by the Jerusalem temple's chief priests to demand the release of Barabbas and the crucifixion of Jesus, Matthew has additional material describing Pilate's proclamation of his own innocence regarding Jesus' fate and the Jewish people's self-proclaimed assumption of all guilt in the matter:

> The governor again said to them, "Which of the two do you want me to release to you?" And they said, "Barabbas!" Pilate said to them, "Then what shall I do with Jesus who is called Christ?" They all said, "Let him be crucified!" And he said, "Why, what evil has he

> done?" But they only shouted all the more, "Let him be crucified!" So when Pilate saw that he was gaining nothing, but rather that a riot was beginning, he took water and washed his hands before the crowd, saying, "I am innocent of this man's blood; see to it yourselves." And all the people answered, "His blood be on us and on our children!" (Mt 27:21-25)

Finally, there is a general lament over Jerusalem:

> "O Jerusalem, Jerusalem, killing the prophets and stoning those who are sent to you! How often would I have gathered your children together as a hen gathers her brood under her wings, and you would not! Behold, your house is forsaken and desolate." (Mt 23:37-38)

Next follows Jesus' prophecy of the destruction of the temple.

After Jesus' death and resurrection the tensions seem to get worse. In Acts 5:17 we read: "The high priest rose up and all who were with him, that is the party of the Sadducees, and filled with jealousy they arrested the apostles and put them in the common prison." In Acts 6-7 we hear the story of Stephen who preached Jesus and was arrested and brought before the high priest. What he said was regarded as blasphemy and he was stoned to death for it. These tensions led to some doleful and extreme language in the New Testament, bitter invectives and denunciations as in 1 Thessalonians 2:14-15 regarding the Jews, "who killed both the Lord Jesus and the prophets, and drove us out, and displease God and oppose all men," or such an epithet as in Revelation 3:9, "the synagogue of Satan."

As for Christianity's encounter with Hellenistic religion, there are several references in the New Testament. For example, there are some passages that describe Jesus' encounter with "the faith" of pagans. One of these is to be found in the narrative of his meeting with the Syrophoenician woman in Mark 7:24-30:

> And from there he arose and went away to the region of Tyre and Sidon. And he entered a house, and would not

have any one know it; yet he could not be hid. But immediately a woman, whose little daughter was possessed by an unclean spirit, heard of him, and came and fell down at his feet. Now the woman was a Greek, a Syrophoenician by birth. And she begged him to cast the demon out of her daughter. And he said to her, "Let the children first be fed, for it is not right to take the children's bread and throw it to the dogs." "Yes, Lord; yet even the dogs under the table eat the children's crumbs." And he said to her, "For this saying you may go your way; the demon has left your daughter." And she went home, and found the child lying in bed, and the demon gone.

And then there is Jesus' encounter with the Roman soldier in Matthew 8:5-13 (cf. Lk 7:2-10). This Roman soldier may have been, like the centurion Cornelius, in Acts 10, a Gentile greatly attracted to Judaism but yet no convert.

References to Christianity's encounter with more formal elements of pagan, Hellenistic religion can be found in the Acts of the Apostles and the epistles of the New Testament. For example, in Acts 14:8-13, we are told of an incident that happened during Paul's and Barnabas' evangelization of Lystra:

Now at Lystra there was a man sitting, who could not use his feet; he was a cripple from birth who had never walked. He listened to Paul speaking; and Paul, looking intently at him and seeing that he had faith to be made well, said in a loud voice, "Stand upright on your feet." And he sprang up and walked. And when the crowds saw what Paul had done, they lifted up their voices, saying in Lycaonian, "The gods have come down to us in the likeness of men!" Barnabas they called Zeus, and Paul, because he was the chief speaker, they called Hermes. And the priest of Zeus, whose temple was in front of the city, brought oxen and garlands to the gates and wanted to offer sacrifice with the people.

In Acts 17:16 we are told that "at Athens, his [Paul's] spirit was provoked within him as he saw that the city was full of idols." And, indeed, in Acts 17:22-23, we are told how Paul used this as an opportunity to preach:

> So Paul, standing in the middle of the Areopagus, said: "Men of Athens, I perceive that in every way you are very religious. For as I passed along and observed the objects of your worship, I found also an altar with this inscription, "To an unknown god." What therefore you worship as unknown, this I proclaim to you."

In Acts 19:21-41, there is an incident referred to as the riot of the Ephesian silversmiths. It tells of Paul's evangelization of the city of Ephesus which was so successful that it put a dent in the trade of artisans who made silver statues of the goddess Artemis whose central shrine was at Ephesus. In 1 Corinthians 8, Saint Paul has to deal with the pastoral problem of Christians who eat "meat sacrificed to idols," since much of the food in that city's markets had been first subjected to pagan religious ceremonies.

Finally, we should note that besides organized and public religious cults, there is also evidence in the New Testament for Christianity's encounter with more discrete and idiosyncratic forms of magic and superstition. In Acts 8:9-13, we are told of Philip the evangelist's encounter with a magician in the city of Samaria:

> But there was a man named Simon who had previously practiced magic in the city and amazed the nation of Samaria, saying that he himself was somebody great. They all gave heed to him, from the least to the greatest, saying, "This man is that power of God which is called Great." And they gave heed to him, because for a long time he had amazed them with his magic. But when they believed Philip as he preached good news about the kingdom of God and the name of Jesus Christ, they were baptized, both men and women. Even Simon himself believed, and after being baptized he continued with Philip.

But later, in Acts 8:14-24, we are told how this same Simon, when he "saw that the Spirit was given through the laying on of the apostles' hands, he offered them money." Two other incidents involving magicians are the story of Bar-Jesus or Elymas the magician in Acts 13:4-12 and the story of the seven sons of Sceva in Acts 19:13-20.

What shall we say about all these passages, what lessons can we take from them? First, as regards Jewish-Christian relations: the story we have told about the encounter between Christianity and Judaism is not the whole truth. In the Christian tradition there are discernible two quite different attitudes toward the Jews. As we have seen from the passages quoted above, one is highly polemical, indeed at times intemperate, irrational and downright malicious. But now we must see that in these same New Testament writings there is yet another, more positive, more reasoned, pious and just attitude toward the Jews.

For example, in some manuscripts of the Gospel according to Luke, in contrast to Matthew's theme of the guilt of the Jews, the dying Jesus is portrayed as exonerating the Jews who opposed him, as he says, "Father, forgive them; for they know not what they do" (Lk 23:34). Moreover, all the textual witnesses to the Gospel according to Luke are at one in witness to Luke's depiction of how the Jewish crowd at the crucifixion departed beating their breasts in remorse: "And all the multitudes who assembled to see the sight, when they saw what had taken place, returned home beating their breasts" (Lk 23:48). And if the authenticity of Luke 23:34 is questioned by some, there is the undisputed witness of Peter in Acts 3:17, "Brethren, I know that you acted in ignorance, as did also your rulers."

But the most important New Testament witness to a more positive evaluation of the Jews is to be found in one of Saint Paul's most important literary works. The Epistle to the Romans is not only the longest but also the most theologically complex of all Saint Paul's epistles. Unlike most of his other epistles which were written to churches he had established, the Epistle to the Romans is written to a church he had never once visited. Indeed, many people see it as a necessary letter written in advance of his visiting the Christians at Rome precisely so as to disarm any apprehensions they may have had as to his attitude toward the Jews. That is, some exegetes have argued, the Christian community at Rome was in large measure made up of former Jews. Moreover, those same Jewish Christians were apprehensive because of what they had heard (or perhaps read in the First Epistle to the Thessalonians?) was Saint Paul's at times harsh indictment of his former co-religionists. Whatever is the truth of the matter, the fact is that the 11th Chapter of the Epistle to the Romans is a long and beautiful, indeed profound, expression of Paul's most mature and comprehensive theology of the Jews. It begins: "I ask, then, has God rejected his people? By no means! I myself am an Israelite, a descendant of Abraham, a member of the tribe of Benjamin. God has not rejected his people whom he foreknew." The foreknowledge theme here is then developed into an explanation of how God in his providence, in his provident wisdom, has used the disbelief of the Jews as a salutary means to allow time for the salvation of the Gentiles. He expresses it as follows in Romans 11:25-29:

> Lest you Gentiles be wise in your own conceits, I want you to understand this mystery, brethren: a hardening has come upon part of Israel, until the full number of the Gentiles come in, and so *all Israel will be saved* [the italics are mine]; as it is written: "The Deliverer will come from Zion, he will banish ungodliness from Jacob" and "this will be my covenant with them when I take away their sins." As regards the gospel, they are enemies of God for your sake; but as regards election, they are beloved for the sake of their forefathers. For the gifts and the call of God are irrevocable.

We must be vigilant to make our own the theology of "the mystery of the Jews" rather than the theology of "the guilt of the Jews." Unfortunately in Christian history this has not always been the case. In fact, it seems that more often than not Christians have based their attitude toward the Jews solely upon the negative passages I have quoted above. I could quote to you lengthy passages from sermons and pamphlets of great Christian figures such as John Chrysostom and Martin Luther, passages that would cause many of us to blush with shame because they read like Nazi diatribes against the Jews. True, once in a while there were glimmers of light. Aquinas followed the lead of Luke in the *Summa theologiae*, the Third Part, question 47, where he treated of the cause of Christ's death, and even more precisely the question of the guilt of the Jews. Aquinas there invokes the position of Luke, citing not only the words of Jesus in Luke 23:34, "Father, forgive them; for they know not what they do," but also Acts 3:17 where Peter says, "Brethren, I know that you acted in ignorance, as did also your rulers." Moreover, we must remember the earliest leadership of the Church — Paul and the Twelve — were all Jews. Remember also the description of the growth of the first Christian community in Jerusalem and the comment in Acts 6:7, "and a great many of the priests were obedient to the faith."

As for the lessons to be learned from the encounter of Christianity and Hellenistic religions, the first phenomenon we should consider is that of Christianity's encounter with the pious Gentile as we have already seen in Jesus' encounters with the Syrophoenician woman and the centurion of Capernaum, and Peter's conversion of Cornelius. A good way to address this issue is to begin by looking at two passages from St. Paul's Letter to the Romans that address in a speculative way the religious motive in human beings. In the very first chapter of that letter Paul asserts his belief that all humankind, Gentiles as well as Jews, will be held accountable by God for their actions. And the Gentiles will be held equally accountable to judgment because, far from being left totally ignorant of God or the moral law, there is present within creation certain clear indications of God and the moral law. Paul points to the first clear indication in Romans 1:19-23:

> For what can be known about God is plain to them, be-
> cause God has shown it to them. Ever since the creation
> of the world his invisible nature, namely, his eternal

power and deity, has been clearly perceived in the things
that have been made. So they are without excuse.

Moreover, besides creation which in the Old Testament words,
"proclaims the glory of God," there is an even more intimate
factor in human beings to be accounted for and Paul addresses
this further factor in Romans 2:14-16:

> When Gentiles who have not the law do by nature
> what the law requires, they are a law to themselves,
> even though they do not have the law. They show that
> what the law requires is written on their hearts, while
> their conscience also bears witness and their conflicting
> thoughts accuse or perhaps excuse them on that day
> when, according to my gospel, God judges the secrets
> of men by Christ Jesus.

What Paul is talking about here is clearly illustrated in the episode of Jesus' encounter with the Roman soldier at Capernaum
(Mt 6:5-13, Lk 7:1-10) of whom Jesus said, "Truly, I say to you,
not even in Israel have I found such faith." That is, this pagan
Roman soldier exhibits a faith in his encounter with Jesus that
Jesus has not always found among his own co-religionists. Moreover, it is arguable that this Roman's soldier's acute sensitivity
to discipline probably fed into his sense of faith. In other words,
we must be prepared to meet at times pious and just pagans, men
and women who even though they do not share our religious
tradition, nonetheless manifest in their lives a measure of justice,
faith and hope that approximates the Gospel tradition.

On the other hand, to be balanced, I think one must also
concede the example of the pious and just pagan is a rarity.
For with the significant exception of Jesus' encounter with the
soldier at Capernaum, the New Testament witness is that most
of humanity is caught up in either religious speculation that is
fruitless or, even worse, beliefs that are not only vain but even
self-destructive. Moreover, this factor of the wayward religious
motive in man is present even today. While many today are
impressed by the phenomenon of atheism in the contempo-

rary world, there is much evidence that suggests superstition still abounds and so too idolatry of such false gods as sex and money.

For example, astrology is still popular today. And its concept of planets and stars influencing us can be seen as but another example of animist religion, that is, the idea that there are many spirits out there that affect our lives. More formal animist cults, such as Santeria, are still strong in many parts of the world and not just in rural areas. While some pagan deities such as Diana have prompted some interest today, for the greater part, the cults of Hellenistic deities like Artemis, Zeus and Hermes are long gone. And, yet, while their formal, historic cults have long faded, some of the devotions they represent are still with us though in different form. That is, while some insist it is atheism that typifies modern man, it can be argued his obsession with sex and money is effectively a form of idolatry. For example, the image of Artemis is well known to students of antiquity from her many surviving images. Indeed, scholars debate whether it is multiple breasts she bears in those images or whether those are instead bulls' testicles. But, whichever is right, the evidence is clear she was a fertility goddess and an example of the ancient world's divinization of sex. Much of modern society continues in this divinization of sex as one of the highest forms of human fulfillment and ecstasy; though, ironically, now the sacred value at stake is not fertility but infertility. However, I would argue the New Testament is most innovative in its identification and exposure of other more subtle religious currents.

Besides its indirect witness to the divinization of sex, the New Testament also introduces us to the concept of material prosperity as an alien God and its pursuit as a deep religious commitment. "Mammon" is a word frequently found in the Aramaic writings of Jesus' day. But when it is found in the *targums* (Aramaic paraphrases of the Hebrew Scriptures), the documents of Qumran (the famous Dead Sea Scrolls) and the Talmud (the later collection of rabbinic teachings going back to the time of Jesus) it is the normal word for "money" or "wealth" or "profit." Moreover, in those literary works it is used there with no essentially bad connotation. However, when Jesus uses the word "mammon" in Matthew 6:24 and Luke 16:13, "You cannot serve God and Mammon," Mammon is personified in the manner of a god, a rival lord to the sovereignty of the God of Israel. Is it too much to claim that in our modern world there is much evidence suggesting worship of "the almighty dollar" often rivals worship of the Almighty Father.

Finally, we must look at the phenomenon of world religions, the fact that in the last three thousand years we have seen arise several intelligent thematic expressions of the religious motive in humankind, religions capable of shaping not only the personal lives of people but even civilizations. With regard to this phenomenon, the Second Vatican Council's 1965 "Declaration on the Church's Relationship to Non-Christian Religions" is a very important summary statement. While it is biblically based, this document also reflects centuries of experience encountering world religions in all their manifestations after the completion of the New Testament. It is a relatively small document and its teachings can be summed up in a few simple principles. First, while the document does indeed recognize the religious motive that seems to have characterized the human race from earliest times, it emphasizes the superior importance of what it describes as "the religions associated with the development of civilization." More precisely in Article 2, paragraph 1, it says:

> From ancient until modern time there is found among various peoples a certain perception of that unseen force which is present in the course of things and in events in human life, and sometimes, even an acknowledgment of a supreme deity or even a Father. This perception and acknowledgment permeates their lives with a deep religious sense. The religions associated with the development of civilization, however, strive to answer these questions with more refined ideas and more highly developed language.

And then it goes on to name, in addition to Judaism, the religious traditions of Islam, Hinduism and Buddhism, as bearers of culture. These great world religions have produced significant bodies of literature and moreover have shaped people's lives in a significant way. However, then it goes on to say (in Article 2, paragraph 2) of these religions something truly remarkable:

> The Catholic Church rejects nothing of those things which are true and holy in these religions. It regards with respect those ways of acting and living and those precepts and teachings which, though often at variance with what it holds and expounds, frequently reflect a ray of that truth which enlightens everyone.

I say this is a truly remarkable statement because at times in the history of Christianity, the Church has not always looked so positively upon other religions. Indeed, there was detectable a strain in earlier Christian thought that tended to demonize all other religions.

However, here is where it is very important that we be balanced, because the Council itself was very carefully balanced in this its attitude toward other religions. While, indeed, the Second Vatican Council concedes to these great world religions a measure of grace and truth, it is, at the same time, equally insistent that the fullness of grace and truth resides with Christianity. Indeed, to get the full sense of this balanced teaching I quote here both the passage just cited along with the very next sentence that balances it and I emphasize the balancing element by putting it in italics:

> The Catholic Church rejects nothing of those things which are true and holy in these religions. It regards with respect those ways of acting and living and those precepts and teachings which, though often at variance with what it holds and expounds, frequently reflect a ray of that truth which enlightens everyone. *Yet, without ceasing it preaches, and is bound to preach, Christ who is "the way, the truth, and the life" (Jn 14:6), in whom people find the fullness of religious life and in whom God has reconciled all things in himself.*

I have made a special point of insisting upon the balance of this important conciliar teaching because there have been some Catholic theologians who after the Council have interpreted this Council's teaching on the relationship of the Church to non-Christian religions as if it implies Christianity is but one of several grace-filled and insightful approaches to God. That is not true. In fact the Council shows itself quite well aware of the fact that alongside these elements of grace and truth there are at times some very erroneous notions destructive of genuine humanity. In the history of the Christian missions there have been individuals who, long ago, realized the importance of dialogue with these other religious cultures. The Spanish layman Ramon Lull (ca. 1233-ca. 1315) and the Italian Jesuit Matteo Ricci (1552-1610) produced significant literary works reflecting that dialogue: Lull's *Dialogue between a Muslim, a Jew and a Christian,* and Ricci's *The One True Faith,* exhibit keen awareness of the religious cultures they were attempting to evangelize and a blessed ability to recognize what was valuable in those cultures and to identify with it. The Second Vatican Council urges the whole Church to attempt this kind of dialogue in a practical fashion. We would do well not to ignore the council's directive.

The importance of this declaration by the Second Vatican Council should not be underestimated. That is even if one is not Catholic and therefore feels no particular need to respect this teaching, basic reason should acknowledge the fact that what it said in its "Declaration on the Church's Relationship to Non-Christian Religions" reflects a phenomenon unknown to the biblical authors, the rise of other intelligent expressions of religion capable of shaping a more humane society. Moreover, while Judaism is still with us to this day, and we must always be conscientious about our respect for the Jews, these other religions have many more adherents and loom even more important politically as well as demographically in the contemporary world. Moreover, while not wanting to approve of any violent rejections of modernity, it is possible to argue that a religion such as Islam exhibits an understandable reaction to modernity. For example, it is not hard to understand how a devout Middle

Eastern Muslim who comes upon MTV by means of satellite television might form an image of America as a libertarian society and thus be quick to accept the labeling of the USA as "the great Satan." While many Westerners will indict the place of women in Muslim societies as constricting, devout Muslims might well find the exploitation of women that characterizes so many videos on MTV a greater cause for consternation.

Further Reading

In Lesslie Newbigin's *The Open Secret: An Introduction to the Theology of Mission* (Grand Rapids, MI: Wm. B. Eerdmans, Revised Edition, 1995), Chapter 10, "The Gospel among the Religions."

J.A. Dinoia's *The Diversity of Religions: A Christian Perspective* (Washington, DC: Catholic University of America Press, 1992).

Two works by Joseph Ratzinger: his *Many Religions, One Covenant: Israel, the Church, and the World* (Ignatius Press, 1999) and his *Truth and Tolerance: Christian Belief and World Religions* (Ignatius Press, 2004).

CHAPTER 19

Church and State

The Church does not exist in a void. There is in this world another large and ambitious social organization. It is called the State. And the State too aspires to a noble task. It attempts to give intelligent direction and just order to human affairs and it even tries to order nature, that is, physical chaos. In other words, it aims to build an organized and just society with well-paved roads. In this sense, the State is one of the greatest of human cultural achievements.

What should be the Church's relationship to the State? Answers to that question have varied greatly over the last two thousand years. These variations have been due to two things. At times it has been the political situation in which the Church has found itself which has dictated the relationship of Church and State. At some other times it has been the varying ideas which people have held of the Church that has dictated what the relationship was between Church and State.

In the earliest period of the Church's history it was political circumstances that dictated the character of the relationship between Church and State. From the period A.D. 30 to A.D. 312, that is, the period from approximately the death of Jesus to the conversion of the Emperor Constantine, it was an adversarial relationship between Church and State. This situation was dictated in large part because of the character of the Roman State. Roman society, and, indeed the Hellenistic world, was profoundly religious but it was also polytheistic. Religious rites accompanied many social and public events. Roman religious toleration is exemplified in a temple in Rome which stands to this day. It is called the Pantheon, "the house of all the gods," precisely because it housed statues and altars to a large variety of deities worshiped throughout the Roman Empire. No doubt, the Romans would have been happy to add a statue of Jesus. But, in addition to this religious tolerance, the Roman State also required acknowledgment of the divinity of the emperor. This situation meant that the Church was largely isolated from official Roman society. It received no support from the Roman public authorities. Quite, the contrary, imperial edicts proscribed Christian worship. And Christian refusal to enter into the imperial cult was regarded as high treason and thus punishable with death.

All of this changed, however, with the conversion of the Emperor Constantine in the year 312. Soon the Church was not only tolerated by the State but even came in for lavish State patronage. Constantine built great churches in Rome, Jerusalem and Constantinople. In 381 Christianity became the official religion of the empire and thus the Church came under direct support of the imperial government. Clergy were given special privileges: financial support, police protection, legal exemptions. The emperor convoked and presided over the first great general council of the Church. The acquisition and disposition of Church property was regulated by imperial laws. This intimate relationship between Church and State only intensified during the Carolingian era (from the 8th to the early 11th centuries) when imperial or, now, royal rule over the Church found further expression: clergy in the West were invested in their spiritual office by kings and feudal lords, and the Church property which the clergy administered was regarded as belonging to the king or feudal lord. This second period of unitary relationship between Church and State ended however in the eleventh century with what some historians describe as "the papal revolution." In the century between 1050 and 1150, a large part of the clergy throughout Western Christendom united under the bishop of Rome to reorganize the Church into a unified, hierarchical, autonomous, political-legal entity, separate from the secular authority of emperors, kings and feudal lords. The "magna carta" of this movement was a document issued by Pope Gregory VII in 1075 called *Dictatus papae* (Dictates of the Pope). It proclaimed that emperors and kings had no authority over the Church, that the bishop of Rome alone had authority to ordain, discipline, depose and reinstate bishops, to convoke and direct general councils of the Church, to establish and administer abbeys and bishoprics. Moreover, it decreed the papal court was to be the last court of appeal for all Christians, to which all Christians had a right to resort in matters within the ecclesiastical jurisdiction. Finally, it claimed that a pope could depose an emperor. This was not a return to an adversarial relationship between Church and State but rather the creation of a dualist theory of Church / State relations, the creation of two separate realms of jurisdiction and authority, the secular and the sacred.

The next major change in the general configuration of Church/State relations came with the Protestant Reformation. Martin Luther (1483-1546) appealed to the German nobility to ameliorate the decadence in the Church and in doing this he gave great authority to secular rulers in the administration of the Church. Luther called upon Christian princes to establish and protect the Church in their domains, to help define its doctrine, regulate its liturgy and discipline its clergy. And thus Lutheranism became the established religion in most of the principalities of Germany and Scandinavia. Through a series of statutes enacted in the 1530's, a State Church was established in England with the monarch as its head. In France in 1598, the edict of Nantes established Gallican Catholicism, under royal rule, as the official religion of France. In the sixteenth century, the State in Spain and in the Netherlands established the Catholic Church under royal patronage.

The French Revolution of 1789, however, with its democratic ideals and Enlightenment theories of religious toleration, led many countries in Europe to adopt disestablishment policies. For example, in France, in 1801, the concordat between Pius VII and the First French Republic relinquished State control but not support of the Church. In 1905, the Law of Separation of Church and State went further and removed State support. However, no country of Europe enacted such strong guarantees of religious freedom as those provided by the United States Constitution. However, even in the United States there remain areas of debate and question regarding Church/State relations. Despite the claim that there is a strict wall of separation between Church and State in the U.S., clergy here are prominent in public life, as chaplains in both the military and the congress. Also, while no Church here receives direct financial support from the State, all religious institutions are exempt from taxation and all clergy are exempt from military service. On the other hand, the Church is often quick to criticize laws and lawmakers regarding war, labor, abortion — even encouraging civil disobedience in such matters. Nor does the Church's involvement in legislation stop at criticism; from time to time Christian legislators attempt to promulgate laws that reflect Christian morality.

In this next section I want to look at passages from the New Testament that arguably address the issue of Church/State relations or have implications for them. I think this is a tricky task. We already have some questionable judgments in this regard, for example, Pope Boniface VIII's papal bull, *Unam sanctam*, dated November 18, 1302. Its use of Luke 22:35-38 to elaborate a "two swords theory" of the relation between Church and State is judged by the great majority of exegetes today (Catholic exegetes included) as a strained, indeed, extremely fanciful, overly imaginative employment of Scripture. But I think the reader will see that the passages I have chosen to treat are not inventive or strained appropriations of Scripture but directly address such patent political issues as taxation and magistracy, and court procedures.

By far the most important New Testament passage on Church/State relations is the account in all three of the Synoptic Gospels (Mk 12:13-17; Mt 22:15-22; Lk 20:20-26) of Jesus' famous dictum regarding the paying of taxes to the Roman State. I quote it here in the Marcan version:

> And they [the chief priests, the scribes and the elders]
> sent to him some of the Pharisees and some of the
> Herodians to entrap him in his talk. And they came and
> said to him, "Teacher, we know that you are true, and
> care for no man; for you do not regard the position of
> men, but truly teach the way of God. Is it lawful to pay
> taxes to Caesar, or not? Should we pay them or should
> we not?" But knowing their hypocrisy, he said to them,
> "Why put me to the test? Bring me a coin, and let me
> look at it." And they brought one. And he said to them,
> "Whose likeness and inscription is this?" They said to
> him, "Caesar's." Jesus said to them, "Render to Caesar
> the things that are Caesar's; and to God the things that
> are God's." And they were amazed at him.

The tax under discussion here is the census tax. It was a particularly explosive issue. There were many kinds of taxes in Israel
in Jesus' day, including religious taxes — elsewhere we hear
Jesus questioned about the temple tax required of all Jews by
their own religious authorities. As in our day, there were property taxes, tolls, sales taxes, inheritance taxes, but this census
tax was most heinous, because it was a reminder of the Jews'
subject status. Indeed, when the poll tax had been first imposed
on the Roman province of Judea in A.D. 6, Judas the Galilean
(see Ac 5:37) had seen this as the Jewish people's introduction to
slavery and an affront to the sovereignty of God (see Josephus'
Antiquities XVIII.i.l). The tax had to be paid using only Roman
coinage. Whether the effigy and title of "the divine Caesar" on
the denarius would have indeed carried with it the impiety Judas
the Galilean attributed to it is a disputed point. Nevertheless,
the question at issue in this Gospel passage would have been of
practical importance to Jews and indeed even Jewish Christians
throughout the period preceding the fall of Jerusalem. And as
for Mark's Roman readers, the story will have been of great
importance to them because of the possibility of interpreting
it as evidence that Christianity need not involve disloyalty to
the State.

Regardless of how one may want to interpret the saying "Render to Caesar," there are several other passages in the New Testament that make it clear there is no conflict between being a devout Christian and respecting the State, both its laws and its magistrates. For example, there is Romans 13:1-7:

> Let every person be subject to the governing authorities. For there is no authority except from God, and those that exist have been instituted by God. Therefore he who resists the authorities resists what God has appointed, and those who resist will incur judgment. For rulers are not a terror to good conduct, but to bad. Would you have no fear of him who is in authority? Then do what is good and you will receive his approval, for he is God's servant for your good. But if you do wrong, be afraid, for he does not bear the sword in vain; he is the servant of God to execute his wrath on the wrongdoer. Therefore one must be subject, not only to avoid God's wrath but also for the sake of conscience. For the same reason you also pay taxes, for the authorities are ministers of God, attending to this very thing. Pay all of them their dues, taxes to whom taxes are due, revenue to whom revenue is due, respect to whom respect is due, honor to whom honor is due.

Several things could be said about this passage. No doubt, Roman law, with its clear articulation of citizenship and magistracy, duties and privileges, is regarded by many as one of humankind's greatest cultural achievements. But one can still be amazed to hear Paul go so far as to claim the State is "God's servant." Martin Luther will take this passage so seriously that in the twentieth century another Protestant theologian, Paul Tillich will accuse Luther of having inculcated in the German people such a respect for civil authority as may have contributed to the success of the Nazi movement. Whatever the truth of that, Paul of Tarsus is far from alone in his teaching Christians basic respect for the State. For example, this is a repeated theme in the secondary Pauline literature. We read in 1 Timothy 2:1-2, "First of all, then, I urge that supplications, prayers, intercessions, and thanksgivings be made for all men, for kings and for all who are in high positions, that we may lead a quiet and peaceable life, godly and respectful in every way." In Titus 3:1, we read: "Remind them to be submissive to rulers and authorities, to be obedient, to be ready for any honest work." Even outside of Pauline literature we find yet another strong exhortation to patriotism in 1 Peter 2:13-17:

> Be subject for the Lord's sake to every human institution, whether it be to the emperor as supreme, or to governors as sent by him to punish those who do wrong and to praise those who do right. For it is God's will that by doing right you should put to silence the ignorance of foolish men. Live as free men, yet without using your freedom as a pretext for evil; but live as servants of God. Honor all men. Love the brotherhood. Fear God. Honor the emperor.

However, what must also be seen is that despite these numerous passages in the New Testament that encourage respect for and obedience to the State, its legal processes and officers, there are at the same time other New Testament passages that reflect a more critical view of the State and its ways.

For example, Jesus as presented in the Gospels is well aware of the authoritarianism present in the political structures of human societies. In Mark 10:42, we hear him say, "You know that those who are supposed to rule over the Gentiles lord it over them, and their great men exercise authority over them." Also, Jesus has a keen eye for the "rough justice" of the civil courts. The warning to his disciples in Mark 13:9, "But take heed to yourselves; for they will deliver you up to councils [legal tribunals]," is given more candid illustration in several passages in Luke and Matthew suggesting Jesus knew well the dubious, at times woeful, procedures of civil courts. The arbitrariness of judges is recalled in the keen depiction of the judge in Luke 18:2-8 who "neither feared God nor regarded man." The severity or harshness of judicial procedures and the penal system is made clear in Luke 12:58: "As you go with your accuser before the magistrate, make an effort to settle with him on the way, lest he drag you to the judge, and the judge hand you over to the officer, and the officer put you in prison. I tell you, you will never get out till you have paid the last copper." The "copper" (*lepton*) was the smallest Greek coin in circulation. When we read these words it is good to keep in mind debtors' prisons remained a prominent element in English society right up into the nineteenth century.

Another subtle but even more challenging view of the State is presented in the Lucan infancy narrative. The birth narrative is set within the context of an imperial decree. Luke 2:1 begins:

> In those days a decree went out from Caesar Augustus that all the world should be enrolled. This was the first enrollment, when Quirinius was governor of Syria. And all went to be enrolled, each to his own city. And Joseph also went up from Galilee, from the city of Nazareth, to Judea, to the city of David, which is called Bethlehem, because he was of the house and lineage of David, to be enrolled with Mary, his betrothed, who was with child.

And thus Joseph and Mary are portrayed here as dutiful subjects of the Roman State, that is, making the inconvenient and arduous journey to be enrolled in a census which was taken precisely for tax purposes. On the other hand, the scene is replete with ironies, for the Roman emperor Augustus is portrayed as the unsuspecting, human tool by which the divine plan is furthered, a plan which will end in the overthrow of Augustus' power. For no sooner is Mary's child born when a choir of angels arrives and the mood of prosaic domestic labor, of peasant bending to the will of the mighty, is broken by the announcement of a cosmic event:

> And while they were there, the time came for her to be delivered. And she gave birth to her firstborn son and

> wrapped him in swaddling cloths, and laid him in a manger, because there was no place for them in the inn.
>
> And in that region there were shepherds out in the field, keeping watch over their flock by night. And an angel of the Lord appeared to them, and the glory of the Lord shone around them, and they were filled with fear. And the angel said to them, "Be not afraid; for behold, I bring you good news of a great joy which will come to all people; for to you is born this day in the city of David a Savior, which is Christ the Lord."

But the drama is not over, for new reinforcements arrive, more angels to help announce a further blessing: "And suddenly there was with the angel a multitude of the heavenly host praising God and saying, 'Glory to God in the highest, and on earth peace among men with whom he is pleased!'"

But the ironies do not stop there, for this theme of peace is particularly portentous. It is invoked several times in the Lucan infancy narrative: Zechariah, the father of John the Baptist, had prophesied that the child to be born whom his son would herald, would "guide our feet into the way of peace" (Lk 1:79). And Simeon upon seeing the child says, "Lord, now lettest thou thy servant depart in peace" (Lk 2:29). This peace motif has special relevance for the Roman emperor Augustus. He took the title *princeps pacis*, prince of peace, because he had inaugurated a reign of peace after forty years of civil war. He erected an altar to peace in Rome, something that can be seen to this day. He initiated a period of great economic prosperity and cultural achievement. And in that sense Luke seems to be offering a considerable challenge, insisting that Jesus is the true prince of peace.

And Paul is well aware of this when he says in Philippians 3:20, "But our commonwealth is in heaven." Christians must realize they have a dual citizenship. Moreover, one final lesson from the New Testament is a late but important one, namely, that the State can become a beast.

Chapter 13 of the Book of Revelation, the Revelation of Saint John, is commonly interpreted as a passage in which the

Roman Empire is symbolized as a beast who is opposed to
Christ. Some exegetes have argued that this represents a position
contradictory to that of Paul. But this is not true. The two positions are not necessarily inconsistent. Both are based on the Old
Testament principal that all human governments are in God's
hands, all are instruments of God's purpose. Therefore, the duty
of obedience to civil rulers is always qualified by the condition
that they are indeed doing their proper work of restraining evil
and promoting peace. When human rulers, like Roman emperors, start to make claims to divine prerogatives and demand to
be worshiped, then they are to be resisted. In the last century,
with the rise of totalitarian States such as Nazi Germany and
Communist Russia, we have seen how true it is that the State
can become a beast.

On the other hand, these passages from the New Testament
can also serve as a warning to us against a simplistic biblicism. In
accord with the ecumenical intentions announced in the preface
to this book, I have tried to base my arguments principally but
not solely upon Scripture. But this evidence of the New Testament witness regarding the question of Church/State relations
shows how we must at times go beyond what can be simply
quoted from Scripture. The New Testament texts supporting and
glorifying the State are preponderantly more impressive than
its more challenging view of the State. I had to dig hard to find
any even indirectly critical of the State. So in the end, I would
like to sum up some principles that might be derived from our
studies so far, a sort of dogmatic summary.

I would argue there are three fundamental elements to all
Christian political theory. But please note: these three elements
while basic to Catholicism, Protestantism and Orthodoxy, nevertheless, find different emphases and even distinctive interpretations in those three traditions.

The first principle is what might be called a fundamental
point regarding "the dualism of Church and State." By "dualism" is meant here the independence of the religious and political orders. The Church's principal sphere of influence and

concern is the spiritual realm where it is the ultimate authority. Similarly, the principal sphere of influence and power for the State should be the social order. And thus theoretically at least there should be a peaceful co-existence between Church and State as long as each respects the rights of the other in its particular sphere. For example, as we saw in the New Testament writings, the Roman Empire could be accepted, indeed must be obeyed when it functioned in purely political matters. In Jesus' dictum, "Give to Caesar the things that are Caesar's," it is arguable we see his acknowledgment of the right of the State to tax all its citizens.

The second principle of Church/State relations might be called "the sovereignty of God over both Church and State." This too is a fundamental concept in Christian political theory and this means that while Christians can and indeed do acknowledge the authority of the State in social matters, nonetheless, we cannot allow an absolute distinction between sacred and profane. That is, we cannot allow the State to become a purely secular sphere with no accountability to God. For example, war can never be seen as a purely political matter.

The third fundamental principle in all Christian political theory is an assumption regarding "the moral ambivalence of all government." Christians must be wary of absolutizing any one political form or structure. No political structure is beyond criticism. In history Christians have at times erred by absolutizing particular forms of government and seeing them as "ordained by God" (cf. the "divine right" of kings). But as an ecclesiologist and not a political theorist I must also point out: there is also the danger of naively applying political forms to religious structures: seeing the Petrine ministry as an absolute monarchy or conceiving of synodal assemblies in simplistic democratic terms, such as in determining Church teaching by means of a simple majority vote.

Further Reading

Chapter XVI, "The Church's Tasks in the World: Church and State, Society, Economy, Science and Culture," in Johann Auer's *The Church: The Universal Sacrament of Salvation* (Catholic University of America Press, 1993)

Chapter III, "The Modern Sense of Freedom and History and the Theological Definition of Human Rights," in Walter Kasper's *Theology and Church* translated by M. Kohl (NY: Crossroad, 1989), pages 54-72.

CHAPTER 20

Introduction to the Concept of Ministry

To mention the word "ministry" today is often to stir up a hornet's nest of controversy, for what is ministry and who ought to be doing it are greatly debated issues in the contemporary Church. And the answers given to those questions are often not just far ranging but contentiously different. For example, classical forms of Christian ministry such as the offices of bishop, priest and deacon are today often indicted as later intrusions upon and distortions of a much more democratic distribution and recognition of talents or gifts which characterized the early Christian Church. Moreover, while these classical forms of ministry are being criticized, new forms of Christian ministry are fast appearing. And these new forms of ministry seem to appropriate for themselves many of the duties that were formerly considered the sole preserve of priests and deacons, monks and nuns, or of pastors. Such so-called "lay ministries" are a great topic of the day. But some critics of them are quick to point out that such expressions as "lay minister" and "lay ministry" are oxymoronic, that is, contradictions in terms. Indeed, many Protestant readers might find the term "lay minister" rather strange in that for them ministers are not laity, they are clergy. But even these issues do not exhaust the contemporary controversies regarding ministry; for there is also a great debate today as to what real ministry is. Here too there is often a polarity between some who insist real ministry is primarily cultic, that is, "church services," leadership in prayer and preaching, and others who insist that "church services" should only prepare one for "service in the streets," service in the community, that is, leadership in social progress and change. Indeed, there are many Christians today who identify themselves almost exclusively with the Church's social justice ministry and have difficulty identifying themselves with any aspect of the Church's teaching and preaching ministry.

To bring some order and light to this contemporary debate, what I propose to do here is a lexical, linguistic, that is, word study of the language of service in the Bible. What we shall see is that ministry in the Bible is service of both God and neighbor. Moreover, we shall see how in the biblical tradition, worship of God in heaven and assistance to one's neighbor in need become not just sacred duties but closely linked such that often one is the test of the integrity of the other.

In the Hebrew of the Old Testament, the language of service takes several forms, but the most important for our interests, the terms with the most strongly theological content, are the terms *abad* and *shereth*. With both of these terms an ordinary, everyday meaning develops into a specialized religious meaning.

Without an object the verb *abad* usually means simply "to work" and often in the sense of physical labor. For example, in the Decalogue, Exodus 34:21, we hear the injunction: "Six days you shall work, but on the seventh day you shall rest." With personal objects, however, *abad* means not just "to work at something" but "to work for someone, to serve." For example, in Genesis 29:30 we are told that Jacob "served Laban for another seven years" tending Laban's flock. In Exodus 21:6 it is used with reference to the service of a slave, "he shall serve him for life." In Job 39:9 we hear the question: "Is the wild ox willing to serve you?" However, this verb *abad* is also used at times to indicate service of God in the sense of worship, as in Exodus 3:12: "When you have brought forth the people out of Egypt, you shall serve God upon the mountain." In Exodus 7:16, God's message to Pharaoh through Moses is: "Let my people go, that they may serve me in the wilderness." In Exodus 20:5, the Hebrew people are warned about graven images in the words: "You shall not bow down to them or serve them." And in Psalm 100:2, we hear: "Serve the Lord with gladness." In addition to its currency as a term for menial labor, personal service, and religious worship, it eventually came to have great theological influence as it shaped such ideas as *sabat*, to cease from work and, because the verb *abad* has a related noun form *ebed*, meaning "slave," it was used to express the important theological concept of "the Servant of the Lord."

We see a similar phenomenon with the Hebrew word *shereth*. But unlike *abad* which meant physical labor, *shereth* was used to describe not menial service, the tending of sheep, or hard labor such as yoked oxen pulling a plow, but personal service rendered by someone who stands in a special relationship to a superior. For example, in Genesis 39:4, we read that "Joseph found favor in his sight and attended him." This is a reference to the biblical patriarch Joseph who came to be so highly trusted a servant of the Egyptian official, Potiphar, that he became Potiphar's principal assistant in charge of his whole household. In Numbers 11:18, we hear Joshua the son of Nun described as "the minister of Moses, one of his chosen men." In 1 Kings 19:21, it is said of Elijah's disciple Elisha, "Then he arose and went after Elijah and ministered to him." Far more frequent, however, is the use of *shereth* and its noun form *mesharet* to designate God's personal attendants. For example, we read in 1 Samuel 3:1, "Now the boy Samuel was ministering to the Lord under Eli." And in Exodus 28:35 we read of the priestly robe, "And it shall be upon Aaron when he ministers (*shereth*)," that is when he serves in the temple cult. We see the same word used in Ezekiel 40:40, "the priests who have charge of the altar; these are the sons of Zadok, who alone among the sons of Levi may come near to the Lord to minister (*shereth*) to him." It is even used to refer to not only angels but even the elements, as in Psalm 104:4: "fire and flame thy ministers." But *shereth* is most commonly used for the service of Levites at the tabernacle in the desert and later in the temple. See Jeremiah 33:21, "the Levitical priests my ministers"; and Joel 1:9, "The priests mourn, the ministers of the Lord."

In addition to the language of service in the Hebrew Scriptures, it is important that we also look at the language of service employed in the famous Greek translation of the Hebrew Scriptures, the work called the Septuagint. This is the title given to the translation of the Hebrew Scriptures into Hellenistic Greek done by Jewish scribes in the city of Alexandria, Egypt around the year 250 B.C. The word "Septuagint" is derived from the Latin word for seventy, *septuagint*. This title is based on the legend that this translation was the work of seventy translators (a legend perhaps influenced by the story of the seventy elders in Exodus 24:1, 9). It became the most widely used and thus most influential translation of the Hebrew Scriptures in the ancient world. Its influence upon Christianity is considerable, witnessed to by the fact that the Septuagint was the Bible for most writers of the New Testament; that is, any citations which the New Testament writers make from the Jewish Scriptures are taken from the Septuagint. When it comes to the language of service in the Bible, the most important contribution by the Septuagint translators was the use they made of the secular Greek term *leitourgia*.

The Greek term *leitourgia* is made up of two other words. It is a combination of the prefix *leitos* meaning "of the people," "for the people," "concerning the people," and the noun *ergon* meaning "service, task, or work." And thus in classical, secular Greek *leitourgia* meant "public service," "service to the nation," "service to the people." As such it is found commonly in classic Attic Greek, the Greek of Homer and Plato and Aristotle, of orators like Demosthenes. For example, Aristotle in his *Politics* V.8 speaks of the common practice in Greek democracies of fleecing the wealthy by demanding that they perform "liturgies," that is, the rich were not only taxed to support the government but pressure was put upon the wealthy to finance additional expensive public works. These expensive works were their "liturgies." But this is precisely the term which the Septuagint translators chose to use whenever the Hebrew Scriptures used the word *shereth*. And thus the work of the priests in the Jerusalem temple came to be called "liturgies," that is, "public service" not just of God but also "for the people."

It is interesting to speculate why the Jewish translators chose to do this. The exegete H. Strathmann in his entry on this term in Vol. IV of *The Theological Dictionary of the New Testament*, gives this reason: "The LXX translators obviously felt a need to try to fix a regular and exclusive term for priestly ministry, and thereby to show that the cultic relation to God is something special as compared with all the other relations of service in which men might stand." But it could also be a particularly sententious use of this secular Greek political term to imply the only true service of the people is the worship of the one true God. But the importance of this Greek term *leitourgia* does not end with the Septuagint, because it is also used significantly in the New Testament.

Sometimes in the New Testament the term *leitourgia* is used precisely as in the Greek Old Testament, that is, to refer to the service of Jewish priests and Levites in the Jerusalem temple. For example, in Luke 1:23 it is said of Zechariah the father of John the Baptist, "And when his time of service [*leitourgias*] was ended, he went to his home." Similarly, in the Epistle to the Hebrews this word *leitourgia* is used several times with reference to the Jewish temple liturgy as in Hebrews 9:21, "both the tabernacle and all the vessels of the service [*leitourgias*]" and in Hebrews 10:11, "And every priest stands daily at his service [*leitourgon*]." And, because the whole theme of the Epistle to the Hebrews is that Christ is the one true high priest this word is applied to Jesus as in Hebrews 8:6, "Christ has obtained a ministry [*leitourgias*]."

However, there are also other times in the New Testament when the term *leitourgia* seems to be used in the old secular, political sense to refer to public works. For example, in Paul's Letter to the Church at Philippi. This letter was apparently written by Paul during his imprisonment. It is written in part as a "thank you" note to the Church at Philippi for their having sent to Paul a financial donation in support of his ministry, a gift which the Philippians had sent in care of one Epaphroditus. In Philippians 2:30, Paul says of this man, "he nearly died for the work of Christ, risking his life to complete your service [*leitourgias*] to me." "Your service" is a reference to their financial gift to Paul. There are yet two other times when Paul uses this word *leitourgia* to refer to the philanthropic generosity (financial assistance) of one Christian congregation toward another. In Chapter 9 of the Second Letter to the Church at Corinth, Paul encourages the Corinthian congregation to be as generous as the churches of Macedonia (Thessalonica, Philippi and Beroea) have been in raising money to be sent to the Church at Jerusalem. In 2 Corinthians 9:12, Paul says of this collection or public offering "the rendering of this service [*leitourgias*] not only supplies the wants of the saints but also overflows in many thanksgivings to God." In Romans 15:27, Paul once again praises the generosity of the Christian communities at Macedonia and Achaia for their financial assistance of the Christian community at Jerusalem, saying "for if the Gentiles have come to share in their spiritual blessings, they ought also to be of service [*leitourgesai*] to them in material blessings."

However, after my conceding that the use of *leitourgia* in these passages seems to reflect the secular, classical use of the term to refer to public philanthropy, there is at the same in these same passages suggestions that Paul is trying to invest these public philanthropic works with a peculiarly religious character that recalls cultic worship in the Jerusalem temple, indeed identifying them with cultic offerings as in a temple. For example, in Philippians 2:17, Paul says: "Even if I am to be poured out as a libation upon the sacrificial offerings [*leitourgia*] of your faith." The original Greek text uses only the verb "poured out." The RSV translators have added "as a libation." A libation is a cultic ritual act, the act of pouring out of a precious liquid — oil, wine or water — as a sacred offering. Such an action was a regular part of Jewish temple observance. Every animal sacrifice in the temple was accompanied by a libation (Nb 15:1-16, 28:7-31). In other words Paul is saying that his ministry and their support of it is like a Jerusalem temple offering. Their financial assistance in support of Paul's ministry is like the wine that the temple priest poured over the flesh offering as it was placed upon the altar. This cultic language makes for a powerful and striking image and Paul resorts to it once again at the end of this letter, though this time it is the image of temple incense offering, when in Philippians 4:18 he says, "I am filled, having received from Epaphroditus the gifts you sent, a fragrant offering, a sacrifice acceptable and pleasing to God." But this is not just a vivid and colorful image; it is also potent in its theological suggestiveness. By that I mean it is possible to argue Paul's manner of speaking here lays the groundwork for a theology of the common priesthood of the faithful. That is, while the author of the Epistle to the Hebrews sets forth in the clearest terms the unique priesthood of Jesus Christ who offered his life once and for all for the salvation of all, it could be argued that here (as also in 1 P 2:5) we see the suggestion of the idea that the personal sacrifices of Christian men and women in the assistance of others are an analogous kind of sacrificial offering, a common priesthood of the faithful taking inspiration from and analogous to that of Christ.

Paul uses this same technical cultic meaning in a more poetic fashion to describe his own ministry when in Romans 15:15-16 he refers to "the grace given to me to be a minister [*leitourgon*] of Christ Jesus to the Gentiles in the priestly service [*hierourgounta*] of the Gospel." This, Saint Paul's poetic use of the language of priesthood to describe his own ministerial labors in preaching the Gospel, may be seen as setting the groundwork for the later development of a concept of ministerial priesthood of certain leaders in the public worship of the Church, bishops and presbyters.

However, there is another term for service used in the New Testament which is even more innovative and even more historic. And this is the term *diakonia*. In its verbal form, *diakoneo* originally meant "to wait on tables," to provide or care for, personal service rendered to another, personal service of the humblest sort: washing another's feet, preparing another's meal, waiting on others at table. In the classical Greek of Plato, such service (*diakonia*) was considered demeaning and thus appropriate only for slaves. While the Septuagint makes no use at all of the term *diakonein*, abundant use is made of it in the New Testament.

For example, sometimes it is used to describe literal domestic table service as in Mark 1:31, where it is said of Peter's mother-in-law whom Jesus has just healed of a fever, "and she served [*diakonei*] them." A similar use occurs in Luke's description of Jesus' visit to the home of two sisters, Mary and Martha. In Luke 10:40 we are told of "Martha who was busy with all the details of hospitality [*diakonian*]" (cf. Jn 12:2). And then in Luke 17:7-8, where Jesus describes the work of a field worker and house servant:

> Will anyone of you who has a servant plowing or keep-
> ing sheep, say to him when he has come in from the field,
> "Come at once and sit down at table?" Will he not rather
> say to him, "Prepare supper for me, and gird yourself
> and serve [*diakonei*] me."

But besides this more or less common use to refer to literal serving at table, we also find in the Gospels that the word *diakonia* is used to refer to religious work, the work of God. Jesus, as presented in the Gospels, often has recourse to the concept of servitude or servanthood. In all three of the Synoptic Gospels (Mk 10:42-45; Mt 20:25-28; Lk 22:25-27) we find an account of Jesus instructing the Twelve on their role in the Church using the language of master/servant. I quote it here in its Marcan version:

> You know that those who are recognized as rulers over
> the Gentiles lord it over them, and their great ones make
> their authority over them felt. But it shall not be so
> among you. Rather, whoever wishes to be great among
> you will be your servant [*diakonos*]; whoever wishes to
> be first among you will be the slave [*doulos*] of all. For
> the Son of Man did not come to be served [*diakonethenai*]
> but to serve [*diakonesai*] and to give his life as a ransom
> for many.

In Romans 15:31 Paul speaks of his ministry to the Church at Jerusalem as "*diakonia mou*." Or in 1 Corinthians 16:15: "You know that the household of Stephanas is the first fruits of Achaia and is devoted to the service [*diakonia*] of the saints." Another example is Ephesians 4:11: "It is he who gave apostles, prophets, evangelists, pastors and teachers in roles of service [*diakonia*] to the faithful." At times it is used as a general description for various Church workers. For example, Saint Paul uses it in several and different ways to describe the work of apostles as "ministers [*diakonous*] of a new covenant" in 2 Corinthians 3:6, or "ministers of God" in 2 Corinthians 6:4, or "ministers of justice" in 2 Corinthians 11:15, and "ministers of Christ" in 2 Corinthians 11:23. He uses it again as a general description of Phoebe in Romans 16:1, "a minister of the Church at Cenchrae" [*diakonon tes ekklesias*], of Timothy in 1 Timothy 4:6 as "a minister of Christ" [*diakonos Christou*], so too Epaphras in Colossians 1:7 is called a *diakonos tou Christou*, and Tychicus in Ephesians 6:21, "a faithful minister in the Lord" [*diakonos in kuriou*]. And then at times it is used to designate a formal ministry or office in the Christian community as in the salutation in Philippians 1:1, "To all the saints in Christ Jesus who are at Philippi, with the bishops and deacons [*diakonois*]," or in the description of the qualifications for the office of deacon in 1 Timothy 3:8-13 (vs. 12 *diakonoi*).

But the history and importance of this term *diakonia* does not end with just its prominence in the Greek New Testament. Another decisive historic moment occurred when the fourth century biblical scholar Jerome in working on a Latin translation of the Greek New Testament chose the Latin word *ministerium* to translate the Greek word *diakonia*. Jerome's translation would come to be called the "Vulgate." This word "vulgate" comes from the Latin *vulgata* meaning "common" (our English word "vulgar" is derived from it) and thus serves to indicate that when Jerome translated the Bible into Latin he employed, not the classical Latin of Cicero, Caesar and Virgil, but the common Latin of the people of his day. This translation of the Bible had great influence in the Western world for more than a thousand years, that is, up until the appearance of modern language translations (German, English, etc.).

But these terms *diakonia* and *ministerium*, however their importance, do not exhaust our survey of terms for ministry or service in the New Testament. There are yet some other New Testament terms that we must look at. For example, the passage we quoted above from Mark 10:42-45 wherein Jesus identifies himself as a servant also serves to introduce us to yet another expression of service in the NT and that is the term "slave." Once again, this is a concept which in the Hellenistic society of Jesus' time would have been totally demeaning. But Jesus, influenced in no small measure by the example of Isaiah the prophet in his image of the servant or slave of God, uses it to express abject, total devotion to God and the work of God. Elsewhere Jesus uses the language not just of menial service but of slavery when he likens discipleship to him with the master/servant relationship as in Matthew 24, "No disciple is above his teacher, no slave above his master." And then look at the number of parables of Jesus wherein a servant figures prominently. In one parable (Mt 21:33ff.), we hear Jesus say, "When vintage time drew near, he sent his servants [*doulos*]." In Matthew 24:45, "Who then is the faithful and wise servant [*doulos*], whom his master has set over his household, to give them their food at the proper time?" Often modern English translations obscure the image of the slave by translating *doulos* as servant. See for example Jesus' words in Matthew 25:23. In the RSV it is: "Well done, good and faithful servant." But the word rendered here as "servant" is really "slave" [*doule*]. Similarly in Matthew 18:21-35, the parable of the unforgiving servant, both the NAB and the RSV constantly translate *doule* as "servant" rather than as "slave." Though the term *doulos* or "slave" is also found in the later New Testament literature to describe Christian service or ministry, it is more often the term *diakonia* which is principally used outside the Gospels to refer to more specific Christian service, namely, the work of serving the Christian faithful.

Yet another New Testament term for service of God and man which we must explore is the Greek word *ergos* meaning "work." This term is employed several times in the New Testament. We find its verbal form in Matthew 9:28, a parable of Jesus wherein the father says to his son, "Go and work [*ergazou*] in the vineyard." In Luke 13:14, the leader of the synagogue says, "There are six days on which work ought to be done" [*ergazesthai*]. In John 5:17, Jesus says, "My Father is working [*ergazetai*] still, and I am working [*ergazomai*]." The noun form is found in Matthew 11:2, "the works of Christ" [*erga tou Christou*]; John 6:28 speaks of "the works of God" [*erga tou theou*]; Romans 2:15 "the works of the law" [*ergon tou nomon*]. Acts 13:7: "The Holy Spirit said, 'Set apart for me Barnabas and Paul for the work [*ergon*] to which I have called them.'" And as "worker" as in Mark 16:20, the "laborer [*ergetes*] deserves his food." But most importantly for our interest is the related word, *sunergos*, that is "co-worker." In Romans 16:3, Paul calls Prisca and Aquila "my fellow workers in Christ Jesus" [*sunergous mou en Christo Iesou*]. In Romans 16:9 he refers to "Urbanus our fellow worker in Christ" [*sunergon hemon en Christou*]. In 1 Corinthians 3:9 we find *sunergoi theou* which the RSV renders as "fellow workers for God" but the NAB's "God's co-workers" is more accurate. 1 Thessalonians 3:2, where Timothy is described as *sunergou tou theou*, is translated in the RSV as "God's servant" but it too could be rendered "God's co-worker." We find it also in Mark 16:20, "And they went forth and preached everywhere, while the Lord worked with them [*sunergountes*]."

Finally, we should not overlook the importance of the New Testament Greek term *kopia*. The Greek *kopia* means "to labor" and its noun version *kopepos* "laborer." We find this word on the lips of Jesus in Matthew 6:28, "Consider the lilies of the field, how they grow, they neither toil [*kopiosin*] nor spin." In Luke 5:5, Simon Peter says, "Master we worked [*kopiasantes*] all night and took nothing!" But in the Pauline letters it used of those who work hard for the Gospel or the Church: in 1 Timothy 4:10, "For to this end we toil [*kopiomen*] and strive," In Romans 16:6, Paul says, "Greet Mary, who has worked hard [*ekopiasen*] among you," and in Romans 16:12, "Greet those workers in the Lord [*kopiosas en kurio*] Tryphaena and Tryphosa."

In the light of this language study, one could argue that Christian ministry is not just a formal religious affair, the worship of God, nor is it the sole preserve of religious professionals. It is also a social duty of justice toward one's neighbor incumbent on us all.

Indeed, while Jesus uses the language of ministry, *diakonia*, principally in his instructions to the Twelve and with reference to their formal responsibilities in pasturing the flock he is attempting to gather, it is still quite possible to argue that Christian ministry is a very simple thing and everyone has a part it in.

Whenever in the New Testament Jesus talks about ministry he always uses examples of domestic service, for example, washing feet (Jn 13:1-7), waiting on people at table (Lk 22:27). True, some of these examples, like the one of waiting on people at table in Luke 22, are capable of a cultic interpretation — distribution of the bread and wine, the body and blood of Christ in a Lord's Supper service — but the primary sense of this action is that of feeding the hungry, answering a basic human need. Similarly, the washing of feet has become a religious ritual in the Holy Thursday service (and among so called "foot-washing Baptists"), a formal religious ritual connected with formal ministerial service, but even so, its primary meaning is that of simple, humble, self-effacing, menial service.

In the Acts of the Apostles 6:1-6, we are told how the leadership of the earliest Christian community at Jerusalem made formal provision so that official ministers, men with an official ministerial charge, were entrusted with the responsibility of feeding widows and orphans. In that authoritative action *diakonia* or "service" of the word is ranked alongside *diakonia* of charity, that is, "service at table" in the sense of literal feeding of the poor is deliberately paralleled with the preaching of the Gospel to make it clear that both are very important ministries:

> And the twelve summoned the body of the disciples and said, "It is not right that we should give up preaching the word of God to serve tables [*diakonein trapezais*]. Therefore, brethren, pick out from among you seven men of good repute, full of the Spirit and of wisdom, whom we may appoint to this duty. But we will devote ourselves to prayer and to the ministry of the word [*diakonia tou logou*]."

But such formalization of a particular ministry does not relieve the rest of the Christian community from its responsibility for informal, personal ministry. A witness to this is James 1:27, where the two duties to God and neighbor are seen as equal responsibilities for all the faithful: "Religion that is pure and undefiled before God and the Father is this: to visit orphans and widows in their affliction, and to keep oneself unstained from the world." "To keep oneself unstained from the world" is the language of cultic purity as practiced by the temple priests. Unfortunately, all too often only the first part of this passage is quoted, that is, the injunction to visit orphans and widows. Though it must be conceded while the New Testament constantly closely links both service of God and service of neighbor, it also makes service of neighbor the litmus test of the legitimacy of one's service of God. Recall Jesus' injunction in Matthew 5:23-24: "So if you are offering your gift at the altar, and there remember that your brother has something against you, leave your gift there before the altar and go; first be reconciled to your brother, and then come and offer your gift."

Are we wrong then to argue that men and women who are trying to be Christian parents are rendering a serious Christian service, exercising a serious ministry toward their children? This may be an informal and unrecognized ministry but a ministry nonetheless. Surely, Christian sons and daughters who are dutifully caring for their aging or infirm parents to the degree that they do this task with a devotion and generosity inspired by the Gospel are performing a ministry, rendering Christian service. Similarly, a Christian doctor, lawyer, used car salesman, barber, baker, *et cetera*, when they see a need and respond to it with Christian generosity beyond the standard ethics of their profession, then they are not merely rendering a professional service but ministering to others. No doubt if asked about their "service" or "ministry", all would respond as in Luke 17:10, "We are unworthy servants; we have only done what was our duty." But moral virtue in a Christian is not just a matter of personal virtue but of public witness, even though such witness may be seen by only a few and is rarely publicly and formally recognized.

This is an important point to make in a time when there has developed a veritable industry of lay ministries. By that I mean formal programs, titles, certifications, degrees, ceremonies of installation, salaried appointments, *et cetera*, that ironically threaten to "clericalize" ministry more than ever before by reserving it to qualified religious professionals. In the face of such a trend, it is good to be reminded that Jesus' conception of ministry is one of simple, humble self-effacing service required of all his disciples. Opportunities for ministry go beyond the programs offered by a formal ministry training program or job openings on a parish staff. Opportunities for ministry occur everyday in people's normal, nor-religious, professional or domestic lives.

No doubt not all ministries are equal. Certain ministries such as those carried out by commissioned or salaried representatives of the Church and in the name of the Church have a visibility and witness value that is of special importance for the Church.

No doubt the responsibilities of some are much greater than those of others and the accountability of some more than others makes for more urgent concern on the part of the community of faith. Indeed, in the following chapters we shall treat of the concept of hierarchy or the ranking of public ministries in terms of their importance and responsibilities. And we shall examine the criteria which the Christian community, the Church, has used for the public calling and appointing of these professional ministers of the cult. But in this chapter it was important to nail down the basic notion of ministry as simple, humble self-effacing service of both God and neighbor.

Further Reading

Chapter 4, "A Ministering Church" in Thomas F. O'Meara's *Theology of Ministry* (Paulist Press, revised edition 1999), pages 139-167.

Chapter 15, "The Intersection of Present Experience and Tradition," in Zeni Fox's *New Ecclesial Ministry* (Kansas City: Sheed & Ward, 1997), pages 219-240.

The article on "Ministry" by N.J. Oppervall in Vol. 3 (K-P) of *The International Standard Bible Encyclopedia* (Grand Rapids: Wm. B. Eerdmans, 1986), pp. 364-365.

Chapter 6, "Christian Service: Charisms of Diakonia," in Ghislain Lafont's *Imagining the Catholic Church,* translation by J. Burkhard (Collegeville, Minnesota: The Liturgical Press, 2000), pages 135-154.

CHAPTER 21

The Ordering of Christian Ministries

When studying the history of Christian ministry or even more generally the history of the Church one soon becomes aware of the fact that very early on in the history of the Church there began the ordering of Christian ministries and that almost equally early on certain ministries attained a preeminent status and in large measure continue to enjoy that preeminence to this day. Many people today, however, are convinced that this historic development sometimes called "the rise of the hierarchy," is a gross injustice, an impingement upon an earlier and original freedom in the Christian community. Moreover, there is much in the Bible and early Christian history to which these modern-day critics can point for support of their judgment on this matter of order in the Church. And so in this chapter we need to examine the historical development of the ordering of Christian ministries so that we can understand more precisely what were the factors, what was the rationale, that went into the ordering of Christian ministries in the early Church. We shall begin here by examining those New Testament texts that witness to the development of ecclesiastical order.

The earliest Church order is found in Paul's First Letter to the Church at Corinth 12:27-28:

> Now you are the body of Christ and individually members of it. And God has appointed in the Church first apostles, second prophets, third teachers, then workers

of miracles, then healers, helpers, administrators, speakers in various kinds of tongues.

In the time of St. Paul, Corinth, located on a coastal plain 48 miles south of Athens, was the richest port and one of the largest cities in Greece. Paul arrived there in A.D. 51 and stayed for 18 months during which time he experienced his greatest missionary success, establishing the largest of his Christian communities. But this success also brought with it several problems, one of which was the problem of order in the Christian community at Corinth. And this he addresses in this letter. The New Testament work called First Corinthians is accepted by all scholars as a genuine work of St. Paul. It was written by Paul from Ephesus in late 56 or early 57. In the passage quoted, Paul's enumeration of the first three ministries — apostles, prophets, teachers — suggests a ranking according to degrees of authority or dignity. The title ranked first, that of apostle, has two meanings in Paul's writings. Either it refers to himself and the historic Twelve, Jesus' inner circle, or Paul uses it at other times to refer to Christian missionaries or itinerant preachers who founded churches. The second title, "prophets," is more difficult to define. This ministry, like that of apostles, seems also to have been itinerant in character. It seems these prophets have oracular instructions, that is, they spoke under direction from the Holy Spirit. The third title, teachers, seems to refer to those who were particularly well versed in the traditions about Jesus, his words and deeds. The remaining five ministries do not seem to be presented in any significant ranking but instead are simply grouped together as prominent ministries in the Christian community at Corinth; however, it is possible to argue that Paul placed last the ministry of speaking in tongues precisely because it was the most problematic in the Church at Corinth. In First Corinthians two of the ministries mentioned in this passage come in for further comment because they have become somewhat problematic in the Corinthian Church. There are too many prophetic voices all wanting to be heard and those who speak in tongues are also numerous but pose a further problem in that no one knows what they are saying. While Paul esteems the prophetic voices and defends them, he is much sterner and judgmental regarding those who speak in tongues, indeed, he seems to have some contempt for them (1 Cor 14:19: "I would rather speak five words with my mind, than ten thousand words in a tongue").

The next Church order we should look at comes from the Epistle to the Ephesians 4:11-12:

> And his gifts were that some should be apostles, some prophets, some evangelists, some pastors and teachers, for the equipment of the saints, for the work of ministry, for building up the body of Christ.

Among modern scholars, the genuine Pauline authorship of Ephesians has been seriously questioned and at times vigorously defended. Raymond Brown says if indeed it was written by Paul, this must have been in the 60's. If not, he says the consensus of doubters claim it was written in the 90's. The important thing to be noted about the passage we have quoted are the ways in which it both resembles and differs from the Church order we saw in First Corinthians 12:27-28. While apostles and prophets are still given pride of place, there is no mention of such charismatic ministries as "speaking in tongues"; moreover, there are two new additions to the list. "Evangelist" seems to be an itinerant ministry or mission, "pastor" seems to indicate a position of domestic leadership, that is, resident leadership of a local Church. As for the absence of any reference to "speaking in tongues," it could be argued that this omission probably indicates this ministry was not prominent in the church at Ephesus.

The third Church order found in the New Testament is not enumerated in any one such compact list as we find in 1 Corinthians 12:27-28 and Ephesians 4:11-12. Rather the third Church order is referred to at various times and in various ways in three New Testament works which are grouped together as the Pastoral Epistles. Individually, these three epistles are called First Timothy, Second Timothy, and the Letter to Titus. These three works claim to be advice written by Paul to his assistants Timothy and Titus, who are portrayed as sort of apostolic delegates, that is, Timothy has been sent by Paul to give direction to the Church at Ephesus, Titus has been sent to the island of Crete. These three epistles are called the Pastoral Epistles because their content is less doctrinal and instead deal almost entirely with rules of order for the organization and running of a local church. There is among exegetes, however, considerable controversy as to the genuine Pauline authorship of these works. For the most part, exegetes tend to see these as later pseudonymous works, that is, not originally written by Paul but instead by a follower of Paul. As for the dating of these works, if they are indeed works of Paul then they were most probably written in the year 65, that is, shortly before Paul's death. However, those who doubt their authenticity date them much later. In the nineteenth century some biblical critics dated them as late as A.D. 150. Nowadays, critics tend more to date them in the 90's. The reason for this more cautious, earlier dating is that there appear to be allusions to the Pastoral Epistles in another early Christian though non-biblical work, the letters of Ignatius of Antioch which were penned about A.D. 107. Moreover, others argue that these Pastoral Epistles should not be dated later that the *First Letter of Clement* (ca. 95), because it exhibits an even more developed hierarchical structure than they do. Whenever one would date them, the fact is that the Church order in the Pastoral Epistles consists of three offices, and I use here the RSV translation, those of "bishop," "elder," and "deacon."

The Church order in the Pastoral Epistles apparently witnesses to an even more dramatic development over the changes we saw from 1 Corinthians 12:27-28 and Ephesians 4:11-12. While the list from Ephesians omitted the more exotic charismatic ministries such as speaking in tongues, in the Pastoral Epistles not only is there no reference to speaking in tongues, but even the hitherto preeminent ministries of apostles and prophets are gone. Nor is there any mention of teachers or evangelists. How can we explain this new ordering? Well, in the case of the apostles and evangelists, it could be argued that their time has long passed. That is, the communities at Ephesus and Crete are long-established communities of which Paul himself or Titus were the principal apostles and evangelists. As for such dramatic not to say spectacular charisms as "speaking in tongues," it could be that, as in the Church at Ephesus, so too in the Church at Crete, this "speaking in tongues" was not a prominent ministry. As for teaching, the author of the Pastoral Epistles is much concerned about right teaching and the threat posed by false teachers and thus the principal responsibility for this seems to have devolved upon the new offices he refers to when using the language of bishops and elders. Indeed, if we look at the descriptions given of the requirements of those who would be given these ministries, we see that the bishops and elders are also the principal preachers and teachers in the community. In First Timothy 3:2-5, while no doubt great stress is placed on the bishop as a moral model and a capable administrator, it is also made clear that he should be a capable teacher:

> Now a bishop must be above reproach, the husband of one wife, temperate, sensible, dignified, and hospitable, *an apt teacher*, no drunkard, not violent but gentle, nor quarrelsome, and no lover of money. He must manage his own household well, keeping his children submissive and respectful in every way; for if a man does not know how to manage his own household, how can he care for God's Church?

And while the elders are also expected to "rule well," special consideration is urged for those who can also preach and *teach* well: First Timothy 5:17: "Let the elders who rule well be considered worthy of double honor, especially those who labor in preaching and teaching."

We can learn more about these two offices if we examine the meaning of their titles. The English word "bishop" is used to translate the Greek, *episkopos*, which literally means "over-seer" for *epi* is the Greek prefix for "over," we see it used in the term "epicenter," that being the point directly over the earth, and in the word "epitomy," meaning "an overview." The Greek word *skopos* contributes to several English words, such as telescope, "to see from a distance." And so the person referred to here as a bishop or *episkopos* is one who exercises oversight of the Christian community. The Greek word which is translated "elder," is the word *presbyteros*, it is the term for the eldest male in a family, in a patriarchal society that meant the head of the family. In the New Testament we cannot always tell when the term *presbyteros* is being used in its generic sense of elder or in its technical sense to indicate a Christian *presiding* elder.

What are we to make of the historical development of the ordering of Christian ministries as seen in these three passages from the New Testament? Some scholars find the development here very ominous, indeed, a wrong turn. A German New Testament scholar and theologian, Ernst Käsemann (1906-1998), at a theological conference in Herborn, Germany in 1949, presented a paper which was later published as "Ministry and Community in the New Testament." In it he presented his idea that the earliest Christian communities were devoid of any kind of ministerial offices and instead these communities were characterized by manifestations of numerous "gifts of grace," *charisma*, on the part of all the baptized. He surveys the Pauline epistles to present evidence that in the Christian communities, the churches Paul established: "all the baptized are 'office-bearers'; they have each his charisma and therefore each his special responsibility." But then he goes on to show how a dramatic change soon occurred: "the Pauline conception of a Church order disappeared in the very Church the Apostle himself created." Using passages from the Pastoral Epistles (First and Second Timothy and Titus) and the two Lucan works, the Gospel and Acts of the Apostles, Käsemann shows how the original Pauline concept of a Church order based on charisma was replaced by a Church order based on authoritative ministerial offices — bishops, presbyters and deacons. And thus we have the advent of the hierarchy and what Käsemann calls *frühkatholizismus*, "early Catholicism." Later he would amplify his thought in an essay entitled "Paul and Early Catholicism" (first published in German in 1963, in English in 1967). One cannot underestimate the influence of Käsemann's thought here even upon Catholic scholarship where the distinction between office and charism becomes a significant theme. However, the eminent Catholic biblical scholar, Raymond Brown in his *The Churches the Apostles Left Behind* (NY: Paulist, 1984) presents an alternative to Käsemann's thesis. Indeed, Brown is quite dismissive of the concept of early Catholicism when he says: "While judgment on that term and topic require nuance, Gaeger is certainly correct in pointing out that 'a good deal of nonsense' has been written about the decline of primitive Christianity into 'early Catholicism'" (pp. 36-37). Instead, Brown in his book sets forth the thesis that there is New Testament evidence for a variety of Church orders, a legitimate diversity of Church orders in the New Testament period. Brown's book originated in a series of lectures which he gave at Union Theological Seminary at Richmond Virginia in January of 1980. I suspect the ecumenical setting encouraged him to look at the New Testament evidence in a way that might reflect the various ecclesial traditions before him. Brown's thesis is open to criticism as being too schematized. But to be fair to Brown he himself cautions in his conclusion, "New Testament diversity cannot be used to justify Christian divisions today" (p. 147). As a corrective to Käsemann's thesis and as a means of forestalling abuse of Brown's thesis, I propose here we look for the evidence for Church order in the earliest work of the Christian movement, Paul's First Epistle to the Church at Thessalonica; for I think we shall see that not only was hierarchical authority present from the beginning, but prophecy was a pastoral problem from the beginning. Moreover, there is evidence for presbyters everywhere in the earliest Christian communities.

The First Letter of Paul to the Thessalonians is not only, indisputably, a genuine Pauline letter but it is also the earliest document of the Christian movement. It is commonly dated as having been written about the year 50. And thus the information it contains regarding Church order really reflects the condition of the Church in the late 40's, within twenty years of the death of Jesus. In terms of Church order, there are two passages in this letter that are of most interest to us. The first is First Thessalonians 5:12: "But we beseech you, brethren, to respect those who labor among you and are over you in the Lord and admonish you, and to esteem them very highly in love because of their work." Here is hierarchical authority already at work, that is, this passage witnesses to the fact that even in the late 40's there are certain members of the local Christian community whose authority is from God for they are "over you *in the Lord*," moreover they exercise more than just oversight — they are not just "over you in the Lord" but they also, if necessary, can stand over and against the community in the sense that they can "admonish you." Who were these people? Acts of the Apostles 17:5-9 supplies us with one precise reference to a significant figure at Thessalonica. According to that passage when Paul and Silas first came to evangelize Thessalonica, they were given hospitality at "the house of Jason." That phrase implies that Jason was indeed an elder or presbyter in the sense of the oldest male in a family, but it hardly indicates that Jason ever functioned as a presiding elder in the Church at Corinth. He was probably a devout Jew who was much taken with Paul and Silas' message and perhaps even converted. But there is another New Testament passage in another genuinely Pauline letter, that provides some matter for thought, for in that letter Paul employs very similar language as to that which he used in 1 Thessalonians 5:12, but this time with relation to a very precise person. At the end of First Corinthians (16:15-18), Paul says:

> Now, brethren, you know that the household of Stephanas were the first converts in Achaia, and they have devoted themselves to the service of the saints; I urge you to be subject to such men and to every fellow worker and laborer. I rejoice at the coming of Stephanas and Fortunatus and Achaicus, because they have made up for your absence; for they refreshed my spirit as well as yours. Give recognition to such men.

Who are these three men? While Paul asks that all three men be given "recognition," he *urges* the Corinthian congregation to "be *subject* to such men" as Stephanas. And thus Stephanas is obviously an important figure in the Church at Corinth, most probably a presbyter in the sense of a presiding elder and not just a *pater familias*, head of a family. It is hardly daring speculation to suggest he probably hosted a house church. It is not at all clear that Fortunatus and Achaicus are presiding elders. They may have accompanied Stephanas out of support, that is, as company and protection on such a long journey, the two hundred miles from Corinth to Ephesus. A comparison with Chloe is perhaps revelatory. Paul had already heard about some problems at Corinth, for he says in 1 Corinthians 1:11, "It has been reported to me by Chloe's people that there is quarreling among you." It is not at all clear whether this Chloe lives in Corinth or Ephesus; if in Corinth then her people perhaps sent a letter, if she lives in Ephesus then her people may have heard gossip that they have passed along to Paul. Either way it is obvious that Chloe is not a presiding elder for surely she would have communicated this news in her own name.

Indeed it is doubtful Chloe is even a Christian. It is more likely she is a pagan matron and her "people" are Christian servants or slaves even. Compare the expression in Philippians 4:22, "All the saints greet you, especially those of Caesar's household." It hardly means to imply that Caesar himself has become a Christian! Nor is it likely that Stephanas has made this two hundred mile journey simply to deliver a letter from the Church at Corinth seeking from Paul instruction about sexual morality. No doubt, he did deliver a letter requesting advice on sexual matters for part of Paul's letter responds precisely to that, the part beginning with 1 Corinthians 7:1, "Now concerning the matters about which you wrote." But that is only one or two chapters in a sixteen chapter letter. Rather it is obvious from the remainder of Paul's First Letter to the Church at Corinth that Stephanas has made a long journey to Ephesus out of a deep sense of personal responsibility, so as to consult with Paul regarding much trouble in the Church at Corinth — a public scandal (incest in 1 Cor 5:1-13), sectarian divisions created in part by the popularity of one itinerant preacher at

Corinth, Apollos of Alexandria (1 Cor 1:12, 3:4-6, 4:6), but also confusion in the worship assembly created by numerous self-styled prophets all with messages from God, and other people who speak in the Christian assembly in unintelligible tongues (1 Cor 14, the entire chapter). Stephanas has made this journey hoping to receive authoritative advice from Paul and perhaps even Paul's personal intervention in these matters. And so, the Church at Corinth is not so unlike the Church at Philippi whom Paul greets, "To all the saint in Christ Jesus who are at Philippi, with the bishops (overseers) and deacons (servants)." While the Church at Corinth was a community in which all were blessed with gifts, it was also a community in which an elder such as Stephanas was exercising a measure of not just pastoral service but also pastoral oversight, episcopacy. One should not underestimate the importance of Paul's endorsement of the authority of Stephanas: while Paul in his letter displays a genuine esteem for the prophetic voices at Corinth (1 Cor 14:4, "he who prophesies edifies the Church") and a near contempt for those who speak in tongues (1 Cor 14:19: "I would rather speak five words with my mind, in order to instruct others, than ten thousand words in a tongue"), he endorses the authority of church workers over that of all these charismatics. In view of this Käsemann's statement seems overdrawn, to say the least: "We may assert without hesitation that the Pauline community had not a presbytery during the Apostle's lifetime."

However, we need to see the ecclesiological implications of a second passage from First Thessalonians that is most revelatory for Church order: "Do not quench the Spirit, do not despise prophesying." This line in 1 Thessalonians 5:19 may be but one small passage but it suggests a great and important drama in the history of the earliest Christian communities, the life of the first generation of Christians. Why do the Christians at Thessalonica despise prophecy? To understand this, we do well to look at the one portrait in the New Testament that we have of an early Christian prophet.

The only New Testament prophet for which we have any descriptive account is that of Agabus who appears but two times in the Acts of the Apostles, but appears there significantly. He is first mentioned in Acts 11:27-30:

> Now in these days prophets came down from Jerusalem to Antioch. And one of them named Agabus stood up and foretold by the Spirit that there would be a great famine over all the world; and this took place in the days of Claudius. And the disciples determined, every one according to his ability, to send relief to the brethren who lived in Judea; and they did so, sending it to the elders by the hand of Barnabas and Saul.

Already we can see why a Christian community might be severely impatient with such itinerant prophets. A Christian community might quickly tire of having people pop up and insist that they have a message from God for the congregation. That community might be especially shy of such characters when, as with Agabus here, they are asking for money. Indeed, it is perhaps especially telling that when this community at Antioch heeds Agabus' request for funds, they do not give the money to Agabus. Rather they entrust their donation to "elders" of their own community.

The next time Agabus appears in the narrative of the Acts of the Apostles it is in Acts 21:10-14. This passage describes an incident that occurred at the end of Paul's third great missionary journey. Paul and his traveling companion (Luke?), after having sailed from Tyre have landed on the coast of Israel at Ptolemais. After having stayed there overnight, they have journeyed to Caesarea where they have stayed with Philip the evangelist. Then we are told:

> While we were staying for some days, a prophet named Agabus came down from Judea. And coming to us he took Paul's girdle and bound his own feet and hands, and said, "Thus says the Holy Spirit, 'So shall the Jews at Jerusalem bind the man who owns this girdle and deliver him into the hands of the Gentiles.'" When we heard this, we and the people there begged him not to go up to Jerusalem. Then Paul answered, "What are you doing, weeping and

breaking my heart? For I am ready not only to be imprisoned but even to die at Jerusalem for the name of the Lord
Jesus." And when he would not be persuaded, we ceased
and said, "The will of the Lord be done."

Several things need to be noted about this passage from
Acts. First, Agabus in his behavior here exhibits characteristics
much like what we have already seen Jesus imitate in such
classical prophets as Isaiah and Jeremiah. That is, not only does
he make oracular utterances but he also makes use of dramatic
gestures, prophetic parables in action, in this case, his dramatic
taking of Paul's belt, sitting on the floor and binding his own
hands and feet. Secondly, though Agabus once again shows himself to be a true prophet, it is interesting that Paul, even so, does
not heed him. We will be able to understand this all the better if
we have a clearer understanding of the whole phenomenon of
prophecy in the biblical tradition.

Prophecy was a prominent feature of ancient Israel. But there
can also be little doubt that false prophecy was a major problem.
The major prophets all lament it (Is 9:15, Jr 14:14, Ezk 13:3) and
the Torah provided advice on how to discern a false prophet (Dt
18:21-22). The situation is not appreciably different in New Testament times. Jesus too warns of false prophets in Mark 13:22, "False
Christs and *false prophets* will arise and show signs and wonders,
to lead astray, if possible the elect." In Matthew 7:15, "Beware of
false prophets, who come to you in sheep's clothing but inwardly
are ravenous wolves." And Jesus gives instruction as to how one
might discern a genuine prophet, instruction quite similar to that
given in Deuteronomy: Matthew 7:16: "You will know them by
their fruits." Paul and Barnabas, on their very first missionary
journey encounter a Jewish false prophet (Ac 13:6-12). 2 Peter
2:1, "But false prophets also arose among the people." 1 John 4:1,
"Beloved, do not believe every spirit, but test the spirits to see
whether they are of God; for many false prophets have gone out
into the world." No wonder that some in the Christian community
at Thessalonica despised prophets and that some other Christian
communities would seek to marginalize the phenomenon, that

is, no longer give prophets the prominence or center of attention that they had for the first generation. However, even when I say this, there are important qualifications to be made. Namely, even in the Pastoral Epistles, prophecy is not entirely absent. Indeed, if we look carefully we will see it is given a significant role, and precisely in the selection of Church leadership. First Timothy 2:18, "This charge I commit to you, Timothy, my son, in accordance with the prophetic utterances which pointed to you." Is this just Paul's remembrance of a passing practice? No doubt prophecy continued for a long time. For example, in *The Shepherd of Hermas*, written at Rome around A.D. 145, the phenomenon of Christian prophets is address in the section on Mandates. There in Mandate 11 the Church is advised to test all prophets, and it is suggested that some marks of false prophets are that often they are "talkative and live in great luxury."

After assessing all this evidence, what can we say for its application today? There are many voices today who want to see a redistribution of Church ministries. First, we should not ignore the lessons of the past; a community cannot be at the mercy of self-proclaimed prophets. Every prophet should be tested. But we should take to heart Paul's words, "Do not despise prophecy." Moreover, we should never try to silence prophetic voices. Also, besides letting prophets speak and testing them, we should also take a lesson from Paul's ignoring the true prophecy of Agabus.

It is interesting to see how the Second Vatican Council handles the issue of charismatic ministries. On the one hand the Council is very approving of such ministries as in this passage from its Dogmatic Constitution on the Church, *Lumen gentium* 12:

> It is not only through the sacraments and Church min-
> istries that the same Holy Spirit sanctifies and leads the
> People of God and enriches it with virtues. Allotting His
> gifts "to everyone according as He will" (1 Cor 12:11),
> He distributes special graces among the faithful of every
> rank. By these gifts He makes them fit and ready to un-
> dertake the various tasks or offices advantageous for the
> renewal and upbuilding of the Church, according to the

words of the Apostle: "The manifestation of the Spirit is
given to everyone for profit" (1 Cor 12:7). These charismatic gifts, whether they be the most outstanding or the
more simply and widely diffused, are to be received with
thanksgiving and consolation, for they are exceedingly
suitable and useful for the needs of the Church.

But what must also be seen is that in the very next paragraph of *Lumen gentium* 12, the Council carefully qualifies what
it has said here:

> Still, extraordinary gifts are not to be rashly sought after,
> nor are the fruits of apostolic labor to be presumptu-
> ously expected from them. In any case, judgment as to
> their genuineness and proper use belongs to those who
> preside over the Church, and to those whose special
> competence it belongs, not indeed to extinguish the
> Spirit, but to test all things and hold fast to that which
> is good (cf. 1 Th 5:12, 19-22).

The lessons here do not just apply to prophecy. There is also
an important lesson here regarding hierarchical authority. The
word "hierarchy" means "sacred order." But what is so sacred
about it? In mathematics order is simply the ranking of objects
according to quantity, that is, according to "more or less." But
in the Church, order is not the ranking of objects according to
more or less but rather for the sake of justice, that justice might
be done to both God and man. Moreover, hierarchical authority
is not exercised only on the level of the highest authority. Even
the director of a modest Christian education program such as
a local church's Sunday school program or catechetical program
exercises a measure of hierarchical authority by choosing the
textbook and at times by selecting or dismissing a catechist. No
doubt, this is never an easy thing. A catechist might be inflamed
with a passion for religious instruction, be convinced that this is
what God is calling him or her to do, but at the same time that
same catechist might be the object of many parents' complaints
that he or she is frightening the children. Similarly a music director may be faced with the problem of a church member who

wants to sing in the choir but has no talent for it. Or the liturgy coordinator might be faced with a parishioner eager to serve as a lector on Sunday but who demonstrably has no talent for reading in public.

Finally, we must also keep in mind that our time is not very comfortable with order and hierarchy. We are still children of the romantic era which exalted freedom over community and celebrated the wildness of nature over the order imposed by human beings. Indeed, in this chapter we have been dealing with two words that are neuralgic for many people, the words "order" and "hierarchy." Neuralgia is a painful thing. At one time or another everyone has experienced a neuralgic point in their teeth, that is, when you eat something very cold, such as ice cream, and suddenly feel a sharp pain at one point in one of your teeth. It is usually because there is a nerve ending close to the surface enamel of that tooth and with the cold of the ice cream, the enamel contracted rapidly and "pinched" that nerve. The reason some people experience neuralgia when "order" and "hierarchy" are mentioned is in some cases quite understandable. Those people may well have experienced overly constricting order or an oppressively authoritarian hierarchy. For example, in the 1991 film, "Sleeping with the Enemy," a passion for order is portrayed as one of the distinguishing marks of a psychopath. This movie tells the story of an abused wife who, in frantic desperation, fakes her own death so that she can start her life anew under a different identity. But her psychopathic (controlling) husband figures out what she has done and stalks her down. At the dramatic climax of the movie, when the woman's husband is about to surprise her with his murderous presence, his obsession with order compels him to pause a moment to neatly arrange the towels on a bathroom rack. There can be no doubt order can be oppressive. That is, no doubt there are people who have experienced such constricting order in their lives that they have an understandable reaction to the very word. However, on the other hand, some degree of order is necessary so that justice may be done to all concerned. When I go to vote I must stand in line and go through an ordered procedure that is tedious. But that is what is needed to guarantee that I am truly eligible to vote and vote no more than once.

More recently, I have been amused by a radio advertisement for a bank in New York City. In this advertisement, a young woman tells us why she likes this particular bank so much. She gives as one reason: "There is no hierarchy." That is, she goes on to explain, the bank representative whom she deals with does not need to go to a "higher up" to get permission for things she and the bank representative are negotiating. This may well be true, but I still suspect there is an effective if unobtrusive hierarchy in her bank. On the other hand, one should also consider the possibility that the hierarchy in this woman's bank is more obvious and numerous than she is ready to admit. That is, it could be argued the reason her bank representative is so efficient is precisely due to the fact that he or she represents and, in fact, exercises hierarchical, ultimate as well as decisive, authority in the matters this woman wants to negotiate.

Further Reading

From Johann Auer's *The Church: The Universal Sacrament of Salvation* translated by M. Waldstein and H.M. Riley (Washington, DC: Catholic University of America Press, 1993), Chapter IX, "The Structures of the Church's Being; Orders and Organization in the Church; The Constitution of the Sacramental Church," pages 148-178.

James T. Burtchaell's *From Synagogue to Church: Public Services and Offices in the Earliest Christian Communities* (NY: Cambridge University Press, 1992).

From Miguel Garijo-Guembe's *Communion of the Saints: Foundation, Nature, and Structure of the Church* translated by P. Madigan (Collegeville, MN: The Liturgical Press, 1994), Chapter IX, "The Hierarchical Composition of the Church," pages 159-196.

CHAPTER 22

Promotion to Ministry

In the Gospel according to Mark 5:1-17, there is the narrative of the healing of the Gerasene demoniac. I have already referred to it in Chapter 15 when I treated of the Church's mission. In that chapter I used the healing of the Gerasene demoniac as biblical evidence to support the idea that the Church's mission is not complete with the personal conversion of individuals, not even with the building up of the community we call Church. But there must also be a witness to the world and a witness that is not just verbal. More precisely, I claimed there were great social implications in Jesus' healing of the Gerasene demoniac. That is, when Jesus exorcized "the legion" of demons from this man and sent them into a herd of swine "numbering about two thousand," he destroyed a considerable personal investment, indeed, perhaps someone's entire livelihood. But I also suggested that since swine were a reprehensible commodity for pious Jews — their dietary laws forbid the consumption of pork — Jesus' action was comparable to how today the effort to save one man from drug addiction might lead to the disclosure and destruction of an entire drug ring. And thus I concluded: a lesson to be learned from Jesus' exorcism of the Gerasene demoniac is that it cannot be "business as usual" when Jesus comes through town. Indeed, anywhere Gospel principles are seriously preached and lived one can well expect radical changes will take place that might affect even the local economy.

The drama of the healing of the Gerasene demoniac, however, does not end simply with his healing. There is appended a further small but, I believe, important drama with more and other theological implications, implications for the theology of ministry. In the very next verses, that is, Mark 5:18-20, we read:

> And as he was getting into the boat, the man who had been possessed with demons begged him [Jesus] that he might be with him. But he refused, and said to him, "Go home to your friends, and tell them how much the Lord has done for you, and how he has had mercy on you." And he went away and began to proclaim in the Decapolis how much Jesus had done for him; and all men marveled.

The Decapolis, Greek for "ten cities," refers to a league of ten Hellenistic, that is, Greek-speaking, non-Jewish, cities in the territory east of Palestine. This league was formed after the Roman conquest of Palestine as a protection against Jewish immigration and aggression. There are two principal ways of interpreting this further drama. Many exegetes say that this passage is an account of the beginning of the Christian mission to the Gentiles. That is, Jesus' own mission and ministry were concentrated solely within Israel. This is what is meant by Matthew 15:4, "I was sent only to the lost sheep of the house of Israel." But here we see him send a man off to witness beyond Israel. However, I side with those exegetes who argue such an interpretation is quite untenable. For they argue it is totally illogical that Jesus would actually send forth to preach the Gospel a man who had received no instruction or preparation for such a mission. Moreover, one might also want to consider the fact that throughout Mark's Gospel Jesus cautions the enthusiasm of the Twelve with his theme of the messianic secret, that the Messiah must first suffer and die. And thus it is much more reasonable to conclude that when this Gerasene asks to become one of Jesus' itinerant followers, Jesus instead directs the man to go home and preach to, witness to his family. But instead, the man in an excess of fervor and enthusiasm mounts a veritable evangelical crusade.

And thus this passage helps explain not just the furtherance of the Christian mission beyond the borders of Israel but also the phenomenon of unauthorized preachers, that is, the fact that the Gospel was preached not just by the Twelve and Paul but also by self-styled preachers and evangelists.

Whichever interpretation is true, the fact is that even today, the whole question of who should minister and under what authority still troubles the Christian community. For to this day there are those who perhaps like the Gerasene demoniac, that is, out of a feeling of grateful enthusiasm for the grace bestowed on them by their faith in Christ, go forth with little or no sponsorship or approbation and set themselves up as a Christian pastor or teacher. For example, currently, the largest Christian congregation in Houston is headed by a preacher who never saw the inside of a seminary, was never assigned there much less "ordained" and his Gospel has been criticized by some as seriously deficient. While the Catholic Church too is from time to time confronted by the phenomenon of self-appointed preachers, the problem there is more often complaint against the upper clergy's sole prerogative regarding ministerial call and pastoral appointment. And thus the Flemish Dominican Edward Schillebeeckx has argued not only for popular election of both bishops and local pastors but of the recognition of personal ministerial calls within the community of faith. Moreover, the growth of lay ministry in the Catholic Church has also raised the issue of how indeed should candidates for ministry be evaluated. Out of the conviction that the Bible still has much to contribute to this debate, I want to survey in this chapter the biblical witness to the idea of vocational or ministerial call and mandate.

As depicted in the Gospels Jesus appears to issue both a ministerial call and a ministerial mandate. That is, while all are called to discipleship, a select few are chosen, trained and sent forth on ministry. Precisely in what manner "many are called, but few are chosen" (Mt 22:4) is well illustrated in the Gospel narratives of Jesus' calling, training and sending forth of the Twelve. For example, Mark 1:17, "And Jesus said to them, 'Follow me and I will make you become fishers of men,'" witnesses to the call of the Twelve. Mark 4:10-11, "To you has been given the secret of the kingdom of God," witnesses to Jesus' private instruction of the Twelve. Mark 6:7, "And he called to him the twelve, and began to send them out two by two," witnesses to the mission of the Twelve. As to what happened after Jesus, the New Testament appears to give a variety of evidence.

No doubt, there is the example of direct appointment by figures other than Jesus himself. For example, Acts 14:21-23 describes Paul and Barnabas on their first missionary journey appointing leaders for the local communities of Christians which had been established through their preaching:

> When they had preached the gospel to that city [Derbe] and had made many disciples, they returned to Lystra and to Iconium and to Antioch, strengthening the souls of the disciples, exhorting them to continue in the faith, and saying that through many tribulations we must enter the kingdom of God. And when *they had appointed elders for them in every Church*, with prayer and fasting, they committed them to the Lord in whom they believed.

Similarly, in the Letter to Titus 1:5, the author says: "For this reason I left you in Crete so that you might set right what remains to be done and *appoint presbyters in every town*." And the Epistle to the Hebrews (5:1-5) supplies us with a veritable theology of vocational calling or divine election when it says:

> For every high priest chosen from among men is appointed to act on behalf of men in relation to God, to offer gifts and sacrifices for sins. He can deal gently with the ignorant and wayward, since he himself is beset with weakness. Because of this he is bound to offer sacrifice for his own sins as well as for those of the people. And *one does not take the honor upon himself*, but he is called by God, just as Aaron was.

So also Christ did not exalt himself to be made a high priest, but was appointed by him who said to him, "Thou art my Son, today I have begotten thee."

And in the Book of Revelation 2:2, Jesus indicts what he calls "those self-styled apostles."

However, the New Testament gives ample evidence of other forms of ministerial call and mandate besides that of direct appointment. For example, Acts 1:15-26 purports to be the account of a promotion to ministry that occurred very early on in the Church's history, shortly after the death, resurrection and ascension of Jesus:

In those days Peter stood up among the brethren (the company of persons was in all about a hundred and twenty), and said, "Brethren, the scripture had to be fulfilled, when the Holy Spirit spoke beforehand by the mouth of David, concerning Judas who was guide to those who arrested Jesus. For he was numbered among us, and was allotted his share in this ministry. (Now this man bought a field with the reward of his wickedness; and falling headlong he burst open in the middle and all his bowels gushed out. And it became known to all the inhabitants of Jerusalem, so that the field was called in their language Akeldama, that is, Field of Blood. For it is written in the Book of Psalms, "Let his habitation become desolate, and let there be no one to live in it"; and "His office let another take.") So one of the men who have accompanied us during all the time that the Lord Jesus went in and out among us, beginning from the baptism of John until the day when he was taken up from us — one of these men must become with us a witness to his resurrection." And they put forward two, Joseph called Barsabbas, who was surnamed Justus, and Matthias. And they prayed and said, "Lord, who knowest the hearts of all men, show which one of these two thou hast chosen to take the place in this ministry and apostleship from which Judas turned aside, to go to his own place." And they cast lots for them, and the lot fell on Matthias; and he was enrolled with the eleven apostles.

This way of selecting someone for service was common in the ancient world. It is called "sortition." Indeed, the casting of lots is used to determine many things in the Old Testament. It was the most famous way to determine the division of land among the Hebrew clans when they entered the land of Canaan (Nb 26:55-56, Jos 18:6). But sortition or the casting of lots was also used for many other practical purposes. In 1 Samuel 14:40-42, Saul used it to determine tactics and strategy for military combat. The priests in the temple used it to decide between the two goats on the day of Atonement (Lv 16:8) and more commonly for the assignment of tasks in the temple (1 Ch 25:8), a practice followed in New Testament times, as in Luke 1:9, where it says of Zechariah the father of John the Baptist, "according to custom of the priesthood, it fell to him by lot to enter the temple of the Lord and burn incense." There are also examples of sortition being employed by secular society. For example, Aristotle, in his *The Athenian Constitution*, written in the year 350 B.C., describes a number of ways in which sortition was used in the government at Athens. In Book 8, Part 62, he describes how certain magistrates were chosen by the casting of lots, the logic being that this method functioned as a practical restraint on personal ambition and the power of wealthy patricians to buy votes. In Book 8, Parts 63-64, he describes how juries for the law courts at Athens were chosen by lottery. Long before Aristotle, in the biblical tradition the casting of lots became a metaphor to describe the will of God as divine election. Our modern English word "election" comes from the Latin *electus* which is the past participle of the verb *eligere*, meaning "to pick out, choose, select." Because of historical factors, the modern English word "election" carries the primary meaning of popular, democratic election. But we must remember that long before the advent of democratic processes there existed a religious notion of divine election. And thus we find such expressions in the Old Testament as in Psalm 16:5: "The Lord is my chosen portion and my cup; you hold my lot" or in Isaiah 34:7: "He has cast the lot for them. His hand has portioned it out to them with the line; they shall possess it forever." Its value as a moral option has not been lost

in modern times. For there is the occasional war story of selecting a man for a dangerous mission by pulling straws from a hat,
the short straw being the choice of the man for the mission. This
presumes all the men involved are capable of the mission, but
it relieves the officer in charge from the onus of selecting one of
his own choices. This incident in Acts is the sole example of this
we have in the New Testament.

Yet another method of election to ministry is illustrated
in Acts 6:1-6 when the apostles instead of resorting to lots rely
instead upon the judgment of the people in a sort of popular election wherein the apostles appeared to have had a rather passive
role of simply "ordaining" the men put forward:

> At that time, as the number of disciples continued to
> grow, the Hellenists complained against the Hebrews
> because their widows were being neglected in the daily
> distribution. So the Twelve called together the com-
> munity of the disciples and said, "It is not right for us
> to neglect the word of God to serve at table. Brothers,
> select from among you seven reputable men, filled with
> the Spirit and wisdom, whom we shall appoint to this
> task, whereas we shall devote ourselves to prayer and to
> the ministry of the word." The proposal was acceptable
> to the whole community, so they chose Stephen, a man
> filled with faith and the Holy Spirit, also Philip, Procho-
> rus, Nicanor, Timon, Parmenas, and Nicolaus of Antioch,
> a convert to Judaism. They presented these men to the
> apostles who prayed and laid hands on them.

At other times there appears to be examples of a more mutual
deliberation as in Acts 15:22, wherein we are told, "Then the
apostles and presbyters, in agreement with the whole Church,
decided to choose representatives and to send them to Antioch
with Paul and Barnabas."

However, while there is indeed a discernible trajectory toward a clear concept of ministerial call and mandate in the New
Testament, we cannot afford to ignore the evidence there for self
appointment. While Jesus did indeed call the Twelve, personally

instruct them and send them forth, even he when confronted by the phenomenon of self-appointed "apostles" does not condemn the man. Here we must look at Mark 9:38-40:

> John said to him, "Teacher, we saw a man casting out demons, and we forbade him, because he was not following us." But Jesus said, "Do not forbid him; for no one who does a mighty work in my name will be able soon after to speak evil of me. For he that is not against us is for us."

This passage has a parallel in Luke 9:49-50. Also one might point to the ministry of the itinerant preacher Apollos of Alexandria who in Acts 18:24-28 pops up in Ephesus after Paul has preached there and the same thing happens in Corinth (see 1 Cor 3:5-6), indeed there soon arise a group of Christians at Corinth with a special allegiance to Apollos (1 Cor 1:12) rather than to Paul. Finally, particularly instructive in this matter of personal vocation versus public ministerial call we have the narrative of Saint Paul's own drama of personal choice of ministry only to be initially rebuffed and only later called.

In Acts 9:26-30, we see how, initially, Paul in the enthusiasm of his new found conversion was eager to preach Jesus and indeed to join the Christian community at Jerusalem and be part of their evangelical efforts. But he soon became such a pastoral problem, that they put him in a boat and send him home:

> And when he had come to Jerusalem he attempted to join the disciples; and they were all afraid of him, they did not believe that he was a disciple. But Barnabas took him, and brought him to the apostles, and declared to them how on the road he had seen the Lord, who spoke to him, and how at Damascus he had preached boldly in the name of Jesus. So he went in and out among them at Jerusalem, preaching boldly in the name of the Lord. And he spoke and disputed against the Hellenists; but they were seeking to kill him. And when the brethren knew it, they brought him down to Caesarea, and sent him off to Tarsus.

Acts 11:19-26 relates how, eventually, Paul was rescued from oblivion by Barnabas:

> Now those who were scattered because of the persecution that arose over Stephen traveled as far as Phoenicia and Cyprus and Antioch, speaking the word to none except Jews. But there were some of them, men of Cyprus and Cyrene, who on coming to Antioch spoke to the Greeks also, preaching the Lord Jesus. And the hand of the Lord was with them, and a great number that believed turned to the Lord. News of this came to the ears of the church in Jerusalem, and they sent Barnabas to Antioch. When he came and saw the grace of God, he was glad; and he exhorted them all to remain faithful to the Lord with steadfast purpose; for he was a good man, full of the Holy Spirit and of faith. And a large company was added to the Lord. So Barnabas went to Tarsus to look for Saul; and when he had found him, he brought him to Antioch. For a whole year they met with the church, and taught a large company of people.

And Acts 13:1-3 shows how Paul's ministerial career as an apostle only began when the Church at Antioch decided to send Paul and Barnabas on mission:

> Now in the church at Antioch there were prophets and teachers, Barnabas, Symeon who was called Niger, Lucius of Cyrene, Manaen a member of the court of Herod the tetrarch, and Saul. While they were worshiping the Lord and fasting, the Holy Spirit said, "Set apart for me Barnabas and Saul for the work to which I have called them." Then after fasting and praying they laid their hands on them and sent them off.

What can we say about the witness of all these biblical texts? Can any consistent rational analysis be made of them? Contemporary exegetical literature evaluates these passages variously, and more specifically, the passages which we have looked at that witness to apostolic appointment have come under severe judgment as anachronistic impositions upon early Church freedom by later and reactionary developments. More precisely, against the alleged "hierarchalism" of such passages, many commentators will cite the passage from the early Christian manual of Church practice called the *Didache*. In Ch. 15 of the *Didache* we read, "You must then, elect for yourselves bishops and deacons who are a credit to the Lord, men who are gentle, generous, fruitful, and well tried." They argue this passage from the *Didache* may be very ancient, indeed, perhaps witnessing to a practice that antedates not just the New Testament Pastoral Epistles such as Titus but also the Gospels and Luke-Acts (some scholars date the *Didache* as early as A.D. 60). Such arguments can also be buttressed by numerous citations of historical examples of popular election of clergy in the patristic era. For example, in the *Apostolic Tradition* of Hippolytus of Rome, written circa A.D. 215, we read, "Let the bishop be ordained after he has been chosen by all the people." However, I advise that here as in some others cases balance is necessary, that is, a truly balanced, catholic, integral, wholesome, systematic theology of the biblical notion of clerical election should incorporate all the elements we have seen.

That is, the texts cited above give historical witness to five apparently distinct methods of promotion to leadership in the Church of the New Testament era: self-promotion, apostolic appointment, prophetic discernment, popular election, consultation. However, I believe it would be wrong to seize upon any one of these methods as the historic precedent for what ought to be Church practice today. Rather it is arguable that all five of these "historic" approaches witness to essential elements that ought to be part of any truly "catholic," that is, integral plan for clerical election. I put quotation marks around the word "historic" in that last sentence to emphasize my conviction that if we could historically examine each of the precedents outlined above, I believe we would find that each of the featured methods was in fact probably but one part of a more complex process of ministerial selection or divine election than is at first apparent.

For example, I doubt that even in the Pauline churches of the Pastoral Epistles presbyters were appointed quite arbitrarily by the apostles. That is, I suspect the apostolic figure who appointed presbyters in every town most probably sought some measure of consultation with the locals as to the soundness of their own choice as to who should or should not be promoted to presbyteral ordination. No doubt in certain historical situations one of these elements might become a more important element in the process than the others. And indeed in some extraordinary cases one element might have prevailed even to the exclusion of all the other elements that normally would go into the promotional process. Certainly this was the case in some situations presented us by later Church history, incidents in which we have much more historical witness with much more historical detail. Perhaps the outstanding example of this from early Church history is the popular election of the layman Ambrose as bishop of Milan. The Arian Bishop Auxentius of Milan had died in 374. The Arians and Catholics fought over the vacant position for three years. This was the only way to end the stalemate. But in the ordinary course of things all five are important. For example, in the contemporary Catholic Church the promotion of a candidate for the presbyterate or priesthood begins with the candidate's self-promotion expressed in his decision to enter a seminary, this is followed by a measure of prophetic discernment by the faculty, consultation of the laity (often when the seminarian is assigned to a periodic or summer pastoral placement in a parish), apostolic appointment (when the bishop decides to ordain the candidate) and popular election when the congregation at the ordination signals its approval by applause. Even the element of a lottery or divine election is there. After all, every ordination is ultimately a gamble in that the bishop and congregation put their faith in God that they indeed have made the right decision in ordaining this man.

Finally, we must consider the phenomenon of self-promotion, both the inherent dangers of it and the possibility that in some cases this may be a genuine working of the Holy Spirit. Most often self-appointed pastors and teachers are a danger.

Despite the fact that Apollos is basically a good man, he does arrive with a half-baked Gospel and his preaching does apparently lead to division. Moreover, there is a narrative in the Old Testament Book of Numbers (Ch 11) that may have relevance for this issue. This passage recalls an incident that occurred during the Hebrew people's march through the wilderness on their way to the Promised Land. At one point Moses complained to God: "I am not able to carry all this people alone, the burden is too heavy for me" (Nb 11:14). The Lord replied instructing Moses: "Gather for me seventy men of the elders of Israel... and I will come down and... I will take some of the spirit which is upon you and put it upon them; and they shall bear the burden of the people with you" (11:16-17). But then, in Numbers 11:26-29, we are told how:

> Two men remained in the camp, one named Eldad, and the other named Medad, and the spirit rested upon them; they were among those registered, but they had not gone out to the tent, and so they prophesied in the camp. And a young man ran and told Moses, "Eldad and Medad are prophesying in the camp." And Joshua the son of Nun, the minister of Moses, one of his chosen men, said, "My lord Moses, forbid them." But Moses said to him, "Are you jealous for my sake? Would that all the Lord's people were prophets, that the Lord would put his spirit upon them!"

This passage has prompted much comment from earliest Christian times, for example, it is quoted in *The Shepherd of Hermas*, Vision 2, Part 3, and it is commented on in the Talmud's tractate Sanhedrin 17a. Joshua's complaint and concern seems to be that Eldad's and Medad's "prophesying" outside the camp is inappropriate because such should only be done at the tabernacle and under the leadership of Moses. But Moses' dismissal of Joshua's complaint seems to approve of or respect the fact that sometimes the Spirit of God does indeed work outside the formal boundaries of right order. In some ways this passage seems to parallel that of the Gospel incident wherein the disciples of

Jesus take umbrage at finding someone other than themselves performing wondrous deeds in the name of Jesus. This might be taken by some as endorsement for a liberal attitude such as might be inferred from John 3:8, "The wind blows where it wills, and you hear the sound of it, but you do not know whence it comes or whither it goes; so it is with every one who is born of the Spirit." But the more relevant Gospel passage might be Matthew 7:16, "You will know them by their fruits" (cf. Mt 12:33, Lk 6:43-45).

Indeed, one should not be naïve about unlicensed preachers or untested prophets. While Paul did not condemn the preaching of Apollos at Corinth, in 1 Corinthians 3:10-11 he does issue an ominous warning:

> According to the commission of God given to me, like a skilled master builder I laid a foundation, and another man is building upon it. Let each man take care how he builds upon it. For no other foundation can any one lay than that which is laid, which is Jesus Christ.

Instructive also is the example of Luther and the Zwickau prophets. In December of 1521, while Luther was absent from Wittenberg, a group of preachers arrived, self-styled "prophets" from Zwickau in Saxony under the leadership of a weaver named Nicholas Storch. Storch and his comrades claimed direct personal inspiration from the Holy Spirit and caused considerable confusion at Wittenberg such that Luther had to return to bring calm. It was such examples of extremes of the Radical Reformation that led Luther to make statements such as the following quotation from his *Lectures on Galatians* of 1535:

> God calls in two ways, either by means or without means. Today he calls all of us into the ministry of the Word by a mediated call, that is, one that comes through means, namely through man. But the apostles were called immediately by Christ Himself, or the prophets in the Old Testament had been called by God Himself. Afterwards the apostles called their disciples, as Paul

called Timothy, Titus, etc. These bishops, called their
successors down to our own time, and so on to the end
of the world. This is a mediated calling, since it is done
by man. Nevertheless, it is divine.

And I suspect it was similar concern that led John Calvin to put
the following caution in his great theological work *The Institutes
of the Christian Faith*, Book 4, Part 3, section 10:

Therefore, that restless and turbulent persons may not
presumptuously intrude themselves into the office of
teaching and governing, it is expressly provided, that no
one shall assume a public office in the Church without
a call.

Further Reading

From Jurgen Moltmann's *The Church in the Power of the
Spirit* translated by M. Kohl (San Francisco: Harper & Row,
1977), Chapter VI, part 2, "The charge to the community and the
assignments within the community," pages 300-314.

From Johann Auer's *The Church: The Universal Sacrament of
Salvation* translated by M. Waldstein and H.M. Riley (Washington, DC: Catholic University of America Press, 1993), Chapter
X, "Vocations or Charisms, Ministries, Offices or Commissionings...," pages 179-194.

From Louis Bouyer's *The Church of God: Body of Christ and
Temple of the Spirit* translated by C.U. Quinn (Chicago, IL: Franciscan Herald Press, 1982), Part II, Chapter 8, "Catholicity and
Apostolicity in the Parochial Community: Laity and Hierarchy,"
pages 407-434.

CHAPTER 23

Priestly Ministry

Among Catholic Christians the term "priest" is a common one. Every Catholic knows what a priest is. He is one of the principal figures in the Church. Every Catholic congregation, that is every local Catholic church, has a priest or at least should have one. It used to be that every parish had not just one priest but often several of them. But nowadays when vocations to the priesthood are few there is the problem of priestless parishes. Moreover, every Catholic knows what their priests are meant to do. While they might do several kinds of pastoral ministry or maybe even have a secular profession, principally they should preside at the Eucharist or Lord's Supper and preach.

This use of the language of "priest," however, does not sit well with all Christians. Indeed, many Christians find it very inappropriate. Their objection to it is, basically, that in their view it has no basis, that is, no precedent, in the New Testament. As we saw in the last chapter, when Christian ministers in the New Testament have a title they are called bishops, presbyters or deacons. None of them is called a priest. These same objectors will point out that even with regard to Jesus we must be very careful in using this title "priest." They insist that the only priests in the New Testament are the Jewish high priests. They will point out that while in one work of the New Testament, the Epistle to the Hebrews, Jesus is called a priest (Heb 4:14) even in that work he offered on earth only one sacrifice, himself, once and for all (Heb 7:27). And now he reigns in heaven (Heb 8). Moreover, when the term "priest" is used of Christians in the NT (1 P 2:5, 9), it refers to all Christians and not just to one particular group of clergy in the Church. These are very formidable arguments and what perhaps not every Catholic knows is that in recent times even some Catholic theologians have begun to argue this way. Moreover, the controversy continues. For example, while at the Second Vatican Council there was a preference for the use of the term "presbyter," the most recent liturgical directives from Rome appear to be returning to the language of "priest." And so it is important that we examine the origin and use of this title "priest" in Christian history and tradition and its relevance today.

The first thing that might be said is that there is a measure of truth in this criticism of the use of the term "priest" by Christians. First, the idea of priesthood is neither indigenous nor peculiar to the Christian tradition. Rather it comes from comparative religion. That is, many religions in the ancient world and in our contemporary world have priests. In the ancient world there were priesthoods in Greece and Rome, Egypt and Babylon. In the contemporary world there are the priests of Hinduism (Brahmins), of Shintoism and the Lamas of Tibet. The basic concept of priesthood is that certain people have attained the skill or been given the gift of knowing how to effectively mediate between others and God. But unlike seers or mystics or mediums who claim to mediate by rising above this world and communicating directly with the transcendent and then returning with a message, the priest is an effective mediator because he knows that for truly effective mediation, a sacrifice must be offered. A priest also knows how to offer the appropriate sacrifice to appease or glorify the deity and thus win the deity's favor. But it must also be seen: priesthood attained a special place in biblical tradition. Ancient Israel appropriated and cultivated the importance of the idea of priesthood. Beginning with the sacrifices offered by Abraham right on up to the destruction of the Jerusalem temple in A.D. 70, priesthood and its attendant notion of sacrifice were prominent, indeed, central aspects of Old Testament religion.

It is also true that apparently none of Jesus' contemporaries thought of him as a priest. By that I mean, if we look in the Gospels we find that Jesus' contemporaries employ various titles or labels in referring to him, they call him prophet, rabbi, teacher, Messiah. At one point, he himself suggests that in view of the healings he performs they might well call him a physician. But no one labels him a priest. This is quite understandable in the sense that in Israel Jesus would never have qualified to be a priest. Priesthood in Israel was not vocational, it was hereditary. You had to be born of the priestly clan of Levi in order to qualify to render priestly service to others. Jesus was born of the house of David. This fact helps us to appreciate how great a work of speculative genius is the Epistle to the Hebrews. Though Paul in 2 Corinthians 5:2 saw Jesus' death as a priestly offering, from the evidence we have, the author of the Epistle to the Hebrews is indeed the first to ever apply this title of priest to Jesus. And respecting history, he finds a way to get around the hereditary character of Israelite priesthood and instead insists Jesus is a priest "in the line" — not of Aaron or Levi — but of a mysterious figure named Melchizedek (Heb 5:6, 10; 6:20; all of Ch. 7). This claim of the Epistle to the Hebrews is therefore not only a remarkable one but an important one. It is an example of profound insight. Insight sees beyond appearances, the surface of things. Though obviously Jesus would not have qualified for temple service in Jerusalem, the author of the Epistle to the Hebrews is saying that the life and death of Jesus is a critique of all other historic forms of priesthood. In the history of religions, throughout the history of mankind, priests have offered all kinds of sacrifice, animal and cereal offerings, even in some cases human lives. But the author of the Epistle to the Hebrews is saying that the life and death of Jesus makes it clear the only truly effective sacrifice is oneself. This is an important teaching to this day. Human beings have always been tempted to think that the sacrifice of another or of some thing can work. In Jesus' own life we see the attractiveness of this kind of thinking when someone suggests that "it is better that one man dies for the people" (Jn 11:50). In modern society people still operate very much under the illusion of the efficacy of sacrifice. For example, some sacrifice spouse and family for success and wealth. They might argue they never self-consciously attempted to do this but all the more reason why we must be made prophetically aware of the subtle attraction to the idea of sacrifice. And, moreover, we need to be made aware of how Jesus has already offered the one perfect sacrifice, and we then must be wary of applying this doctrine in our own lives.

However, we need to return now to the other theme about this use of the language of priesthood and that is with regard to Christian ministers. Once again these critics are right that the only other use of the language of priesthood in the New Testament, that is, other than as applied to Jesus Christ in the Epistle to the Hebrews, is in 1 Peter where it is used to describe the lives of all Christians. Sometimes, in the past, Catholic theologians have made use of a line from Saint Paul to justify the use of priestly language for Christian ministers. In one of Paul's letters he does indeed describe his own ministerial labors using priestly language, "My life is being poured out like a libation" (Ph 2:17; cf. 2 Tm 4:6). However, if we are to truly appreciate how intimately tied the language of priesthood is to the mystery of Jesus Christ and his work, then we must look at the place of cult in his own life and his attitude toward it. That is, I am going to argue here that priestly language for Christian ministry finds its validation not in the brilliant insight of the author of the Epistle to the Hebrews nor in some accommodated, poetic sense as in Paul's phrase or the later Christian adaptation of such language as in 1 Clement where the Christian clergy are closely paralleled to the priestly ministers of ancient Israel. Instead, what we need to recognize is that priesthood is deeply imbedded in the life and death, mission and ministry of the historical Jesus. And it is that which not just occasions but requires our appropriation of the language of priesthood.

Unlike the sectarians of Qumran, who rejected the temple cult, and unlike John the Baptist who, though the son of a priest, himself kept a distance from the temple cult, there are several passages in the Gospels that suggest that Jesus was not only raised in a temple-observant family but the temple and its

cult continued to be an important reference point and indeed
a focus of his ministry. There were three foci for the religious life
of devout Jews in Jesus' day: the home, the synagogue and the
temple. Moreover, there was no major antipathy among these,
that is, most Jews found it easy to employ all three in their devout life. We see this in Jesus too. When the Gospel describes
Jesus, Mary and Joseph as going to Jerusalem for the feast of
Passover, we must recall that though Joseph indeed went to
the temple to obtain the lamb for the seder, this ritual supper
itself was celebrated in "the home," that is in a domestic setting
and not in a synagogue or the temple. And this was but one of
several religious observances that would characterize a Jewish
home. As for synagogue observance, the Gospel several times
points to the fact that Jesus was a synagogue observant Jew
but it is also careful to point out that the temple also played an
important part in the spirituality of the family from Nazareth.
Luke 2:22 describes Mary and Joseph as conscientiously going
up to the temple to offer the appropriate sacrifices (Lv 12:1-8)
after the birth of Jesus. In Luke 2:41-52, the one incident in the
Gospels describing the adolescence of Jesus, we are told, "Each
year his parents went to Jerusalem for the feast of Passover." As
for Jesus' own adult attitude toward the temple, the Synoptic
Gospels conflate his ministry to just one year. Moreover, there is
a repeated motif of anticipation that his ministry will climax in
his going up to Jerusalem at the end of that one year ministry.
John's Gospel, which is considered more reliable in this matter,
suggests Jesus' ministry lasted over a two-and-a-half (maybe as
much as three) year period. In John's Gospel there are several
descriptions of Jesus during his public ministry going up to
Jerusalem for temple observances. In John 2:13, Jesus goes up
to Jerusalem for Passover. In John 5:1, Jesus goes to the temple
for the observance of the Jewish feast of Shavuot, "weeks" or
the Jewish "Pentecost" (fifty days). In John 7:1-10, we hear
how Jesus was so determined to observe the feast of Sukkoth
or "tabernacles" in the temple at Jerusalem that he went there
despite the fact that opposition to him and his ministry had
grown to a hostile point. In John 10:26, we find Jesus in the

temple at Jerusalem in the middle of winter in order to observe the fest of the dedication or in Hebrew Hanukkah.

Beyond these suggestions that Jesus himself was a temple-observant Jew, there is also some incidental evidence in the Gospels that suggests not only festival observance (which some might want to discount as merely a concession to tradition or social convention on Jesus' part), but also a personal concern on the part of Jesus for the correct observance of the temple cult. For example, Jesus' words in Matthew 5:23-24, "If you bring your gift to the altar, and there recall that your brother has anything against you, leave your gift there at the altar, go first and be reconciled with your brother, and then come and offer your gift." Obviously, Jesus' words here seem to imply he himself has no objection to one's participation in the temple cult as long as one has a good conscience about one's own proper moral disposition. One could also invoke as a witness to Jesus' attitude toward the temple cult Matthew 23:16-22, a passage wherein Jesus refers to the pious practice of swearing by the altar of the temple. Once again, Jesus' attitude is not to indict the practice but rather to insist on its observance with purity of motive. Perhaps an even more revealing witness is Matthew 17:24-25, wherein Jesus is portrayed as paying the temple tax. This should not be confused with Jesus' judgment on the validity of paying taxes to Rome (we discuss this at length in the chapter on Church-State relations). Rather here we are referring to the tax imposed upon all devout Jews by the Jewish community itself for the support of the temple cult. In Matthew 17:24-25 Jesus conscientiously pays it for Peter and himself. There is yet one more thing we must note: Jesus' positive attitude toward the temple and participation in its cult appear even more remarkable when we note that many of Jesus' contemporaries in Israel took a much more casual, at times even hostile, attitude toward the temple cult. For example, John the Baptist's ministry appears to have had no particular relationship to the temple cult despite the fact that he himself is described as having been born into a priestly family (J. Meier, *A Marginal Jew*, II, 24, makes much of this). And the sectarians of Qumran had their own priestly class and they repudiated the Jerusalem temple cult as hopelessly corrupt.

However, we would be remiss if we did not also call attention to the fact that there are also some Gospel passages that suggest Jesus, despite his own general respect for the temple and its cult, also harbored a more ambiguous, at times downright critical, attitude toward the temple. For example, there are Jesus' comments regarding temple sacrifice and its limitations. In Mark 12:32-33, we hear him say, "To love him [God] with all your heart, with all your understanding, with all your strength, and to love your neighbor as yourself is worth more than all burnt offering and sacrifices." In Matthew 12:7, "If you knew what this meant 'I desire mercy, not sacrifice,' you would not have condemned these innocent men." Many exegetes have suggested the parable of the Good Samaritan in Luke 10:30-37 is Jesus' anti-clerical joke regarding the temple personnel's obsession with Levitical, that is, cultic purity. And then there are those passages where Jesus is recorded as having predicted the destruction of the temple. For example, Mark 13:1-2: "As he was making his way out of the temple area one of his disciples said to him, 'Lord, teacher, what stones and what buildings!' Jesus said to him, 'You see these great buildings? There will not be one stone left upon another that will not be thrown down.'" Moreover, Jesus' words there belie no sense of regret. At another time, Jesus appears to say something that effectively exalts himself over the temple: Matthew 12:6: "I say to you, something greater than the temple is here" (cf. Jn 2:19-21). Finally, in the trial leading to his death, Jesus was accused of having threatened the destruction of the temple by his own initiative! See Mark 15:58: "We heard him say, 'I will destroy this temple made with hands and within three days I will build another not made with hands'" (cf. Mt 26:61).

What can we say of all this evidence? In one sense it is not very remarkable. That is, it appears from this survey that Jesus' attitude toward the temple cult was ultimately ambiguous. He was tolerant of it – indeed even himself observant of it — but at the same time he exhibits an acute awareness of the limitations of the temple cult both in terms of its observance (the priests' obsession with cultic purity) and in itself (how mercy is worth more than any burnt offering or sacrifice). In this regard, Jesus' attitude toward the temple and its cult is neither innovative nor particularly remarkable. It is rather an ambiguity which we might expect from any thoughtful religious person. The prophetic literature of the Hebrew Scriptures often exhibits the same ambiguity. Indeed, some of Jesus' criticism of the temple is not much more than a quotation of prophetic critiques. For example, his "I desire mercy, not sacrifice" is a direct quotation of Hosea 6:6. However, these incidental remarks and actions on the part of Jesus do not exhaust the evidence for his attitude toward the temple cult or priesthood in the Israel of his day. We have yet to look at what might well be called strategic acts of Jesus directed toward the temple and its cult, that is, actions not prompted by his observance of the cult. First, it is significant that his ministry self-consciously ends in Jerusalem. He need not have gone there, he could have stayed away. This is brought out most strongly in the Synoptic Gospels where Jesus intentionally makes his way to the temple and makes it the final focus of his teaching and miracles.

However, what is probably most revelatory of Jesus' attitude toward temple and cult are two great prophetic actions. The first takes place in the temple itself. The second self-consciously makes reference to the temple cult. I am referring to the first incident called "the cleansing of the temple." This incident is related in all four Gospels: Mark 11:15-19, Matthew 21:12-17, Luke 19:45-48, John 2:14-16. The historicity of this event cannot be denied. No doubt there is a discrepancy as to when it occurred: the Synoptics have it at the end of Jesus' ministry, John at the beginning. And no doubt the incident is capable of several different interpretations. For example, Mark sees it as an illustration of Jesus as Messiah come in judgment against Jewish religion. But some exegetes give it a social justice interpretation. That is, Jesus' cleansing of the temple was an expression of his anger aroused by the greed and dishonesty of the money changers and the way they were fleecing the poor. Another interpretation sees this action as not Jesus' concern for the poor; rather he is outraged by the profanation of the temple by commercialism. Lightfoot in the nineteenth century claimed that in this prophetic action Jesus was showing himself to be the Messiah not only of the Jews but of the Gentiles. That is, Lightfoot claims it is no accident that this incident occurs in that part of the temple precinct called "the court of the Gentiles."

The second great prophetic action is an incident that occurred at his last supper with his disciples, the special use he made of bread and wine at that supper and the words of his that accompanied those actions. As with the cleansing of the temple, this incident also has multiple attestations in the New Testament. It is found in all three Synoptic Gospels (Mk 14:22-25; Lk 22:19-20; Mt 26:16-30) and in Paul's First Letter to the Church at Corinth 11:23-25:

> For I received from the Lord what I also handed on to you, that the Lord Jesus, on the night he was handed over, took bread, and, after he had given thanks, broke it and said, "This is my body that is for you. Do this in remembrance of me." In the same way also the cup, after supper, saying, "This cup is the new covenant in my blood. Do this, as often as you drink it, in remembrance of me."

I quote the Pauline account for several reasons. It is the earliest witness. Most scholars agree this epistle was written about the year 55, probably 15 years earlier than the earliest written Gospel, Mark. Moreover, it is witness to an even earlier tradition. That is, the language that Paul uses to introduce his teaching here is a clear signal that this is no invention of his own but is a tradition which he himself received. Moreover, it is a tradition coming from the Lord Jesus himself. The important words are the opening ones, "For I received from the Lord what I also handed on to you." Compare this with the phrase Paul uses elsewhere, "For I hand on to you what I myself received, namely, that Jesus died and rose." That is the apostolic tradition, or the Christian tradition. But what is most important in this passage is the fact that Jesus employs cultic language to describe what he is doing, "This is the new covenant in my blood." Jesus with this language pits himself over against the temple cult. He is saying: Before others will violently take my life, I here and now, through this prophetic ritual, offer it up to the Father as a sacrifice, and, moreover, I charge you to repeat this prophetic action whenever you gather as the right way to remember me and my work for you. Therefore it is appropriate that when the Lord's Supper service is celebrated certain elements be employed that can visually underline the fact that this is not simply a fellowship meal but rather the memorial of a great self-sacrifice. Thus, the table upon which it is celebrated should be obviously an altar and not just a table. Moreover, the officiant who presides over this table should visibly appear as more than just a *pater familias*.

The Second Vatican Council did indeed attempt to incorporate some of the demands of the Protestant Reformers. More precisely, in its Dogmatic Constitution on the Church, *Lumen gentium*, there is present a Catholic version of the doctrine of the priesthood of all believers. But implicit in that conciliar document and others such as the Constitution on the Liturgy is a well-balanced, integral, and thus a truly Catholic doctrine of priesthood. The Christian doctrine of priesthood, if it is to be truly balanced and integral, must acknowledge three realities and do justice to each: the original and unique priesthood of Jesus Christ, the common priesthood of all the baptized, and the ministerial priesthood of bishops and presbyters. The baptized, through the lives they lead, morally represent the unique sacrifice of Christ. This is the spiritual sacrifice referred to in such biblical passages as Romans 12:1: "I appeal to you therefore, brethren, by the mercies of God, to present your bodies as a living sacrifice, holy and acceptable to God, which is your spiritual worship." 1 Peter 2:5, "And like living stones be yourselves built into a spiritual house, to be a holy priesthood, to offer spiritual sacrifices acceptable to God through Jesus Christ." Bishops and presbyters, following the directive in 1 Corinthians 11:25, "Do this… in remembrance of me," sacramentally represent the unique sacrifice of Christ. The baptized through holy lives mediate the sacrifice of Christ to the world; bishops and presbyters mediate the sacrifice of Christ to the congregation of the faithful.

Finally, it is true that the Second Vatican Council intentionally preferred to use the language of "presbyter" instead of "priest." Early drafts of its Decree on the Ministry and Life of Priests employed such titles as *De clericis* (regarding clerics), *De sacerdotibus* (regarding priests), *De vita et ministerio sacerdotali* (regarding priestly life and ministry), but the final form was *Presbyterorum ordinis*, "the order of *presbyters*." This was no concession to the Protestant Reformers nor was it an attempt to lessen or distance themselves from the sense that the presider at the Eucharist is a priest. Rather it was to insist that Catholic priests do not simply preside at an altar, they preside over a community. No doubt such presidency has a juridical aspect to it in that as *Lumen gentium* makes clear "the ministerial priest, by the sacred power he enjoys, molds and rules the priestly people" (Article 10). The Council further specifies something of what is meant in that statement when it treats of the charismatic gifts that characterize the Spirit's work in the lives of all the baptized and says of those gifts, "judgment as to their genuineness and proper use belongs to those who preside over the Church" (Article 12). This is consonant with the Old Testament doctrine of priesthood, in that, in ancient Israel the priest was never simply the officiant of cultic sacrifice. Old Testament priests were Israel's principal religious teachers, custodians of Israel's historical traditions and the source of instruction regarding the law. Indeed, the most daring work of theological speculation in the Old Testament, the creation narratives of Genesis 1-2:4, is a product of the Pentateuch's priestly source. No doubt in Jesus' day there were social factors that had worked to mitigate this original, broader notion of priesthood. That is in Jesus' day the role of the temple priest had come to be more taken up with the cult, and teaching was now principally the work of the scribes. We must be careful not to allow social factors today to have the same effect. That is, there are factors at work today that would so reduce the role of the priest as to make him little more than a chaplain to the community. I have in mind those places where the administration of the parish, pastoral oversight, is totally given over to a layperson and the priest merely comes on Sunday to say Mass and to let someone else preach, or those situations where a bishop appears to rely more upon the advice of lay professionals rather than the members of his presbyteral council who should be his principal consultors.

Further Reading

William R. Millar's *Priesthood in Ancient Israel* (Chalice Press, 2001) is a Protestant exegete's intriguing attempt to recover the notion of priesthood for his religious tradition.

In Joseph Ratzinger's *Called to Communion: Understanding the Church Today* translated by A. Walker (San Francisco: Ignatius Press, 1996), Chapter IV, "On the Essence of the Priesthood," pages 105-131.

Gisbert Greshake's *The Meaning of Christian Priesthood* translated by P. MacSeumais (Westminster, Maryland: Christian Classics, 1989).

CHAPTER 24

Diaconal Ministry

I use the term "diaconal ministry" to refer to two historic expressions of Christian ministry that arose in the early Church and are still present in some form among us today, namely, the ministries of deacon and deaconess. The origin, history and meaning of these two ministries are complex and sometimes even controversial. As an aid to our understanding of these two ministries, we begin by examining biblical passages that provide some insight into the origin and development of these ministries and perhaps even their meaning and relevance today.

Our English words "diaconal," "deacon," and "deaconess" derive from a Greek word that appears often on the lips of Jesus as he is presented in the canonical Gospels. In both the classical Greek of Homer and Aristotle and in the Koine or common Greek of the time of Jesus, the word *diakonos* meant a house servant, literally "one who waited on tables." This word and other language of service, both free and compulsory, figure prominently in the Gospel accounts of the preaching of Jesus of Nazareth. For example, several times in the Gospels Jesus speaks of himself as being a "servant" to others and the importance of his disciples' "serving" each other. In Luke 22:27, Jesus says, "I am among you as one who *serves* [*diakonon*]." In Mark 10:43-45 (and its parallels Mt 20:24-28, Lk 22:24-27), Jesus uses this same language of service to temper the ambition of some of the Twelve by making it clear to them that if they are to effectively lead God's people they must not imitate secular rulers who "lord it over" their peoples. And, no doubt, for dramatic effect and sharpest contrast Jesus even uses the metaphor of slavery, an institution heinous and repulsive to Jewish sensitivities. In Mark 10:43-45, Jesus says: "But it shall not be so among you; but whoever would be great among you must be your servant [*diakonos*], and whoever would be first among you must be slave [*doulos*] of all. For the Son of Man also came not to be served [*diakonethenai*] but to serve [*diakonesai*]."

The Greek word *diakonos* while meaning literally "one who serves at table" is used metaphorically in the New Testament not just by Jesus to describe his own role, as we have seen above, but also at several places it is used by others to describe the work of various people in the Christian community. For example, Saint Paul makes much use of the word *diakonos* in his Second Letter to the Church at Corinth. In 2 Corinthians 3:6 he uses it to describe himself and his assistant, Timothy: "God… has qualified us to be ministers (*diakonoi*) of a New Covenant." Similarly, in 2 Corinthians 6:4, he says of himself and Timothy "as servants (*diakonoi*) of God we commend ourselves in every way." But there are other times in the New Testament writings when the term appears to be used to describe a particular office or ministry or responsibility in the Christian community. Apparently, the earliest example of this is in the Letter to the Philippians, written about the year 61. That letter begins with the greeting, "Paul and Timothy, servants [*douloi*] of Christ Jesus, to all the saints in Christ Jesus who are at Philippi, with the bishops [*episkopoi*] and deacons [*diakonoi*]." I say "apparently" because in our chapter on the ordering of Christian ministries we already treated the theme of how titles and offices of Christian ministry first arose and how it is difficult at times to discern whether a term such as "elder" or "servant" in a New Testament passage is indeed being used to refer to a formal Christian ministry or as a simple moral descriptive. And so it is here. For example, I have quoted the RSV translation of Philippians 6:1, but the New American Bible translation of that same passage renders the terms *episkopoi* and *diakonoi* not as "bishops and deacons" but as "overseers and ministers." In a lengthy footnote, the NAB translators explain

at Philippi "this office had not yet developed into the form that
it later assumed." It is not possible to discern which translation
more nearly reflects the actual situation in Philippi. Are the
people referred to by *episkopoi* and *diakonoi* formal office holders
in the Church at Philippi or are they merely generous, hardwork-
ing members of the community whom Paul is singling out for
honor? It can be argued Paul is being particularly adept in his
use of this term in this his opening salutation of his Letter to the
Philippians. That is, Paul foregoes here the title of apostle that
he uses to describe himself in the opening salutation of his other
letters (Rm 1:1, 1 Cor 1:1, 2 Cor 1:1, Gal 1:1), and instead here he
employs the humblest title possible — calling himself a "slave"
of Christ. The reason for his choice of this very humble title is
most probably not simply because he did not found the Church
at Philippi but because he wants to defer to, to acknowledge, to
"spotlight" the local Church leadership. In that sense it can be
claimed: no doubt in this opening salutation of the Letter to the
Philippians, we see the language first used by Jesus as a term of
general spirituality now becoming a precise technical reference
for a particular responsibility in the Christian community: the
humble domestic servant is fast becoming a responsible Church
officer, a deacon! But surely the *episkopoi* and *diakonoi* here are
not identical with the bishops and deacons as we find those
ministries fully developed in the post-apostolic Church.

The next passage from the New Testament that any student
of diaconal ministry should be aware of is a passage from the
Acts of the Apostles. The passage is Acts 6:1-6, and it purports to
be a description of a crisis which arose in the life of the earliest
Christian community at Jerusalem. But it is also a passage that
in the early Church came to be regarded as the historical account
of the foundation of the ministry of deacons. For examples, it
is cited as such in Irenaeus' *Against Heresies* (1.26; 3.12; 4.15),
in Cyprian's Epistle (3.3) and in Eusebius' *Ecclesiastical History*
(6.43). The Synod of Neo-Caesarea in 315 mandated the limit
of seven deacons for each metropolitan see citing Acts 6:1-6 as
the historic precedent for diaconate ordination. Here is how the
passage reads:

> Now in these days when the disciples were increas-
> ing in number, the Hellenists murmured against the
> Hebrews because their widows were neglected in the
> daily distribution [*diakonia*]. And the Twelve summoned
> the body of the disciples and said, "It is not right that
> we should give up preaching the word of God to serve
> [*diakonein*] tables. Therefore, brethren, pick out from
> among you seven men of good repute, full of the Spirit
> and of wisdom, whom we may appoint to this duty. But
> we will devote ourselves to prayer and to the ministry
> [*diakonia*] of the word." And what they said pleased the
> whole multitude, and they chose Stephen, a man full of
> faith and of the Holy Spirit, and Philip and Prochorus,
> and Nicanor, and Timon, and Parmenas, and Nicolaus,
> a proselyte of Antioch. These they set before the apostles,
> and they prayed and laid their hands on them.

There are several things the reader needs to know about this
passage. For one thing, while this passage was traditionally held
to be the historical account of the foundation of the diaconate,
that claim is much disputed by modern exegetes and theologians. The principal objections raised are two. The formal title
of deacon (*diakonos*) is nowhere used in this passage. And, while
these seven men were set aside, ordained for charitable work,
when we hear of them later they are not doing charitable work;
rather they are portrayed as prominent preachers and teachers,
evangelists (Stephen in Acts 7, Philip in Acts 8:4-40). These objections can be answered.

While it is true the word "deacon" is never used in Acts
6:1-6, nevertheless, there is considerable and varied, one might
even say, sententious use made of variations on that term such
as the cognate noun "service" (*diakonia*) and the verb "to serve"
(*diakonein*). Of course, one could argue no one should be surprised that the formal title of deacon is not used here. Formal
titles for Christian ministries are a late development in the New
Testament. For example, most often those whom we later call
the twelve apostles are in the earliest Gospel simply called "the
Twelve" (Mk 3:14, 4:10, 6:7, 9:35, 14:10, 17:20). Similarly, those

men set apart for charitable ministry in Acts 6:1-6 are simply called "the Seven." There can be little doubt that Luke's use of the various forms of the words for service is meant to underscore the importance but difference between liturgical service and pastoral service.

As for the fact that Stephen and Philip are never again seen laboring in charitable ministry: James 1:7 witnesses to the importance of both charity and worship and their close identification: "Religion that is pure and undefiled before God and the Father is this: to visit orphans and widows in their affliction, and to keep one unstained from the world." That is, true religion consists of two things, doing justice to God and neighbor, more precisely, charity toward one's neighbor; and reverence for God, due worship of God, for the phrase "keep one unstained from the world" is a poetic reference to the cultic purity required for the integrity of liturgical worship in the Jerusalem temple. While no Christian minister is exempt from either task, even so, Acts 6:1-6, suggests that the earliest division of labors in the Church, of ministries in the Church, was to insure that the charitable task be clearly marked out as a major responsibility by being given a sacramental, that is, a revered even reverenced visible public prominence. And if Stephen and Philip are portrayed as preaching and teaching, in no small measure dramatic circumstances dictated this. In Stephen's case the defense of the faith, in Philip's his flight from Jerusalem meant he no long had widows to provide for.

1 Timothy 2:8-13 is yet another passage any and every student of diaconal ministry needs to be acquainted with. This passage comes after a description of the qualifications for the office of bishop, and it gives the qualifications for the office of deacon:

> Deacons likewise must be serious, not double-tongued, not addicted to much wine, not greedy for gain; they must hold the mystery of the faith with a clear conscience. And let them also be tested first; then if they prove themselves blameless let them serve as deacons. The women [*gunaikas*] likewise must be serious, no slanderers, but temperate, faithful in all things. Let deacons be the husband of

one wife, and let them manage their children and their
households well; for those who serve well as deacons gain
a good standing for themselves and also great confidence
in the faith which is in Christ Jesus.

The most intriguing aspect of this passage is its mention
of women, the *gunaikas* of verse 11. Acts 6:1-6 specifies men.
But here women are mentioned. There is much controversy as
to the identity of these women. In the past, this reference was
most often interpreted as referring to the wives of deacons. More
recent scholarship has suggested it might well refer to women
deacons. But caution is appropriate here. For, if indeed we are
reading the qualifications for women deacons, we must take into
consideration the fact that there are other parts of this letter that
would put severe restrictions on the extent of women's diaconal
ministry. For example, in 1 Timothy 2:12, we read: "I permit no
woman to teach or to have authority over men." And thus if like
Stephen and Philip these women in 1 Timothy ever preached or
taught, it must have been to other women they addressed their
words. And this would not be unlike the ministry of deaconesses in the later Church, something which we will describe in
detail later.

Those who interpret 1 Timothy 3:11 as referring to women
deacons are often quick to cite another New Testament passage
that apparently describes a woman deacon. This is Romans
16:1-2:

I commend to you our sister Phoebe, a deaconess of the
church at Cenchreae that you may receive her in the Lord
as befits the saints, and help her in whatever she may
require from you, for she has been a helper of many and
of myself as well.

The first thing that must be noted about Romans 16:1-2 is that
the RSV translation which we cite here employs an anachronism. It calls Phoebe a "deaconess" when in fact Paul uses the
masculine noun *diakonos*, deacon. The first literary evidence for
the use of the term "deaconess" (*diakonissa*) is not found until

the year A.D. 325, when the Council of Nicea uses it to address a rank of women ministers in the Church. Are the RSV translators doing the same thing here that they did in Philippians 1:1, which is employing a much later concept to an earlier situation? It is interesting to compare once again the RSV and NAB translations. The NAB, as with its treatment of Philippians 1:1, describes Phoebe as "a minister of the church at Cenchreae." And the reason it gives is to refer the reader to the reason it gave for the translation of Philippians 1:1. They do not want to read into the earlier historical situation the later fully developed office when here it is only in nascent form. Moreover, I think a careful consideration of Paul's precise words in Romans 16:1-2 supports the NAB translation.

As for Paul's description of Phoebe as a *diakonos*: I think here too we must exercise the same care as we did in identifying the sense of his use of the word *diakonoi* in Philippians 1:1. I think here too Paul is trying to give some recognition and honor to Phoebe for her generous service to him, the Christian community at Cenchrae from which she comes and to others. But I do not think he means to imply Phoebe is the bearer of the title of a formal office in the Church at Cenchrae, part of a hierarchy of orders, a virtual ecclesiastic or Church leader. Rather I think Paul uses the term here to refer to Phoebe simply as an esteemed but humble servant of the community. Moreover, there is another term in addition to *diakonos* that Paul uses here to describe Phoebe. And it is probably more revealing of the true character of her work. I am referring to Romans 16:2 where Paul calls Phoebe a *prostates*, that is, a helper, or advocate or benefactor "of many and myself as well." This is probably indirect evidence that it was Phoebe's wealth that enabled her to be generous to many. Indeed, some exegetes have argued the fact that Phoebe could afford to travel from Cenchrae to Rome is clear indication of her personal wealth. And still others have suggested that it is not unlikely that as the bearer of Paul's Letter to the Romans, Phoebe, not only paid her own way to Rome to deliver it, but she may well have paid for all the parchment on which Romans, Paul's longest literary effort, had been written.

But to be fair to the translators of the RSV, I do not think they are totally wrong in their interpolating this anachronistic term into the text. It could be that the women referred to in 1 Timothy 3:8-13, with the restrictions on their range of preaching and teaching, and the prominently charitable ministry of Phoebe in Romans 16:1-2, might well be seen the forerunners of the later Church office of deaconess.

At this point, I think it would be better if we leave the Bible behind for a moment and trace the historical development of both the ministries of deacon and deaconess in the history of the early Church.

That deacons were an important part of Church leadership from early on is witnessed to by several references to them in the Letters of Ignatius of Antioch (*Ephesians* 2.1; *Magnesians* 2; 6.1; 13.1; *Trallians* 3.1;7.2; *Philadelphians* 4;7; 10.1;11.1; *Smyrnians* 8.1, 12.2, *Polycarp* 6.1). But while they are mentioned there as an essential element in every Church, their function is not entirely clear. There is but one passage that suggests deacons preached (*Philadelphians* 11.1): "Philo, the deacon from Cilicia, a man of attested merit, who even now assists me in the ministry of the Word of God." However, we have much more witness to their role in the later centuries.

In order to cover the huge extent of the history of male diaconal ministry in the last two thousand years, what I shall do here is to schematize it into three periods, an initial golden age, followed by a long period of slow decline into obscurity, and then, most recently, a period of gradual restoration to prominence.

The first period, the golden age, when the diaconal office was at its greatest prominence and power, extends from about 95 A.D., the death of the last apostle, to 325 A.D., the date of the first Ecumenical Council, the Council of Nicea, whose strictures against deacons signal the beginning of the historic decline of this ministry into relative obscurity. During the hundred years after the death of the last apostle, the diaconal office which we saw in Acts 6:1-6, originally given over to the protection and care of the poor, rapidly developed into an important position of great responsibility in government of the Church. That is, in this period, not only did the deacons have a prominent role in the liturgy — male deacons assisted the bishop with baptisms, in the Eucharistic Assembly male deacons chanted the Gospel, led the prayer of the faithful, received the offerings from the people, and helped to distribute communion. But they had a, perhaps, even more important role in the life of the Church outside the liturgical assembly. The custom soon arose to have no more than seven male deacons in any major church and one of them, the first deacon or "archdeacon" often became the bishop's chief administrative officer. In some places, these deacons had complete control over the goods of the church. They served as official inspectors for the local bishop, his principal counselors and diocesan functionaries. They were often sent as emissaries or legates by their bishops. And owing to their experience and prominence, many of them were subsequently elected bishops. The problem is the power of archdeacons soon came to be an irritant not only to presbyters but even to some bishops. Soon we begin to find evidence of arrogant deacons. Cyprian of Carthage (d. 258), in his Epistle 64, wrote "to Rogatianus, about the deacon who contended against the bishop." The Council of Arles in A.D. 314, says that some deacons not only assisted but even at times were so bold as to preside at a Eucharist (Canon 15). The Council of Nicea, in one of its canons (juridical directives), more precisely Number 18, specifically addressed the problem of arrogant deacons in the liturgical assembly:

> It has come to the attention of this holy and great synod that in some places and cities deacons give communion to presbyters, although neither canon nor custom allows this, namely that those who have no authority to offer should give the body of Christ to those who do offer. Moreover, it has become known that some of the deacons now receive the Eucharist even before the bishops. All these practices must be suppressed. Deacons must remain within their own limits, knowing that they are the ministers of the bishop and subordinate to the presbyters. Let them receive the Eucharist according to their order after the presbyters from the hands of the

bishop or the presbyter. Nor shall permission be given
for the deacons to sit among the presbyters, for such
an arrangement is contrary to the canon and to rank. If
anyone refuses to comply even after these decrees, he is
to be suspended from the diaconate.

In the West the actual period of decline extended from the
Council of Nicea in 325 to the Council of Trent in the sixteenth
century, a period of more than a thousand years. But the decline
became quite rapid in the early part of this era when theologians
like Jerome (d. 419) and Chrysostom (d. 407) became "sacer-
dotalists," that is, exalted the importance of the presbyteral or
"priestly" office over that of the deacon (see especially Jerome's
Epistle 146 and Chrysostom's Second Homily on 1 Tm 2:8-10).
During this period the role of the deacon was reduced more
and more to that of a mere liturgical assistant. Moreover, it
even disappeared as a permanent office and instead was now
seen as but one step on the way to the priesthood. However, the
permanent diaconate never wholly vanished from the West. For
example, Francis of Assisi (d. 1226) was initially a lay preacher.
The Church's concern regarding unlicensed preachers led to
Francis being offered to be ordained a presbyter. Francis refused
but agreed to be made a deacon. Even so, in the last will and
testament of Francis we see how the deacon was regarded as
totally inferior to those who presided at the Lord's Supper. In
his will Francis wrote, "Even though I had all the wisdom of
Solomon, if I should find poor secular priests, I would not preach
in their parishes without their consent. I will not consider their
sins, for in them I see the Son of God and they are my lords." It
is probably an expression of genuine humility on Francis' part,
but nonetheless, it can also be taken as the apt expression of the
now chastened office of a deacon, a deacon who "knows his
place." The lesson of Nicea has been learned.

In the post-apostolic Church, frequent mention is made
of deaconesses. This office was especially common in the Eastern Churches. But what is clear is that while their ministry is
somewhat analogous to that of the male diaconate, it was not

its equivalent, indeed, it was something quite different. There is a passage from a letter by Pliny the Younger, governor of the Roman province of Bithynia (today the region of Anatolia in North Central Turkey) written to the Emperor Trajan in the year A.D. 112. It is often cited as the earliest reference outside the New Testament to women exercising a diaconal ministry. This is because in his letter Pliny uses the Latin word *ancillae*, meaning "servants," to describe the role in the Christian community of two Christian women, former slaves, who had been arrested and tortured. Pliny's use of this term *ancillae* has been interpreted by some to be a reference to these women's particular role of service in the Christian community, in other words, a diaconal ministry. Other early sources are more precise in describing a ministry of women both of charity and in the liturgy.

The *Didascalia Apostolorum*, III.2, an early third century document, makes clear the responsibilities of deaconesses: they guarded the door through which women entered the church, they escorted women worshipers to the place designated for them, and they communicated to the bishop the needs and desires of women. Yet another important liturgical role for deaconesses was to assist the bishop at the baptism of women. Baptism of adults at that time included the baptismal candidate's disrobing and being total immersed in the waters of baptism; this and some other parts of the baptismal ceremony such as the anointing of the head and chest, were ceremonies that could not be performed with propriety for women by male ministers. And so it was one of the principal functions of deaconesses to assist in the baptism of women. While these women were given great respect they were not the equivalent of male deacons. This was made very obvious at the celebration of the Eucharist wherein the male deacons stood in the sanctuary with the priests and bishop while the deaconesses either stood as a group at the women's entrance or sat scattered among the women.

Liturgical custom regarding the installation of deaconesses varied, and no doubt in some places it was similar to if not identical to the installation of male deacons, that is, it was an ordination rite. For example, while the Roman presbyter Hippolytus in the middle of the second century, in his *Apostolic Tradition*, warns against the use of the imposition of hands and insists upon only the blessing of deaconesses, Canon 19 of the Council of Nicea in 325 is an indirect witness to the use of the imposition of hands for the installation of deaconesses. And Canon 15 of the Council of Chalcedon (A.D. 451) uses the formal language of ordination (*cheirotoneisthai*). Even so, these elements merely serve to indicate that deaconesses were regarded as a minor order. For the imposition of hands was used for the installation of other minor orders such as that of lector, as in the *Apostolic Constitutions* (VIII, 2) at Syria in the fourth century. Nevertheless, the ministry of a deaconess was not the same as that of a deacon, indeed, it was much more limited.

Even though the office of deaconess was not the equivalent of that of a deacon it was a prominent and honored ministry. For example, at Constantinople in the time of Chrysostom, there were no fewer than forty deaconesses in that Church and Olympia the archdeaconess was no doubt Chrysostom's most esteemed personal advisor. But it could also be that much of Olympia's prominence was due to personal distinctions such as the fact that she was one of the richest women in the world. And, even though Olympia was high in Chrysostom's personal esteem, there was still an archdeacon at Constantinople, Serapion. If Serapion's influence was much less than that of Olympia's, that might well have been due to a crisis in the office of the male deacon. We have already seen how, early on in the history of Christianity, male deacons became so prominent and powerful that a bishop like Chrysostom saw it as one of his duties to tame that office and confine it to a more humble role.

The period of gradual restoration of diaconal ministry as a permanent and recognizable if not entirely prominent ministry in the Church began with the Protestant Reformation and its Catholic response, the Council of Trent (ca. 1560). The actions of the Reformers varied. Luther, though he recognized the NT office as a vital charitable ministry, wasted no time in trying to restore it. On the other hand, Calvin, in his theological compendium called *The Institutes of the Christian Faith* (4.3.9 and 4.4.5), gave more careful and scholarly consideration to the idea of restoring diaconal ministry. Indeed, he sketched for the Reformed Church a concept of diaconal ministry based on the classical biblical texts and his keen research into the male and female diaconate, the deacons and deaconesses of the early Church. Calvin thus distinguished "two distinct orders of deacons," that is, men with responsibility for the wealth of the Church and thus the distribution of alms to the poor, but women who give personal care for the sick and the poor (and with only the men to be ordained). But Calvin's vision, for all its scholarly weight and careful consideration, was rarely put into practice.

As for the Catholics, the Council Fathers at Trent seriously debated the restoration of diaconal ministry to a permanent and responsible position in the Church. But it was a recent and glaring abuse of the office that worked to prevent its restoration. That is, as already noted, the office had never totally disappeared and in fact during the Renaissance it resurfaced in a new form when it was given to the sons of princely families so that the son might enjoy an ecclesiastical income and title long before priestly or episcopal ordination.

It was in the Churches of the Radical Reformation, the Anabaptists and Mennonites, that diaconal ministry found its most notable restoration. The "Concept of Cologne" (1591) states: "Deacons shall be chosen according to the example of the Apostolic Church, to whom is to be assigned the care of the poor. They are to distribute to the poor the gifts received for this purpose so that the giver shall remain unknown as Christ teaches." Among Anabaptists the deaconess office, based on Romans 16:1 and 1 Timothy 5:9-10, was preserved from the beginning. The Dordrecht Confession of April 1632, Article 9, Section 5, says, "Also that honorable old widows be ordained and chosen as servants, who besides the almoners, are to visit, comfort, and take care of the poor, the weak, the afflicted, and the needy." Among the Mennonites at first all groups maintained the office of deacon, though not every congregation had one. Early on deacons were ordained and served for life and often shared with the bishop in exercising oversight of the community of faith, for example, deacons kept the Church membership record. But in later times, in many cases deacons came to be elected for a term, several served together and the work was more charitable ministry. It was not until the nineteenth century that Lutherans and Anglicans made serious efforts to restore the ministry and office and when they did it was not the male order of deacon but the women's ministry. In the wake of the social havoc wrought by the Napoleonic wars, Lutheran Churchmen sought to establish a form of charitable ministry among the poor similar to that supplied by Catholic religious orders. In 1836, Theodore Flidner, a Lutheran pastor in the village of Kaiserwerth on the Rhine, spurred by the example of the charitable work of Catholic religious orders in his town, bought a house to be used as a hospital and training place for a deaconess association, young women who would promise at least five years of charitable service. This house at Kaiserwerth rapidly became the model for others in Lausanne (1841), Strasbourg (1842), Dresden and Utrecht (1844), Bern and Berlin (1845), Stockholm (1851) and St. Petersburg (1859). In England in 1862, the order of deaconess was revived for the Anglican Church when Bishop Tait of London ordained Elizabeth Ferard. And by the end of the nineteenth century, the Lutheran Churches in America had adopted a similar program. To this day the Lutheran Church-Missouri Synod's Concordia Seminary in St. Louis advertises a graduate level program for deaconess preparation. It describes a deaconess as "a woman with a theological and practical preparation who is called to serve as a support to a pastor in his ministry."

As for the Orthodox Church, there the male diaconate as a permanent ministry never disappeared. But its administrative functions were severely reduced. Indeed, in most cases a deacon's duties were solely liturgical. For example, in Orthodox monasteries to this day at least one monk is a deacon and he will probably remain a deacon for life, as other monks are chosen to be ordained priests. This deacon, however, does have a very prominent role in the liturgy, chanting many prayers and biblical passages. Outside the monastery, the lifelong deacon is usually found in a bishop's household where he functions as personal secretary and valet to the bishop as well as the bishop's principal assistant at all liturgies. And as for deaconesses, across the centuries into modern times there has always been a canonical provision for them and their role in baptismal liturgies was never revoked. But for all practical purposes the female diaconate, deaconesses, disappeared from the Orthodox Church by the end of the twelfth century. In the nineteenth and twentieth centuries there were some attempts to revive the order of deaconess. For example, in the nineteenth century the Grand Duchess Elena Pavlovna led a movement to restore the order of deaconesses in the Russian Orthodox Church. Most recently, on October 8, 2004, the Synod of the Church of Greece voted a limited restoration of the female diaconate, that is, specifying "the regional bishop may consecrate senior nuns of holy monasteries of their eparchy in order to address the needs of these holy monasteries."

As for the Catholic Church, it was not until the Second Vatican Council (1962-1965) that a serious effort was made to restore the ministry of deacon as an ordained and permanent ministry rather than just a transition stage on the way to priestly ordination. Even before the Council, in the late 1940's and 1950's in Germany, a movement to restore the diaconate had gotten under way and it was accompanied by considerable support from renowned theologians like Karl Rahner. Rahner's essay on diaconal ministry shows a keen knowledge of the biblical background for this ministry and follows it in its insistence upon evidence of outstanding charitable ministry as the principal qualification for promotion to this office. At the Council itself, the proposal to restore the diaconate as a permanent office got a mixed reception and so, as a compromise, the restoration was not mandated for the universal Church but rather left as an option for regional episcopal conferences to implement. The division was not doctrinal but on pastoral grounds in that the most divisive issue was the proposal that the rule of celibacy not be a requirement of permanent deacons, but that they be allowed the option to marry before ordination. Predictably, after the Council response to this invitation was mixed. The West German and US bishops' conferences were quick to implement the idea, but most other national episcopal conferences either shrugged off the opportunity or took much more limited measures to implement it. Moreover, it is arguable that the diaconal ministry implied in the Council documents was not so much the restoration of the classical diaconate of the early Church whereby there were but a few deacons, prominent principally for their charitable ministry, while also serving as liturgical attendants and advisors to their bishop. Rather what resulted was a pastoral deacon assigned to assist a priest in the pastoral ministry of a parish and to assist more liturgically and sacramentally than charitably (see Vatican II's Constitution on the Church 3.29). Further developments have ensued of a very mixed if not contradictory character. For example, some voices have been raised urging that deacons be given even further sacramental powers such as to anoint and absolve, on the grounds that there is possibly an historic precedent in the actions of Cyprian of Carthage who during the persecutions, when he and his presbyters fled the persecution, allowed the deacons who remained behind with the people to anoint and even absolve those near death (see his Epistle 18). However, in contrast some bishops in the US, disappointed in the preaching performance of their permanent deacons, no longer give them faculties to preach. And, even more recently, feminists have also weighed in urging the extension of this ministry to women. But on February 11, 2005, a decision of the Vatican's Congregation for the Doctrine of the Faith ruled out anointings by deacons or laity.

What can we say in conclusion? First, it is important that someone give formal witness as in the Bible and in the early Church to the importance of charity as well as communion, of material assistance to the poor as well as sacramental communion from the Table of the Lord. The Church must be vigilant to retain the diaconate as a clear sacramental sign that she places, like Jesus, love of neighbor not only a par with (Mk 12:30-31) but as a litmus test of the genuineness of our love of God (Mt 5:23-24).

While deacons did assist at the Table of the Lord with sacramental communion, it was the apostolic figures, the Twelve, who principally represent the liturgical task of worship as sacramental communion. In this regard, Catholics might well take a lesson from those ecclesial traditions in the East (the Orthodox) and the West (the Reformation heritage) which have preserved not only the offices of deacon and deaconess and their distinction but also the strongly charitable character of diaconal ministry whether exercised by men or women. And, while the office of deaconess has no real roots in the Western Church, it could be adapted.

Further Reading

Edward P. Echlin's *The Deacon in the Church: Past Time and Future* (Staten Island, NY: ST PAULS/ Alba House, 1971).

James Monroe Barnett's *The Diaconate: A Full and Equal Order* (New York: Seabury, 1981).

Aimé Georges Martimort's *Deaconesses: An Historical Study* (San Francisco: Ignatius Press, 1986).

Jeannine Olson's *Deacon and Deaconesses Through the Centuries* (Revised Edition, St. Louis: Concordia Publishing House, 2006).

Karl Rahner's "The Theology of the Restoration of the Diaconate" in *Theological Investigations* Vol. V (New York: Seabury Press, 1968), pp. 268-314.

CHAPTER 25

The Petrine Ministry

In 1868, Pope Pius IX summoned all the bishops of the Catholic world to come together in solemn assembly at Rome for a special kind of meeting which is called a world or "ecumenical" Council (from the Greek *oikumene*, meaning "the inhabited world"). There had not been such a meeting since the sixteenth century when all Catholic bishops were summoned to a small city named Trent in the north of Italy to figure out some kind of response to the Protestant Reformation.

In 1868, London's principal newspaper, *The Times*, thought this Council summoned by Pope Pius IX an important enough event that it sent a reporter to cover it. He was an Anglican clergyman by the name of Thomas Mozley. His reports to *The Times* were eventually published as a two-volume work, *Letters from Rome on the Occasion of the Oecumenical Council, 1869-1871*. Mozley was a keen observer; moreover, he wrote very well. One of the most dramatic and entertaining passages from Mozley's *Letters...* is his description of an awesome thunderstorm that raged over St. Peter's Basilica — the place where this Council was held — during the final vote on the dogma of papal infallibility:

> The storm, which had been threatening all the morning, burst now with the utmost violence, and to many a superstitious mind might have conveyed the idea that it was the expression of Divine wrath, as "no doubt it will be interpreted by numbers," said one officer of the Palatine Guard. And so the *placets* [affirmative votes] of the Fathers

struggled through the storm, while the thunder pealed above and the lightning flashed in at every window and down through the dome and every cupola, dividing if not absorbing the attention of the crowd. *Placet*, shouted his Eminence or his Grace, and a loud clap of thunder followed in response, and then the lightning darted about the baldacchino and every part of the Church and Conciliar Hall, as if announcing the response. So it continued for nearly one hour and a half, during which time the roll was being called, and a more effective scene I never witnessed. Had all the decorators and all the getters-up of ceremonies in Rome been employed, nothing approaching to the solemn splendor of that storm could have been prepared, and never will those who saw it and felt it forget the promulgation of the first Dogma of the Church.

If, indeed, there were "numbers" who interpreted the electrical storm that arose during the voting on papal infallibility as a sign of God's wrath, yet another "number" might well have interpreted that electrical storm as signaling not divine wrath but divine revelation. By that I mean anyone acquainted with the Bible knows that the principal metaphor for God's wrath is torrential rain that produces disastrous floods (in this regard see not only the universal deluge in Gn 6:5-9:17, but also Job 22:28; Ps 69:2, 5, 124:4; Is 8:7; Dn 9:26, 11:10, 11:40; Ho 5:10). Whereas thunder and lightning accompany divine revelation, like the thunder and lightning that accompanied God's revelation of the Law to Moses on Mount Sinai (Ex 19:16, 19; 20:18, 21). In the New Testament thunder accompanies the voice of God (Jn 12:29) and lightning the coming of the Son of Man (Lk 17:24) and thunder and lightning issue from the throne of God in heaven (Rv 4:5). Here, however, we are not going to argue over the correct interpretation of the portents of nature that were displayed over St. Peter's during the voting on papal infallibility or whether indeed they were "portents" in any sense. Nor are we going to consider the dogma of papal infallibility as promulgated by the First Vatican Council. Instead, and more consistent with the announced style of this book, we are going to look at certain biblical passages that are often presented, as they were at Vatican I, as supporting the idea of a special ministry in the Church, a ministry which, in dialogues on Christian unity, is called the Petrine Ministry. The word "petrine" comes from the Latin word "Petrus" for the name Peter. "The Petrine Ministry" is a technical phrase from the language of modern ecumenical dialogue where it means "a Peter-like ministry," Peter being a reference to one of Jesus' principal disciples and the figure to which popes relate their own ministry. That is, all popes claim that the ministry they offer the universal Church is but a continuation of that ministry which in the Gospel accounts we see Jesus accord to Peter, and which, in the rest of the New Testament, we see Peter carrying out in relation to the earliest Christian communities.

And so what we are going to do here is to survey New Testament references to Peter, seeking out the passages that appear to be most revelatory of Peter's role during the life and death of Jesus and then later in the life of the early Christian movement. We must be somewhat selective, because Peter's name appears often in the New Testament. It is invoked there no less than 189 times. We shall look first at the portraits of Peter during the public ministry of Jesus and then at the portraits of Peter in the life of the early Church. The first group of portraits comes from the Gospels, and the second from the Acts of Apostles and the New Testament epistles.

The first thing to be noted about the Gospel portrayal of Peter is the peculiar prominence given in the Gospels to Peter's place amid the disciples of Jesus. For example, when at the beginning of Jesus' public ministry he begins to gather about him the central or core group, indeed, as we have seen, the signal group of his disciples, "the Twelve," the call of Peter is featured first (Mk 1:16; Mt 3:18; Lk 6:14). Moreover, later on, when Christian tradition preserved the list of names of this original and signal group, Peter's name always appears at the top of the list. Here we look at that list as it appears in Mark 3:13-19:

> And he went up into the hills, and called to him those
> whom he desired; and they came to him. And he ap-

> pointed twelve, to be with him, and to be sent out to preach and have authority to cast out demons; Simon whom he surnamed Peter; James the son of Zebedee and John the brother of James, whom he surnamed Boanerges, that is, sons of thunder; Andrew, and Philip, and Bartholomew, and Matthew, and Thomas, and James the son of Alphaeus, and Thaddeus and Simon the Canaean, and Judas Iscariot, who betrayed him.

Similar lists, with Peter's name always at the top, can be found in Matthew 10:1-4 and Luke 6:12-16.

Also, among the Twelve there is observable what appears to have been an even more intimate, select group of three (an inner-inner circle?) who at times are privileged to have experiences of Jesus which the other nine have not. Here too when mention is made of this select group, Peter's name is always mentioned first. For example, Mark 5:37 tells us, "And he allowed no one to follow him except Peter and James and John, the brother of James." Mark 9:2 tells us, "And after six days Jesus took with him Peter and James and John, and led them up a high mountain apart by themselves; and he was transfigured before them." Mark 14:32-33: "And they went to a place which was called Gethsemane; and he said to his disciples, 'Sit here, while I pray.' And he took with him Peter and James and John, and began to be greatly distressed and troubled."

Another notable highlighting of Peter in the Gospel narratives is the fact that Peter is often portrayed as taking the initiative in conversations with Jesus. For example, in Mark 11:21, "Peter remembered and said to Jesus, 'Rabbi, look! The fig tree you cursed has withered!'" In Matthew 18:21, "Then Peter came up and said to him, 'Lord, how often shall my brother sin against me, and I forgive him?'" Or consider Luke 12:41, "Peter asked, 'Lord, are you telling this parable to us, or to everyone?'" At other times Peter is portrayed as acting as spokesman for the Twelve, especially when he is expressing a consensus of opinion as in Mark 10:28: "Peter said to him, 'We have left all we had to follow you.'" Or John 6:66-68:

> After this many of his disciples drew back and no longer went about with him. Jesus said to the twelve, "Will you also go away?" Simon Peter answered him, "Lord, to whom shall we go? You have the words of eternal life. And we have believed, and have come to know, that you are the Holy One of God."

Similarly, in Mark 8:27-29, though this question by Jesus is addressed to them all, and they variously respond as to the opinion of outsiders, it is Peter who pronounces the consensus of their own judgment, the opinion of the Twelve:

> And Jesus went on with his disciples, to the village of Caesarea Philippi; and on the way he asked his disciples, "Who do men say that I am?" And they told him, "John the Baptist; and others say, Elijah; and others one of the prophets." And he asked them, "But who do you say that I am?" Peter answered him, "You are the Christ." And he charged them to tell no one about him.

Moreover, there are other times when, though the other apostles are present, Jesus singles out Peter for particularly pointed reference. For example, after the miraculous draft of fish in Luke 5:8-10:

> But when Simon Peter saw it, he fell down at Jesus' knees, saying, "Depart from me, for I am a sinful man, O Lord." For he was astonished, and all that were with him, at the catch of fish which they had taken; and so also were James and John, sons of Zebedee, who were partners with Simon. And Jesus said to Simon, "Do not be afraid; henceforth you will be catching men."

And if it is Peter who is singled out in Luke 5:8-10 as having now become the prime example of a fisher of souls, so in John 21:15-17, it is Peter who is the intense focus of Jesus' attention, though this time it is to use him as the prime example of a shepherd of God's people:

> When they had finished breakfast, Jesus said to Simon Peter, "Simon, son of John, do you love me more than these?" He said to him, "Yes, Lord; you know that I love you." He said to him, "Feed my lambs." A second time he said to him, "Simon, son of John, do you love me?" He said to him, "Yes, Lord; you know that I love you." He said to him, "Tend my sheep." He said to him a third time, "Simon, son of John, do you love me?" Peer was grieved because he said to him the third time, "Do you love me?" And he said to him, "Lord, you know everything; you know that I love you." Jesus said to him, "Feed my sheep."

Arguably, this peculiar highlighting of Peter, this focus upon Peter, the prominence given to him in the Gospels reaches a high point in Luke 22:31-32. For in this passage Peter is neither the spokesman for the Twelve, nor the initiator of dialogue with Jesus, nor being held up by Jesus as an example for the rest (for the others are also to be fishers of men and shepherds of the flock). But here Peter is charged by Jesus with the task of being the strength and support of his brethren:

> "Simon, Simon, behold, Satan demanded to have you that he might sift you like wheat, but I have prayed for you that your faith may not fail; and when you have turned again, strengthen your brethren."

Of course, the most famous example of this special prominence given to Peter in the Gospel narratives, and the passage most often cited in Catholic theology as the foundation for the Petrine ministry, is Matthew 16:15-19:

> He said to them, "But who do you say that I am?" Simon Peter replied, "You are the Christ, the Son of the Living God." And Jesus answered him, "Blessed are you, Simon Bar-Jona! for flesh and blood has not revealed this to you, but my Father who is in heaven. And I tell you, you are Peter, and on this rock I will build my Church, and the powers of death shall not prevail against it. I will give

you the keys of the kingdom of heaven, and whatever
you bind on earth shall be bound in heaven, and whatever you loose on earth shall be loosed in heaven."

heavy, official

It is a passage freighted with sententious language. For example,
the language of the power of the keys: in the Old Testament a key
is a symbol of power and authority, not just divine power as in
Job 12:14, but also the power given to certain servants of God (Is
22:22). The language of binding and loosing became traditional
rabbinic language for authority (cf. 2 Baruch 11:2; *Talmud: Ta'anit*
12a; Josephus' *Wars of the Jews* 1.5.2). No doubt, elsewhere some
of this language is used more broadly of the entire Christian community (Mt 18:18). But, even so, here it is particularly powerful
for it suggests, since in Mathew's Gospel Jesus is portrayed as
the new Moses, and the Church as the new Israel, then, it seems
obvious, Peter is the new chief rabbi.

There are yet two more categories of Petrine portraiture
from the Gospels that we must examine. In striking contrast to
these exalted or flattering portrayals of Peter which we have been
looking at, there are also much more humbling and, in once case,
a downright humiliating portrait of Peter in the Gospel accounts
of Jesus' life and death. I call one group "the presumptuousness
of Peter" because in these three portraits he is overconfident in
his own capacity for leadership. With regard to this kind of portraiture of Peter, it is perhaps significant that in Matthew's Gospel
where, as we have just now seen, Peter is portrayed, at one point,
as being given immense authority by Jesus, there are also no less
than three rather chastening portraits of the presumptuousness
of Peter. The first of these more humbling portraits occurs in the
Matthean narrative of a storm on the Sea of Galilee. In Matthew's
account of this incident, Jesus' disciples are without Jesus in a boat
being tossed about on the Sea of Galilee in a sudden storm. When
Jesus appears walking on the waters towards them telling them to
"Take heart, it is I, have no fear." We are told in Mt 15:22-33:

And Peter answered him, "Lord, if it is you, bid me come
to you on the water." He said, "Come." So Peter got out

of the boat and walked on the water and came to Jesus;
but when he saw the wind, he was afraid, and beginning
to sink he cried out, "Lord save me." Jesus immediately
reached out his hand and caught him, saying to him, "O
man of little faith, why did you doubt?" And when they
got into the boat, the wind ceased.

In the second portrayal, Matthew 17:1-6, there is no verbal rebuke of Peter comparable to Jesus' calling him "O man of little
faith." Nevertheless Peter does appear rather impetuous and
foolish. Moreover, the voice of God the Father is heard with an
admonition which, though addressed to all, appears to have
particular application to Peter in view of his presumptuous talk
about constructing tents:

And after six days Jesus took with him Peter and James
and John his brother, and led them up a high mountain
apart. And he was transfigured before them, and his face
shone like the sun, and his garments became white as
light. And behold, there appeared to them Moses and
Elijah, talking with him. And Peter said to Jesus, "Lord,
it is well that we are here; if you wish, I will make three
booths here, one for you and one for Moses and one for
Elijah." He was still speaking, when lo, a bright cloud
overshadowed them, and a voice from the cloud said,
"This is my beloved Son, with whom I am well pleased;
listen to him." When the disciples heard this, they fell
on their faces, and were filled with awe.

The third portrayal of Peter's presumptuousness occurs in Matthew 26:31-35:

Then Jesus said to them, "You will all fall away because
of me this night; for it is written, 'I will strike the shepherd, and the sheep of the flock will be scattered.' But
after I am raised up, I will go before you to Galilee." Peter
declared to him, "Though they all fall away because of
you, I will never fall away." Jesus said to him, "Truly,
I say to you, this very night, before the cock crows, you

will deny me three times." Peter said to him, "Even if I must die with you, I will not deny you." And so said all the disciples.

Of course this is prelude to the final and humiliating portrait of Peter's denial of Christ in Matthew 26:69-76:

> Now Peter was sitting outside in the courtyard. And a maid came up to him, and said, "You also were with Jesus the Galilean." But he denied it before them all, saying, "I do not know what you mean." And when he went out to the porch, another maid saw him, and she said to the bystanders, "This man was with Jesus of Nazareth." And again he denied it with an oath, "I do not know the man." After a little while the bystanders came up and said to Peter, "Certainly you are also one of them, for your accent betrays you." Then he began to invoke a curse on himself and to swear, "I do not know the man." And immediately the cock crowed. And Peter remembered the saying of Jesus, "Before the cock crows, you will deny me three times." And he went out and wept bitterly.

The passion narrative in John's Gospel contains yet another example of Peter's presumptuousness. In John 18:10-11, we are told that when the soldiers came to the garden of Gethsemani to arrest Jesus, "Simon Peter, who had a sword, drew it and struck the high priest's servant, cutting off his right ear." Jesus responds by rebuking Peter, "Put your sword into its sheath; shall I not drink the cup which the Father has given me?"

But, besides these humbling portraits of the impetuosity of Peter, the Gospels also narrate events in which Peter is not just humbled but humiliated. For example, in Mark 8:31-33 (and its parallel Mt 16:21-23), we hear Jesus rebuke Peter in the most severe terms:

> And he began to teach them that the Son of Man must suffer many things, and be rejected by the elders and the chief priests and the scribes, and be killed, and after three

days rise again. And he said this plainly. And Peter took
him, and began to rebuke him. But turning and seeing
his disciples, he rebuked Peter, and said, "Get behind me,
Satan! For you are not on the side of God, but of men."

In the portrayal of Peter after the death of Jesus, there are
three kinds of portraits we must look at: first, those of his eminent
ministry; second, those of his cooperative ministry; and finally one
indicting or humiliating portrait. In the portrayal of Peter after the
death and resurrection of Jesus, despite his denial of Jesus, Peter
appears as still holding his preeminent status among the disciples.
Paul in a work ante-dating the written Gospels by at least ten to
fifteen years, says Peter was the first to see the risen Christ (1 Cor
15:5) and Luke 24:34 agrees with this. In the Acts of the Apostles,
after the account of the ascension of Jesus, Peter is portrayed as
exercising the principal leadership role among the disciples in
Jerusalem. This is seen in several ways. It is Peter who suggests
getting a replacement for Judas (Ac 1:15ff). It is Peter who casts
judgment on Ananias and Sapphira (Ac 5:1-11). It is Peter who
preaches at Pentecost (Ac 2:14-41), and Peter who speaks before
the Sanhedrin in defense of himself and John (Ac 3:5-12). There
are yet more passages in the Acts of the Apostles where Peter not
only appears, once again, as spokesman for the Twelve (Ac 2:14,
38), but now his ministry, like that of Jesus' original ministry, is
characterized by spectacular graces and divine interventions. For
example, Peter raises the dead (Ac 9:36-43), he is the recipient
of special revelation (Ac 10:9-16)), and he is miraculously delivered from prison (Ac 12:6-19). Moreover, Acts shows Peter as
prominent not only in the Jerusalem community but he quickly
becomes well known to many other Christian communities, for
in Acts 9:31-32 we are told "the Church throughout all Judea and
Galilee and Samaria had peace and was built up… [and] Peter
went here and there among them all." Another even more impressive witness to the stature of Peter among the earliest Christian
communities occurs in Paul's First Letter to the Corinthians.
Indeed, it is an amazing witness to the stature of Peter in the
early Church, that, though, unlike Paul and Apollos, Peter most

probably had never been to Corinth, even so there was a group at Corinth who identified themselves as indebted specifically to Peter's witness to Christ (1 Cor 1:12). And there is more to be learned by a comparison of Peter's relationship to Paul. After his conversion, Paul went up to Jerusalem precisely to meet with Peter and indeed spent two weeks with him (Gal 1:18). Paul later compares himself to Peter, "I had been entrusted with the task of preaching the Gospel to the Gentiles just as Peter had been to the Jews" (Gal 2:7). Finally, Peter, like Paul, appears in the New Testament as the author of epistles. But while Paul's epistles are to precise Christian communities, Peter's have the character of encyclical letters, that is, circular letters meant to be distributed to a number of churches. The First Epistle of Peter opens with the salutation: "Peter, an apostle of Jesus Christ, to the exiles of the Dispersion." And the opening salutation of the Second Epistle of Peter signals an equally broad audience: "Simon Peter, a servant and apostle of Jesus Christ, to those who have obtained a faith of equal standing with ours." And while the latter salutation might be interpreted in an egalitarian sense, yet later in that same letter peculiar authority is claimed for Peter when it is insisted: "We have that prophetic word made more sure. You will do well to pay attention to this" (1 P 1:19).

As we have seen, in the Gospels there is a balanced portrayal of both the preeminence of Peter and the humiliation of Peter. So too while most of the New Testament portraits exhibit Peter's continuing preeminence in the post-Ascension early Church, there are several that portray Peter's cooperation with others, and even one portrait of his correction by another apostolic figure. Peter, though the recipient of divine revelation, consults with the other apostles and is even sent by them (Ac 8:14). Peter is portrayed working with John almost as a team (Ac 3:1-11, 4:1-22, 8:14). Peter, though an awesome apostolic figure, humbly ranks himself as "a fellow presbyter" (1 P 5:1-4). Peter is portrayed as using Paul's scribe Silvanus, implying intimate cooperation and unity of doctrine and effort between Peter and Paul (1 P 5:12). Indeed, Peter refers to Paul as "our beloved brother" (2 P 3:15), and this despite the fact that Paul once challenged Peter. Indeed, the final image of Peter we refer to is the humbling one from Paul's Letter to the Galatians 2:11-14:

> But when Cephas came to Antioch I opposed him to his face, because he stood condemned. For before certain men came from James, he ate with the Gentiles; but when they came he drew back and separated himself, fearing the circumcision party. And with him the rest of the Jews acted insincerely, so that even Barnabas was carried away by their insincerity. But when I saw that they were not straightforward about the truth of the gospel, I said to Cephas before them all, "If you, though a Jew, live like a Gentile and not like a Jew, how can you compel the Gentiles to live like Jews?"

And thus for all Peter's eminence in the early Church, he still could be challenged by another.

What are we to make of all this portraiture of Peter in the New Testament? The first thing I would say is beware of sentimentalizing these portraits. What I mean by that is I feel certain there are some readers who would be quick to challenge me, "Oh, no doubt, in the early Church Peter exercised great authority but woe to any one who is so presumptuous as to assume that role today." In response, however, I would point out that such an attitude trivializes Sacred Scripture by reducing such passages to merely charming recollections of how it once was. But the Bible never just tells us charming stories of how it once was. The stories preserved in the Bible were preserved precisely out of the conviction that they contain enduring lessons, perennial lessons for us all. For example, in the narrative of the bestowal of the keys, this is not just some recollection of how Peter exercised immense moral authority among the Christians of his generation. We will always need someone to bind and loose our consciences. And precisely at those times when Christian pastors themselves are divided on such matters, there is need for one among them who can call them all to account. Moreover, there is biblical evidence of an intention to provide a means for continuing guidance after Peter's death.

For example, 2 Peter 1:12-15:

> Therefore I intend always to remind you of these things,
> though you know them and are established in the truth
> that you have. I think it right, as long as I am in this body,
> to arouse you by way of reminder, since I know that the
> putting off of my body will be soon, as our Lord Jesus
> Christ showed me. And I will see to it that after my depar-
> ture you may be able at any time to recall these things.

This passage may indeed be nothing more than the clear statement of intention to have Peter's teaching preserved in literary
form for the next generation to read. But the fact is that from
early on the overseers, the presiding elders of the Church at
Rome were conscious of preserving the apostolic heritage of
Peter and Paul not just in literary form but also by continuing
direction. There is an early Christian literary work entitled the
First Letter of Clement to the Church at Corinth. This letter was
written by an overseer, a presiding elder of the Church at Rome,
in the early 90's. He writes to intervene in a dispute dividing
the Church at Corinth. No doubt it might have been Paul's and
not Peter's identification with Rome as the final venue of his
ministry that occasioned and gave this letter a peculiar measure
of authority, since the Christian community at Corinth had been
founded by Paul. But in his letter Clement invokes not just the
memory of Paul but together the memory of the Roman ministry
of both Peter and Paul:

> Let us set before our eyes the good apostles: Peter, who
> because of unrighteous jealousy suffered not one or two
> but many trials, and having given his testimony went to
> the glorious place which was his due. Through jealousy
> and strife Paul showed the way to the prize of endur-
> ance. (1 Clem 5.3-5)

And, indeed, it is important to see that the Church of Rome
has never seen itself as just the preserver of the Petrine ministry.
The Church of Rome came to refer to itself as *the* Apostolic See

precisely because it claims to preserve the doctrinal heritage of both Peter *and* Paul. Therefore one must be very careful about trying to drive a wedge between those two apostolic traditions. Indeed, many scholars believe the Silvanus of 1 Peter 5:12 — "By Silvanus, a faithful brother as I regard him, I have written briefly to you" — is one of Paul's most faithful co-workers, Silas in Aramaic, Silvanus in Greek, who accompanied Paul on his second missionary journey (Ac 15:36-41), shared Paul's imprisonment at Philippi (Ac 16:19-29), and helped Paul preach the Gospel at Corinth (2 Cor 1:19). If this is true then 1 Peter 5:12 is an important witness to the unity of doctrinal tradition shared by Peter and Paul.

In the end, I suggest we need to be careful what use we make of Galatians 2:11-14. Rather than seizing upon it as an open invitation for other Churches to challenge Rome, we would do better to see it is a warning against the pressures placed on all Christian teachers and preachers to compromise doctrinal principle in order to appease or mollify some special interest group in the Church. For the protagonists in the narrative of Galatians 2:11-14 are not just Peter and Paul. Indeed, the principal protagonist in the drama of Paul's confrontation with Peter is a third party, the insidious "certain men" of "the circumcision party," theological partisans and intransigents who seek, not so much to challenge any one authority in the Church, as to get all to follow their partisan lead.

Further Reading

Pheme Perkins' *Peter: Apostle for the Whole Church* (Augsburg Fortress, 2000).

Petrine Ministry: Catholics and Orthodox in Dialogue edited by W. Kasper (Newman Press, 2005).

William Farmer's *Peter and Paul in the Church of Rome: The Ecumenical Potential of a Forgotten Perspective* (New York: Paulist, 1990).

CHAPTER 26

The Teaching Ministry

In the New Testament there are a variety of titles given to Jesus by his contemporaries. For example, at various times we hear him called "prophet," "teacher," "rabbi," "Messiah," "king," "holy one." But among these various titles there is one that is given to Jesus more than any other and that is the title "teacher." Moreover, within twenty-five years of the death of Jesus the title "teacher" is given to certain members of the Christian community and the bearers of this title are accorded a high and honorable place in the community. For example, in 1 Corinthians 12:27-28 we are given a veritable hierarchical ordering of ministries in that Church, and third after apostles and prophets and well before several other ministries comes the office of teacher:

> Now you are the body of Christ and individually members of it. And God has appointed in the Church first apostles, second prophets, third teachers, then workers of miracles, then healers, helpers, administrators, speakers in various kinds of tongues.

However, there is also considerable evidence in the New Testament that this office of teacher in the early Church rapidly became a very problematic one. For example, in another Church order, the one related in the Epistle to the Ephesians 4:11-12, the title and office of teacher seem to have been somewhat diminished in authority and respect. For in Ephesians 4:11-12, it is not just apostles and prophets but also evangelists and pastors who are given precedence before teachers: "And he gave some as apostles, others as prophets, others as evangelists, others as pastors and teachers." In fact, in the latest Church order given in the New Testament, the Church offices designated in the so-called Pastoral Epistles, 1 and 2 Timothy and Titus, the office of teacher is nowhere mentioned but rather appears to have been taken over completely by that of the ordained hierarchy of bishop, presbyter, deacon.

The reason for this circumspection or restriction of the title of teacher is not difficult to understand. False teachers appear to have arisen very quickly in the Christian movement. At several points in the New Testament there are warnings about them and sometimes with precise descriptions of their errors and in one instance a precise identification of the perpetrators of these errors. In Galatians 1:7 Saint Paul tells that congregation, "There are some who trouble you and want to pervert the gospel of Christ." Colossians 2:18 warns "Let no one disqualify you, insisting on self-abasement and worship of angels, taking his stand on visions." 2 Timothy 2:17-18 indicts "Hymenaeus and Philetus, who have swerved from the truth by holding that the resurrection is past already." 2 John 7 laments the fact that "many deceivers have gone out into the world, men who will not acknowledge the coming of Jesus Christ in the flesh." No wonder then that James 3:1 carries a stern warning to anyone who might aspire to the teaching ministry: "Let not many of you become teachers, my brethren, for you know that we who teach shall be judged with greater strictness."

In the Church today, teaching of Christian doctrine is done on various levels and by various people. Of course, parents are the first teachers of their children in the ways of the faith. Indeed, the Catholic rite for the baptism of children contains a notice and a prayer for the parents of these children: "You will be the first teachers of your child in the ways of the faith. May you also be the best of teachers." But parents are not alone in this effort at Christian education. Most Christian communities have catechists or religious instructors who continue the education of children and of converts and even adults who want to grow in their knowledge of the faith, its teachings and traditions. Pastors who preach from pulpits at Sunday worship and other times and events such as weddings and funerals also participate in the teaching ministry of the Church. Then there are the more formal teaching roles of degreed faculty in schools, colleges and seminaries. Then still in the Catholic Church there is the teaching authority of the principal pastors of the Church, the pope and bishops. Upon all these people — parents, catechists, theologians, exegetes, pastors, popes and bishops — falls the responsibility of what has been described as "authentically interpreting the word of God." On the other hand, while the Church's teaching ministry is shared by a large group, there are important distinctions to be made among these teachers. For example, it is obvious that the responsibility of some of these teachers is greater than that of others even if just for numerical reasons. That is, a parent or a catechist has a relatively small charge as compared to a pastor who instructs numerous families. A bishop has the responsibility of instructing not just many families but also the pastors in his jurisdiction. A pope at times addresses all the bishops. With this in mind, we begin our study of the Church's teaching ministry by examining the more general concept of Christian teaching in the New Testament. We begin our study by looking at the teaching authority and teaching method of both Jesus and Paul; for, while we all would like to teach as Jesus did, audiences differ and the way Paul taught a Gentile audience might appreciably differ from how Jesus taught his fellow Jews.

As for the way that Jesus taught, the first thing we should notice is that all four authors of the canonical Gospels make observations about the quality of Jesus' teaching style, the impression which Jesus' teaching left on his audiences. Indeed, in a rare unanimity of witness these four Gospel writers claim that Jesus' teaching had a sensational effect on his audience. I place in parallel juxtaposition here representative comments from all four canonical Gospels so that the reader can see the unanimity of this witness:

Mark 1:22: "And they were astonished at his teaching,
for he taught them as one who had authority and not as the scribes."

Matthew 7:28-29: "And when Jesus finished these sayings, the crowds were astonished at his
teaching, for he taught them as one who had
authority, and not as their scribes."

Luke 4:32: "And they were astonished at his teaching,
for his word was with authority."

John 7:15: "The Jews marveled at it [the teaching of
Jesus], saying, 'How is it that his man has
learning, when he has never studied?'"

All four passages claim Jesus' audiences were astonished and
marveled at his teaching. While John is satisfied to record the
marvel of the crowds, the Synoptics are quick to specify the
reason for the crowd's astonishment. They claim it was the authoritative style with which Jesus handled the text of the Scriptures that distinguished Jesus from the other Jewish religious
teachers of his day. But there is a phrase in our quotation here
from John 7:15 that is more revelatory than just the Synoptics'
comparison of Jesus' teaching method with that of the scribes.
And that is the comment about Jesus that "he has never studied."
At first glance, this is a rather strange statement. Jesus could
read from the Scriptures (Lk 4:16-17 portrays Jesus as reading
in a synagogue service) and the accounts in the Gospel portray
him as engaging in learned rabbinic, scribal or pharisaic debate
over the interpretation of certain biblical passages (Mk 2:23-28,
10:1-12). Most exegetes would argue these are evidence that Jesus
had at least attended an elementary synagogue school and that
he perhaps even progressed in his synagogue school education
to the point of having studied not just the text of Scripture but
learned something of the historic traditions of interpretation
(*midrash* and *halakhah*). Thus when in John 7:15 we hear it said of
Jesus "he has never studied," John does not mean to imply that
Jesus was illiterate in the sense of never having gone to school.
Rather John is indicating that though Jesus teaches with a command and insight worthy of a well-trained rabbi, he himself was

not known to have ever studied under one. Young Jewish boys who excelled in their studies in the synagogue schools of Jesus' time were often noticed by the local rabbi and encouraged to go on to study with one of the great rabbinic teachers in Jerusalem. We know that this is what happened with Saint Paul, because he says as much when he makes it clear that he studied with Gamaliel (Acts 22:3). And thus John's comment about Jesus' "never having studied" casts some light on the contrast which the Synoptic authors draw between Jesus' teaching and that of the scribes, the learned class in Israel. The authority of the scribes came from their careful examination of the text of Scripture and their intimate acquaintance with the teachings of the elders, but Jesus does not indulge in word splitting or the careful weighing of literary or rabbinic authorities. The authoritative character of his teaching does not rest on superior scholarship, greater intellectual acumen, or a more clever exegesis as did the authority of the scribes (and rabbis). Rather the authoritative character of Jesus' teaching comes from his original intuitive genius and an original or lived experience. That is, his teaching is not only confident but exhibits an inner logic that appears to derive from his personal encounter with the text and, even more importantly, with the object to which the text witnesses, the transcendent itself.

But there is a passage in the Gospel according to Luke that reveals yet another aspect of Jesus' teaching method, and that is the famous parable of the Good Samaritan in Luke 10:25-37, a narrative found only in Luke. Its value for our concern is more in the pedagogical context and use which Jesus makes of this parable. And so I quote it in its entirety:

> And behold, a lawyer stood up to put him to the test, saying, "Teacher, what shall I do to inherit eternal life?" He said to him, "What is written in the law? How do you read?" And he answered, "You shall love the Lord your God with all your heart, and with all your soul, and with all your strength, and with all your mind; and your neighbor as yourself." And he said to him, "You have answered right; do this, and you will live."

But he, desiring to justify himself, said to Jesus, "And who is my neighbor?" Jesus replied, "A man was going down from Jerusalem to Jericho, and he fell among robbers, who stripped him and beat him, and departed, leaving him half dead. Now by chance a priest was going down that road; and when he saw him he passed by on the other side. So likewise a Levite, when he came to the place and saw him, passed by on the other side. But a Samaritan, as he journeyed, came to where he was; and when he saw him, he had compassion, and went to him and bound up his wounds, pouring on oil and wine; then he set him on his own beast and brought him to an inn, and took care of him. And the next day he took out two *denarii* and gave them to the innkeeper, saying, 'Take care of him; and whatever more you spend, I will repay you when I come back.' Which of these three, do you think, proved neighbor to the man who fell among the robbers?" He said, "The one who showed mercy on him." And Jesus said to him, "Go and do likewise."

The literary characteristics of Luke's Gospel suggest an author well acquainted with both Hellenistic and Jewish literary and intellectual conventions. Here, specifically, Luke appears to be contrasting the classical Greek conception of teaching as a dialogue wherein the teacher stimulates the student to exercise his own intellectual or reflective powers and the Hebrew or biblical notion of teaching as a body of truths which the student needs to learn by "revelation" of his teacher. No doubt this Gospel passage begins with Jesus' giving a Socratic-like response to the young scholar's question by turning it back on him and making him to "think for himself." However, what is really happening is that Jesus, in classic Jewish pedagogical style, is inviting the young scholar to recite from memory a passage of Scripture. And thus Jesus is not really urging this student to think for himself but rather to quote the tradition, to recognize the truth which the Scripture reveals. But instead the young man wants to dialogue.

Indeed, the truly Semitic, non-speculative, anti-dialogical character of the exchange between Jesus and this student of the law is even more apparent in the young man's further question, "And who is my neighbor?" This question is obviously an opening for what could become endless speculation. And, moreover, there is evidence that rabbinic scholars did indeed debate precisely such questions with numerous scholarly opinions and distinctions as to what constitutes "being a neighbor," for example, living next door, living in the same town, living several miles away, and so forth. Jesus, in contrast, refuses this invitation to dialogue, to enter into endless speculations or intellectual and legal distinctions like a rabbinic scribe or teacher of the law. Instead he tells a story whose meaning is so dramatically obvious that it not only puts an end to all such vain speculations but also humbles, even shames the student into admitting the obvious literalness of the scriptural teaching which he has already quoted and thus to forego any rationalization of the text.

This anti-speculative, anti-dialogical character can also be seen in Saint Paul. In his First Letter to the Church at Corinth 2:1-6, Paul contrasts the wisdom he preaches with what the world calls wisdom, and he does this in a way that makes clear the power of religious teaching is not its rational character but its personal and moral force:

> When I came to you, brethren, I did not come proclaiming to you the testimony of God in lofty words or wisdom. For I decided to know nothing among you except Jesus Christ and him crucified. And I was with you in weakness and in much fear and trembling; and my speech and my message were not in plausible words of wisdom, but in demonstration of the Spirit and power, that your faith might not rest in the wisdom of men but in the power of God.
>
> Yet among the mature we do impart wisdom, although it is not a wisdom of this age or of the rulers of this age, who are doomed to pass away.

Moreover, this anti-speculative theme is common in other letters of Paul and in the secondary Pauline literature. For example in Colossians 2:8, we read, "See to it that no one makes a prey of you by philosophy and empty deceit, according to human tradition, according to the elemental spirits of the universe, and not according to Christ." In the Pastoral Epistles this theme becomes more strident. In 1 Timothy 1:3-11, there is a strong contrast between "speculations" on the one hand and "the plan of God which is to be received by faith" on the other. There is also an insistence that the aim of religious instruction is not so much intellectual satisfaction but moral edification:

> As I urged you when I was going to Macedonia, remain at Ephesus that you may charge certain persons not to teach any different doctrine, not to occupy themselves with myths and endless genealogies which promote speculations rather than the divine training that is in faith. Certain persons by swerving from these have wandered away into vain discussion, desiring to be teachers of the law, without understanding either what they are saying or the things about which they make assertions.

And then there is 1 Timothy 6:2-4, with its stern warning about avoiding scholastic disputes:

> Teach and urge these duties. If any one teaches otherwise and does not agree with the sound words of our Lord Jesus Christ and the teaching which accords with godliness, he is puffed up with conceit, he knows nothing, he has a morbid craving for controversy and for disputes about words.

Now it might be objected that this aversion to speculation is more a pastoral initiative occasioned by the humble intellectual resources of Paul's congregants. Surely, in part, this can explain Saint Paul's words. On the other hand, however, such an explanation fails to recognize a basic element in all Christian instruction. For example, this anti-speculative bent in Saint Paul is equally apparent in his teaching method. That is, in this same letter when he presents the doctrine of the Eucharist (1 Cor 11:23ff.), there is no attempt made to explain its meaning.

Rather the injunction is simply passed on: "For I received from the Lord what I also delivered to you, that the Lord Jesus on the night when he was betrayed took bread, and when he had given thanks, he broke it." Compare also 1 Corinthians 15:3ff. which uses the same technical language of "receiving... delivering": "For I delivered to you as of first importance what I also received, that Christ died for our sins in accordance with the Scriptures, that he appeared to Cephas, then to the twelve." What we have here in this formulaic expression is the concept of tradition. Our English word "tradition" comes from the Latin *traditio* meaning to deliver. However, the technical biblical word is "catechesis" or "to catechize." Our English words "catechesis," "catechist" and "catechism" are derived from a Greek composite word *kata-echein* which means literally, *kata*, according to, *echein* to echo, reflecting the basic mechanics of elementary religious instruction, the rehearsal of rote answers. The word *katecheo* is rare in profane Greek. Some have conjectured it is a theatrical term whereby the actor makes his voice resound, sound again as an echo within the amphitheater. But more important for our interests is the use of this term in the New Testament. In Luke 1:4, in the prologue to his Gospel, Luke tells the dedicatee, Theophilus, that he has written this Gospel so "that you may know the truth concerning the things of which you have been informed [*katechethes*]." In Acts 18:25, it is said of one Apollos of Alexandria "he had been instructed [*katechemenos*] in the way of the Lord." In 1 Corinthians 14:19, Paul rebukes the charismatics at Corinth when he insists "in church I would rather speak five words with my mind in order to instruct [*katecheso*] others than ten thousand words in a tongue." In Galatians 6:6, he advises those being instructed in the Christian faith to give material support to their instructors when he says, "Let him who is taught [*katechoumenos*] the word share all good things with him who teaches [*katechounti*]." All these uses of the term *katecheo* refer to basic instruction in the fundamentals of the Christian faith. The same method was used in ancient Israel. The Decalogue (Ex 20:1-17) is a collection of moral tenets that can be easily memorized and passed on. The questions with formulaic answers that are part of the Passover Seder are yet another example (see Ex 12:27).

But to summarize: what we have been seeing is that in the New Testament basic religious instruction has little if any speculative or dialogical form or content but is rather more in the style of a passing on of traditions and stories. This is because the form and content of religious instruction in the Bible aims to witness not so much to speculative teaching but rather to a lived experience — in the Old Testament it is Moses' encounter with God on Sinai that leads to the liberation of the Hebrews from bondage in Egypt, in the New Testament it is the encounter of Galilean fishermen or a tax collector (Matthew) with the lay preacher from Nazareth, an encounter that gives a radical new direction to those men's lives. This primitive, primary, fundamental lived experience must come first. Its intellectual elaboration comes after the experience and must always remain subservient to that primitive, primal experience. However, on the other hand, to be balanced, one must also recognize that within the New Testament though primacy is given to this lived experience, its intellectual exploration and speculative elaboration also have an important place.

Though Jesus refused to enter into speculation with the lawyer in Luke 10:25-37, elsewhere in the Gospels there is ample portrayal of his entering into religious dialogue. In Luke 2:46 we see how Jesus as a youth was attracted to religious discussions: "They found him in the temple, sitting among the teachers, listening to them and asking them questions." Jesus is portrayed being questioned by others, Mark 7:5, "The Pharisees and the scribes asked him, 'Why do your disciples not live according to the tradition of the elders?'" In Matthew 9:14, "The disciples of John came to him, saying: 'Why do we and the Pharisees fast, but your disciples do not?'" In Matthew 17:10, his own disciples challenge him when they ask, "Then why do the scribes say that first Elijah must come?" In Mark 9:32 the Twelve are portrayed as negligent because when Jesus taught that the Son of Man must die, "they did not understand the saying, and they were afraid to ask him." Jesus himself was often ready to answer objections and insinuations against him and his teaching (cf. Jn 8:41-58; 18:19-24), which later he developed and justified against his opponents (cf. Mk 2:6-12, 10:2-9; Lk 4:22-28).

Similarly, one must be careful not to misread Paul's indictment of philosophy in Colossians 2:8.

"Philosophy" in the classical Greek tradition denoted the highest effort of the human intellect. But in Hellenistic times, the time of Jesus and Paul, this term had come to be debased to mean all sorts of subtle dialectics and pseudo-philosophical speculation that had little or nothing in common with the critical thinking and discerning knowledge of classical Greek philosophy. More precisely, scholars have claimed to detect in Paul's description of the false teachers at Colossae similarities to Pythagorean, or Cynic, or popular Stoic thought or even to Middle Platonism. For example, such a phrase as "the elemental powers of the universe" has been extensively debated by scholars. Most seem to conclude it is a reference to constellations or heavenly bodies conceived as living beings that influence, indeed control, not just peoples' lives but even nature. Also, Stoic thought included a determinant outlook in which astrology and naturalistic science governed the world in cyclic fashion. And thus the only reason Paul uses the term "philosophy" here is because the false teachers at Colossae used this term to bestow upon their arguments a measure of intellectual pretension when it fact what they taught was not really philosophy but only a syncretistic and mystic theosophy, a pseudo-philosophy.

Moreover, we need to take into account the admonition in 1 Peter 3:15, "Always be prepared to make a defense to any one who calls you to account for the hope that is in you." The word that the RSV translators render as "defense" is the Greek *apologian*. *Apologia* was the traditional term for a particular form of forensic oratory, namely, a defense speech in a courtroom proceeding. And, no doubt, 1 Peter 3:15 can be read as a warning that Christians might indeed be hauled before civil courts to defend their beliefs and practices, arrested and charged for being a Christian, the adherent to a mysterious cult. However, there is much here that suggests it is not merely juridical defense that is implied here. For example, the phrase "to account for the hope that is in you" hardly suggests a magistrate's interest and procedure. More precisely, the verb *aitounti*, "asking," and which the RSV translates as "calls you," suggests ordinary conversation rather than juridical inquiry. And then there is the fact that the word which the RSV translates as "account" is the Greek *logon*, literally "word" but meaning "rational speech," and thus, "reason." All these suggest that what the author of 1 Peter 3:15 has in mind is more a reasoned explanation of one's faith before a general public audience than merely a legal defense of one's faith in a courtroom proceeding. Moreover, while the *apologia* continued to be principally the term for a defense speech in a courtroom proceeding, there was also the most famous literary example, Socrates' answer to the charge of impiety brought against him as recorded in Plato's dialogue *Apology*. I am not suggesting that the author of 1 Peter had Plato's *Apology* in mind. But it was precisely that document and this passage from 1 Peter that eventually gave birth to a movement in early Christian thought called apologetics, or the reasoned defense of Christian faith, the whole great movement of Christian speculative science, speculative theology, which would begin with Justin Martyr's *Apology* (A.D. 150) and reach something of an apex with the *Summa contra gentiles* of Saint Thomas Aquinas. As Christianity grew, its religious teaching quickly began to go beyond mere commentary on revelation (Scripture) and soon enlarged to include apologetic demonstration from the Scriptures that Jesus is the Messiah and later apologetic demonstration from reason (dialectic logic, philosophy). Augustine of Hippo will show that a knowledge of Platonism can help one discuss Christian doctrine, and Aquinas will recruit the assistance of Aristotelianism. In our own time, German Jesuit Karl Rahner made adroit use of the thought of Kant and Hegel. The value of philosophical speculation and rational demonstration in both our investigation and defense of the Christian faith cannot be underestimated. Without rational inquiry and elaboration, the Christian faith would be in danger of becoming a mere mysticism or, worse still, enslaved to fideism and authoritarianism.

Though reason and intellectual argument are of great importance in the presentation of the Christian faith, we must not underestimate the even greater challenge that is the human heart. We must not forget the lesson in Jesus' reluctance to engage in useless dialectics when he discerned that the inquirer's heart was not in the right place. The challenge posed by our affective nature is of paramount importance for the Church's teaching ministry. For example, we must never forget the limitations of intellectual argument in the face of passion. Without genuine conversion of heart even the most cogent intellectual arguments will be of little avail. In the New Testament much reference is made to the role of the heart in matters of both faith and understanding. 1 Timothy 1:5, "a clean heart" [*kithara kardia*] is the way to the truth. And in the rest of the New Testament it is the heart that is the principal source not just of faith but of right thinking. In Mark 3:5, Jesus is "grieved at their hardness of heart [*porosai tes kardias*]." Mark 6:52, "but their hearts were hardened." Mark 11:23, "doubt in his heart." Luke 8:12, "the devil comes and takes away the word from their hearts." Luke 8:15, "those who, hearing the word, hold it fast in an honest and good heart." The RSV's Romans 1:21 "they became futile in their thinking, and their senseless minds were darkened" is really "they became vain in their reasonings [*dialogismois*] and their undiscerning heart [*kardia*] was darkened." In Romans 10:9, we are urged to "believe in your heart." In Romans 10:10, we are told, "For man believes with his heart" and in Romans 16:18, "by fair and flattering words they deceive the hearts of the simple minded." In Ephesians 1:18, it is "having the eyes of your heart enlightened," and in Ephesians 4:18 we read "they are darkened in their understanding, alienated from the life of God because of the ignorance that is in them, due to their hardness of heart." Hebrews 3:12 uses the term "unbelieving heart." In Mark 4:12 and Matthew 13:15 Jesus explains that the reason he casts so much of his teaching in the form of parables was precisely so that his hearers might "understand with their hearts." Implicit is the idea: mere appeal to their minds with ideas would not have been sufficient. Instead, emotive, sensual visual images were required because they could appeal to the heart as well as the mind.

This distinction between the intellectual understanding of and moral disposition or openness to the Christian message has important ramifications for our understanding of the teaching office of the Church. For example, this results in modern times in the Catholic concept of *magisterium* and the distinction between two kinds of teaching authority in the Church, the authentic or living magisterium of pastors (priests and bishops) and the academic or studied magisterium of experts or scholars (theologians and exegetes).

In classical Latin, *magister* meant "master," not only in the sense of "schoolmaster" or teacher, but in the many senses in which a person can be a "master," for example, of a ship, of servants, of an art or trade. But in the Medieval Latin of the schoolmen it came to mean simply the role and authority of a teacher. The traditional symbol of teaching authority was the chair, and Aquinas speaks of two kinds of magisterium: that of the pastoral chair of the bishop, and that of the academic chair of the university professor (see his *Quodlibet* III, 9, ad 3). We call pastoral teaching authority "authentic and living" not to suggest that the academic or studied authority of experts and scholars is dead or inauthentic but rather to suggest that the engagement of these pastors with the Gospel is not so much intellectual comprehension as it is openness to mystery, a certain patience in the presence of the intellectually defiant or incomprehensible character of the Gospel. That is, the teaching of a bishop or priest is not a mere notification of an historical event but a judgment and sanctification of its hearer, in other words more an appeal to conversion of heart than to satisfaction of the mind or curiosity. In contrast, a theologian or exegete presents speculative or historical data meant to inform the mind of the hearer. As for the description of the teaching authority of pastors as "living" (rather than studied), what we are referring to here is the idea that, while all theol-

theologians vs. bishops

ogy should be faith in search of understanding, the subjective faith commitment of scholars is not always discernible in their work nor is the quality of their scholarship necessarily linked to any public or personal profession of faith. But a Christian pastor must again and again publicly witness to his personal engagement with the faith not only by leading a congregation in its profession of faith but also by his witness not just to the literary and historical sources of faith but also to the risen Christ and his Spirit present among us. In other words, it could be said: priests and bishops witness primarily to faith while theologians and exegetes witness primarily to scholarship and study. Admittedly, these two witnesses are not by nature mutually exclusive. Thomas Aquinas was a saintly scholar and mystic and Augustine a learned bishop. Nevertheless, it could be argued: the authority of bishops and priests is based not simply on a study of texts but upon the frequency of sacramental encounter, personal knowledge and experience of the risen Christ, daily encounter with him in liturgical worship and sacramental celebration.

That a certain priority is given to the teaching authority of pastors over that of theologians is obvious from both the teaching of the Second Vatican Council and certain traditions in the very conciliar process. For example, the Second Vatican Council in its Dogmatic Constitution on Divine Revelation, *Dei verbum* 10, says, "The task of authentically interpreting the word of God has been entrusted exclusively to the living magisterium whose authority is exercised in the name of Jesus Christ" and, one might add, not in the name of scholarship or linguistic skill, etc. Also while theological experts are a necessary and prominent part of the conciliar process, conciliarists even at the height of their power (the Council of Constance, 1414-1418) refrained from giving theologians an equal vote in the conciliar assembly. This instead is reserved only to the chief pastors of the Church, and appropriately so. For while it is very important that pastors listen attentively to the speculations and findings of theologians, ultimately, however, all these must be judged by the practical experience of pastors. In this regard it is worthwhile quoting a statement from German Jesuit Karl Rahner, one of the great theologians of the twentieth century:

> I set more store by the unrelieved mediocrity of a stupid bishop — who will deny that there are such? — because it is more open to the *whole* truth, than I do by the brilliant ideas of a scholar who in the intoxication of discovery cuts down truth to the dimensions of *his* system (in *Servants of the Lord* translated by R. Strachan [NY: Herder and Herder, 1968, p. 53]; the emphases are Rahner's own).

But here I must make an important distinction. While I agree in principle with what Rahner says, I also want to make it clear: all the bishops I have met have been not only intelligent but they sing well, too. *extends to all christians*

Finally, in my chapter on ministry I tried to argue there is a sense in which all Christians are involved in ministry. So too with the Church's teaching ministry, all Christians teach. And though most teach unselfconsciously and by example, one should never underestimate the power of the quiet witness that is good example. For instance, if, as we saw earlier, parents are the first teachers of their children in the ways of the faith, they need to teach as much by example as by word, otherwise they will be only indulging in moralistic chatter that their children will learn to ignore. While parents might and indeed should take the time to teach their child the mechanics of prayer, instruct them regarding the proper words and gestures, much more effective is their demonstration or modeling of such piety as their regular and faithful observance of Sunday worship and such moral precepts as honesty and integrity in word and deed. Even as great a preacher as Saint Paul did not rely merely on verbal eloquence but recognized that actions speak louder than words and thus the importance of his personal example. In 1 Corinthians 4:14, he says:

> I do not write this to make you ashamed, but to admonish you as my beloved children. For though you

have countless guides in Christ, you do not have many
fathers. For I became your father in Christ Jesus through
the gospel. I urge you, then, be imitators of me.

In a time when television, film and popular music are quick to
challenge religious tradition, social convention and the authority
of parents, one should not underestimate the power of a parent's
good example. While children may indeed be fascinated and
for a while even fall victim to wrong messages from the entertainment industry and media stars eager to set themselves up
as models for imitation (Is there anything more unctuous than
a pop idol who has found a moral cause?), the good example
of devout and conscientious parents can provide a fallback
for recovery. While some among the laity pursue catechetical
certification or degrees in ministry, parents should be alerted to
the fact they preside over the domestic Church for which they
need no formal authorization or specialized training. Instead,
in the measure to which they model for their children an image
of piety, love and justice worthy of imitation, this will make
them the most effective teachers of the Christian faith. Popes
and bishops will mandate and define, but it will be for naught
unless parents have first set a good example.

Further Reading

Avery Dulles' *A History of Apologetics* (revised edition; San
Francisco: Ignatius Press, 2005).

Francis A. Sullivan's *Magisterium: Teaching Authority in the
Catholic Church* (Mahwah, NJ: Paulist Press, 1983).

Maxwell Johnson's *The Rites of Christian Initiation: Their
Evolution and Interpretation* (Collegeville, MN: The Liturgical
Press, 1999).

CHAPTER 27

Women and Ministry

From the beginning women have always had a significant role in Christian ministry. Indeed, the presence of women in Christian ministry despite social restrictions in secular society was a mark of the Church from the beginning. And the biblical evidence is particularly strong in this regard.

That Jesus often went beyond the social conventions of his day regarding a man's relationship to a woman is suggested by several Gospel passages. For example, in John 4:27, we are told the Twelve "marveled that he was talking with a woman." Indeed, some interpret John 12:3, "Mary took a liter of costly perfumed oil made from genuine aromatic nard and anointed the feet of Jesus and dried them with her hair," as indication that Jesus upon occasion would indulge not just conversational intimacy but permit even a measure of physical intimacy with a woman in a public setting.

Moreover, that women played a prominent role not just in the social life but even in the public ministry of Jesus there can be little doubt. For example that a woman as much as any man could be a disciple of Jesus seems to be quite evident from Luke 10:38-42:

> Now as they went on their way, he entered a village;
> and a woman named Martha received him into her
> house. And she had a sister called Mary, who sat at the
> Lord's feet and listened to his teaching. But Martha
> was distracted with much serving; and she went to him

> and said, "Lord, do you not care than my sister has left
> me to serve alone? Tell her to help me." But the Lord
> answered her, "Martha, Martha, you are anxious and
> troubled about many things; one thing is needful. Mary
> has chosen the good portion, which shall not be taken
> away from her."

To appreciate the remarkable character of this passage it is important that we recognize the technical character of some of its language, more precisely, the phrase "sat at the Lord's feet." This is the technical language of discipleship. That is, unlike in the modern classroom where mass produced seats are provided for everyone, in the ancient world only the teacher sat in a chair. His pupils sat on the floor "at his feet." And thus in this passage Mary is being graphically, unmistakably, portrayed as a disciple of Jesus. No rabbi in Jesus' time would ever have taken on a woman disciple. Anyone who has read Isaac Bashevis Singer's 1983 novella *Yentl* or seen its cinematic adaptation knows that even in modern times women were not allowed to study Torah.

But Jesus appears even more iconoclastic regarding the social conventions of his time when we consider the evidence that Jesus had not only women domestic followers such as Mary and Martha of Bethany but also women itinerant followers. Luke 8:1-3 is clear witness to the fact it was not only men who traveled with Jesus on the road:

> Soon afterward he went on through cities and villages,
> preaching and bringing the good news of the king-
> dom of God. And the Twelve were with him, and also
> some women who had been healed of evil spirits and
> infirmities: Mary, called Magdalene, from whom seven
> demons had gone out, and Joanna, the wife of Chuza,
> Herod's steward, and Susanna, and many others, who
> provided for them out of their means.

Finally, one should not doubt the quality of commitment from Jesus' women disciples. Gospel passages such as Mark 15:40, 47 and Luke 23:37, 55 witness to the fact that while all but one of Jesus' male disciples deserted him in the great crisis at the end of his life, several women stayed with him. Moreover, it is Jesus' women disciples who go to his tomb, find it empty, experience visions there, and later go to announce the resurrection to Jesus' male disciples (Mk 16:1-9; Mt 28:10; Lk 24:1-11; Jn 20:1-18).

As for the role of women in the ministry of Saint Paul, here too we find substantial evidence of their significant presence. For example, there is a passage in Paul's Epistle to the Church at Philippi that evidently acknowledges the assistance given him by two women in the evangelization of that city. For, in Philippians 4:2-3, Paul commends the work of Evodia and Syntyche, saying, "I ask you... help these women, for they have labored side by side with me in the gospel together with Clement and the rest of my fellow workers, whose names are in the book of life." The final chapter of the Epistle to the Romans begins with Paul's commendation of yet another woman actively involved in service to yet another church (Rm 16:1-2):

> I commend to you our sister Phoebe, a deaconess [*diakonos*] of the Church at Cenchreae, that you may receive her in the Lord as befits the saints, and help her in whatever she may require from you, for she has been a helper [*prostasis*] of many and of myself as well.

In a previous chapter herein on the historic mission of the Church, we already introduced the husband and wife catechetical team, Prisca and Aquila, referred to by Paul in 1 Corinthians 16:19. They are mentioned once again by Paul in the concluding chapter of the Epistle to the Romans, this time for their hosting a house church in Rome (Rm 16:3-5):

> Greet Prisca and Aquila, my fellow workers in Christ Jesus, who risked their necks for my life, to whom not only I but also all the churches of the Gentiles give thanks; greet also the church in their house.

To this day there is a church on Rome's Aventine hill bearing

Prisca's name. And archeological evidence suggests there has been a church there since earliest Christian times.

There is also New Testament evidence that women played a prominent role in the ministries of non-Pauline Churches. For example, at the conclusion of the Epistle to the Romans, Paul greets not only women who assist him now (Phoebe) or assisted him in the past (Prisca), but he also sends greetings to a woman in the Church at Rome whom, apparently, he has never met but knows only by reputation. In Romans 16:6, Paul says, "Greet Mary who has worked hard for you." Nor is this Mary the only woman prominent in ministry at Rome. For in Romans 16:12, Paul says, "Greet those workers in the Lord, Tryphaena and Tryphosa." Moreover, it is not just Paul who witnesses to women prominent in ministry. There are several passages in the Acts of the Apostles that point to women prominent in ministry. While in Acts 1:14 it is noted that women were with the apostles in the upper room at the Pentecost event, in Acts 12:12 we hear that one of them, John Mark's mother Mary, hosts a house church at Jerusalem. In Acts 21:9, we are told that the evangelist Philip had "four virgin daughters gifted with prophecy."

And thus what can we conclude at the end of this our survey of the New Testament evidence for women in ministry? First, it is obvious everything in the New Testament points to the equality of women and men in nature and salvation. Jesus' teaching is addressed to both sexes. Indeed, many of the most powerful images of salvation employed by Jesus in his preaching feature wise, generous, determined, industrious women — the wise virgins (Mt 25:1-13), the widow who gives her last penny (Mk 12:41-44), the persistent widow who assails the unjust judge (Lk 18:1-8), the woman who takes a bit of leaven and kneads it into some dough (Mt 13:33), the woman who sweeps her house to find a lost coin (Lk 15:8-10). Women who respond to the preaching of Jesus figure prominently in the Gospels whether it is Mary Magdalene (Lk 8:2), Mary and Martha of Bethany (Lk 10:38-42), the woman afflicted with a hemorrhage (Mk 5:25-34), the woman who anoints Jesus' feet (Mt 26:7), the Syrophoenician woman (Mk 7:24-30), the Samaritan woman at the well (Jn 4). Moreover, a number of New Testament passages illustrate how the spirit of prophecy was given to women as well as men (Lk 2:36; Acts 2:17; 1 Cor 11:5). And so Paul is absolutely right when he says in Galatians 3:28, "There is neither Jew nor Greek, there is neither slave nor free, there is neither male nor female; for you are all one in Christ Jesus."

When we come to the early history of the Church, there is a similar story. It is possible to cite numerous references from patristic literature all insisting upon the equality of men and women in nature and salvation. For example, Clement of Alexandria, head of the first great catechetical institute, argues in his *Paedagogus* or "The Instructor," his treatise on the instruction of a Christian (Bk I, Ch. 4) written about A.D. 195:

> The virtue of man and woman is the same. For if the God of both is one, the master of both is also one; one Church, one temperance, one modesty; their food is common, marriage an equal yoke; respiration, sight, hearing, knowledge, hope, obedience, love all alike. And those whose life is common, have common graces and a common salvation; common to them are love and training.

Tertullian, in a work of his called *On the Apparel of Women*, written about the year A.D. 198, says in Bk I, Ch 2: "For you women, too, have the same angelic nature promised as your reward, and the same sex, as do men. The Lord promises you the same advancement to the dignity of judging." We find a similar sentiment in the writings of a great archbishop in North Africa. Cyprian of Carthage (d. 258), in a letter written in A.D. 255 (Epistle 75), says (in paragraph 14):

> For if the day rises alike to all, and if the sun is diffused with like and equal light over all, how much more does Christ, who is the true sun and the true day, bestow in his Church the light of eternal life with the like equality! ... The mercy of Christ, and the heavenly grace that would subsequently follow, was equally divided among all;

> without difference of sex, without distinction of years,
> and without distinction of persons, upon all the people
> of God the gift of spiritual grace was shed.

The Apostolic Constitutions 7.281, a collection of ecclesiastical law dating from the latter half of the fourth century, celebrates the extraordinary gifts of grace in women:

> Women prophesied also. Of old, there was Miriam, the
> sister of Moses and Aaron; and after her, Deborah. Then
> there were later Huldah and Judith — the first under
> Josiah, the second under Darius. The mother of the Lord
> prophesied as well, as did Anna and Mary's kinswoman,
> Elizabeth. Furthermore, in the days of the apostles, there
> were the daughters of Philip.

As for women in the ministries of the patristic era Church, there are considerable historical, literary and epigraphic references to the prominence of Christian women in such forms of ministry as orders of widows, consecrated virgins and deaconesses. Macrina, sister to Basil and Gregory of Nyssa, not only founded a monastery of women but appears to have been equally as learned as her illustrious brothers. Benedict's sister Scholastica and the Spanish abbess Etheria are yet more examples of learned nuns. As for devout lay women, it could be argued that several of the greatest figures from the patristic era — Jerome and Augustine — had women co-workers much as did St. Paul. Indeed, Roman matrons appear almost as a specific rank of ministry. Jerome's co-workers were the widowed Roman matrons Marcella, Paula and Fabiola. Paula founded two monasteries at Bethlehem, one for men, one for women. And she headed the one for women. Augustine fostered a group of devout women gathered around the aristocratic and wealthy Roman matron Anicia Faltonia Proba. Another Roman matron, Melania (342-410), working with Rufinus, founded a double monastery on the Mount of Olives. Her daughter Melania the Younger went to Africa with her husband Pinian and founded two monasteries at Thagaste. But it was not just ascetic women.

In his Letter #304, Augustine shows a keen respect for the vocation of married couples. Finally, numerous Greek epigraphic inscriptions throughout Asia Minor from the fourth to the sixth centuries honor deaconesses. The most celebrated was Olympias, deaconess of Constantinople, not just an intimate friend, but chief advisor and principal consultant of the Patriarch John Chrysostom.

Toward the end of the patristic era, the English Benedictine Wynfrith of Devonshire, later known as St. Boniface, introduced a significant innovation when he recruited cloistered nuns to leave their monastery and accompany him on missionary journeys. In the year 716, he undertook a mission to the Germanic tribes. On his first journey he took with him only Benedictine monks. And he had no success. On his second journey he took with him several Benedictine nuns. This time his mission succeeded and set a precedent for women's greater role in the Church's ministry.

Later, when Vincent of Beauvais (1190-1264), Dominican friar and author of the principal encyclopedia of the Middle Ages, was asked to write a book on the education of princes (*De eruditione principium*), he went on to offer another book instructing noble parents to educate their daughters (*De educationis filiorum nobelium*). But it was not just the daughters of nobility who were educated. In the Middle Ages learning to read and write was basic training for any young woman pursuing her vocation as a nun. This perhaps accounts for the fact that religious women such as Mechtild of Magdeburg (c. 1210-c. 1280), Angela of Foligno (c. 1248-1309), Gertrude "the Great" (1256-c. 1302), Bridget of Sweden (c. 1303-73), Julian of Norwich (c. 1342-c. 1413), Margery Kempe (c. 1373-c. 1433) and Catherine of Genoa (1447-1510) were able to articulate their religious visions in such a way that we now have a veritable library of women mystics in the Middle Ages. Besides literary mystics, the Middle Ages also provide us examples of women in charismatic or prophetic ministries. Hildegard of Bingen (1090-1179) created enduring works of music and art as well as literature. Catherine of Siena (1347-1380) broke with the tradition of cloistered nuns to carry on a public ministry to the poor. She even ventured on a diplomatic mission to lecture to the pope at Avignon on his duties to the Church. At the time of the Reformation, Teresa of Avila (1515-1582) worked alongside John of the Cross in the reform of the Carmelite order and in fact often led him. She has left a literary legacy as great as John's. Indeed, the preface to George Eliot's (Mary Ann Evans') *Middle-march* (1872), one of the finest of English novels and, arguably, one of the first literary works of feminism, is a panegyric to the achievements of Teresa of Avila. In fact, long before secular society admitted women to the ranks of leadership, women's religious orders in the Catholic Church provided women with opportunities for not just education but also leadership and achievement in the local church and in the foreign missions. An outstanding example of this is Maria Francesca Cabrini (1850-1917) who founded schools, hospitals and orphanages on three continents, in Europe, North and South America.

Finally, one should not ignore the teaching ministry of Christian mothers who throughout the Middle Ages and into modern times often taught the faith as much by their example as with words and at times they did this in the face of absent or errant, not to say perfidious, husbands and fathers.

However, after having said all this there still remains the obvious fact that from the beginning, while women have indeed had an appreciable place in Christian ministry, there have always been certain limitations to women's ministry, limitations to which the historic Catholic and Orthodox communities still adhere even to this day (e.g., recent Vatican strictures against the ordination of women).

For example, while I have presented much evidence of women's position in the ministry of both Jesus and Paul and the early Church, one must be very careful not to exaggerate this evidence or read too much into it. While there can be no doubt Jesus accepted the voluntary ministry of women to himself and to the Twelve, it appears equally evident it was only men whom he personally recruited, summoned away from their work and family, to follow him and become a sign of God's new action among his people and for the world (see the call of the Twelve in Mk 1:16-17). It was only these men and not his women disciples that Jesus sent forth on mission to announce the Gospel (Mk 6:7 and its parallels). Indeed, in stark contrast, Jesus' women disciples appear to have served him and the Twelve in an important but relatively ancillary capacity, more precisely, by funding the evangelical efforts of Jesus and the Twelve (Lk 8:3).

As for the argument that it was the women disciples who first announced the empty tomb and resurrection: one must be very careful here because the import of this event for ministry is not entirely clear. For one thing, Paul, if he knew of this event saw little significance in it. For in 1 Corinthians 15:5, the earliest literary reference to post-resurrection appearances, Paul makes no mention of the women's discovery of the empty tomb or of their encounter with the risen Christ. As for the four Gospels: they present widely varying accounts of the discovery of the empty tomb. True, in Mark angels mandate the women a message for the Eleven, and in Matthew it is Jesus himself. But in Luke and John, the women are given no mandate at all; instead it seems to come from personal initiative. Moreover, Luke 24:11 seriously limits the significance of the women witnesses to the resurrection: "The words of the women seemed to the Eleven an idle tale and they did not believe them." Instead, the Eleven will have to experience the resurrected Christ themselves. And, finally, whatever the interpretation of the source of a preaching mandate for his women disciples at the time of Jesus' resurrection, this mission was a very limited one. While the Gospels supply us with accounts claiming both the historical Jesus (Mk 6:7; Mt 10:5) and the resurrected Christ (Mk 16:5; Mt 28:19) sent the Twelve *into the world*, Mary Magdalene and the women at the tomb are sent *only to the Eleven*.

As for the ministry of women in the Pauline churches, all too often in contemporary literature the evidence is exaggerated and the real and obvious assistance offered by women in the early Church is interpreted as not simply assistance but oversight and even presidency in those assemblies. For example, that

Prisca's name is always presented before her husband's (Acts 18:18, 26; Rm 16:3) is, no doubt, an indication of her higher social standing. Nevertheless, one is not thus justified in concluding that if she hosted a house church, it was she rather than her husband who presided at the Eucharist. It could very well be that neither she nor her husband presided, but instead a visiting apostolic or prophetic figure broke the bread.

A similar exaggeration is common regarding the Phoebe mentioned in Romans 16:1-2. When citing this passage above, I quoted from the RSV, but at two points I inserted the corresponding New Testament Greek words *diakonos* and *prostasis*. The reason that I included those Greek words is that some modern exegetes insist they are technical terms indicating Phoebe is an ordained minister who exercises oversight. But as an indication of just how arbitrary a judgment that is, consider the fact that often those very same exegetes who insist Phoebe is an ordained deacon also insist that when Paul uses that same term *diakonos* of men in the Church at Philippi, they are merely pastoral assistants because the formal office had not yet developed: Philippians 1:1, "Paul and Timothy, slaves of Christ Jesus, to all the holy ones in Christ Jesus who are in Philippi, with the overseers and ministers (*diakonoi*)." As to why the Christian community at Cenchrae should have been so much more ecclesiastically developed than that at Philippi no explanation is offered. As for the word *prostasis*, the evidence strongly suggests Phoebe "led" the Church at Cenchrae in generosity rather than oversight. The witness of Romans 16:1-2 is that Phoebe is yet another example of the women described in Luke 8:2-3, that is, a wealthy woman who could afford to travel and thus not only delivered Paul's letter to Rome but maybe even paid for the parchment on which this, his longest letter was written.

A similar caution against exaggeration must be observed in evaluating the ministry of certain other women in the New Testament. For example, the Lydia mentioned in Acts 16:14f. While she gave Paul hospitality, there is no indication she hosted a house church. And, while some have taken the reference to

"Chloe's people" in 1 Corinthians 1:11 as referring to a woman who presides over a house church, it could just as well be a reference to a pagan woman who owned slaves, some of whom were members of a Christian assembly at Corinth. Moreover, while Paul is always conscientious to acknowledge the assistance of women, when he refers precisely to those members of a Christian community who are exercising pastoral oversight, it is only to men that he refers (Stephanas in 1 Cor 16:15, Epaphroditus in Ph 2:25-30). And as for Colossians 4:15-17, even though the Pauline authorship is disputed, there is a big difference between Nympha who, out of her generosity, hosts a house church and Archippus who labors under a divine mandate:

> Give my greetings to the brethren at Laodicea and to Nympha and the church in her house. And when this letter has been read among you, have it read also in the church of the Laodiceans; and see that you read also the letter from Laodicea. And say to Archippus, "See that you fulfill the ministry you have received in the Lord."

Finally, while there is much evidence in the Pauline literature as to the prominence of women in such ministries as hospitality, there is also witness in those same letters to specific restrictions regarding a woman's role in the worshiping assembly. For example, in 1 Corinthians 14:33-35:

> As in all the churches of the saints, the women should keep silence in the churches. For they are not permitted to speak, but should be subordinate, as even the law says. If there is anything they desire to know, let them ask their husbands at home. For it is shameful for a woman to speak in church.

Yet another restriction appears in 1 Timothy 2:11-15:

> Let a woman learn in silence with all submissiveness. I permit no woman to teach or to have authority over men; she is to keep silent. For Adam was formed first,

then Eve; and Adam was not deceived, but the woman
was deceived and became a transgressor. Yet a woman
will be saved through bearing children, if she continues
in faith and love and holiness, with modesty.

When we come to the patristic era we see a similar phenomenon. While women were indeed considered equal in nature and
grace, and they figured prominently in various forms of ministry,
even so none of these same authorities ever advocated the ordination of women to major orders. Indeed, when patristic works
address the issue of women's ordination they are firmly against
it. We have just cited the enthusiastic celebration of the prophetic
voices of women of the Old and New Testaments in *The Apostolic
Constitutions*. But that same work forbids women to preach in the
assembly or to celebrate sacraments such as baptism normally
reserved to a priest (427, 428, 429). The *Didascalia Apostolorum*,
composed in northern Syria in the early half of the third century,
while acknowledging that women were called to discipleship,
argues that women were not appointed to teach and to preach
(3.6.2). *The Apostolic Church Order*, an Egyptian work compiled
about A.D. 300, contains a dialogue between male and female
disciples on whether or not women can celebrate the Eucharist.
Here, it is not just men such as Peter, Andrew, James and John, but
even Mary Magdalene argues against it. And, while women were
prominent as deaconesses, the female diaconate was considered
a minor order. As we have already seen in our chapter on diaconal
ministry, it was not equivalent to the order of deacon.

Reliable evidence for women in roles of ordained ministry
even among the heterodox is scant or questionable. For example,
no doubt Montanus, founder of an apocalyptic movement about
the year 172, ranked alongside himself as mouthpieces of the
Holy Spirit two of his women followers. But Priscilla and Maxi-
milla were prophetesses, not priestesses. True, Irenaeus of Lyons,
about the year 180, in his four-volume work, *Against Heretics* (Bk
I, Ch 13) describes a Gnostic named Marcus who has women
ritual assistants (they held the chalices when he consecrated).
But there is no doubt it is still Marcus who presides at the rite. In

the same letter of Cyprian of Carthage that we have cited above, he claims (in paragraph 10) to have known of a prophetess who baptized and celebrated the Eucharist. But he insists she was in league with Satan. The most ambitious reference to women acting as priests and bishops occurs in the principal literary work of Epiphanius, bishop of Salamis. In his *The Panarion* (49.2-3), the most important and extensive heresiological encyclopedia from the early Church, written ca. 374-377, Epiphanius describes heretical or enthusiastic groups such as the Cataphyrgians as installing women as bishops or presbyters. However, several modern scholars have argued this reference may be nothing more than an exaggerated slander. In recent times, some other scholars have put forward claims they have discovered evidence of women presbyters in ancient times. For example, Giorgio Otranto in 1982 published a work in which he claimed to show how a letter of Pope Gelasius I and some contemporary funerary inscriptions can be interpreted to demonstrate the existence of women presbyters in the Church in Southern Italy in the fifth century. Such claims have yet to receive universal scholarly acceptance. Indeed, they appear to be little more than highly imaginative and inventive interpretations of obscure texts.

What then are we to make of these historic limitations on the role of women in ministry? It is possible to give some theological arguments in support of them. For example, there is much that suggests: with the religion of the Bible, while there has always been an absolute equality between women and men with regards to human nature and salvation, as regards mission and ministry, there has always been a peculiarly arbitrary element and this has been so even when mission and ministry has involved only men. The arbitrary character of the biblical concept of sacred mission in a general sense is encapsulated in the old adage, "How odd of God to choose the Jews." The arbitrary character of individual missions provides us with much more cause for wonder and perhaps even consternation. Though Miriam exhibited a talent for leadership and a charismatic eloquence (Ex 15:20), it was her reluctant and inarticulate brother Moses (Ex 4:10), who was called to lead Israel. Indeed, in the Bible often among the men called to mission, their native capacities are at odds with their mission. David was the youngest and least impressive of Jesse's sons (1 S 16:6-12). Paul was nowhere near as eloquent as Apollos (cf. Ac 18:24 and 1 Cor 2:1). Timothy appeared to some far too young to be given leadership responsibilities (1 Tm 4:12).

There is yet another theological argument that is current today. In defense of this restriction of ordination for males only, several recent pronouncements of the Church have borrowed from Aquinas the idea that the celebrant of the Eucharist performs *in persona Christi*, that is, functions "in the person of Christ." Thomas uses this phrase in his *Summa theologiae*, Part 3, Questions 82-83, where he treats of both the minister and the rite of the Eucharist. But there has arisen some controversy regarding the proper interpretation of Aquinas' phrase. While some insist Aquinas means the celebrant of the Eucharist to effectively represent Christ must be a male, others have insisted the imitation of Christ implied here by Aquinas is moral self-effacement and not physical or sexual conformity. They argue thus: A woman as much as any man can represent Christ at the Last Supper, his consummate act of self-effacement, self-sacrifice.

However, the most popular explanation in modern times is that these historic restrictions on women in ministry are all due to cultural prejudices. Indeed, modern exegetes have found ways of explaining away these limitations of women in the ministry of Jesus and Paul. For example, it is at times alleged that the reason Jesus did not include women among the Twelve, his prophetic sign of a New Israel, was a practical one, an exigency. That is, he knew a woman would not be acceptable as a preacher in his time. The problem with this argument is that its thesis is totally out of character with Jesus' forthright personality as witnessed to in a passage like Mark 22:16, "Teacher, we know that you are true, and teach the way of God truthfully, and care for no man; for you do not regard the position of men." Indeed, it is hard to think that this Jesus who was so boldly innovative in other ways would hesitate to include women among the Twelve simply because he thought others would take offense at it.

As for those passages in the Pauline literature that put severe restrictions on women in the assembly, the standard response is to claim that in the case of both 1 Corinthians 14:34-35 and 1 Timothy 2:11-15, these are not original with Paul but are later interpolations, later reversals of the original freedom that characterized the first Pauline churches. Here we are working on more plausible ground, that is, the literary evidence does indeed strongly suggest 1 Corinthians 14:34-35 is a later interpolation and, moreover, an interpolation not easily reconcilable with 1 Corinthians 11:5, 13, where Paul takes it for granted that women do pray and prophesy aloud in the assembly. However, it is possible to argue that these interpolations are far from illegitimate. Rather they represent a further reflection on experience and consequent refinement of pastoral practice. That is, it can be argued that even when there are interpolations in Pauline letters this is but an analogy to the multiple redactions the Gospel traditions themselves have undergone. More precisely, it could be that in the earliest Christian assemblies women's prophetic voices were very prominent and, perhaps, in some cases all too prominent. Indeed, if the example of Philip the evangelist and his "four virgin daughters gifted with prophecy" (Ac 21:9) is any indication it could be that women's voices far outnumbered those of men in the earliest Christian assemblies. And, so, some measure had to be taken to insure that men's voices would be heard. But even here one must note: the Pauline restriction on women teaching men has long been overcome. Women now teach men, not just in Catholic elementary and secondary schools but in Catholic colleges, university departments of religion and in seminaries.

In conclusion, I want to suggest another possible answer. This historic exclusion of women from the most prominent ministries may not be due entirely to cultural biases. Instead, it might well be a strategic maneuver, a necessary response even, to two important social phenomena: in every time and place on earth the socialization of the male of the human species has proven to be a more formidable challenge than the socialization of the female; and in the Church from the beginning the number of women disciples has always far outnumbered the men. More precisely, the modern sciences of physical and cultural anthropology supply considerable data that suggest the male of the human species is a much greater challenge to any community, secular or religious, in terms of socialization. While the female of the human species is equipped for both conception and nurture, in contrast the male of the human species, with no womb and only vestigial nipples, is at a physical and emotional remove from both of these vital processes of nature and nurture. Moreover, the human male must not only learn responsibility in those areas, but can readily shirk such responsibilities. A man never has to bear the results of intercourse that leads to conception, only the female in a cohabiting relationship can ever get pregnant. And, while the female can be equally sexually aggressive, she cannot be invasive. The male alone is capable of violent penetration. It is most probably biological factors such as these, reinforced by the bad example of males who selfishly capitalize upon their biological remoteness and natural incapacities, that account for the phenomenon that in every nation on earth the number of males in prison far exceeds the number of females in prison and the number of single parent families headed by a female far outstrips those headed by a male. All the evidence suggests a responsible male, ready and able to make significant emotional and social commitment is a rarity in any society. A similar phenomenon is observable in the history of the Church. All four Gospels witness to the greater responsiveness and commitment of Jesus' women disciples who, according to John's Gospel, outnumbered the men three to one at the foot of the cross (Mk 15:40-41; Mt 27:55; Lk 23:49; Jn 19:25-26). And so it has continued throughout history. Historically and to this day, women far outnumber men in both Christian worshiping assemblies and in the service ranks of the Church. In the face of this patent and dramatic evidence of women's more ready and prominent religious engagement, the historical tradition of calling only males to ordained ministry, the promotion of men to the most visible positions of leadership in the community of faith, might well be seen as a type of affirmative action aimed at securing for the Christian community at least a few examples of the prominent engagement of men in the social leadership of the Church. Moreover, it could well be argued this constitutes not just a social exigency but a unique and important sacramental sign value. That is, in view of the profoundly ambiguous physical and emotional capacities of the male of the human species, if a Christian community can produce a male who is willing to publicly preside at the table of the Lord this is, indeed, a uniquely eloquent sign of grace overcoming the limitations of human nature.

Further Reading

Kenneth Woodward's "Gender and Religion: Who's Really Running the Show?" in *Commonweal* (November 22, 1996), 9-14.

John Paul II's Apostolic Letter, *Mulieris dignitatem* (The Dignity of Women), 15 August 1988.

John Paul II's Apostolic Letter, *Ordinatio sacerdotalis* (Priestly Ordination), 22 May 1994.

Sara Butler's *The Catholic Priesthood and Women: A Guide to the Teaching of the Church* (Chicago, 2007).

CHAPTER 28

The Ministry of a Consecrated Life

Among the historic forms of Christian ministry consideration must be given to those men and women who, from early Church history to the present day have given over their lives totally and completely to the service of the Gospel. These people, by means of a pledge or vow, a public promise to God, have denied themselves many good things so as to make real for others certain Gospel values and something of a foretaste of the blessings of the kingdom. For example, often by simply or solemnly foreswearing marriage and family, personal wealth and self-determination, these Christians were able to give themselves totally to the service of the poor by providing them schools, hospitals and orphanages. They brought the Gospel to dangerous or neglected places at home and the most exotic and remote places abroad. Though there are not many of them with us anymore, much of the finest cultural accomplishments of Christianity — art, music, architecture and pedagogy — were due to their generous and personal sacrifices. In order to understand these people, their ministerial method and religious motivation, we shall look first at the phenomenon of vows in both Old and New Testaments and then trace something of the development in Christian history of this ideal of Christians who consecrate their lives to service of the Gospel.

Vows are mentioned frequently in the Old Testament and rank among the oldest Israelite religious practices. In biblical usage one might swear an oath to another person but one vowed only to God, for a vow was a deliberate, solemn promise to God. One example of a solemn vow in the Old Testament is Jacob's solemn promise to build an altar to God at Bethel. We read in Genesis 28:20:

> Then Jacob made a vow, saying, "If God will be with me, and will keep me in this way that I go, and will give me bread to eat and clothing to wear, so that I come again to my father's house in peace, then the Lord shall be my God, and this stone, which I have set up for a pillar, shall be God's house; and of all that Thou givest me I will give the tenth to Thee."

Other prominent examples are Israel's vow to obtain victory in battle (Nb 21:2) and Hannah's vow in order to obtain a son (1 S 1:11). The psalms of the Old Testament contain numerous allusions to the duty of fulfilling a vow: Psalm 22:25, "My vows I will pay before those who fear Him"; Psalm 50:14, "Offer to God a sacrifice of thanksgiving. And pay your vows to the Most High"; Psalm 56:12, "My vows to thee I must perform, O God"; Psalm 61:8, "So will I ever sing praises to thy name, as I pay my vows day after day"; Psalm 65:1, "Praise is due to thee, O God, in Zion and to thee shall vows be performed"; Psalm 66:13-14, "I will come into thy house with burnt offerings; I will pay thee my vows, that which my lips uttered and my mouth promised when I was in trouble"; Psalm 76:11, "Make your vows to the Lord your God, and perform them."

An entire chapter (6) of the book of Numbers is given over to precise description of one particular kind of vow, the Nazirite vow. The word *nazir* meant "one set apart." The man or woman who made this vow abstained from intoxicating beverages, the use of the razor and contact with the dead (in Jg 16:17, Samson's great length of hair is the result of the Nazirite vow he had taken). All such vows were for only a period of time, and at the end the Nazirite offered a burnt sacrifice in the temple sanctuary and had his or her long hair shorn and burnt along with the sacrificial offering.

There are two passages in the Acts of the Apostles that witness to the fact Jewish Christians still made such vows. Acts 18:18 describes Paul as having made such a Nazirite vow sometime after his Christian conversion and during his days of public ministry: "After this Paul stayed many days longer, and then took leave of the brethren and sailed for Syria, and with him Priscilla and Aquila. At Cenchreae he cut his hair, for he had a vow [*euzen*]." In Acts 21:23-24, James and the elders of the Jerusalem Christian community recommend to Paul four Christians of Jerusalem who had made such a vow and they ask Paul to help these men: "We have four men who are under a vow; take these men and purify yourself along with them and pay their expenses."

For our interests, however, there is a later passage in the New Testament, which, though it does not use the precise language of a vow, yet describes a similar solemn promise to God. Moreover, this passage witnesses to a novelty in the Christian use of vows. For now a vow is used not to gain a personal favor from God but as an aid to Christian ministry. In 1 Timothy 5:3-16, Paul gives instructions for the care and status of widows in the Christian community:

> Honor widows who are real widows. If a widow has children or grandchildren, let them [the widow's children] first learn their religious duty to their own family and make some return to their parents; for this is acceptable in the sight of God. She who is a real widow, and is left all alone, has set her hope on God and continues in supplications and prayers night and day; whereas she who is self-indulgent is dead even while she lives. Command this, so that they may be without reproach. If anyone does not provide for his relatives, and especially for his own family, he has disowned the faith and is worse than an unbeliever.
>
> Let a widow be enrolled if she is not less than sixty years of age, having been the wife of one husband; and she must be well attested for her good deeds, as one who has brought up children, shown hospitality, washed the feet of the saints, relieved the afflicted, and devoted

herself to doing good in every way. But refuse to enroll younger widows; for when they grow wanton against Christ they desire to marry, and so they incur condemnation for having violated their first pledge [*pistin*]. Besides that, they learn to be idlers, gadding about from house to house, and not only idlers but gossips and busybodies, saying what they should not. So I would have younger widows marry, bear children, rule their households, and give the enemy no occasion to revile us. For some have already strayed after Satan. If any believing woman has relatives who are widows, let her assist them; let the Church not be burdened, so that it may assist those who are real widows.

It is important that we understand the social background of this passage. In the sexist society of the ancient world, a deceased man's goods went not to his widow but to his eldest son. And thus penniless widows were abundant and a major social problem. In ancient Israel widows were readily recognizable because they wore specific clothing, "widow's weeds" (Gn 38:14, 19). Because they had no man to defend them, they could be easily exploited and victimized, for example, by creditors (see 2 K 4:1ff.; Jb 24:3). In the Old Testament, the widow was considered the epitome of the lonely and helpless. Popular biblical tradition speaks of God defending widows (Ps 146:9; Ml 3:5) and commanding their protection (Ex 22:22; Dt 16:14). Jesus displays his concern for widows in several ways: the raising of the only son of the widow of Nain (Lk 7:11-15), he points to the poor widow who gave as her temple offering her last two coins (Mk 12:41-44; Lk 21:1-4), he castigates those who "devour the houses of widows" (Mk 12:40; Lk 20:47). The care of widows is identified in the New Testament (Jm 1:27) as one of the constituent elements of religion that is pure and undefiled.

As for the specific teaching of 1 Timothy 5:3-16, there are two points made, one in each of the two paragraphs quoted. In the first paragraph the author reminds Christians of their duty to care for their widowed mothers. In the second paragraph, the author describes a special group of widows admission to which required three things. First, a widow must be at least sixty years of age. Second, she must have proven herself dedicated to acts of charity. Third, she must make a pledge not to marry again. He calls this group of women "enrolled widows" which many exegetes feel refers to a public ceremony in which such widows would verbally make their pledge. And thus the enrollment of widows is not just a remedy for a general social problem but a specific form of ministry or public witness in the local church.

That some sort of institution of consecrated women, women who would forego marriage in order to serve the Gospel or the Church, the community of faith, continued in the early Christian Church is indicated by several passages in the early Church Fathers. For example, Ignatius of Antioch (died ca. 101), in his *Letter to Polycarp* 5.27, speaks of the "virgins who are called widows." Justin Martyr (died ca. 165), in his *Apology* 6.15, refers to "groups" of virgins. Part I of a Church order called *The Apostolic Tradition* (ca. 230) describes a state or order of virgins. The Church handbook called *The Apostolic Constitutions*, written about 380, deals extensively with virgins.

Apparently, it was somewhat later that men began to seek some institutional form of exclusive consecration, total devotion to the Christian life apart from marriage and secular profession. In the third century, we see the beginning of a life of special asceticism practiced by the "fathers of the desert," Christian men who retired to the solitude of the Egyptian desert to lead a life of prayer and mortification. They left the world in order to seek God and to serve the world at the level of its deepest need: prayer. This ascetical movement began about the mid third century and flourished into the fourth century. It began in no small measure as a counter-cultural movement, a critique of contemporary Christianity. That is, with the conversion of the Roman emperor Constantine and the public legitimation of Christianity, the Christian faith had suddenly become not only free but socially attractive, even fashionable. These hermits opted out of this emerging "Christian society" in part as protest. Though at first most of these men were hermits and anchorites, soon they began to gather around a charismatic figure such as Anthony of Egypt (ca. 250-356). Another important "master" of the devout life or revered charismatic figure, Pachomius (ca. 290-346), introduced the idea of cenobitism. This word is derived from two Greek words meaning "common life." A cenobite was a monk who lived in community, in contrast to a hermit who lived separately from others. Basil the Great (329-379) not only founded several monastic communities but wrote down directions for them. He wrote two volumes that to this day are the principal historic guides to monasticism in the Orthodox tradition. The *Great Asceticon* consists of 35 questions and answers dealing with basic concepts of spiritual and monastic asceticism. His *Small Asceticon*, despite its title, consisted of 313 questions and answers. In the West, Augustine of Hippo (354-431) drew up his rule for the common life of clerics. Then Benedict of Nursia (ca. 480-ca. 550) drew up a rule for men and women, clerics and laity who wanted to live in community and pursue the religious life exclusively. There was but one vow requiring stability of residence, obedience and monastic zeal. The chief task of the community was a form of communal prayer called the "Divine Office" (*opus dei*) supplemented by personal spiritual reading (which led to scholarly research) and manual labor (not always physical labor, for example, the copying of manuscripts and the production of art, the illumination of manuscripts). An added note was hospitality to travelers. From the eighth to the twelfth centuries, Benedictine monasticism was the only form of the religious life known in the West. While the Benedictine tradition underwent radical reform in the Middle Ages in such movements as the Carthusians (a lessening of the communal sense due to new emphasis on strict silence and contemplation) and Cistercians (remoteness from society and simplicity of life, return to manual labor), the next truly innovative variation on the vowed life or consecrated Christian life occurred in the thirteenth century with the rise of the mendicant orders, the Franciscans, Dominicans and Carmelites, who, while keeping the Divine Office, dispensed with stability of residence in favor of strategic itinerancy. Also their rejection of community of goods in favor of poverty, that is, simplicity of life style and begging for a living, dependence upon charitable support by generous laity, was in no small measure a prophetic critique of wealthy Benedictine abbeys (community of goods can make for individual poverty but corporate wealth and, consequently, large and wealthy monasteries have attracted the attention of rapacious governments — England's Henry VIII, the French Revolution, Peter the Great in Russia). The sixteenth century saw the rise of orders of clerics regular who now freed themselves from the obligation of choral office (prayers chanted together) so as to be even more dedicated to pastoral ministry, educational and missionary efforts. The most prominent example of this innovation was the Jesuits, or Society of Jesus, who not only abandoned community worship but also made much of the vow of obedience. In the seventeenth century, St. John Baptist de la Salle instituted non-clerical, that is, lay congregations of teaching brothers. In the nineteenth century, secular institutes were created.

In all of these expressions of the religious life, the most prominent element was not just the total dedication, the public profession, but also the idealism of realizing certain Gospel values associated with Jesus' preaching of the kingdom of God. In that sense, these consecrated Christian men and women were "professionals," that is, people who made a public profession of their faith both for their own salvation and for the good of the wider Church. As we have seen, the rise of a professed life for men, the desert fathers, was motivated by a desire to offer an alternative to the bourgeois Christianity of the urban masses. This idealism resulted in the concept of "perfection," or the more perfect way of the three vows, what will come to be called the "evangelical counsels," a classic statement of which can be found in Aquinas' *Summa theologiae*, Part 2, question 184.

The term "evangelical counsels" refers to certain teachings or examples, object lessons regarding the Christian life, set forth by Jesus himself. These teachings were deemed "evangelical" because they were found in the Gospels, and "counsels" because they were not formal precepts like the Ten Commandments, basic moral requirements demanded of all, but rather they were seen as a personal invitation from the Lord to a sort of evangelical idealism. This evangelical idealism found expression in the three vows of poverty, chastity and obedience, the rationale for which was anchored in certain Gospel passages. For example, the concept of religious or Christian "poverty," the renunciation of material wealth and goods, was based on Jesus' encounter with the rich young man. This Gospel narrative occurs in Mark 10:17-22 and its parallels in Matthew 19:16-22 and Luke 18:18-24. I quote here the Marcan version because it is probably the more primitive:

> And as he [Jesus] was setting out on his journey, a man ran up and knelt before him, and asked him, "Good Teacher, what must I do to inherit eternal life?" And Jesus said to him, "Why do you call me good? No one is good but God alone. You know the commandments. 'Do not kill, Do not commitment adultery, Do not steal, Do not bear false witness, Do not defraud, Honor your father and mother.'" And he said to him, "Teacher all these I have observed from my youth." And Jesus looking upon him loved him, and said to him, "You lack one thing; go, sell what you have, and give to the poor, and you will have treasure in heaven; and come, follow me." At that saying his countenance fell, and he went away sorrowful; for he had great possessions.

In Matthew's Gospel, Jesus' response to the rich young man is to say, "If you would be *perfect* [*teleios*], go, sell what you possess and give to the poor, and you will have treasure in heaven; and come, follow me." I have quoted Matthew here because his variant on the saying of Jesus here will have tremendous influence on the developing theology of the religious life.

The ideal of chastity in the form of celibacy, that is, not periodic sexual abstinence for cultic purposes as the temple priests practiced bur rather total abstention from sex and thus marriage, was based upon two other passages from Scripture, one from the Gospels, the other from a Pauline epistle. The Gospel passage is the famous "eunuch logion" of Matthew 19:10-12. The nineteenth chapter of Matthew begins with Jesus' teaching on marriage and divorce. Jesus inveighs against an attitude that would make divorce easy. Jesus' disciples appear amazed at the strictness of Jesus' teaching:

> The disciples said to him, "If such is the case of a man with his wife, it is not expedient to marry." But he said to them, "Not all men can receive this precept, but only those to whom it is given. For there are eunuchs who have been so from birth, and there are eunuchs who have been made so by men, and there are eunuchs who have made themselves eunuchs for the sake of the kingdom of heaven. He who is able to receive this, let him receive it."

Some exegetes have argued that in this passage Jesus' use of the image of the eunuch was probably motivated by someone's crude and dismissive comment on the fact that Jesus himself did not marry. That is, someone might have scoffed that the reason Jesus did not marry was that he was incapable of sexual performance. The social institution of the eunuch, common in some societies outside Israel, was heinous to Jewish thought and so it is amazing that Jesus would resort to this fantastic image.

The other passage most often cited in support of the ideal of celibacy is Paul's First Letter to the Church at Corinth 7:1-8. There Paul treats of questions posed to him by that Christian assembly regarding marriage:

> Now concerning the matters about which you wrote. It is well for a man not to touch a woman. But because of the temptation to immorality, each man should have his own wife and each woman her own husband. The husband should give to his wife her conjugal rights, and likewise the wife to her husband. For the wife does not rule over her own body, but the husband does; likewise the husband does not rule over his own body, but the wife does. Do not refuse one another except perhaps by

agreement for a season, that you may devote yourselves
to prayer; but then come together again, lest Satan tempt
you through lack of self-control. I say this by way of
concession, not command. I wish that all were as I myself am. But each has his own special gift from God,
one of one kind and one of another. To the unmarried
and the widows I say that it is well for them to remain
single as I do.

As for obedience: there are no New Testament texts that
specifically recommend, much less require, the form of obedience to which vowed Christians commit themselves. But there
can be no doubt obedience as a spiritual theme looms large in
the New Testament both in the personal spirituality of Jesus and
the Christian spirituality preached in the epistles. Despite the
attempt on the part of some modern-day interpreters of the life
of Jesus to portray him as a revolutionary, in the Gospels Jesus
is portrayed as conspicuously obedient to the claims of human
authority and religious custom. He is subject to his parents (Lk
2:51). He acknowledges the right of the State to tax people (Mt
17:24). He is observant of religious ordinances such as attendance
at synagogue on the Sabbath (Lk 4:16) and at the temple on major
feasts (Jn 2:13; 5:1; 7:10; 10:22). And Jesus himself acquiesced in
paying not just government taxes but also the temple tax (Mt
17:24-25). Indeed, several Gospel passages suggest obedience
was a major characteristic of Jesus' self-identity. His personal
spirituality can be summed upon in such expressions as Mark
14:36, "Not my will but Thine be done," or John 4:34, "My food
is to do the will of him who sent me." Jesus' whole life work is
often described in terms of his obedience, as in Romans 5:19: "As
by one man's disobedience many were made sinners, so by one
man's obedience many will be made righteous." Paul, in Philippians 2:8, describes Jesus as "obedient unto death." A similar
spirituality of obedience is recommended to all Christians in
the epistles of the New Testament. In Ephesians 6:1, "Children,
obey your parents in the Lord, for this is right." In 1 Peter 2:13
we hear the admonition, "Be subject to every human institution for the Lord's sake, whether it be the king as supreme or

to governors as sent by him." Obedience to Church authority is also enjoined, as in Hebrews 13:17: "Obey your leaders and submit to them; for they are keeping watch over your souls as men who will have to give account." Moreover, in Matthew 8:8-10, Jesus commends the centurion of Capernaum's strong sense of obedience to orders as equivalent to great faith:

> But the centurion answered him, "Lord, I am not worthy to have you come under my roof; but only say the word, and my servant will be healed. For I am a man under authority, with soldiers under me; and I say to one, 'Go,' and he goes, and to another, 'Come,' and he comes, and to my slave, 'Do this,' and he does it." When Jesus heard him, he marveled, and said to those who followed him, "Truly, I say to you, not even in Israel have I found such faith."

After having mustered all these passages as biblical foundation for the theology of a consecrated Christian life, that is, for the institution of religious life, monastic, clerical and lay, however, I must also acknowledge that the interpretation of the passages I have cited here have been hotly contested, disputed by exegetes and theologians. For example, the passages presented here in support of the concept of celibacy have been given quite different interpretations, at odds with everything I have said. Moreover, we should also consider that one of the prominent features of the Protestant Reformation was its searing critique of the Catholic concept of the religious life and especially religious life's claim to be the way of perfection. But one should also be very careful in assessing the Reformation critique. By that I mean if one realizes the historical situation of that critique much of the criticism is blunted. For example, John Calvin wrote a comprehensive four-volume systematic theology entitled *The Institutes of the Christian Religion*. Book 4, Chapter 13 of *The Institutes* is entitled, "Vows and How Everyone Rashly Taking Them Has Miserably Entangled Himself." No doubt, Calvin is unrelentingly condemnatory of religious life as lived in his day, but what must also be seen is that Calvin does not totally reject the idea of religious life; indeed, he duly recognizes its importance and value in the history of the early Church. Religious life in Calvin's day was decadent and deserved censure, and that is why part of the Catholic Counter-Reformation was the precise reform of such abuses as in Teresa of Avila's Carmelite reform movement or the reform measures mandated by the Council of Trent.

No doubt, a reaction against monasticism constituted a principal emphasis of the Protestant Reformation, exemplified in Luther's own abandonment of the Augustinian Order in which he once made solemn profession. And where Protestantism triumphed all religious orders were suppressed. Even so, the disciplined community life of consecrated Christian men and women never totally disappeared even within Protestantism. For example, in the eighteenth century, the religious society called "The Moravian Brethren" arose. The nineteenth century witnessed the establishment of several communities of professed Christians within the Anglican and Lutheran traditions. In the twentieth century the interdenominational and ecumenical monastic order, the Taizé community, was founded. Nevertheless, the vowed life is a very marginal, not to say eccentric, phenomenon within contemporary Protestantism. And perhaps this is its future even in Catholicism.

Until very recently, here in America it was common to see nuns, monks, friars, "religious brothers" or "religious sisters," communities that called themselves, "Christian Brothers," "Daughters of Charity," "The Order of Preachers, "The Society or Company of Jesus," "The Sisters of Mercy," living a consecrated Christian life among us. They often staffed our schools, hospitals, orphanages, assisted in our parishes or were prominent in the missions, home as well as foreign. Eschewing contemporary fashions of dress, they were easy to recognize because of their quaint, distinctive, uniform garb. But now their number has become greatly reduced. And, even if some are still with us, they are not so readily discernible, that is, they no longer dress uniformly and distinctively. The reason for the decline in their numbers is not entirely clear. In some measure their precipitous decline may be due to the growth of secular-ism in the Western world, the aggressiveness of a society that challenges many of the ideals to which these Christian men and women dedicate themselves. The materialism, narcissism, obsession with sex that characterizes modern culture are not easily reconciled with the ideals of poverty, obedience and chastity. But one should not simply blame the world. For there have also been serious changes within the Catholic Church itself which may have, though no doubt unintentionally, con-tributed to the decline in the number of vowed religious. For example, in certain documents of the Second Vatican Council, great emphasis was placed on the dignity of the laity, including their capacity for ministry. It could be that, in view of this, many Catholics have been quick to realize one need not take vows to assume a significant role in the liturgical assembly, teach the faith, feed the poor, work as a missionary or in campus or hospital ministry. The effect of these two disparate phenom-ena — secularism and a renewal of Christian lay spirituality — work to raise the question: What place does the vowed life have in the Church?

It could be the answer to that question is a precise and strategic one. That is, just as the practice of the Nazirite vow in ancient Israel began as a counter-cultural statement — the Nazirite's abstinence from wine was a pointed rejection of one of the principal features of Canaanite culture — and the flight to the desert of Christian hermits in the early Church was a criti-cism of the new all too fashionable Christian faithful, so too the consecrated Christian life today might function as a prophetic critique of laxity or worldliness in the lives of Christian clergy and laity. To give but one example, the experience of the peace, the silence, and the chaste music of monastic liturgies — stylistic choices that aim at creating a palpable sense of communion with the sacred — can be a salutary alternative to those garrulous parish liturgies whose sensuous songs strive to create a sense of contemporaneity and human community.

Further Reading

Johannes B. Metz's *Followers of Christ: Perspectives on the Religious Life* translated by T. Linton (Paulist Press, 1978), is an imaginative rethinking of the rationale for the vowed life.

The essay, "Protestant Religious Orders," in Donald G. Bloesch's *The Church: Sacraments, Worship, Ministry, Mission* (Downers Grove, IL: InterVarsity Press, 2002), pages 211-218.

J.F. Hardy's "Pledges" in Volume 3 of *The International Standard Bible Encyclopedia* (Grand Rapids, MI: Wm. B. Eerdmans, 1986), 886-887.

Part III

APPENDICES

The Blessed Virgin Mary and the Church

Some readers might be surprised to find that in a book on the Church there is a chapter on the Blessed Virgin Mary. But there is a reason for this. The Blessed Virgin Mary has long figured significantly in the piety and devotional life of many of the Christian traditions. Throughout their long history, the ancient Churches, the Catholic and Orthodox, have always exhibited as a prominent feature of their liturgical as well as devotional life the celebration of not just moments in the life and death of the Blessed Virgin Mary but even her "blessed" or divinely favored character. Moreover, even so revolutionary an event as the Protestant Reformation did not totally obliterate all examples of Marian devotion. That is, even in some of the Christian assemblies stemming from the Protestant Reformation of the sixteenth century, there is evident to this day a significant measure of devotion to the Blessed Virgin Mary, for example, in the Anglican and Lutheran traditions. Johann Sebastian Bach's musical setting of the *Magnificat* (Lk 1:46-55) is an eloquent example of this strain of piety among Lutherans. But in this chapter we need to make clear: Mary, the mother of Jesus, is not just a significant figure in piety and devotion but she also figures significantly as an element in Catholic ecclesiology where she is seen not only as a prominent member, nor even as just the most prominent member of the communion of saints, but as also having a very special relationship to all the faithful. What precisely is that relationship and what is its theological basis will be the theme of this essay.

In order to illustrate this theme, what I will do here is to take the biblical-historical approach which I have employed throughout this book. That is, here we shall begin by examining those passages in the New Testament wherein the Blessed Virgin Mary appears and examine them so as to see what significance has been or should be given them. There can be little doubt much modern day Catholic devotion to the Blessed Virgin Mary finds its impetus in visionary appearances of the Virgin at Lourdes, Fatima, Guadalupe, *et cetera*. But, long before these modern-day appearances of the Virgin Mary, she also appeared significantly in the Bible. No doubt, what significance should be given to these New Testament references to Mary is a hotly debated point to this day. An informed Christian should be aware of these passages and the controversies they have provoked. So what I shall do here is, first, to review in a cursory fashion all the passages in the New Testament that refer to Mary, references no matter how oblique or, for some, how farfetched. After a brief evaluation of them, I shall treat more precisely of the more sententious and substantial portrayals of Mary in Luke and John especially with regards to their ecclesiological significance. In surveying the image of the Blessed Virgin Mary in the New Testament, I shall proceed chronologically.

The earliest reference to the Blessed Virgin Mary occurs in an epistle of Saint Paul and it is a very indirect reference. In Galatians 4:4-5, Paul says, "God sent forth his Son, born of a woman." Mary gets equally sparse and indirect reference in the earliest Gospel, that of Mark. Moreover, it is not just indirect but apparently dismissive. In Mark 3:31-39, we discover that while Jesus was preaching to a large crowd, he was told:

> "Your mother and your brethren are outside, asking for you." And he replied, "Who are my mother and my brethren?" And looking around on those who sat about him, he said, "Here are my mother and my brethren! Whoever does the will of God is my brother, and sister, and mother."

Mary is referred to three times in the Gospel according to Matthew. Matthew's Gospel, unlike Mark's, has an infancy narrative. And there we find two references to Mary, one rather oblique and seemingly inconsequential, but the other quite sententious. We begin with the more sententious reference because it occurs first. Matthew's infancy narrative is written from the point of view of Joseph who is portrayed as a conscientiously devout Jew, a "just man," who is quite perplexed when he finds his espoused, Mary, has already conceived a child. In Matthew 1:18-25 an angel appears to him in a dream, saying:

> "Joseph, son of David, do not fear to take Mary your wife, for that which is conceived in her is of the Holy Spirit; she will bear a son, and you shall call his name Jesus, for he will save his people from their sins." All this took place to fulfill what the Lord had spoken by the prophet: "Behold, a virgin shall conceive and bear a son, and his name shall be called Emmanuel" (which means, God with us). When Joseph woke from sleep, he did as the angel of the Lord commanded him; he took his wife, but knew her not until she had borne a son; and he called his name Jesus.

I said this passage is quite sententious because in it Mary is presented as the prophetically announced instrument of the Holy Spirit, a fact underlined by Matthew's quotation of the Septuagint translation's "virgin" as opposed to the original Hebrew, "young woman."

The other, briefer, reference to Mary in Matthew's infancy narrative occurs in the story of the magi. When the magi arrive at the house in Bethlehem, we are told in Matthew 2:11, "and going into the house they saw the child with Mary his mother."

Finally, in Matthew 12:45-60, there is an almost verbatim quotation of the incident we first saw described in Mark's Gospel, Jesus' dismissal of his mother and his brethren.

When we come to the Gospel according to Luke we find a much more extensive portrayal of Mary, in fact the most extensive in any one New Testament work. In Luke we find no less than six portrayals of Mary. In some of these passages she is the central figure. The first, in Luke 1:26-38, is a narrative of the visit of the angel Gabriel to Mary to announce to her that not only has she already been much favored by God but that now, if she but co-operate, God will make of her the instrument for a much greater thing: the advent of the Messiah. The next fulsome Lucan portrait of Mary is in 1:39-56. In this passage we are told of a visit of the pregnant Mary to her cousin Elizabeth. The two women rejoice in their miraculous pregnancies and this occasions a particularly poetic response from Mary called the Magnificat wherein Mary celebrates the wonders God is working through her and how these redound to her own everlasting glory (1:48). The next appearance of Mary in Luke's Gospel is in the narrative of the annunciation to the shepherds. Angels appears to shepherds to tell them of the birth of the Messiah. And then in Luke 2:15-19, we are told:

> When the angels went away from them into heaven, the shepherds said to one another, "Let us go over to Bethlehem and see this thing that has happened, which the Lord has made known to us." And they went with haste, and found Mary and Joseph, and the babe lying in the manger. And when they saw it they made known the saying which had been told them concerning this child; and all who heard it wondered at what the shepherds told them. But Mary kept all these things, pondering them in her heart.

Yet another notable mention of Mary is in Luke 2:27-35, a passage often called the presentation in the temple. This tells of Mary and Joseph bringing the infant Jesus to the Jerusalem temple so as to fulfill Jewish dedication and purification rites. There in the temple Joseph and Mary encounter an old man, Simeon, who stops and pronounces a prophetic utterance not only about the child Jesus but also about Mary his mother: "Behold, this child is set for the fall and rising of many in Israel, and for a sign that is spoken against (and a sword will pierce through your own soul also), that thoughts out of many hearts may be revealed."

Yet another passage from Luke wherein Mary figures as a significant secondary character is the passage called the finding of the child Jesus in the temple. This is the only account in all four Gospels of an incident from the so-called hidden years of Christ. It tells of how it was the custom of Joseph and Mary to go up to Jerusalem each year for the Passover festival. When Jesus was 12 years of age he went with them but was inadvertently left behind when the family caravan started back to Nazareth. Joseph and Mary return to Jerusalem to look for him. After three days they find him in the temple in the company of the elders. This narrative ends with a short but intriguing dialogue between Jesus and Mary. In Luke 2:41-51, we are told:

> And when they [Joseph and Mary] saw him they were astonished; and his mother said to him, "Son, why have you treated us so? Your father and I have been looking for you anxiously." And he said to them, "How is it that you sought me? Did you not know that I must be in my Father's house?" And they did not understand the saying when he spoke to them. And he went down with them and came to Nazareth, and was obedient to them; and his mother kept all these things in her heart.

The Gospel according to Luke not only shares with Mark and Matthew a near identical narrative of the incident wherein Jesus dismisses Mary and his relations (Lk 8:19-21), but Luke has, in addition, an interesting variation on the same theme. In Luke 11:27-28 we are told of a woman who hearing Jesus preach shouts a compliment to him which is an indirect praise of his mother. The passage goes:

> As he said this, a woman in the crowd raised her voice and said to him, "Blessed is the womb that bore you, and the breasts that you sucked." But he said, "Blessed are those who hear the word of God and keep it."

The New Testament work called the Acts of the Apostles is regarded by all modern biblical scholars as a companion piece

to the Gospel according to Luke. In the first chapter of Acts we
are given a description of the disciples of Jesus gathered in Jerusalem shortly after his ascension into heaven. They are in an
upper room. the Twelve are featured but we are also told in Acts
1:14 of the presence of Mary and the brethren of Jesus: "All these
with one accord devoted themselves to prayer, together with the
women and Mary the mother of Jesus, and with his brothers."

    In the Gospel according to John reference is made to Mary,
the mother of the Lord, three times. The first time is in an incident called the wedding feast at Cana. In John 2:1-11, we are told
that there was a marriage at Cana in Galilee and the mother of
Jesus was there. And then, almost parenthetically, we are told,
Jesus and his disciples were also invited. And, indeed, Mary is
the principal dramatic agent in this biblical narrative, for when
the wine runs out Mary draws this to the attention of Jesus.
Jesus responds with the words, "O woman, what have you to
do with me? My hour has not yet come." But then he goes on
to multiply the wine anyway. The second reference to Mary in
John's Gospel follows immediately from the Cana narrative. For
at the end of that narrative we are told in John 2:12, "After this
he went down to Capernaum, with his mother and his brothers
and his disciples; and there they stayed for a few days." This
is intriguing because it is the only passage in the Gospels that
seems to suggest Mary and the relations for a while at least
were among Jesus' itinerant followers. But John later makes it
clear some of the relations turned against him (Jn 7:5). The third
and final reference to Mary in the Gospel according to John is
in 19:25-27, that part of John's passion narrative describing the
death of Jesus. In John 19:25-27, we are told:

> But standing by the cross of Jesus were his mother, and
> his mother's sister, Mary the wife of Clopas, and Mary
> Magdalene. When Jesus saw his mother, and the disciple
> whom he loved standing near, he said to his mother,
> "Woman, behold, your son!" Then he said to his disciple,
> "Behold, your mother!" And from that hour the disciple
> took her to his own home.

There is one last passage from the New Testament that at times has been interpreted as a reference to the Blessed Virgin Mary. This is an apocalyptic image from the very last book of the Bible, the Revelation of John. There, in 12:1-6, we read:

> And a great portent appeared in heaven, a woman clothed with the sun, with the moon under her feet, and on her head a crown of twelve stars; she was with child and she cried out in her pangs of birth, in anguish for delivery. And another portent appeared in heaven; behold a great red dragon, with seven heads and ten horns, and seven diadems upon his heads. His tail swept down a third of the stars of heaven, and cast them to the earth. And the dragon stood before the woman who was about to bear a child, that he might devour her child when she brought it forth; she brought forth a male child, one who is to rule all the nations with a rod of iron, but her child was caught up to God and to his throne, and the woman fled into the wilderness, where she has a place prepared by God, in which to be nourished for one thousand two hundred and sixty days.

What are we to make of all these references to Mary? No doubt, some of these references are extremely brief even oblique. But I would caution: one should be careful about dismissing references to Mary however indirect or fleeting. Indeed, some of the most terse and indirect have proven theologically valuable or intellectually probative and suggestive. For example, all Christologists recognize that the phrase "born of a woman" in Galatians 4:5 is a telling qualification insuring the genuine humanity of Jesus. And Matthew's "the child with his mother" occasioned one of the major genres of Western art expressing a deep psychological bond. And, no doubt, while some of these references to Mary appear on the surface at least censorious and dismissive of her, those same passages also lend themselves to deeper, more probative meanings. For example, modern exegetes have made it clear that Jesus' dismissive remark at the appearance of Mary and his relations is part of an "anti-familial polemic" on the part of the Gospel writers. Apparently, after Jesus' death and resurrection, some of Jesus' relations sought to assume importance in the Christian assembly simply because of their biological link to him. Moreover, from patristic times it has been argued that Jesus' dismissive remark, far from denigrating Mary, actually serves to make clear that her dignity and importance is not based solely upon the fact that she was his biological mother; her dignity resides in the fact that she not only heard the word of God but submitted to it. As for the value to be placed on any of these references to Mary, especially the more extended and portentous ones, no doubt historic interpretations vary between the extremes of a prosaic minimalism and what some would regard as an overenthusiastic, overly imaginative maximalism. And this continues to this day. For example, most modern exegetes claim that the reference to Mary at Pentecost (Ac 1:14) is devoid of doctrinal or devotional meaning. They insist the passage is a frequent Lucan compositional technique, a minor summary. And mention of Mary there is merely due to Luke's conscientious attention to historical accuracy: his research made clear Mary was there and so he dutifully notes her presence with no suggestion that there is any particular significance to be attached to it. On the other hand, a contemporary exegete, Luke Timothy Johnson, can argue Luke's mention of Mary at this point is not accidental; rather it is to bring out a doctrinal theme first broached in the infancy narrative of his Gospel. There the Spirit overshadowed her (Lk 1:35) so that she might give birth to the prophet-Messiah, so she is now portrayed as present at that gift of the Spirit that now gives birth to the Church, she is one of those "daughters of Israel" who have the Spirit of prophecy (Ac 2:17).

But here I want to concern myself only with those passages that are indisputable references to Mary and moreover those passages that deal with her precise relation to the Christian faithful, the disciples of her Son. In that regard, we need to look again and more carefully at the portraits of Mary in the Gospels of Luke and John.

All the portraits of Mary in Luke work to present her as a model of Christian faith, a woman who despite doubts and

confusion, perseveres in the faith. For example, in the very first
Marian narrative in Luke, Mary is portrayed as considerably
troubled by Gabriel's words. She mentally wrestles with the
idea. Gabriel, perceiving her inner turmoil, begins to supply
an explanation. Gabriel's explanation includes a lengthy and
poetic description of the nature of this child who will be born
of Mary, if she but co-operate. At the end of Gabriel's rhapsodic
description of the child, Mary responds with a contrasting sober
realism, a very prosaic but powerfully logical question, "How
can this be, since I have no husband?" But when Gabriel goes on
to explain that, if Mary will consent, the Holy Spirit will descend
upon her and make her the agent of a miraculous conception,
Mary final concedes to this divine proposal.

Mary's *fiat* in verse 38 is essentially an act of faith. While
she now, because of Gabriel's explanation, knows the divine purpose, she still does not fully understand it. She concedes to God's
action in her life even though it is mind-boggling to her. Though
she is a sober and realistic person, she is no skeptical rationalist.
However, it is even more important that we see here and now
that this portrayal of Mary as a woman who believes despite
the fact that she does not totally understand, who lives by faith
despite many things she does not understand, becomes a motif
in Luke's Gospel. For example, Luke concludes his narration of
the visitation of the shepherds to the new born infant Jesus with
the note, "But Mary kept all these things, pondering them in her
heart" (2:19). Luke 2:41-52, in the narrative of the finding in the
temple, concludes with the words, "and his mother kept all these
things in her heart." This language of "keeping in the heart" is
the opposite of keeping in mind. What one keeps in mind, one
understands. What one holds in the heart is a mystery.

In Luke's presentation of Mary as a woman of great faith
despite doubts and questions we find the image of the model
Christian, the model for all who would believe in Christ. And
there is, indeed, a great lesson here for us all. Christian faith is
not an irrational leap in the dark. It asks probative questions.
But in the end, after having been given a measure of explanation, it has the humility to admit there are things it will never

completely understand. But it does not allow questions, doubts and fears to lead to agnosticism or atheism. Moreover, it is Mary rather than Peter or Paul who stands as the pre-eminent model for the faithful, the believer. Peter and Paul might indeed be models for ministry of various types, but Mary is the model for the faithful. However, we must also wrestle with other Gospel passages that suggest Mary is more than just a model for believers. If Luke's portrait of Mary is that of a troubled woman of great faith, John's portrait of Mary is that of the confident mother ever solicitous for her children, indeed, the mother of us all.

Mary first appears in John's Gospel in John 2:1-11 in what is almost a Marian pericope. That is, we have already seen how its beginning focuses more upon her. But the first thing to be noted is the remarkable contrast with what we have seen in Mark. While Luke's Mary is always troubled and uncomprehending, here she knows her son, knows what he can do, and moreover knows that he will do whatever she asks of him. No doubt, Jesus makes his point. "O woman what have you to do with me" has always been noted as a rather harsh rebuke. It certainly makes clear the complete independence of Jesus. But is that all that is happening here? John's Gospel is unlike the Synoptics in that his Gospel often functions on a highly symbolic level in addition to its literal historical narrative. For example, at the basis of John's narrative in 2:1-11 was probably a miracle account of Jesus changing water into wine. But John in his telling of it does it in such a way as to make it resonate with allusions to Old Testament prophecies and themes. More specifically: the huge amount of wine. The quantity is enormous — six jars each containing 18 to 24 gallons, as much as 144 gallons of wine! This is probably not a precise historical memory but rather a literary allusion. For it serves to recall those Old Testament passages wherein the messianic banquet is described as a time when the wine will flow (Is 25:6, 55:1; Jr 31:5, 31:2; Am 9:13; Ho 2:22; Jl 2:24). But John is also setting up Mary for symbolic expansion by his use of the enigmatic language of "O woman" and "my hour." The term "woman" has deep Old Testament resonances. This starts with the Genesis creation narrative: Genesis 1:23, "She shall be called

Woman." Genesis 3:2, "And the woman said to the serpent." Genesis 3:12, "The man said, 'The woman thou gavest to be with me, she gave me fruit of the tree, and I ate.'" Genesis 3:15, "I shall put enmity between you and the woman." Similarly the language of "hour" is also peculiarly freighted with meaning. It is used in the Old Testament (Ec 9:12) and the Gospels to refer to the time of trial, death, or God's judgment. It is particularly abundant in John's Gospel (Jn 7:30; 12:23, 27; 13:1; 17:1).

Moreover, this language of "mother" "son," "hour," "woman" finds a significant echo in the final portrait of Mary in John's Gospel. Similarly John 19:25-27 may have at its basis a precise memory that Jesus gave care of his mother to John. But if that is all it was this would be no more than a sentimental memory: oh, how nice that he thought of providing for his mother. Rather the same elements that in John 2:1-11 made that passage so dramatic and enigmatic combine now here to suggest John the Gospel writer sees a much deeper meaning in this last gesture of Jesus than merely that he was the thoughtful son who would provide for his mother. Epiphanius of Salamis saw this passage as principally a witness to the claim Jesus was an only child. We see it rather as suggesting Mary has now become the mother of us all, just as Eve once became the mother of all the living.

Further Reading

Carl Braaten's *Mary Mother of God* (Eerdmans, 2004).

John MacQuarrie's *Mary for All Christians* 2nd edition, T. & T. Clark, 2001.

Karl Rahner's *Mary, Mother of the Lord* (Herder and Herder, 1963).

E. Schillebeeckx's *Mary, Mother of the Redemption* (Sheed and Ward, 1964).

The Second Vatican Council:
The Church as Deliberative Assembly

In Part I, Chapter 2 of this book, we undertook a word-study of the New Testament term, *ekklesia*, which we translate as Church. We saw how this term originally meant "assembly." That is, from its Greek roots in two words, a verb "to call" and a preposition meaning "forth" it was used in classical Greek to designate the Hellenistic civic assembly and in the Septuagint, the Greek translation of the Hebrew Scriptures made by diaspora Jews, it was used to designate the Hebrew sacred assembly and then in the New Testament to designate the Christian worship assembly. We concluded that one of the things that marks a significant difference between the Hellenistic civic assembly and the biblical worship assembly, whether Jewish or Christian, was the fact that in the *ekklesia tou theou*, the "assembly of God," people gathered principally to hear the Word of God and not each other. However, there is a sense in which, at certain times, the Word of God is communally discerned by Christians who assemble to listen to each other. The great prototype of this kind of sacred assembly is described for us in the fifteenth chapter of the Acts of the Apostles. In that chapter we are told of a controversy that arose within the first generation of Christians, a controversy as to whether Christians should be required to observe such traditional Jewish practices as dietary laws and the circumcision of males. This controversy grew to be so divisive that a special assembly of the brethren was called at Jerusalem to make some definitive judgment. Of that assembly we are told, "the apostles and the presbyters met together to see about this matter" (Ac 15:6) and that "after much debate had taken place" (Ac 15:7), "the apostles and presbyters, in agreement with the whole Church, decided…" (Ac 15:22). Moreover, what they decided was then sent "to the brethren in Antioch, Syria, and Cilicia" (Ac 15:23) and the message began with the words, "It is the decision of the Holy Spirit and of us" (Ac 15:28). At several times in history, the leadership of the Church has met in a similar fashion to decide issues important to the whole community of faith and to come to decisions they meant to be binding on the whole community. In the twentieth century, the outstanding example of this type of general assembly of the Church is an event that is called the Second Vatican Council. Between 1962 and 1965 all the bishops of the Catholic world were summoned to Rome along with invited theologians, Catholic laity and representatives of other Christian assemblies. This assembly issued several statements. We study that event here and its processes for two reasons. First, it has great ecumenical importance. Second, I believe we can learn much from it about the nature of the Church.

This sacred assembly came about because of a decision by then bishop of Rome, Pope John XXIII. Bishops of Rome, upon their election take a special name to indicate their new role among the people of God. There is a biblical precedent for doing this. In Gn 17:5, Abram when called by God was given the new name Abraham. In Mk 3:16, Mt 16:18, Lk 6:14, Jesus gives "Simon son of John" the name Peter. Pope John XXIII's baptismal name had been Angelo Giuseppe Roncalli. Born in 1881 into a humble, farming family in the north central part of Italy, Angelo Roncalli went to the seminary in his hometown of Bergamo and was ordained a priest in 1904. Shortly after, he became secretary to the bishop of Bergamo. During the First World War he served as a military chaplain. After the war, he was called to Rome for administrative service. Eventually he served in several Foreign Service positions for the Church (Bulgaria, Greece, Turkey, and France). At the age of 71 he was made Patriarch of Venice. At the death of Pope Pius XII in 1958, Roncalli was the 77-year-old Cardinal Patriarch of Venice. And it was Roncalli that the cardinals chose on October 28, 1958, to succeed Pius XII as bishop of Rome. Since that election there has been a great deal of speculation as to why the cardinals chose to elect such an aged man. Several reasons have been given. Some argue that the cardinals were motivated by the longevity of the previous pope's reign. That is, Pius XII had served from 1939 to 1958, almost twenty years. And thus some suspect the cardinals did not welcome the prospect of another long papal reign. Others have argued since Pius had been a cold, austere aristocrat and intellectual, the cardinals felt this time it would be good to have a warm, expansive, and, if not a downright "republican" type, at least a pastor with the common touch. Some few, and with less charity, have suggested the cardinals could find no outstanding candidate and so they opted for a "throne warmer," that is, someone to sit in the Chair of Peter till better talent (or greater ambition?) came along. John XXIII, though not particularly ambitious — he had a long career as a dutiful and competent functionary in the papal diplomatic corps — turned out to be an amazing "mover and shaker," a charismatic figure who raised the papacy to international esteem and a decisive Church leader whose deeds have had tremendous implications both in and outside the Catholic Church. And he did all of this in less than five years!

Without question, his most historic act was his summoning of the twenty-first Ecumenical Council or world assembly of the Catholic Church. At Rome, on January 25, 1959, at the conclusion of the annual week of Prayer for Christian Unity, in an address to seventeen cardinals gathered in the Abbey of Saint Paul-Outside-the Walls, John XXIII announced his intention to call an Ecumenical Council. At that time he said his intentions in doing this were two. First, to update (he used the Italian word "aggiornamento") the Church. His second goal was to update the Church with an eye toward Christian unity. In his opening speech at the Council, John XXIII would add to these two original intentions the further intention of fostering unity among all peoples. On May 17 (Pentecost Sunday), 1959, slightly more than three months later, Pope John announced his creation of a group called the "Ante-Preparatory Commission." This commission was to consult the Roman curia, the bishops of the world, and the faculties of theology and canon law in Catholic universities and seminaries throughout the world so as to determine the subjects to be treated by the Council and to recommend the composition of the various committees that would more directly prepare the material for conciliar deliberation. A year later, on June 5 (Pentecost Sunday), 1960, in a *motu proprio* (a personal directive) entitled *Superno Dei nutu* he established ten preparatory commissions, a central commission to coordinate the work of the ten individual commissions, and two secretariats, one for mass media of communication, the other for promoting the unity of Christians. Over the next year, that is, from June 12, 1961 to June 20, 1962, the central commission examined the preparatory commission's proposed *schemata*, that is, working papers or draft documents. Eventually, it approved 73 draft documents, most of which never reached the Council floor, at least not in their original form.

On October 11, 1962, at Saint Peter's Basilica in Rome, in solemn splendor, Pope John XXIII presided over the opening ceremonies of the Second Vatican Council. Among those present in the basilica that day were the three principal groups who would be most instrumental in the work of the Council. The first group, "the Fathers of the Council," consisted mostly of bishops. By virtue of his office every bishop in the Catholic world had a right to be there. But the Council Fathers also consisted of some men who, though they were not bishops, held positions of great responsibility in the Church, men such as the heads of religious orders, for example, the Father General of the Jesuits and the abbot primate of the Benedictines. I call this the first group because their responsibility was unique in that they alone could speak and debate on the Council floor and they alone could vote. The second group is called by its technical name, the *periti* (from the Latin word for experts). These were theologians and canonists, canon law experts. They were numerous because while each bishop was allowed to bring his own personal theologian, the working commissions of the Council also had theologian members. These theological experts, though they had neither the right to speak on the Council floor nor to vote on the final form of Council documents, could be very influential. For example, they assisted in the initial drafting and considerable revision of the Council documents. Moreover, though they could not speak on the Council floor, nevertheless they spoke in other venues where their expert opinion could be well heard, giving conferences at the Vatican, at the Roman seminaries and the places where the attending bishops were lodging. The third group consisted of "the auditors." This group was made up of Catholic laity and representatives of Protestant and Orthodox traditions. The title "auditor" serves to indicate not so much their role but their capacity, that is, this group though it had no direct voice or vote in the deliberations of the assembly, had prime seats in St. Peter's Basilica where they could view and hear all the public debates, and thus their observations on the proceedings were not only sought out but sometimes simply inferred by their non-verbal reactions to debate. Present at the opening on October 11, 1962, were 2,540 Council Fathers and attendance by this group held well above 2,000 throughout the three years of deliberation, debate and voting. While the work of the commissions was nigh continuous throughout the three years, the full Council met only in the fall of those years. And thus we can say the Second Vatican Council met in four sessions in the four successive autumns of 1962-1965:

The First Session – October 11, 1962 to December 8, 1962
The Second Session – September 29, 1963 to December 4, 1963
The Third Session – September 14, 1964 to November 21, 1964
The Fourth Session – September 14, 1965 to December 8, 1965

During these four autumnal sessions, the Council Fathers met in 168 "General Congregations," that is, working sessions, and 10 "Public Congregations," that is, ceremonial sessions. In that time they produced sixteen formal documents. Here I present them with the technical genre description of each document, followed by each document's formal Latin title. All the documents promulgated by this Council were written in Latin and the title of each is taken from the first two or three words of the document's text:

1. Dogmatic Constitution on the Church, *Lumen gentium* (Light of Nations)
2. Dogmatic Constitution on Divine Revelation, *Dei verbum* (Word of God)
3. Constitution on the Sacred Liturgy, *Sacrosanctum concilium* (Most Sacred Council)
4. Pastoral Constitution on the Church in the Modern World, *Gaudium et spes* (Joy and Hope)
5. Decree on the Instruments of Social Communication, *Inter mirifica* (Among the Wonderful)
6. Decree on Ecumenism, *Unitatis redintegratio* (The Restoration of Unity)
7. Decree on Eastern Catholic Churches, *Orientalium ecclesiarum* (Eastern Churches)
8. Decree on the Bishops' Pastoral Office in the Church, *Christus dominus* (Christ the Lord)
9. Decree on Priestly Formation, *Optatam totius* (The Desired [Renewal] of the Whole [Church])
10. Decree on the Appropriate Renewal of the Religious Life, *Perfectae caritatis* (The Perfection of Charity)
11. Decree on the Laity, *Apostolicam actuositatem* (Apostolic Efficacy)
12. Decree on the Ministry and Life of Priests, *Presbyterorum ordinis* (The Order of Presbyters)
13. Decree on the Church's Missionary Activity, *Ad gentes* (To the nations)
14. Declaration on Christian Education, *Gravissimum educationis* (The Supreme Importance of Education)
15. Declaration on the Relationship of the Church to Non-Christian Religions, *Nostra aetate* (In Our Age)
16. Declaration on Religious Freedom, *Dignitatis humanae* (The Dignity of the Human Person)

The technical genre descriptive that precedes the Latin title of each document here is important because it serves to point out the peculiar theological significance of each document. The title "Constitution" implies a constitutive statement of the faith and thus a document of doctrinal importance. The title, "Dogmatic Constitution" was reserved for those documents of the Council that carry the most dogmatic weight, that is, those documents that contain solemn teaching. A "Decree," though not a constitutive statement of the faith, has juridical authority, that is, the enforcement of law in the Church. "Declarations" are neither dogmatic pronouncements nor juridical decrees but they, nonetheless, are important statements of the Council, documents in which the Council wants to "go on record," as it were, or "go on notice" for having said something. Finally, this Council created a fourth genre. The document on the Church in the Modern World is called a "Pastoral Constitution" rather than a "Dogmatic Constitution" because its aim was practical direction rather than dogmatic pronouncement.

However, for our interests here it can be argued while the Council documents contain much important teaching, there is an equally important lesson to be learned from a study of the way the Council worked, the process employed to create those documents. At Vatican II the work of the Council Fathers in deliberating and voting upon the working papers (*schemata*) presented to them by the conciliar commissions combined two processes or procedures for deliberating and voting. One was a democratic process, the other a consensual process. The democratic process or simple majority vote was employed for all procedural matters, for example, when to schedule or end debate on an issue or topic. The consensual process was employed for all substantive matters. In the consensual process a simple majority is not enough, rather what is aimed for is genuine consensus. The English word "consensus" is the past participle of the Latin verb *consentire*, a verb which quite literally means "to feel together." Consensus is harmony, cooperation or sympathy in different parts of an organism; it is group solidarity in sentiment and belief. A striking example of this is the voting on Vatican II's Dogmatic Constitution on the Church, *Lumen gentium,* which was promulgated at the close of the Council's third session, November 21, 1964. It passed by a final vote of 2,151 to 5, not a precisely unanimous vote but certainly a vote indicating a very solid consensus, practical unanimity. How such unanimity was achieved can be seen from the more precise voting procedure employed in deliberation and debate of this text. When the Council Fathers were deliberating upon the working papers (*schemata*) presented to them by the conciliar commissions, in assessing the proposed text of each document, the Council Fathers could vote one of three ways. If the Council Father liked the text as is, he could vote *placet*, a Latin word meaning, "It pleases." Or, if he found the text totally unacceptable he could vote, *non placet*, "It does not please." But there was a third alternative and even more helpful response than just a *non placet* vote. This third alternative was a vote called, *placet juxta modum*. This means literally "It pleases with the following change." The employment of such a procedure several times — the documents went back to committee for revision more than once — meant that everyone had an opportunity and more than once to refine the conciliar statement and thus what resulted was truly a consensus statement. No doubt, in the end, some bishops could say that the final draft went a little farther than they themselves might have gone, but it was still something they could live with. Other bishops, no doubt, probably could have said the final draft was in some measure a little disappointing in that it did not go as far as they had wished it might go. But they too could not only live with the statement but go home and promulgate it, see to it that it took effect in the lives of the faithful. Obviously, the evidence of five Council Fathers who still voted nay in the matter of the Council's Dogmatic Constitution on the Church indicates quite clearly that one will probably never be able to achieve universal consent. There will always be a few holdouts.

One cannot overestimate the importance of this principle of consensus rather than simple majority rule. I want to quote in this regard the words of one of the most important, most influential, conciliar *periti* (theological experts) at least with regards to *Lumen gentium,* Vatican II's Dogmatic Constitution on the Church. Monsignor Gérard Philips was a *peritus* or expert from the theological faculty at Louvain University. After the

Council, the Catholic publishing house of Herder and Herder came out with a multi-volume edition of the Council statements with introductions and line for line commentary. Gérard Philips was chosen to do the commentary on *Lumen gentium*. At one point in his commentary Philips says:

> A Council does not in fact try to establish the view of a majority against that of a minority; by its very nature it must strive to bring about practical unanimity. Paul VI was tireless in his efforts to achieve this end, so persistent in fact that he evoked a psychologically understandable reaction among the large numbers who were favorably disposed to the draft. He could congratulate himself finally on having brought the opposition to consent, without their being oppressed by a sense of defeat.

Philips' words here are very important. The Second Vatican Council lasted almost four years; in fact, when we add in the years of preparation it took even longer. If a purely democratic process had been employed it could have been over in much shorter time, but it might also have resulted in a schism, for without doubt there would have been a minority who would have felt defeated by a simple democratic process. This should stand as a warning to us all about the danger of misapplying democratic processes in the Church. We have indeed seen the damage that can be done in Christian assemblies when a sizeable minority is overruled by simple democratic procedures. By that I refer to the fact that in recent times some ecclesial traditions have been torn apart when major pastoral or even doctrinal changes were implemented with little regard for a significant dissenting minority, for example, in the question of the ordination of women or of practicing homosexuals in the ministry. It is not good to make decisions when a simple majority has been reached or even when a sizeable majority has arisen. Also, it should be kept in mind that in some cases — such as those just mentioned — the Holy Spirit is with the minority resisting such changes. In this matter it is appropriate to recall an observation by Canadian Jesuit philosopher and theologian Bernard Lonergan which can be found in the epilogue to his work *Insight*. I give it here in the quip form in which it often circulates: "Holy Mother Church always seems to arrive a little late and a little out of breath." Some use this paraphrase of Lonergan as a reproach alleging the Church's tardiness with regards to modernity; others more loyal to Lonergan's original meaning realize it is that Jesuit's sage observation of one of the dynamics of sound doctrinal development.

Americans, especially, ought to be sensitive to this problem of the tyranny of the majority. The political thinking that went into the founding of this nation produced several speculative works that state clearly the dangers of the tyranny of the majority. There are several references to this idea in the writings of Thomas Jefferson. It is the essence of *The Federalist Papers*, a series of 85 essays published between 1787 and 1788 on the proposed new Constitution of the United States. This theme is addressed by James Madison in *The Federalist Papers #10* and *#51* and by Alexander Hamilton in *Paper #85*. Alexis de Toqueville's masterpiece, *Democracy in America* (1831), is all about the dangers of crude majoritarianism.

One more area in which patience plays an important part in the work of an Ecumenical Council is in the matter of the implementation of its teachings. It takes years for the decisions of an Ecumenical Council to be realized or take effect. For example, Trent mandated the creation of seminaries (before Trent the training of candidates for the diocesan priesthood had been in the style of an apprenticeship). But it required more than a hundred years of trial and error after Trent before the Church was able to figure out just what a seminary should be.

But our treatment of the Church as deliberative assembly would not be complete without two more considerations: on the role of the pope in an Ecumenical Council and Paul VI's creation of yet another deliberative assembly, the World Synod of Bishops.

I did not mention the pope as one of the three principal groups in an Ecumenical Council simply because he is not a group. Even so, the role of the pope cannot be underestimated. Though in the past lay people have called Ecumenical Councils (the first seven Ecumenical Councils were summoned by Roman or Byzantine emperors), now only the pope can. And indeed when John

XXIII died, Vatican II was automatically "prorogued," a technical legal term meaning it was suspended *sine die*, that is, without setting a date for reassembling. This was to take care not to saddle the next pope with the previous pope's agenda and thus allow the new pope to make his own decision as to whether to continue with a Council. Moreover, a Council can legislate all it wants but until the pope signs off on its decrees those decrees have no authority whatsoever. But it is important that we also consider the role of the pope in the deliberations of an Ecumenical Council. Here the important thing to be aware of is the fact that traditionally popes do not attend Ecumenical Councils. True, Pius IX at Vatican I and John XXIII and Paul VI at Vatican II presided at the ceremonial opening and closing of each session. But during the working sessions they never appeared on the Council floor. And there is good reason for this tradition: it allows freedom for debate, the speakers need not feel they are under direct papal scrutiny. However, these popes were never totally absent from the conciliar process because they were kept informed daily as to both how the Council was going and what was happening. No doubt, this "behind the scenes" role of the pope in an Ecumenical Council can be given a sinister interpretation as has been given by some, unfairly, regarding the role of Pius IX at Vatican I. But that the pope should remain "behind the scene" and not "on the scene" is an important part of the dynamics of an Ecumenical Council.

Finally, we should consider the fact that on 15 September 1965 at the beginning of the final session of the Second Vatican Council, Pope Paul VI issued a personal directive mandating the creation of a World Synod of Bishops which, after the conclusion of the Council, would meet at Rome with some regularity. The term "synod" is derived from two Greek words: *syn* meaning "together" and *hodos* meaning "road" or "way" and thus indicating a "common path." Early in the history of the Church bishops began to come together for mutual consultation on important issues. These meetings were called synods. Paul VI's creation of a World Synod of Bishops to meet with regularity at the Vatican was meant to be a remedy for two things, the length of times between Ecumenical Councils which are such massive undertakings and also as a way to remedy the criticism that the some popes have appeared to be captive to the opinions of their curia, the cardinals in charge of the Vatican administrative bodies. This World Synod of Bishops now meets every three years and it consists of about 200 bishops, some appointed by the pope, others elected to represent various regions of the Church throughout the world. While it functions principally as a consultative body who bring to the pope's attention important issues, Paul VI first saw the World Synod of Bishops as not merely consultative but deliberative. And indeed the first two meetings of this body, in 1969 and 1971, resulted in the issuance of formal statements by the Synod. However, that practice was soon curtailed and ever since the third World Synod of Bishops the practice has been that the Synod ends without making any formal statements. Instead, the pope about a year later issues a summary statement of what was discussed. This seems appropriate in that, unlike an Ecumenical Council, the World Synod of Bishops is no way near as representative — no theological experts, no laity, no representatives of other Christian traditions — nor does it have enough time to produce truly consensus statements, certainly as regards seriously controverted issues.

Further Reading

From Joseph Ratzinger's *Principles of Catholic Theology* translated by M.F. McCarthy (San Francisco: Ignatius Press, 1987), "A Review of the Postconciliar Era — Failures, Tasks, Hopes," 367-378, and "Church and World: An Inquiry into the Reception of Vatican Council II," 378-393.

From Walter Kasper's *Theology and Church* translated by M. Kohl (New York: Crossroad, 1989), Chapter VIII, "The Continuing Challenge of the Second Vatican Council: The Hermeneutics of the Conciliar Statements," 166-176.

From Paul Ramsey's *Who Speaks for the Church?* (Nashville: Abingdon, 1967) the essay "Toward an Ecumenical Ethics," pages 124-147, is an insightful appraisal of the methods of the Second Vatican Council in composing faith-based public statements.

Biblical Index

Author Index

ST PAULS

This book was produced by ST PAULS, the publishing house operated by the Society of St. Paul, an international religious congregation of priests and brothers dedicated to serving the Church through the communications media.

For information regarding this and associated ministries of the Pauline Family of Congregations, write to the Vocation Director:

Vocation Director of the Society of St. Paul
2187 Victory Blvd., Staten Island, NY 10314

Phone us at (718) 865-8844
E-mail: vocation@stpauls.us
www.stpauls.us

That the Word of God be everywhere known and loved